Readings in
International Business

Readings in International Business: A Decision Approach

edited by Robert Z. Aliber
and Reid W. Click

The MIT Press
Cambridge, Massachusetts
London, England

© 1993 Massachusetts Institute of Technology

All rights reserved. No part of this book may be reproduced in any form by any electronic or mechanical means (including photocopying, recording, or information storage and retrieval) without permission in writing from the publisher.

This book was set in Palatino by Asco Trade Typesetting Ltd., Hong Kong, and was printed and bound in the United States of America.

Library of Congress Cataloging-in-Publication Data

Readings in international business: a decision approach / [edited] by Robert Z. Aliber and Reid W. Click.
    p.   cm.
  Includes bibliographical references and index.
  ISBN 0-262-01132-8.—ISBN 0-262-51066-9 (pbk.)
  1. International business enterprises. I. Aliber, Robert Z. II. Click, Reid W.
HD2755.5.R38   1993
658'.049—dc20   92-21502
                                                                      CIP

Contents

.

Introduction

In the last few years, much as in the 1960s, a great deal of attention has been paid to the globalization of business. In the 1960s the attention to global business was triggered by the surge in the foreign investments of U.S. firms in Western Europe and in various developing countries with petroleum reserves and other mineral resources. In the 1980s the large number of takeovers of U.S. firms by firms headquartered in Great Britain, Japan, and other industrial countries has reinforced this attention. Sony bought Columbia Records and then Columbia Pictures, and Matsushita bought MCA. British Petroleum became the largest producer of crude petroleum in North America through its subsidiary, Standard Oil of Ohio. Grand Metropolitan, a London-based firm in the food and lodging services, acquired Pillsbury and its Burger King subsidiary. Taken together, foreign purchases of U.S. firms totaled nearly $200 billion in the 1980s. The share of U.S. output of a number of industries accounted for by foreign firms ranged up to 35 percent. Japanese-owned auto factories in the United States were producing nearly 15 percent of the cars in the United States—and appeared likely to increase their share to 25 percent. Siemens, the large German electronics firm, employs tens of thousands of Americans in its various U.S. factories.

Moreover, the initiative to "complete the common market" in the European Community in 1992 has placed more attention on rationalization of production and marketing arrangements in the community's twelve member countries. U.S. and Japanese firms are seeking to position themselves to compete effectively in this integrated market of 300 million people.

The economic success of Japan, Taiwan, Korea, Hong Kong, and Singapore has focused attention on economic potential in the Pacific Rim. Will there be a Japanese yen bloc, and a new set of trading arrangements based on Japan? How should U.S. and European firms approach these markets—

and how should they source to take advantage of the remarkable capacity of these countries to produce a wide range of quality consumer goods?

In the late 1980s firms headquartered in the newly industrializing countries (NICs) of Korea, Singapore, Venezuela, Brazil, Argentina, Kuwait, and Mexico began to expand abroad, partly to protect their access to foreign markets and partly to reduce production costs. Petroven, the government-owned petroleum firm in Venezuela, bought Champlin Oil, a U.S. gasoline distributor. Vitro, one of the most vibrant of the Mexican industrial firms, acquired Anchor Hocking, one of the largest U.S. firms producing glass containers. Gold Star, one of the leading business firms in Korea, has more than fifteen U.S. factories.

The rapid shift toward a market economy in Poland, Hungary, and Czechoslovakia has led to many questions about how the firms and productive facilities in these countries will be integrated into the world economy. The engineering skills of the labor force in some of these countries are impressive, but the capital equipment and some elements of the infrastructure are obsolete. And the work habits of much of the labor force in a competitive environment are untested.

The United States and Canada have formed a free trade area; tariffs on their trade with each other are being eliminated. And the U.S. and Mexican governments have moved to develop a free trade area; Canada almost certainly will be a participant in this large North American free trade area. Earlier, Mexico had moved to develop a free trade area with Chile. Inevitably Brazil will seek to join this free trade area. A free trade area for all the Americas seems just over the horizon.

Most of the developments noted in the previous several paragraphs are recent. The cliché is that the world is shrinking rapidly because of the Fax machine—a metaphor for the sharp declines in the costs of economic distance. The costs of transportation and communication have fallen sharply relative to the costs of production and marketing.

Increasingly firms in each industry view their competitors in a global rather than a national context. Competition in automobiles is among about twelve firms headquartered in the United States, Japan, Germany, France, Italy, and Sweden—and these firms have plants in thirty or forty countries. And six or seven auto firms account for 70 percent of global output. Similar statements can be made about the structure and organization of many industries, including aluminum, electronics, publishing, air transport, and food. Some industries—chemicals, banking, food—are remarkably competitive; although many firms are large in terms of number of employees and assets and have name recognition, no firm has more than 2 or 3 percent of global sales. Firms headquartered in the United States and Japan, Germany, Great Britain, the Netherlands, and a few other foreign countries compete in each other's national markets, and in many third-country markets, even though each firm is subject to the tax and regulatory policies of its national government.

The economic significance of some of the traditional barriers associated with the boundaries among nation-states is declining, especially in the context of regional trading arrangements. The significance of other boundaries —and of the distinctions among currency areas—is increasing. A large number of industrial products are subject to "voluntary" export quotas; very few Japanese-made automobiles are sold in Italy because of trade barriers. And automobiles made in Japan are subject to import barriers in most foreign countries.

Approaches to International Business

The response in business schools in the United States, Canada, and various European countries to the growing importance of globalization of business has been the development and extension of courses in international marketing, international financial management, international taxation and accounting, and international business policy. Most of these courses are extensions to a multicountry context of traditional marketing, finance, and accounting courses. For example, many courses in international finance extend portfolio diversification and capital budgeting to an international setting. A few courses are internationalized by adding foreign content in the last week or two. There is a periodic effort to internationalize a larger share of the content of these courses.

These international business courses highlight that the international environment is more diverse than the domestic environment, because the differences among countries in per capita income, language, culture, consumer preferences, and the regulation of business are much larger than the differences in these attributes within a country. Corporate tax rates differ by countries, and exchange rates between national currencies change— frequently by large amounts.

Finance, marketing, production, and tax management decisions in the global context are more than extensions of these same decisions in the domestic context, and for several different reasons. The foreign exchange value of the German mark and the Japanese yen varies in terms of the U.S. dollar, so that the U.S. dollar equivalents of the German and Japanese earnings of U.S. firms change (as do the Japanese yen and the German mark equivalents, of the U.S. earnings of the U.S. subsidiaries of German and Japanese firms). Corporate tax rates within a country change frequently; there were two significant changes in the effective U.S. corporate tax rate in the 1980s, and comparable changes in many foreign countries. As the differentials in national tax rates change, so the ranking of countries by after-tax production costs and after-tax rates of return may also change. Per capita incomes in individual countries increase at different rates, so tastes and the demand for particular types of products increase at more rapid rates in some countries than in others. In Spain and Brazil and Mexico and numerous other countries, automobile demand is growing several times more rapidly than population, with the consequence that unit production costs of autos are declining. In contrast, the market for automobiles in the United States has been mature for several generations; automobile sales increase slightly more rapidly than population, and unit production costs are stable.

Decisions in the global economy are more complex than those in the domestic economy, partly because the range of firms competing is wider and more diverse, and partly because the business and political environment changes at a more rapid rate. Business is all about decisions, and international business is all about the same decisions encountered by domestic firms—in a more complex environment, one characterized by significant changes in the basic relationships among national economic variables such as per capita income, price levels, interest rates, and tax rates. There are a few unique decisions that firms encounter in the international context that have no close domestic counterparts, primarily those associated with dealing with host-country governments.

Most of the decisions that managers encounter in the global context are extensions or counterparts of decisions they make in the domestic economy. Each of the basic marketing decisions featured in domestic marketing textbooks—the product, package, promotion, place (distribution), and price—has a counterpart in international marketing management. The implication of the "global marketing" cliché is that these national borders should be ignored or at least slighted, primarily to achieve economies of scale in the various marketing functions. But global marketing downplays the extensive differences in tastes and preferences of consumers in different countries. The central question for a cost-effective international marketing program becomes how to group countries to realize scale economies in the various marketing activities, while recognizing the national differences in the attributes of consumers.

Similarly the capital budgeting, cash management, capital structure, and portfolio decisions that are at the core of textbooks on corporate finance all have international counterparts. Perhaps one unique international financial decision is the debt denomination decision: should the firm denominate its debt in its domestic currency or in a foreign currency? (The debt denomination decision is the dual or mirror of the portfolio decision, which centers on how risky securities should be systematically combined in a portfolio.) The debt denomination decision is linked to the foreign exchange exposure that firms encounter because of their production and marketing activities. Managers must determine how a firm's economic income, its accounting income, its net worth, and its market value will be affected by changes in exchange rates; then they must decide whether the firm should hedge its foreign exchange exposure by arranging the currency denomination of its debt to neutralize or offset the foreign exchange exposure of its payments and receipts. Each of these decisions—the debt denomination decision, the cash management decision, the capital budgeting decision—must necessarily reflect a view on the relationship between interest rates on comparable securities denominated in different currencies and the anticipated, and realized, changes in exchange rates in the short as well as long run.

These decisions in the global context are more complex than in the domestic context because the uncertainty about the environment for business is significantly greater. Part of the greater uncertainty reflects the richer diversity of the political environment; national governments come and go, and the policies of the governments frequently differ from those of their predecessors. Moreover, the relationship among the rates of economic growth of various countries changes; during virtually every decade a few countries grow more rapidly than most others, and so the relative size of their domestic markets for various goods increases more rapidly than the markets in most other countries.

Purpose of This Book

This book highlights the major decisions that managers encounter in the global context; its organization emphasizes both the pattern of international transactions in goods, services, and securities and the types of decisions that managers make in the course of these transactions. It conveys both the rich diversity of the global environment and the systematic relationships among national price levels, per capita incomes, corporate tax rates, and interest rates in different countries. And it integrates the complex diversity of the global environment by relating the range of international managerial decisions to the values governing the various economic and business variables of different countries.

We compiled this volume to achieve several objectives. We wanted a book that would help graduate and upper level business school students develop their understanding of business decisions in the global context by building on their prior knowledge of the functional fields of business. We wanted a book that would highlight the richness of the diversity of the global business enviroment without burdening the reader with a large amount of institutional detail. And we wanted to use the organization of the book as a device for a systematic approach to the key decisions—and as a way to demonstrate how these individual decisions are related to each other.

We believe this book has several advantages. The headings of its six parts present an outline of what international business is all about—the mix of attributes associated with particular countries such as income per capita, resources, and tax rates; the pattern of international transactions in goods, services, and securities, including the foreign investments of particular firms; and the types of marketing, production, and finance decisions that managers of firms encounter in the international context. The introductions to its parts identify and discuss the decisions managers must deal with in each of the functional areas, such as marketing, production (or sourcing), and finance, and the relations among these decisions.

We also wanted to present classic readings where available, such as Levitt's "The Globalization of Markets." Selecting twenty articles from a set of several thousand was a challenge. Our first objective in choosing articles was to illustrate particular approaches to international business decisions—even though we did not always agree with the basic assumptions of each article. We hope our introductory comments highlight the assumptions implicit in many of the readings.

We use the introductions to each of the six parts to emphasize the set of relevant decisions in each functional area. For example, the introduction to part 5, on international taxation, frames the particular decisions concerning organizational choices (branch versus subsidiary, formation of holding companies), the dividend decision, the transfer pricing decision, the designation of payments decision (royalty versus tax, dividend versus loan), and the competitive location decision. Similarly part 4, on multinational corporate finance, outlines the range of financial decisions in the international context, such as capital budgeting, debt denomination, and foreign exchange hedging decisions.

Organization of This Book

Physical science, social science, and domestic business are all about patterns in events. Similarly there are patterns in international business, even though a number of events and decisions may seem random. Research in business schools and within firms seeks to expand knowledge of these patterns. Our organizational rationale was to highlight the broad themes of patterns in the growth of national markets, and then to consider how the demands in the various national markets might be satisfied.

Changes in international ownership patterns are highlighted in part 1. The most dramatic change is the rapid growth of Japanese foreign investment, in the United States, Great Britain, and other countries in Western Europe, as well as in the developing countries. British investment in the United States also has increased by almost as much as Japan's, although from a much larger base. These changes in the pattern of ownership provide background for evaluating competing approaches to the theory of direct foreign investment.

Corporate strategy and organization are examined in part 2. The strategic question involves how a firm maintains and expands its unique advantages in foreign markets, and protects its advantages in domestic markets, as its industry becomes increasingly international. From the 1920s through the 1970s the foreign expansion of U.S. firms suggests they shared an advantage which they were able to exploit in many foreign markets. The large purchases of U.S. firms by Japanese and British and other foreign firms in the 1980s suggests that U.S. firms have been at a strategic disadvantage. Strategy involves exploiting an advantage, and compensating for the strategic advantage of others.

International marketing issues are considered in part 3. International marketing recognizes that there are economies of scale in developing a marketing program for more than one country. Global marketing seeks to develop a standardized marketing program for all countries. The competing corner position is that managers customize a marketing approach for each of n countries; n might be two or ten or more. There are numerous intermediate positions, which involve alternative ways to group countries for a standardized approach to one or several aspects of the marketing program.

The basic financial decisions for a multinational firm are discussed in part 4. The key to these decisions is the relationship between interest rates on comparable securities denominated in U.S. dollars and various foreign currencies and realized changes in exchange rates. Where the annual changes in interest rates do not differ significantly from the realized annual changes in exchange rates, international financial decisions do not differ significantly from domestic financial decisions. Interest rate differentials obviously differ from changes in exchange rates both in the short run (less than three or four years) and in the long run.

International taxation issues are highlighted in part 5. Governments in most countries set their tax rates with only a casual understanding of the impacts of these rates on the international competitive positions of domestic firms and foreign firms. Once tax rates are known, the key question for corporate managers is how to organize and arrange activities so as to maximize after-tax income.

Part 6 deals with political risk—the uncertainty that multinational firms encounter because of arbitrary and capricious actions of host-country governments. Many firms, especially those in the raw material production industries, have incurred significant losses because their properties have been taken over by host country governments. But there are thousands of less dramatic actions of host-country governments that have the effect of significantly reducing the profit rate—such as currency controls, local business laws, and equity dilution requirements.

Terry Vaughn, the economics editor at The MIT Press, has been most supportive of this project. Peter Geib provided useful feedback on the first set of readings. And Cathy Coursey patiently typed the n drafts of these introductions and helped us with much of the photocopying.

I

Patterns of
International Business

Patterns dominate the world economy—patterns that reflect the comparisons of the data from different countries. The patterns in the data led to efforts to develop theories that describe the economic forces behind these patterns.

One of the most fascinating patterns involves the growth in income of individual countries. For fifty years or more, from 1920 through the 1970s, the United States was the richest country, with higher levels of per capita income than in any other country. For most of this century, the United States had experienced a more rapid rate of economic growth than any other country. By the late 1980s, however, the levels of per capita income in Norway, Sweden, Switzerland, and a few other industrial countries were as high as those in the United States; for most of forty years their rates of growth of per capita income had been higher than those in the United States, in part because they were making up for much slower growth in the 1940s. And although per capita income in Japan was below that in the United States, and per capita income in Korea, Mexico, Brazil, and other newly industrializing countries (NICs) was below that in Japan, these countries also had been experiencing rates of growth of per capita income significantly higher than in the United States. One reason these countries have achieved higher rates of economic growth is that output in their manufacturing sector has increased. Rapid economic growth is associated with a movement of excess labor from farms to industry, and many of these NICs have more excess labor than the United States.

A second pattern in the world economy involves increases in the ratios of imports and of exports to national income. This ratio for the United States more than doubled from 1970 to 1990, from 4 percent to 9 percent. Similar increases are evident for many other countries. One reason that imports have been growing more rapidly than income is that the costs of transportation and communication have declined sharply relative to the costs of production.

The increase in the ratio of imports to national income is more dramatic for manufactured goods. Many countries are significant importers and exporters of the same types of goods. For example, the United States is the world's largest producer of commercial jet aircraft; U.S. exports of jet aircraft parts and accessories in were $20 billion. Yet total U.S. imports of aircraft in 1990—from countries like France, the Netherlands, Sweden, and Brazil—totaled $5 billion. In both consumer goods and producer goods like jet aircraft, countries import goods similar to those they produce at home, and export, because foreign goods and domestic goods are not perfect substitutes—and there is more of a demand for diversity. Germany

Table I.1
Per capita incomes

1970		1980		1987	
United States	4,922	Qatar	34,078	Switzerland	26,155
Sweden	4,139	United Arab Emirates	29,162	Iceland	21,617
Canada	3,973	Brunei	26,065	Norway	19,895
Kuwait	3,858	Switzerland	16,060	Denmark	19,881
Switzerland	3,308	Sweden	14,935	Japan	19,471
Luxembourg	3,238	Norway	14,121	Sweden	19,109
Denmark	3,208	Iceland	14,087	United States	18,374
Australia	3,133	Germany	13,213	Germany	18,354
Germany	3,042	Denmark	12,943	Finland	18,110
United Arab Emirates	2,964	Luxembourg	12,455	Luxembourg	16,285
Norway	2,884	Saudi Arabia	12,372	Canada	16,200
France	2,814	France	12,333	United Arab Emirates	15,889
Qatar	2,696	Belgium	12,237	France	15,854
Belgium	2,653	Netherlands	11,970	Qatar	15,783
Netherlands	2,568	United States	11,804	Austria	15,688

Source: United Nations.

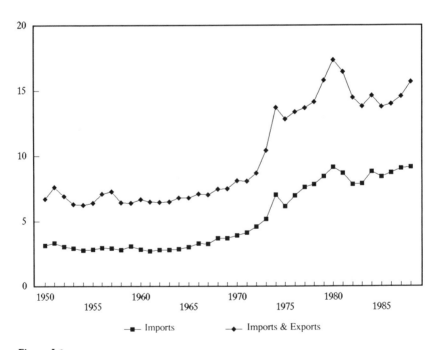

Figure I.1
Ratios of U.S. imports and exports to GNP, 1950–1988

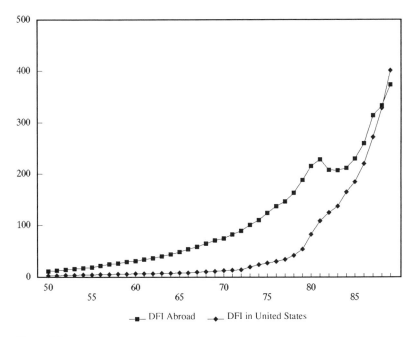

Figure I.2
U.S. direct foreign investments (billions of dollars)

exports Mercedes, Porsches, BMWs, and Volkswagons; and imports Saabs, Volvos, Fiats, and Renaults.

The rapid growth of trade in manufacturers has been associated with a much more extensive integration of manufacturing production in different countries. Hyundai Motors imports various electrical components from Japan to incorporate into the automobiles that it will ship to the United States. Ford Motor produces its Escort line in Mexico, utilizing some components made in the United States and in other countries.

The third pattern is the increase in foreign ownership of manufacturing plants, and the changes in the pattern of international ownership. The 1960s was identified with *Le Défi Américain* (*The American Challenge*)—U.S. firms were investing abroad at a rapid rate and acquiring many long-established foreign firms. U.S. firms continued to invest abroad at a rapid rate in the 1970s, and at a less rapid rate in the 1980s. The surprise, however, has been the surge in foreign investment, including foreign acquisition of some very well-known and well-established U.S. firms. Firestone Tire, the number three U.S. tire maker, was acquired by Bridgestone, the leading tire company in Japan. At the end of 1980, direct foreign invest-

Table I.2
Metal manufacturing: Top 10 companies and sales as percent of top 50 companies

	1975		1980		1984	
1	Nippon Steel (Japan)	5.79	Thyssen (Germany)	5.58	IRI (Italy)	9.80
2	Thyssen (Germany)	5.77	Nippon Steel (Japan)	4.80	Nippon Steel (Japan)	5.04
3	U.S. Steel (U.S.)	5.38	U.S. Steel (U.S.)	4.57	Thyssen (Germany)	4.94
4	British Steel (U.K.)	3.52	PechineyUgineKuhlmann (France)	3.31	Canadian Pacific (Canada)	4.74
5	Bethlehem Steel (U.S.)	3.28	Canadian Pacific (Canada)	3.13	LTV (U.S.)	2.96
6	PechineyUgineKuhlmann (France)	2.88	LTV (U.S.)	2.93	Fried Krupp (Germany)	2.69
7	Sumitomo Metal (Japan)	2.79	Fried Krupp (Germany)	2.81	Nippon Kokan (Japan)	2.50
8	Nippon Kokan (Japan)	2.77	EBTEL (Netherlands)	2.58	Aluminum Co. of America	2.41
9	Kawasaki Steel (Japan)	2.51	British Steel (U.K.)	2.48	Kobe Steel (Japan)	2.30
10	Krupp-Konzern (Germany)	2.50	Bethlehem Steel (U.S.)	2.47	Alcan Aluminium (Canada)	2.30

	1987		1990*	
1	IRI (Italy)	14.37	IRI (Italy)	16.57
2	Nippon Steel (Japan)	5.10	Thyssen (Germany)	5.80
3	Thyssen (Germany)	4.94	Nippon Steel (Japan)	5.71
4	INI (Spain)	4.43	Usinor-Sacilor (France)	4.76
5	Usinor-Sacilor (France)	3.89	Preussag (Germany)	4.04
6	Canadian Pacific (Canada)	3.21	Pechiney (France)	3.81
7	Fried Krupp (Germany)	2.73	Barlow Rand (So. Africa)	3.68
8	Aluminum Co. of America	2.70	Sumitomo Metal (Japan)	3.45
9	LTV (U.S.)	2.64	Viag (Germany)	3.28
10	Nippon Kokan (Japan)	2.55	Matallgesellschaft (Germany)	3.23

*Percent of Top 41 Companies

Table I.3
Computers: Top 10 companies and sales as percent of top companies

	1975*		1980*		1984*	
1	IBM (U.S.)	37.17	IBM (U.S.)	37.09	IBM (U.S.)	39.81
2	Litton Industries (U.S.)	8.83	Honeywell (U.S.)	6.97	Honeywell (U.S.)	5.32
3	Sperry Rand (U.S.)	7.83	Sperry (U.S.)	6.77	Hewlett-Packard (U.S.)	5.24
4	Honeywell (U.S.)	7.11	IBM Deutschland (Germany)	5.75	Digital Equipment (U.S.)	4.84
5	NCR (U.S.)	5.58	NCR (U.S.)	4.70	Sperry (U.S.)	4.54
6	IBM Deutschland (Germany)	5.30	IBM France	4.59	Fujitsu (Japan)	4.44
7	IBM France	4.39	Burroughs (U.S.)	4.04	Control Data (U.S.)	4.36
8	Burroughs (U.S.)	4.32	Rank Xerox (U.K.)	4.02	Burroughs (U.S.)	4.17
9	Rank Xerox (U.K.)	3.59	Control Data (U.S.)	3.91	NCR (U.S.)	3.53
10	Olivetti (Italy)	3.38	Fujitsu (Japan)	3.71	IBM Deutschland (Germany)	3.43
	*Percent of 15 Companies		*Percent of 18 Companies		*Percent of 24 Companies	

	1987*		1990*	
1	IBM (U.S.)	38.40	IBM (U.S.)	30.85
2	Fujitsu (Japan)	10.00	Fujitsu (Japan)	6.37
3	Unisys (U.S.)	7.36	Hewlett-Packard (U.S.)	5.50
4	Digital Equipment (U.S.)	7.28	Digital Equipment (U.S.)	5.34
5	Hewlett-Packard (U.S.)	6.79	Canon (Japan)	4.60
6	IBM Japan	5.62	Unisys (U.S.)	4.17
7	Canon (Japan)	4.20	Olivetti (Italy)	3.84
8	IBM Deutschland (Germany)	3.56	Bull (France)	3.66
9	IBM France	3.56	NCR (U.S.)	3.55
10	IBM United Kingdom	3.31	Ricoh (Japan)	3.25
	*Percent of 30 Companies		*Percent of 15 Companies	

Table I.4
Electronics: Top 10 companies and sales as percent of top 50 companies

	1975		1980		1984	
1	General Electric (U.S.)	9.34	General Electric (U.S.)	9.07	A. T. & T. (U.S.)	9.30
2	I. T. & T. (U.S.)	7.92	I. T. & T. (U.S.)	6.73	General Electric (U.S.)	7.84
3	Philips (Netherlands)	7.49	Philips (Netherlands)	6.69	Matsushita (Japan)	5.61
4	Siemens (Germany)	5.41	Siemens (Germany)	6.52	Hitachi (Japan)	5.18
5	Western Electric (U.S.)	4.59	Hitachi (Japan)	4.68	Philips (Netherlands)	5.00
6	Hitachi (Japan)	4.12	Matsushita (Japan)	4.61	Siemens (Germany)	4.67
7	Westinghouse (U.S.)	4.09	Western Electric (U.S.)	4.37	I. T. & T. (U.S.)	3.93
8	AEG-Telefunken (Germany)	3.62	Générale d'Elect (France)	3.94	Toshiba (Japan)	3.17
9	RCA (U.S.)	3.34	Thomson-Brandt (France)	3.15	Samsung (South Korea)	2.89
10	Idemitsu Kosan (Japan)	3.26	Westinghouse (U.S.)	3.09	Westinghouse (U.S.)	2.88

	1987		1990*	
1	General Electric (U.S.)	7.47	General Electric (U.S.)	9.13
2	A. T. & T. (U.S.)	6.39	Hitachi (Japan)	7.92
3	Hitachi (Japan)	5.77	Samsung (South Korea)	7.04
4	Siemens (Germany)	5.22	Matsushita (Japan)	6.80
5	Matsushita (Japan)	5.20	Siemens (Germany)	6.13
6	Philips (Netherlands)	4.95	Philips (Netherlands)	4.82
7	CBE (France)	4.03	Toshiba (Japan)	4.72
8	Samsung (South Korea)	4.00	Alcatel Alsthom (France)	4.13
9	Toshiba (Japan)	3.87	NEC (Japan)	3.81
10	NEC (Japan)	2.91	Daewoo (South Korea)	3.48

*Percent of Top 45 Companies

Table I.5
Petroleum refining: Top 10 companies and sales as percent of top 50 companies

	1975		1980		1984	
1	Exxon (U.S.)	12.24	Exxon (U.S.)	10.79	Exxon (U.S.)	9.71
2	Royal Dutch/Shell (U.S./Neth.)	8.76	Royal Dutch/Shell (U.S./Neth.)	8.07	Royal Dutch/Shell (U.S./Neth.)	9.07
3	Texaco (U.S.)	6.68	Mobil (U.S.)	6.23	Mobil (U.S.)	5.99
4	Mobil (U.S.)	5.62	Texaco (U.S.)	5.36	British Petroleum (U.K.)	5.41
5	National Iranian Oil	5.14	British Petroleum (U.K.)	5.03	Texaco (U.S.)	5.06
6	British Petroleum (U.K.)	4.72	Standard Oil of CA (U.S.)	4.23	Standard Oil of IN (U.S.)	2.88
7	Standard Oil of CA (U.S.)	4.59	ENI (Italy)	2.84	Chevron (U.S.)	2.86
8	Gulf Oil	3.89	Gulf Oil	2.77	ENI (Italy)	2.76
9	Standard Oil of IN (U.S.)	2.72	Standard Oil of IN (U.S.)	2.73	Atlantic Richfield (U.S.)	2.64
10	Française des Pétroles	2.50	Française des Pétroles	2.50	Shell Oil (U.S.)	2.21

	1987		1990	
1	Royal Dutch/Shell (U.S./Neth.)	10.13	Royal Dutch/Shell (U.S./Neth.)	11.52
2	Exxon (U.S.)	9.88	Exxon (U.S.)	11.37
3	Mobil (U.S.)	6.62	British Petroleum (U.K.)	6.40
4	British Petroleum (U.K.)	5.84	Mobil (U.S.)	6.32
5	Texaco (U.S.)	4.44	ENI (Italy)	4.49
6	Chevron (U.S.)	3.36	Texaco (U.S.)	4.43
7	ENI (Italy)	3.13	Chevron (U.S.)	4.22
8	Elf Aquitaine (France)	2.74	Elf Aquitaine (France)	3.54
9	Shell Oil (U.S.)	2.70	Amoco (U.S.)	3.04
10	Amoco (U.S.)	2.61	Total (France)	2.53

Table 1.6
Food: Top 10 companies and sales as percent of top 50 companies

	1975		1980		1984	
1	Unilever (U.K./Neth.)	10.78	Unilever (U.K./Neth.)	10.26	Unilever (U.K./Neth.)	6.45
2	Nestle (Switzerland)	5.08	Nestle (Switzerland)	6.35	Nestle (Switzerland)	3.95
3	Kraftko (U.S.)	3.49	Dart & Kraft (U.S.)	4.09	Dart & Kraft (U.S.)	2.91
4	Esmark (U.S.)	3.40	Beatrice Foods (U.S.)	3.60	Beatrice Foods (U.S.)	2.78
5	LTV (U.S.)	3.10	Esmark (U.S.)	2.65	General Foods (U.S.)	2.56
6	Beatrice Foods (U.S.)	3.01	General Foods (U.S.)	2.59	Barlow Rand (So. Africa)	2.20
7	Greyhound (U.S.)	2.68	Consolidated Food (U.S.)	2.32	Consolidated Food (U.S.)	2.09
8	General Foods (U.S.)	2.64	Ralston Purina (U.S.)	2.12	Nabisco Brands (U.S.)	1.86
9	Borden (U.S.)	2.42	Greyhound (U.S.)	2.07	General Mills (U.S.)	1.67
10	Ralston Purina (U.S.)	2.26	George Weston (U.K.)	2.04	Dalgety (U.K.)	1.60

	1987		1990*	
1	Unilever (U.K./Neth.)	8.48	Philip Morris (U.S.)	11.59
2	Nestle (Switzerland)	7.39	Unilever (U.K./Neth.)	10.45
3	Occidental Petrol (U.S.)	5.35	Nestle (Switzerland)	8.72
4	Kraft (U.S.)	3.44	Occidental Petrol (U.S.)	5.74
5	Sara Lee (U.S.)	2.86	Conagra (U.S.)	4.06
6	Conagra (U.S.)	2.82	Grand Metropolitan (U.K.)	3.86
7	Beatrice (U.S.)	2.79	Feruzzi Finanziaria (Italy)	3.65
8	Hanson Trust (U.K.)	2.78	Sara Lee (U.S.)	3.05
9	Dalgety (U.K.)	2.39	BSN (France)	2.54
10	Barlow Rand (So. Africa)	2.38	A-D-M (U.S.)	2.06

*Percent of Top 48 Companies

Table I.7
Motor vehicles and parts: Top 10 companies and sales as percent of top 50 companies

	1975		1980		1984	
1	General Motors (U.S.)	18.98	General Motors (U.S.)	14.95	General Motors (U.S.)	19.14
2	Ford Motor (U.S.)	12.76	Ford Motor (U.S.)	9.61	Ford Motor (U.S.)	11.95
3	Chrysler (U.S.)	6.22	Fiat (Italy)	6.52	Toyota Motor (Japan)	5.50
4	Daimler-Benz (Germany)	4.35	Renault (France)	4.92	Chrysler (U.S.)	4.47
5	Renault (France)	4.16	Volkswagenwerk (Germany)	4.75	Nissan Motor (Japan)	4.00
6	Volkswagenwerk (Germany)	4.08	Daimler-Benz (Germany)	4.43	Volkswagenwerk (Germany)	3.66
7	Toyota Motor (Japan)	3.82	Peugeot (France)	4.36	Daimler-Benz (Germany)	3.48
8	Nissan Motor (Japan)	2.91	Toyota Motor (Japan)	3.69	Mitsubishi Heavy (Japan)	3.21
9	Fiat (Italy)	2.59	Nissan Motor (Japan)	3.59	Fiat (Italy)	3.10
10	Ford Motor of Canada	2.32	Mitsubishi Heavy (Japan)	2.85	General Motors of Canada	2.87

	1987		1990*	
1	General Motors (U.S.)	15.47	General Motors (U.S.)	15.72
2	Ford Motor (U.S.)	10.89	Ford Motor (U.S.)	12.34
3	Toyota Motor (Japan)	6.30	Toyota Motor (Japan)	8.10
4	Daimler-Benz (Germany)	5.71	Daimler-Benz (Germany)	6.82
5	Volkswagenwerk (Germany)	4.62	Volkswagenwerk (Germany)	6.00
6	Fiat (Italy)	4.51	Fiat (Italy)	5.49
7	Chrysler (U.S.)	3.99	Chrysler (U.S.)	5.05
8	Nissan Motor (Japan)	3.90	Nissan Motor (Japan)	3.88
9	Renault (France)	3.73	Renault (France)	3.77
10	Peugeot (France)	2.99	Peugeot (France)	3.69

*Percent of Top 40 Companies

ment in the United States totaled $83 billion; at the end of 1989, the comparable figure was over $400 billion, exceeding the book value of the foreign investments of U.S. firms by several tens of billions of dollars. The change in this pattern is dramatic—which suggests a change in the underlying factors that determine the pattern of direct foreign investment.

A fourth pattern is the changes in the importance of firms headquartered in different countries in the hit parade ranking of their industries. Consider the lists of the world's largest banks for 1969, 1979, and 1989, ranked by assets. Japanese banks now dominate the hit parade of the world's largest banks; they have achieved a significant increase in their rankings in the hit parade. Or consider the sales of automobile firms for these same years. Japanese auto firms have increased their share of the world market from 10 percent in 1975 to 15 percent in 1980 to 25 percent in 1990; Japanese auto plants in the United States are scheduled to have capacity of 2.5 million units per year, while U.S. firms have the capacity to produce 5 million units a year in the United States. The rise of Japanese firms to the top of the hit parade in many industries reflects three factors. The first is that the Japanese economy has grown more rapidly than most other industrial economies in the 1950–1990 period; the second is that the Japanese yen appreciated relative to the U.S. dollar, so that values in Japan increased relative to values in the United States and in other industrial countries; and the third is that Japanese firms rapidly increased their foreign investments in the 1980s. This change in ranking of firms headquartered in different countries is dramatic in a few industries—banking and financial services, electronics, information technology, and automobiles—and far less dramatic in others such as petroleum and chemicals.

Among the articles in part 1, "The Process of Transnationalization in 1980s" looks at broad trends in the world economy, focusing on patterns of direct foreign investment and shifts in ownership, especially in service industries. The growing importance of Japanese and Western European multinationals and the role of the United States as a host country are highlighted. Changes in the patterns of direct foreign investment are traced to changes in the international competitiveness of firms headquartered in different countries; it is argued that the firms that have achieved an increase in their standing in the hit parade have developed more effective technologies and organization skills.

Michael E. Porter's "Changing Patterns of International Competition" focuses on industry trends and the strategic implications of global competition. Porter distinguishes multidomestic industries, in which competition within a country is independent of competition in other countries, from global industries, in which competition is on worldwide basis. Some industries that have previously been multidomestic are becoming global. Porter urges multinational corporations to achieve global platforms rather than to compete country by country, and discusses strategic responses that overcome multidomestic parochialism.

Theories of direct foreign investment have been developed to explain changes in the pattern of international ownership. One set of theories involves firm-specific advantages, a second set certain economies of transactions costs, and a third set differentials across countries in the cost of capital. J. Saúl Lizondo's "Foreign Direct Investment" presents a taxonomy of these theories. He first examines theories identified with perfect markets, then considers theories identified with market imperfections, and finally focuses on theories based on differences in various financial variables across countries.

1

The Process of Transnationalization in the 1980s

U.N. Center on Transnational Corporations

A.   Transnational Corporations in the World Economy

Transnational corporations (TNCs) are perhaps the most important actors in the world economy. They straddle national boundaries, and the biggest TNCs have sales which exceed the aggregate output of most countries. The foreign content of output, assets and employment in many of them is large, in some instances ranging from 50 per cent to over 90 per cent. All told, adding their home-country output and their production abroad, they account for a significant proportion of total world output. It is estimated, for example, that the largest 600 industrial companies account for between one-fifth and one-fourth of value added in the production of goods in the world's market economies. Their importance as exporters and importers is probably even greater. For example, between 80 and 90 per cent of the exports of both the United States of America and the United Kingdom of Great Britain and Northern Ireland is associated with TNCs. TNCs also loom large in international capital flows. Transnational banks (TNBs) and other non-bank financial companies account for the bulk of international lending. Moreover, owing to the transnational character of their operations, non-financial TNCs hold liquid assets in several currencies and, in recent years, they have become important participants in world financial markets. And, of course, TNCs are responsible for the vast majority of foreign direct investment (FDI) and production abroad (see box 1.1 for a brief discussion of the motivations for foreign production).

The largest 56 TNCs have sales ranging between $10 billion and $100 billion. This does not mean that the universe of the transnational corporation is confined to very large corporations. In fact, most TNCs are medium-

From *Transnational Corporations in World Development*, United Nations Center on Transnational Corporations, 1988, pp. 15–31. Reprinted by permission.

Box 1.1
Why Do Firms Invest Abroad?

For an individual firm to invest abroad, it must have some firm-specific advantages that enable it to operate in foreign countries, where local firms have the advantages of better knowledge of consumer and factor markets and the favour of local governments. While these firm-specific assets are a necessary condition for direct investment, they may not be a sufficient condition; if trade were free, a company might exploit its advantages by exporting to each market.

What is the reward that tempts firms to produce outside their home countries? The literature on direct investment provides a variety of answers (see Caves, 1982, chap. 1; and Dunning, 1981, chap. 2). Many answers may be needed because there may be many motivations, varying with the firm involved, the industry, the home country, the host country and the time at which the decision is made.

One extreme case is an industry in which trade is impossible or is impeded by legal or institutional restrictions; that case is probably characteristic of most service industries and public utilities. A railroad, for example, must produce in a country in order to sell there. And when the search for raw materials is an important factor, they must, of course, be produced or extracted where they are found.

A more common case is that in which trade can take place, but local production is the cheapest, most efficient or most profitable way of serving a market, even though it could be served by exporting from the home country. The reasons might be a reduction in transport or tariff costs to that market, as in the case of automobile assembly, as compared with the export of fully-assembled cars.

A third case is that in which a host country is the cheapest location for production to serve the world market, sometimes including the home market. An example might be semiconductor assembly in South-East Asia.

Finally, there is the situation in which a firm can expand its market in a country by producing there, as opposed to exporting. One reason might be that, for certain types of products, particularly complex or intricate ones for which after-sales service, consulting and advice are important, the implicit assurance of the firm's continued presence in the market is an important selling point. A commitment to distribution facilities in a country is probably more convincing in this respect than selling through agents, and a commitment to complete production in a country more convincing than distribution facilities.

It is said that buyers of complex machinery often prefer to buy from sellers producing in their countries for those very reasons. A production facility in a country may also gain for the firm the advantage of familiarizing local buyers with the firm's name and reputation, so that production of one product in a host country may increase the demand there for other products of the same firm, even imported products. Whereas the reasons for TNCs to

Box 1.1 (continued)

venture abroad in order to supply host-country markets are varied, only countries with sizeable domestic markets are able to attract that kind of investment. In addition, the availability in a prospective host country of adequate economic and human infrastructure is often important for TNCs considering an investment.

While these factors could all be described as pulling firms away from their home bases, there also may be forces originating at home that push them to foreign production if they possess firm-specific advantages. For example, Swedish TNCs in the clothing and textile industries shifted production to Portugal and other low-wage countries as Swedish wages became too high for home production. There were many reports of United States firms shifting production to foreign locations when the exchange value of the dollar made production in the United States too expensive and uncompetitive. And recently there have been reported cases of Japanese firms shifting their production to lower-cost Asian countries to mitigate the effects of the large rise in the exchange value of the yen. Thus, an increase in the extent to which a country's firms produce abroad could reflect a gain in their competitiveness, but it could also reflect a loss in the competitiveness of the country itself as a location for production.

Another influence on the extent of internationalization of a country's enterprises is the composition of the country's production and shifts therein. Although data are fragmentary, there is evidence that service industries have typically been less international in their operation than primary production or manufacturing industries. That may be a consequence of the higher degree of national regulation in service industries, but it may also represent a greater degree of difficulty in those industries in transferring a company's competitive advantages from one location to another (Lipsey, 1987, p. 54). Whatever the reason, the result may be that the extent of internationalization tends to be reduced by the world-wide growth in the importance of service industries. An offsetting influence is the increasing degree of direct investment within the service industries.

size companies, with typical sales running well below $1 billion. While the vast majority of TNCs are based in the developed market economies, a new phenomenon that has received considerable attention in recent years has been the growing importance of corporations from developing countries as foreign investors. Most of those companies are relatively small, although 33 of them have sales of $1 billion or more. And, in today's increasingly interdependent world economy, even enterprises from centrally planned economies have found that equity investments abroad can help them achieve their economic objectives. It should be noted, though, that those investments are still a very small proportion of the world stock of FDI.

FDI is undoubtedly the most important manifestation of transnationalization.[1] Information on FDI stocks in a country indicates the value of the stock of productive capital owned by foreign companies in that country. And data on FDI stocks owned by a particular company yield a first glimpse of the importance of that company's foreign activities.

But TNCs influence the world economy not only through investing equity capital abroad. The essence of transnationalization is the internalization of international market transactions within an individual decision-making unit, the transnational corporation, which engages in such activities whenever markets are non-existent or function imperfectly or where the risks involved in market transactions are too high. But internalization of markets across national boundaries does not necessarily require equity investment. Thus corporations can extend their capacity to internalize markets abroad through borrowing by their affiliates rather than through investing in them. In addition, certain forms of quasi-internalization, which require little or no investment, have proliferated in recent years.

Two such types of non-equity arrangements have become very important in the 1980s .... One of them is collaborative arrangements between TNCs based in different countries. These have taken the form of cross-licensing of new technologies and products, joint ventures between TNCs, and joint research and development (R & D) programmes. The purpose of these arrangments has been to take advantage of each corporation's strengths and to share the costs of developing new products and technologies. The shortening of the life cycle of both end products and state-of-the-art technologies, the need to innovate continuously in order to remain competitive and the sharp increase in the cost of technological innovation have all pushed corporations to seek collaboration with selected rivals in their own home countries and abroad.

Many firms have also been in the process of substituting purchasing of components for in-house production. Rapid technological change and the danger of being locked into inefficient in-house supplies are leading corporations to concentrate on the production of key components or those which are difficult to buy on the open market. In order to reduce the risks involved in contractual arrangements, corporations at the same time have tended to establish much closer, long-term relationships with their contractees, which often take the form of quasi-integration. In many cases, corporations have entered into joint ventures with their suppliers. And, even where no equity links are involved, suppliers often participate in production design and planning, and are often tied to the user firm by means of long-term contracts.

The international dimension of this second development arises because TNCs prefer the international sourcing of components. By nature, most TNCs have a global outlook, and they cast their net wide. Firms from some developing countries, particularly those in South-East Asia, have been large sub-contractees to TNCs from the developed market economies. Sub-contracting has been an important source of exports for several countries in that area, particularly in consumer electronics, textiles and clothing.

It can thus be hypothesized that new forms of transnationalization have been emerging that are different from the well-publicized non-equity forms of relationship between TNCs and firms in host countries (for example, licensing, management contracts). Those new developments, together with the gradual increase in the importance of foreign-owned production in world output, could mean that the world economy may be witnessing the emergence of corporate clusters or galaxies whose members are linked together by both equity and non-equity relationships (Dunning, 1985).

B.   World Economic Environment of the 1980s

The strategies and behaviour of TNCs are conditioned to a large extent by the world economic environment in which they operate. At the broadest level, one can identify a series of economic, institutional and technological factors that have influenced the world economic scene of the 1980s. The salient economic features of the 1980s have been an accentuation of the slow-down in world economic growth that appears to have begun in 1973, growing disparities in economic performance among developing countries, a marked increase in international economic instability and significant changes in the origin and destination of net international financial flows. At the level of economic policies, two broad trends stand out. One has been a heightening of protectionism in, and trade frictions among, the major industrialized market economies. The second major policy change has been the rapid liberalization of the domestic financial markets of the developed market economies. In the realm of technology, the increasing application of information technologies, based on micro-electronics, in the production processes of goods and services has gathered a strong momentum. To be sure, all of those trends were discernible in the 1970s, but they have become more accentuated in the 1980s.

The current decade has been a difficult period for the world economy, particularly for its weakest members. As shown in table 1.1 and figure 1.1,

Table 1.1
Growth rates of world output, by region, 1960–1986 (percentage)

Region/country group	1961–1973	1974–1980	1981–1986
World output[a]	**5.5**	**3.6**	**2.7**
Developed market economies	**5.0**	**2.5**	**2.2**
United States	4.0	2.2	2.4
Western Europe	4.8	2.4	1.5
Japan	9.8	3.8	3.6
Developing countries	**6.3**	**5.1**	**1.5**
Africa	5.5	4.4	−0.9
Asia	5.1	6.0	4.8
Middle East	8.2	3.9	−0.9
Developing Europe	5.5	6.4	2.9
Latin America and the Caribbean	6.7	5.2	1.0
Centrally planned economies of Europe	**6.6**	**4.6**	**3.3**
China	**3.8**	**5.6**	**8.8**

Source: United Nations Department of International Economic and Social Affairs.
a. Gross domestic product for all country groups, except for China and the centrally planned economies of Europe. For the latter, the rates of growth shown are for net material product.

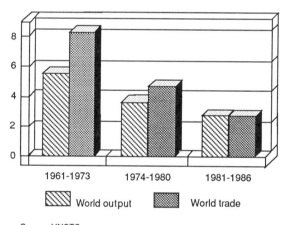

Source: UNCTC.
Note: Annual average rate of growth.

Figure 1.1
Growth of world output and trade, 1961–1986 (percentage)

it now seems clear that the world economy entered a period of slower economic growth around 1973. All groups of countries, regardless of their economic system or level of development, have been affected. In this regard, there are two striking differences between the 1970s and the 1980s. The first is that growth rates have decelerated a notch further during the current decade. Second, the developing countries have experienced the most dramatic decline in growth rates. Whereas in the 1970s they had been able to evade, at least in part, the generalized slow-down in economic growth that took place among the developed market economies, during the 1980s, on average, they have recorded the lowest rates of growth in the world economy. In fact, per capita output for the developing countries as a whole has fallen by almost 1 per cent per annum during the course of the current decade. Thus, while developing countries had historically recorded growth rates that exceeded those of the developed market economies, during the 1980s, their growth rates have been very significantly inferior to those of all industrialized countries, whether market or centrally planned economies.

Among developing countries, there has also been an increasing differentiation in growth performance. While some countries have continued to industrialize at a rapid pace, in many others, there has been stagnation or even retrogression. This is clearly in evidence in table 1.1. On the one hand, growth performance improved dramatically in China and did not deteriorate significantly in Asia (excluding the Middle East); on the other hand, in other developing regions, the growth rates of output were well below those of the population or were even negative.

It is too soon to tell whether the world-wide retardation of economic growth since 1973 is of a conjunctural nature or whether it is a phenomenon with long-term implications for the world economy.[2] To be sure, cyclical factors have exerted an influence: the most recent period includes the two most serious recessions since the 1930s. But recoveries from those recessions have also been uncharacteristically weak, and it has proved increasingly difficult for the economies of individual countries to sustain an upward momentum. There have clearly been other factors at work. In the developed market economies, growth performance has been affected by economic policies that emphasize the control of inflation rather than the expansion of demand and by the failure of the major industrial countries to co-ordinate their policies so as to ensure steady growth combined with internal and external equilibrium. As regards the developing countries, in the 1980s they have been affected by a number of adverse external factors, including the slow-down in the developed market economies, wide fluctuations in primary commodity prices (including petroleum) and a downward trend in a number of them, high international interest rates and the drying up of lending by transnational banks. Undoubtedly, economic policies in a number of developing countries have not been conductive to growth, but the pervasiveness of the deceleration in the growth of output indicates that factors of an external nature have been paramount.

Since the breakdown of the Bretton Woods system, exchange rates among major currencies and the interest rates for instruments denominated in those currencies have become very unstable. That instability has increased during the 1980s, a period that has witnessed post-war highs for international interest rates. In addition, between 1980 and 1985, the United States dollar appreciated by 50 per cent in effective terms (as calculated by the International Monetary Fund), but those gains had dissipated by mid-1987.

Generally, the high degree of instability prevailing in the international economy has discouraged export-oriented production and, therefore, has been a force working against the integration of national economies. It should be noted, however, that international economic instability has not prevented the integration of the domestic financial sectors of the developed market economies. In fact, one of the salient economic features of this decade has been the rapid pace of international financial integration among the developed market economies, which has far outstripped world economic integration through trade or FDI.

Since the mid-1970s, the progressive liberalization of international trade under the aegis of successive rounds of multilateral negotiations has been reversed. Although tariffs among industrial countries are now low, non-tariff barriers have become an increasingly important aspect of the world economic environment.

Rising international economic instability and growing protectionism may have had an adverse impact on world economic growth. In fact, it can be argued that the strong economic growth that characterized the post-war period until the early 1970s was made possible by a high degree of predictability in exchange rates and the progressive dismantling of tariff barriers to trade in the major trading nations. During that period, world trade grew considerably faster than world output, controls on international capital flows were gradually relaxed and production abroad by TNCs grew faster than domestic production. Thus, high growth went hand in hand with the rapid internationalization of production, capital flows and investment.

The deceleration in the growth of world trade since the early 1970s has been more marked than that of world output (see figure 1.1). Clearly, world trade and output are interdependent, and it is not possible to claim that slower growth in world trade has caused world output growth to decelerate. However, the evidence does seem to indicate that world trade has been progressively less of an engine of growth in the world economy, perhaps as a result of growing protectionism and international economic instability.

The 1980s has also witnessed large shifts in the location of the financial surpluses in the world economy. Until the early 1970s, the United States was the major exporter of capital (in the form of both equity and debt-generating flows). During the 1970s, however, the pre-eminent position of the United States was gradually eroded; with the oil price increases of 1973–1974 and 1979, the location of world financial surpluses shifted temporarily towards the low-absorption oil-exporting developing countries. During the 1980s, the current-account surpluses (as well as the excesses of domestic saving over domestic investment) in the world economy have come to be located primarily in Japan, the Federal Republic of Germany and some other Western European countries. On the other hand, the United States has become the largest net absorber of foreign financing in the world economy; in 1985, it became a net international debtor for the first time since the end of the First World War. The large financial surpluses located in Japan and the Federal Republic of Germany have contributed to the expansion abroad of TNCs based in those countries, and they have also underpinned the growing prominence of Japanese transnational banks and other non-bank financial institutions in international capital markets.

In recent years there have been extremely significant developments in the area of technology. While information technologies based on microelectronics were well developed in the 1970s, what is remarkable about the 1980s is the speed with which they have been introduced into the production processes of goods and services. Those technologies are rapidly becoming core technologies of the entire economic system in the industrialized market economies. Their growing utilization, the dramatic improvements of efficiency which they yield, together with developments in biotechnology and new materials, allow one to speculate that the world economy may be entering a new technological era, with unforeseen economic repercussions for all groups of countries. If this is so, the current period of slow world economic growth may eventually come to be seen as a kind of "breathing space," prior to a period of more rapid growth. However, whether the potential of those technologies for faster economic growth will be realized, and whether the benefits will be widely shared, are still in question. So far, in an environment of slow growth in demand, those innovations have led mostly to improvements in efficiency and to the rationalization of existing production. In other words, technological innovations have become embodied in capital-deepening, rather than production-expanding, investments.

TNCs are playing a key role in the development of the new technologies. Most technological innovations are the result of either the R & D activities of TNCs or of research undertaken by others, but funded by TNCs. Even in the numerous cases where innovations are made by smaller national firms on their own, those firms are often eventually taken over by TNCs, or sometimes they grow rapidly and become TNCs in their own right. The role of TNCs in technological change can be more readily appreciated when one begins to view technological innovation not as something exogenous or disembodied, but as one of the fundamental ways in which firms respond to competitive pressures and to other stimuli stemming from the environment in which they operate. Thus, technological innovations are highly firm-specific intangible assets, which tend to diffuse throughout the economy only with the passage of time. Moreover, since technological innovations require increasingly large volumes of resources, only firms of a certain size are able to undertake or fund them.

The economic environment of the 1980s, characterized by slow growth and intensifying competition, has placed a premium on reducing costs and increasing efficiency. As a result, technological considerations have gained in importance in the strategics of TNCs. There has been a proliferation of take-overs of smaller, innovative firms and foreign investments to gain access to the host country's technological know-how. And collaborative agreements among TNCs in the research and development area have also proliferated.

C. Transnationalization in the 1980s: The Broad Trends

Has the transnationalization of world economic activities decelerated in the current decade? The available information shows that, in spite of the slow-down in world economic growth and the heightening of international economic uncertainties, growth in the activities of TNCs continued at a steady pace. The relative importance of TNCs from different home countries as foreign investors, and of different countries as hosts to FDI, did, however, undergo significant changes. Foreign production and investment by TNCs based in Japan and in a number of Western European countries grew considerably faster than foreign production and investment by United States-based TNCs. The United States emerged as the largest host country to TNCs from Western Europe and Japan, and investment flows to developing countries declined substantially.

Long-term changes in stocks of FDI can be used as an initial proxy for the importance of TNCs in the world economy. Shares in world FDI stocks by countries (outward investment) and in countries (inward investment)[3] can be taken to represent the extent to which individual home and host countries and regions participate in the transnationalization of world production. Under certain assumptions, changes in the ratios of outward and inward FDI stocks to the gross domestic product (GDP) of home and host countries yield a preliminary notion of the direction of change in the role of TNCs in the world economy as producers and investors abroad.[4] The quality of the data varies considerably between countries, and therefore the ratios of FDI stocks to GDP need to be interpreted with caution.[5]

It should also be noted that FDI seriously underestimates the extent to which TNCs own or control foreign assets. Affiliates of TNCs can finance the purchase of foreign assets through means other than FDI, such as borrowing or raising equity in host country capital markets (where allowed), or borrowing directly from international capital markets. Usually, considerably less than full ownership is needed for a foreign company to be in a position to control the activities of an affiliate abroad. Even in the complete absence of equity investment, non-equity relationships with foreign firms, such as technology licensing, management contracts or subcontracting, allow TNCs to earn foreign rents from their firm-specific assets.

In spite of those shortcomings, the data on FDI stocks can be used to identify some of the major changes over time in the extent of transnationalization for individual home countries and host regions. The major changes between 1975 and 1985 are summarized in figure 1.2, which shows clearly the declining importance of TNCs from the United States as foreign investors and the increase in the role of the United States as a host country. Whereas in 1975 the stocks of FDI located in Western Europe were almost four times those in the United States, in 1985 the stocks in the United States had aleady surpassed those in Europe. During the period from 1975 to 1985, the ratios of outward FDI stocks to the GDPs of their respective home countries did, indeed, exhibit a sharp upward trend for all countries except the United States (see table 1.2). As regards the ratios of inward FDI stocks to host regions, the trend has also been consistently upward for both developed and developing countries, with the exception of Africa (see table 1.3).[6] The increase in the latter ratio was particularly strong for the United States.

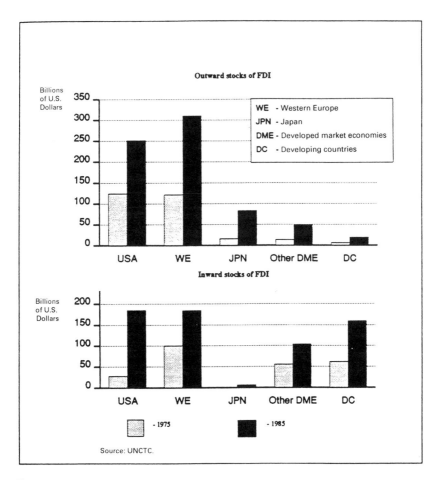

Figure 1.2
Outward and inward stocks of FDI (billions of U.S. dollars)

Although the aggregate ratios of FDI stocks to world output (excluding the centrally planned economies of Europe) have increased, the fragility of the data underlying those ratios do not really allow one to state unambiguously that foreign production has increased as a proportion of the aggregate output of home countries or of host regions. Perhaps the only conclusion that one can derive from the data is that production abroad by TNCs has expanded at least as rapidly as the world economy. But there have been important changes in the national origin of the companies that are investing abroad.

Table 1.2
Outward stocks of foreign direct investment, by major home country and region, 1960–1985 (billions of U.S. dollars)

Countries/regions	1960 Value	1960 percentage of total	1960 GDP	1975 Value	1975 percentage of total	1975 GDP	1980 Value	1980 percentage of total	1980 GDP	1985 Value	1985 percentage of total	1985 GDP
Developed market economies	**67.0**	**99.0**	**6.7**	**275.4**	**97.7**	**6.7**	**535.7**	**97.2**	**6.7**	**693.3**	**97.2**	**8.0**
United States	31.9	47.1	6.2	124.2	44.0	8.1	220.3	40.0	8.2	250.7	35.1	6.4
United Kingdom	12.4	18.3	17.4	37.0	13.1	15.8	81.4	14.8	15.2	104.7	14.7	23.3
Japan	0.5	0.7	1.1	15.9	5.7	3.2	36.5	6.6	3.4	83.6	11.7	6.3
Germany, Federal Republic of	0.8	1.2	1.1	18.4	6.5	4.4	43.1	7.8	5.3	60.0	8.4	9.6
Switzerland	2.3	3.4	26.9	22.4	8.0	41.3	38.5	7.0	37.9	45.3	6.4	48.9
Netherlands	7.0	10.3	60.6	19.9	7.1	22.9	41.9	7.6	24.7	43.8	6.1	35.1
Canada	2.5	3.7	6.3	10.4	3.7	6.3	21.6	3.9	8.2	36.5	5.1	10.5
France	4.1	6.1	7.0	10.6	3.8	3.1	20.8	3.8	3.2	21.6	3.0	4.2
Italy	1.1	1.6	2.9	3.3	1.2	1.7	7.0	1.3	1.8	12.4	1.7	3.4
Sweden	0.4	0.6	2.9	4.7	1.7	6.4	7.2	1.3	5.8	9.0	1.3	9.0
Other[a]	4.0	5.9	3.1	8.5	3.0	1.7	17.4	3.2	1.9	25.6	3.6	3.3
Developing countries	**0.7**	**1.0**	—	**6.6**	**2.3**	—	**15.3**	**2.8**	—	**19.2**	**2.7**	—
Centrally planned economies of Europe	—	—	—	—	—	—	—	—	—	**1.0[b]**	**0.1**	—
Total	**67.7**	**100.0**	—	**282.0**	**100.0**	—	**551.0**	**100.0**	—	**713.5**	**100.0**	—

Source: United Nations Centre on Transnational Corporations, based on J. Dunning and J. Cantwell, *IRM Directory of Statistics of International Investment and Production* (New York: New York University Press, 1987); and official national and international data.
a. Australia, Austria, Belgium, Denmark, Finland, Greece, Ireland, New Zealand, Norway, Portugal, South Africa, Spain.
b. 1983. Rough estimate.

Table 1.3
Inward stocks of foreign direct investment, by major host region, 1975–1985 (billions of US dollars)

Countries/regions/areas	1975			1983			1985		
	Value	percentage of total	GDP	Value	percentage of total	GDP	Value	percentage of total	GDP
Developed market economies	**185.3**	**75.1**	**4.5**	**401.0**	**75.6**	**5.1**	**478.2**	**75.0**	**5.5**
Western Europe	100.6	40.8	5.8	159.6	30.1	5.6	184.3	28.9	6.6
United States	27.7	11.2	1.8	137.1	25.9	4.2	184.6	29.0	4.7
Other[a]	57.0	23.1	7.0	104.3	19.7	6.0	109.2	17.1	5.7
Japan	1.5	0.6	0.3	5.0	0.9	0.4	6.1	1.0	0.5
Developing countries and territories	**61.5**	**24.9**	**6.4**	**138.4**	**24.4**	**7.4**	**159.0**	**25.0**	**8.5**
Africa[b]	16.5	6.7	15.7	19.6	3.7	9.4	22.3	3.5	10.8
Asia[c]	13.0	5.3	3.2	40.1	5.8	4.9	49.6	7.8	5.7
Latin America and the Caribbean[d]	29.7	12.0	8.9	73.2	13.8	11.9	80.5	12.6	13.6
Other[e]	2.3	0.9	2.1	5.4	1.0	2.4	6.6	1.0	3.4
Total[f]	**246.8**	**100.0**	**4.9**	**539.4**	**100.0**	**5.5**	**637.2**	**100.0**	**6.1**

Source: See table 1.2.
a. Australia, Canada, Japan, New Zealand, South Africa.
b. Botswana, Cameroon, Central African Republic, Congo, Côte d'Ivoire, Egypt, Gabon, Ghana, Kenya, Liberia, Libyan Arab Jamahiriya, Malawi, Mauritius, Morocco, Nigeria, Senegal, Seychelles, Sierra Leone, Togo, United Republic of Tanzania, Zaire, Zambia, Zimbabwe.
c. Bangladesh, China, Hong Kong, India, Indonesia, Malaysia, Pakistan, Philippines, Republic of Korea, Singapore, Sri Lanka, Taiwan Province, Thailand.
d. Argentina, Barbados, Brazil, Chile, Colombia, Dominican Republic, Ecuador, Guyana, Jamaica, Mexico, Panama, Paraguay, Peru, Trinidad and Tobago, Uruguay, Venezuela.
e. Fiji, Papua New Guinea, Saudi Arabia, Turkey, Yugoslavia.
f. Excluding the centrally planned economies of Europe, for which no precise data are available.

It would appear from table 1.2 that the importance of United States TNCs as foreign investors peaked in the late 1960s or early 1970s. Thus the share of the United States in total outward FDI shows some decline in 1975 as compared to 1960 and, since 1975, that trend has accelerated. While United States-based TNCs still account for 35 per cent of total world FDI stocks, their weight has declined sharply since 1975. Moreover, the ratio of outward FDI stocks to GDP for the United States peaked in the second half of the 1970s and has subsequently declined.

By contrast, the ratio of outward FDI stocks to GDP has increased sharply in Japan, Canada, and almost all the Western European countries. As regards shares in the world stock of FDI, the big gainers have been Japan and the Federal Republic of Germany. Companies from those two countries had relatively small amounts of FDI in 1960, reflecting the fact that both countries were still recovering from the effects of the Second World War. Since then, corporations based in those countries have become increasingly important foreign investors. There are differences, however, between these two home countries. While the share of the Federal Republic of Germany in total FDI stocks did, in fact, rise less than that of Japan, FDI as a share of GDP has increased faster in the Federal Republic of Germany than in Japan.

Enterprises from developing countries have tended to increase their small share of world FDI stocks, but this trend appears to have peaked in the early 1980s. With regard to enterprises from the centrally planned economies, no precise figures are available. The most recent estimate places the cumulative value of capital contributions by enterprises from the Soviet Union and Eastern Europe in the developed market economies at $500 million (McMillan, 1987, p. 44). FDI stocks, of course, are larger, since they also include the value of reinvested earnings. The above figure underestimates the world stocks of FDI owned by enterprises from the centrally planned economies for an additional reason: they exclude stocks in developing countries, which could be almost as large as those in the developed market economies. One source has placed the value of the stocks of FDI owned in 1983 by enterprises from socialist countries at $1 billion (United States, Department of Commerce, 1984, p. 8). While the figure is likely to be somewhat larger today, it still accounts for less than 0.2 per cent of the world total.

The data for host regions shown in table 1.3 also show some significant changes between 1975 and 1985. The share of the developed market economies in inward FDI stocks remained at three quarters of the world total. Among the developed market economies, the Western European countries, which up to the 1970s had been the preferred region of destination for FDI, saw their share decline, while the share of the United States increased dramatically. In 1985, the stocks of FDI in the United States were equivalent to almost 5 per cent of its GDP, as compared to less than 2 per cent in 1975. By contrast, owing to official barriers, inward FDI stocks in Japan are a negligible proportion of GDP, and this has remained unchanged over time.

Among the developing countries, Africa's share of inward FDI stocks declined by one half. The nationalization of foreign mining and petroleum assets that took place in Africa during the early 1970s, together with the lack of interest on the part of TNCs in investing in projects directed to the small domestic markets of most African countries, account for the falling share of Africa in the world stock of FDI. The Asian countries (including China) increased their participation by 2.5 percentage points, reflecting the relatively strong economic performance of that region. The share of Latin America and the Caribbean rose slightly.

The proxy for the degree of transnationalization used here (the ratio of the stocks of FDI to the GDPs of home countries and host countries or regions) could be affected by exchange-rate fluctuations. For example, the decline observed during the 1980–1985 period in the United States' outward stocks of FDI relative to its GDP could be partly accounted for by the strong appreciation of the dollar. A large share of the foreign investments of United States corporations is in Western Europe and, as the dollar appreciated with respect to the currencies of those countries, the stocks of FDI owned by United States corporations in Western Europe, when converted back to dollars, declined in value. The opposite is probably true of Japanese and Western European corporations; the depreciation of their currencies during the same period probably overstates somewhat the rise in their ratio of FDI stocks to GDP. The change in this ratio for Japan and the major Western European countries was probably less affected by currency fluctuations than that of the United States, since a considerable share of their investments abroad are in countries whose currencies moved together with theirs.

In spite of possible biases imparted by the measure chosen to assess broad trends in the transnationalization of the world economy, the basic conclusions that were derived from examining the data appear to be quite robust. The decline in the relative importance of TNCs based in the United States, the increasing transnationalization of Japanese and Western European companies and the surge of investment into the United States appear to be actual long-term phenomena, even though their precise measurement is rendered difficult by swings in exchange rates. Thus the United States lost ground as a home country—and, conversely, Japan, the Federal Republic of Germany, the United Kingdom and Canada gained—both when the dollar was depreciating (in the second half of the 1970s), as well as when it was appreciating (the first half of the 1980s). At the same time, the United States has been steadily becoming a more important destination for FDI since the mid-1970s.

D.   What the Data for the Major Home Countries Show

These preliminary results about the changing importance of TNCs based in different home countries are confirmed when one examines various measures of transnationalization in four major home countries for which data are available: the Federal Republic of Germany, Japan, the United Kingdom and the United States. The measures that were estimated are (a) the ratio of outward FDI stocks to total corporate assets, (b) the ratio of assets abroad controlled by affiliates of TNCs to total corporate assets, and (c) employment in affiliates abroad to domestic private employment. The results of those calculations are shown in tables 1.4, 1.5 and 1.6, respectively. Since the methods used to estimate the data that went into the calculation of the ratios vary greatly from country to country, cross-country comparisons of the ratios are not meaningful. What is of significance is their movement over time for each individual country.

The two financial ratios (FDI stocks and assets controlled by foreign affiliates to total corporate assets) are affected by the exchange-rate problem noted above. The ratio of FDI stocks to domestic assets has the drawback that it does not reflect the extent to which the corporations based in a country control production abroad. For example, it is conceivable that United States corporations, whose ratio of FDI stocks to domestic assets has declined in the 1980s, may have reduced their risk capital abroad (by, say, entering into joint ventures with local companies), while still increasing the output of their affiliates. That problem is taken into account to some extent by the second and third measures of transnationalization. Of course, even these measures do not fully account for the possible impact of non-equity forms of relationship between TNCs and firms in host countries.

Unfortunately, the only measure for which data are available for a fairly long-time span in the four home countries is the first one, which is probably the most inadequate of the three. As table 1.4 suggests, the transnationalization of United States firms peaked somewhere between 1965 and 1975. Owing to small year-to-year variations in the ratio, it is difficult to identify

Table 1.4
Selected home countries: ratio of outward foreign direct investment stocks to total corporate assets (percentage)

Year	United States All corporations	Non-financial corporations	Japan	Federal Republic of Germany	United Kingdom[a]
1945	1.8	—	—	—	—
1950	2.1	4.2	—	—	—
1955	2.4	5.6[b]	—	—	16.0
1960	2.9	—	—	—	18.0
1965	3.1	6.8	—	1.4	18.3[c]
1970	3.2	6.8	0.4[d]	2.3[e]	22.7
1975	3.1	6.4	0.9	3.4	21.8
1980	3.0	5.3	0.9	4.8	22.6
1981	2.9	5.6	1.2	5.6	27.1
1982	2.6	5.4	1.4	5.9	29.0
1983	2.2	4.8	1.4	6.3	31.0
1984	2.1	4.7	1.7	7.2	—
1985	2.1	4.7	1.5	—	—

Source: United Nations Centre on Transnational Corporations, based on official national sources.
a. 1957.
b. 1966.
c. 1971.
d. 1969.

a peak within this period. During the entire post-war period up to the early 1970s, the ratio of United States FDI stocks abroad to total corporate assets increased continuously. In the early 1970s the ratio began to decline, and this fall accelerated during the period from 1980 to 1985.

Exactly the opposite is true of the Federal Republic of Germany, Japan, and the United Kingdom. In all of those countries, the available data suggest that companies based there have become increasingly transnational in orientation since at least the early 1970s.[7]

Information on the other two indicators of transnationalization is considerably less abundant. Ratios of foreign assets controlled by affiliates to total corporate assets are available only for the United States and the Federal Republic of Germany. Employment data are available for those two countries and for Japan. For the United States, data are unavailable except for the years 1976, 1977 and 1982, the years for which bench-mark surveys of direct investment abroad were conducted.

Table 1.5
United States and the Federal Republic of Germany: ratio of assets of foreign affiliates to
total corporate assets (percentage)

Year	United States		Federal Republic of Germany	
	All industries	Non-financial industries	All industries	Non-financial industries
1950	—	4.8	—	—
1957	5.3	7.0	—	—
1966	7.6	14.6	—	—
1976	—	—	19.5	20.4
1977	16.9	20.0	21.5	21.4
1980	—	—	31.6	29.2
1981	—	—	36.2	33.6
1982	15.6	16.7	38.3	34.7
1983	—	15.5	39.6	37.1
1984	—	14.6	43.5	41.7
1985	—	15.2	—	—

Source: United Nations Centre on Transnational Corporations, based on official national
sources.

Table 1.6
United States, the Federal Republic of Germany and Japan: Employment in foreign
affiliates, as percentage of total domestic employment

Year	United States		Federal Republic of Germany[c]	Japan
	Non-financial affiliates[a]	Manufacturing affiliates[b]		
1957	7.3	9.9	—	—
1972	—	—	—	0.9
1974	—	—	—	1.6
1976	—	—	5.1	2.0
1977	11.3	24.7	5.3	1.9
1980	—	—	7.2	1.8
1981	—	—	7.3	2.1
1982	9.5	23.6	7.1	2.1
1983	9.1	22.9	6.9	2.1
1984	8.6	22.6	7.2	2.0
1985	8.4	22.6	7.6	—

Source: United Nations Centre on Transnational Corporations, based on official national
sources.
a. Total domestic employment refers to private sector non-agricultural employment.
b. The denominator is domestic manufacturing employment.
c. The denominator is total non-agricultural employment.

The asset indicator (table 1.5) tells much the same story as the ratio of FDI stocks to total corporate assets. Among bench-mark survey years, the ratio of assets controlled by affiliates of United States corporations to total corporate assets appears to have peaked in 1977 and to have fallen substantially since then. On the other hand, for the Federal Republic of Germany, the ratio shows a steady increase beginning in 1976, the earliest possible time for which such calculations can be made.

Although the change in the asset indicator is in the same direction as that of the ratio of FDI to total corporate assets, there are some interesting differences. For United States corporations, the decline in the asset ratio has been substantially less than the decline in the FDI ratio. In addition, the long-run changes in those two indicators for United States corporations have been quite different. While by 1985 the ratio of FDI to total corporate assets had returned to its 1950 level, in 1985 the ratio of assets of affiliates to total corporate assets was about three times its 1950 level. This means that affiliates of United States firms have tended to finance an increasing share of their expansion from sources other than their parent companies. Such sources include joint-venture partners in host countries, borrowing in local currencies and borrowing from international capital markets without the guarantee of the parent company. In fact, in 1985, FDI by United States companies represented only 31 per cent of the value of their affiliates' assets, down from 35 per cent in 1977 and from 63 per cent in 1950. By contrast, corporations based in the Federal Republic of Germany do not seem to have moved extensively towards financing of affiliates from non-parent sources, since the increase in the assets of affiliates roughly paralleled the increase in FDI stocks of the parent companies in the period from the mid-1970s to the mid-1980s.

The employment ratio (table 1.6) exhibits the same pattern of variation over time as between the major home countries, but to a lesser extent, perhaps because this indicator is not affected by currency changes. Two significant points emerge from this table. In the first place, most of the increase in employment abroad for corporations from Japan and the Federal Republic of Germany appears to have occurred during the 1970s. In fact, Japanese employment abroad, as a share of total domestic employment, was practically unchanged over the 1980–1985 period, after having doubled between 1972 and 1980.

Second, the decline in the share of United States employment abroad has been substantially less pronounced than the drop in the two financial indicators. In the case of manufacturing, the ratio of employment abroad to total private employment dropped by barely 2 percentage points (or about

10 per cent) between 1977 and 1985. This suggests that part of the apparent decline in transnationalization, as measured by economy-wide indicators, was owing to changes in the composition of economic activity. It is a well-known fact that the share of services in total output has been expanding rapidly. Although FDI in services has also grown faster than total FDI, the production of services is still less transnationalized than that of goods.

The data for the four individual home countries analysed are remarkably consistent with those presented earlier in the present chapter. They show a fairly general movement towards the increasing transnationalization of corporations other than those based in the United States. FDI positions have grown relative to their domestic assets, while the proportion of assets located outside their home countries has increased. The proportion of employment in their foreign affiliates has also increased. The exception to these generalizations is the United States. After a rapid growth in transnationalization by United States firms throughout the post-war period up to the mid-1970s, those firms appear to have drawn back somewhat and to have reduced their overseas employment and assets relative to those in the United States.

E.   A Pausible Explanation of Transnationalization Trends

What accounts for the simultaneous increase in the transnationalization of non-United States corporations and the decline in that of United States corporations? A great deal more research is needed before one can advance a definitive hypothesis. For the time being, the most plausible explanation lies in changes that could have taken place in the relative competitiveness of corporations from different industrialized countries.

The period of the Second World War and the post-war reconstruction had opened up a wide gap between United States firms and those of other industrialized countries. United States firms emerged from that period with an accumulation of the technological and organizational assets that are the basis for a firm's ability to operate in foreign countries. That gap between United States and non-United States companies led to an increase in the level of foreign operations and in the share of foreign operations in the total activity of United States companies.

Since the early 1970s, however, corporations based in home countries other than the United States have probably been in the process of catching up with United States TNCs. If the transnational expansion of United States firms in Western Europe was, in fact, based on technological superiority, the recovery of Western European corporations would have worked to diminish the capability of United States corporations to expand further in Western Europe. At the same time, it would have increased the incentives for Western European companies to become transnationals.

The transnational expansion of Japanese corporations appears to be due to superior technological and organizational factors. Japanese corporations are still at the beginning of their process of transnational expansion and many firms are now not only catching up technologically with the leading international corporations in their field, be they United States-based or Western European, but in a number of sectors the locus of technological innovation (in a broad sense, encompassing management techniques and the organization of production) may be gradually shifting towards Japanese corporations. If this is so, many Japanese corporations would now possess the intangible assets required for international leadership of their respective industries.

The hypothesis that non-United States TNCs have been gaining in competitiveness relative to their United States counterparts is in agreement with the dramatic increase observed in FDI in the United States in the 1980s. TNCs from industrialized countries other than the United States are now strong enough to compete with United States corporations on their own home ground, and they have been anxious to position themselves in the huge United States market, where their presence before 1980 was relatively small.

Increasing protectionism in the United States and Western Europe and exchange-rate instability have undoubtedly encouraged Japanese investments in other developed market economies and Western European investments in the United States. While protectionism threatens companies with the loss of export markets, exchange-rate instability renders profits from export-oriented investment more uncertain. Both of those characteristics of world economic development in the recent period probably encouraged TNCs from Japan and Western Europe to invest in countries where they sell their products.[8] However, the rapid transnationalization of Japanese corporations and the aggressive thrust of Western European companies into the United States economy might have occurred even in the absence of protectionism and international economic uncertainties, albeit at a considerably slower pace.

The catch-up hypothesis is also consistent with the observed decline in the ratios of foreign to total assets and employment for United States corporations. These ratios have fallen because the increase in those corporations' investment and employment at home has outstripped the rise in their foreign activities. Thus it would appear that United States TNCs have emphasized investments at home over foreign investment, perhaps with a view to defending themselves against competition by foreign corporations.... those investments appear to have been related to the quest for greater productive efficiency, the reduction of costs and the rationalization of operations.

There have also been other factors at work. The liberalization of exchange controls in Japan and a number of Western European countries during the second half of the 1970s could have induced a once-and-for-all increase in the stocks of FDI by companies based in those countries. In addition, slow economic growth in their home countries may have encouraged foreign investments by corporations based in Western Europe and Japan, but particularly in the United States, a country which has the largest domestic market in the world and one in which foreign investors still have a relatively small position.

To some extent, the growing international position of companies from Japan and several Western European countries, particularly the Federal Republic of Germany and the United Kingdom, and the decline in that of United States corporations, is a reflection at the corporate level of the shifts in the location of world current-account imbalances. As already noted, Japan and the Federal Republic of Germany have emerged as the strongest surplus countries, and the United States has swung from being the world's largest creditor to being its largest debtor. Western European and Japanese corporations have accumulated substantial amounts of cash, and they have been investing it in foreign ventures, particularly in the United States.

The United States could continue to exert a powerful attraction for companies based in other industrialized countries in the medium-term future, especially in view of the steep decline in the dollar since early 1985, which is now very likely to be viewed as permanent by TNCs from Japan and Western Europe. Moreover, the stock market crash of October 1987 has made the acquisition of United States companies very attractive. Since the ratio of inward FDI stocks to GDP in the United States is still well below the average for the Western European countries, it would appear that there is still plenty of "room" for further growth of inward investment in the United States by companies based in Japan and Western Europe.

The international economic environment has had other effects on TNCs.... services, particularly the financial sector, have been absorbing a growing proportion of new FDI. The main cause for the huge foreign investments by transnational banks and non-bank financial companies in the 1980s has been the rapid liberalization of domestic capital markets that has taken place in all of the large money-centre countries. The instability of exchange rates and interest rates may have also been contributing factors.

The liberalization of domestic financial markets in the industrial countries has led to the emergence of an international financial market with a high degree of integration (see Bryant, 1987, chap. 5). The greater integration of the financial sectors of the industrialized countries, and the strong incentives either to speculate on or hedge against the impact of changes in key international parameters, have resulted in a veritable boom in international capital flows intermediated by transnational financial institutions. Thus FDI in banking and finance has grown very rapidly during the 1980s, as most transnational commercial and investment banks have been eager to position themselves in all major financial markets. Of course, the vast majority of such activities has been centred in the developed market economies, while most developing countries have been entirely excluded therefrom.

International economic instability has undoubtedly led to an increase in the weight of purely financial transactions in the sum total of activities of TNCs and may have also had an impact on the sectoral composition of investment, both foreign and domestic, in favour of the financial sector of the major-currency countries and to the detriment of investments in other sectors. Rapid and unforeseen changes in the value of internationally traded currencies and in interest rates on financial investments denominated in various currencies foster international capital flows of a speculative nature. A large corporation with significant liquid balances denominated in different currencies can make larger and quicker profits from guessing the direction of movements in international interest rates and exchange rates than from investments in the expansion of productive capacity, which normally take several years to mature. On the other hand, the greater uncertainty attached to international transactions in goods and capital has led to an increase in the demand for new financial instruments which would allow risk-averse corporations and individuals to protect the value of their assets in their home-country currencies. The greater demand for international financial instruments has been, therefore, an additional spur to foreign investments in the banking industry.

As host countries, the developing countries have maintained their historic proportion in world FDI stocks of about one quarter. This has been due to the growth of stocks located in China and in South-East Asia. Among developing regions, the major destination of FDI flows in the past was Latin America. The countries of that region have been in chronic difficulties since the eruption of the debt crisis in 1982, and this has discouraged new investments. Generally, total investments by TNCs in their

home economies and in other developed countries may have grown substantially faster than their investments in developing countries. The rush by
non-United States corporations to invest in the United States, rapid processes of technical change in the industrial economies requiring large volumes of capital-deepening investment, together with the deceleration in
the rates of economic growth of many developing countries in Africa, Latin
America and the Middle East, may explain this phenomenon. While it is
too early to predict that the recent changes in the location of investment
by TNCs constitute a new trend, there is the danger that, in the future,
developing countries may become increasingly marginal to TNCs. If this
were the case, it would reduce the number of option available to developing countries, and it would increase their difficulties in obtaining access to
foreign capital and modern technology.

Notes

1. Strictly speaking, the term "transnationalization" is meant to denote the extent
to which a country's production of goods and services can be accounted for by
enterprises based in other countries, or the extent to which individual enterprises
produce abroad relative to their total production.

2. Angus Maddison has recently argued that the period 1950–1973 was unusual,
and that the slow-down after 1973 represented a return to growth rates that were
more in line with long-term historical experience. See "Growth and slowdown in
advanced capitalist economies: Techniques of quantitative assessment," Journal of
Economic Literature, vol. XXV, No. 2 (June 1987).

3. Stocks of FDI abroad by countries and foreign-owned stocks of FDI in countries
are henceforth referred to as "outward stocks" and "inward stocks," respectively.

4. If one assumes a constant capital-output ratio in the home economy, an increase
in the ratio of outward FDI stocks to home-country GDP would indicate that the
capital stock held abroad has grown at a faster pace than the domestic capital stock.
Conversely, assuming a constant capital-output ratio for capital stocks abroad, an
increase in the ratio would be a sign that output abroad by affiliates of TNCs has
been growing faster than output in the home country. By the same token, under
similar assumptions, changes in the ratio of inward FDI stocks to the GDP of a host
country would indicate the extent to which production by foreign companies (or
the foreign-owned capital stock) was growing faster than production or the capital
stock owned by nationals of the host country.

5. The stocks of FDI as reported by home and host countries tend to differ for a
variety of reasons. Different countries have different criteria for distinguishing
between direct and portfolio investment, depending on the extent of foreign ownership. Many countries define FDI differently. For example, some countries do not
collect statistics on reinvested earnings. In most countries, FDI stocks are measured
at book value, a method which tends to underestimate real replacement value.

When stocks of FDI are estimated as the sum of flows in current values (usually measured in United States dollars), the resulting stocks can be seriously underestimated, since, owing to international inflation, a dollar of investment several years ago is worth a great deal more than a dollar of investment at a point closer to the present. On the other hand, this method of measuring investment stocks ignores depreciation and changes in the valuation of existing assets.

6. In the case of the developing countries, the ratios are affected by the real depreciation of the currencies of a large number of countries vis-à-vis the dollar since the beginning of the debt crisis in 1982, which caused their GDPs to fall in dollar terms.

7. The large differences in the absolute value of the ratio from country to country are due to differences in the methods used to estimate FDI stocks and, particularly, in the number of companies included in the denominator. In the case of the United Kingdom, the total assets figure is that of "large corporations" (as defined in United Kingdom, *Annual Abstract of Statistics*).

8. The incentives to expand productive capacity in foreign markets have probably been less for United States corporations than for corporations based in other home countries, since the former already had significant foreign positions prior to the mid-1970s.

References

Bryant, Ralph C. *International Financial Intermediation* (Washington, D.C., The Brookings Institution, 1987).

Caves, Richard E. *Multinational Enterprise and Economic Analysis* (Cambridge, England, Cambridge University Press, 1982).

Dunning, John H. *International Production and the Multinational Enterprise* (London, Allen and Unwin, 1981).

Dunning, John H. "International business, the recession and economic restructuring." University of Reading Discussion Papers. *International Investment and Business Studies* No. 88 (Reading, England, September 1985).

Lipsey, Robert E. "Changing patterns of international investment in and by the United States." NBER Working Paper No. 2240 (New York, National Bureau of Economic Research, May 1987).

McMillan, Carl H. *Multinationals from the Second World—Growth of Foreign Investment by Soviet and East European State Enterprises* (London, Macmillan Press, 1987).

United States, Department of Commerce. *International Direct Investment—Global Trends and the U.S. Role* (Washington, D.C., 1984).

2

Changing Patterns of International Competition

Michael E. Porter

When examining the environmental changes facing firms today, it is a rare observer who will conclude that international competition is not high on the list. The growing importance of international competition is well recognized both in the business and academic communities, for reasons that are fairly obvious when one looks at just about any data set that exists on international trade or investment. Figure 2.1, for example, compares world trade and world GNP. Something interesting started happening around the mid-1950s, when the growth in world trade began to significantly exceed the growth in world GNP. Foreign direct investment by firms in developing countries began to grow rapidly a few years later, about 1963.[1] This period marked the beginning of a fundamental change in the international competitive environment that by now has come to be widely recognized. It is a trend that is causing sleepless nights for many business managers.

There is a substantial literature on international competition, because the subject is far from a new one. A large body of literature has investigated the many implications of the Heckscher-Ohlin model and other models of international trade which are rooted in the principle of comparative advantage.[2] The unit of analysis in this literature is the country. There is also considerable literature on the multinational firm, reflecting the growing importance of the multinational since the turn of the century. In examining the reasons for the multinational, I think it is fair to characterize this literature as resting heavily on the multinational's ability to exploit intangible assets.[3] The work of Hymer and Caves among others has stressed the role of the multinational in transferring know-how and expertise gained in one country market to others at low cost, and thereby offsetting the unavoidable extra costs of doing business in a foreign country. A more recent stream of literature extends this by emphasizing how the multinational firm

From *California Management Review*, Winter 1986, pp. 9–40. Reprinted by permission.

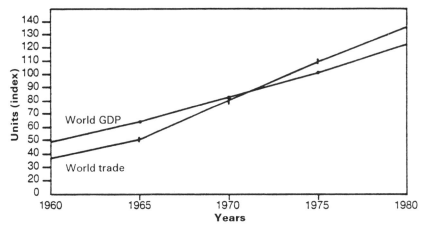

Source: United Nations, *Statistical Yearbooks*.

Figure 2.1
Growth of world trade

internalizes transactions to circumvent imperfections in various intermediate markets, most importantly the market for knowledge.

There is also a related literature on the problems of entry into foreign markets and the life cycle of how a firm competes abroad, beginning with export or licensing and ultimately moving to the establishment of foreign subsidiaries. Vernon's product cycle of international trade combines a view of how products mature with the evolution in a firm's international activities to predict the patterns of trade and investment in developed and developing countries.[4] Finally, many of the functional fields in business administration research have their branch of literature about international issues—e.g., international marketing, international finance. This literature concentrates, by and large, on the problems of doing business in a foreign country.

As rich as it is, however, I think it is fair to characterize the literature on international competition as being limited when it comes to the choice of a firm's international strategy. Though the literature provides some guidance for considering incremental investment decisions to enter a new country, it provides at best a partial view of how to characterize a firm's overall international strategy and how such strategy should be selected. Put another way, the literature focuses more on the problem of becoming a multinational than on strategies for established multinationals. Although the distinction between domestic firms and multinationals is seminal in a literature focused on the problems of doing business abroad, the fact that a firm is multinational says little if anything about its international strategy except that it operates in several countries.

Broadly stated, my research has been seeking to answer the question: what does international competition mean for competitive strategy? In particular, what are the distinctive questions for competitive strategy that are raised by international as opposed to domestic competition? Many of the strategy issues for a company competing internationally are very much the same as for one competing domestically. A firm must still analyze its industry structure and competitors, understand its buyer and the sources of buyer value, diagnose its relative cost position, and seek to establish a sustainable competitive advantage within some competitive scope, whether it be across-the-board or in an industry segment. These are subjects I have written about extensively.[5] But there are some questions for strategy that are peculiar to international competition, and that add to rather than replace those listed earlier. These questions all revolve, in one way or another, around how a firm's activities in one country affect or are affected by what is going on in other countries—the connectedness among country competition. It is this connectedness that is the focus of this article and of a broader stream of research recently conducted under the auspices of the Harvard Business School.[6]

Patterns of International Competition

The appropriate unit of analysis in setting international strategy is the industry, because the industry is the arena in which competitive advantage is won or lost. The starting point for understanding international competition is the observation that its pattern differs markedly from industry to industry. At one end of the spectrum are industries that I call *multidomestic*, in which competition in each country (or small group of countries) is essentially independent of competition in other countries. A multidomestic industry is one that is present in many countries (e.g., there is a consumer banking industry in Sri Lanka, one in France, and one in the U.S.), but in which competition occurs on a country-by-country basis. In a multidomestic industry, a multinational firm may enjoy a competitive advantage from the one-time transfer of know-how from its home base to foreign countries. However, the firm modifies and adapts its intangible assets to employ them in each country and the outcome is determined by conditions in each country. The competitive advantages of the firm, then, are largely specific to each country. The international industry becomes a collection of essentially domestic industries—hence the term "multidomestic." Industries where competition has traditionally exhibited this pattern include retailing, consumer packaged goods, distribution, insurance, consumer finance, and caustic chemicals.

At the other end of the spectrum are what I term *global* industries. The term global—like the word "strategy"—has become overused and perhaps under-understood. The definition of a global industry employed here is an industry in which a firm's competitive position in one country is significantly influenced by its position in other countries.[7] Therefore, the international industry is not merely a collection of domestic industries but a series of linked domestic industries in which the rivals compete against each other on a truly worldwide basis. Industries exhibiting the global pattern today include commercial aircraft, TV sets, semiconductors, copiers, automobiles, and watches.

The implications for strategy of the distinction between multidomestic and global industries are quite profound. In a multidomestic industry, a firm can and should manage its international activities like a portfolio. Its subsidiaries or other operations around the world should each control all the important activities necessary to do business in the industry and should enjoy a high degree of autonomy. The firm's strategy in a country should be determined largely by the circumstances in that country; the firm's international strategy is then what I term a "country-centered strategy."

In a multidomestic industry, competing internationally is discretionary. A firm can choose to remain domestic or can expand internationally if it has some advantage that allows it to overcome the extra costs of entering and competing in foreign markets. The important competitors in multidomestic industries will either be domestic companies or multinationals with stand-alone operations abroad—this is the situation in each of the multidomestic industries listed earlier. In a multidomestic industry, then, international strategy collapses to a series of domestic strategies. The issues that are uniquely international revolve around how to do business abroad, how to select good countries in which to compete (or assess country risk), and mechanisms to achieve the one-time transfer of knowhow. These are questions that are relatively well developed in the literature.

In a global industry, however, managing international activities like a portfolio will undermine the possibility of achieving competitive advantage. In a global industry, a firm must in some way integrate its activities on a worldwide basis to capture the linkages among countries. This will require more than transferring intangible assets among countries, though it will include it. A firm may choose to compete with a country-centered strategy, focusing on specific market segments or countries when it can carve out a niche by responding to whatever local country differences are present. However, it does so at some considerable risk from competitors with global strategies. All the important competitors in the global industries listed earlier compete worldwide with coordinated strategies.

In international competition, a firm always has to perform some functions in each of the countries in which it competes. Even though a global competitor must view its international activities as an overall system, it has still to maintain some country perspective. It is the balancing of these two perspectives that becomes one of the essential questions in global strategy.[8]

Causes of Globalization

If we accept the distinction between multidomestic and global industries as an important taxonomy of patterns of international competition, a number of crucial questions arise. When does an industry globalize? What exactly do we mean by a global strategy, and is there more than one kind? What determines the type of international strategy to select in a particular industry?

An industry is global if there is some competitive advantage to integrating activities on a worldwide basis. To make this statement operational, however, we must be very precise about what we mean by "activities" and also what we mean by "integrating." To diagnose the sources of competitive advantage in any context, whether it be domestic or international, it is necessary to adopt a disaggregated view of the firm. In my newest book, *Competitive Advantage*, I have developed a framework for doing so, called the value chain.[9] Every firm is a collection of discrete activities performed to do business that occur within the scope of the firm—I call them value activities. The activities performed by a firm include such things as salespeople selling the product, service technicians performing repairs, scientists in the laboratory designing process techniques, and accountants keeping the books. Such activities are technologically and in most cases physically distinct. It is only at the level of discrete activities, rather than the firm as a whole, that competitive advantage can be truly understood.

A firm may possess two types of competitive advantage: low relative cost or differentiation—its ability to perform the activities in its value chain either at lower cost or in a unique way relative to its competitors. The ultimate value a firm creates is what buyers are willing to pay for what the firm provides, which includes the physical product as well as any ancillary services or benefits. Profit results if the value created through performing the required activities exceeds the collective cost of performing them. Competitive advantage is a function of either providing comparable buyer value to competitors but performing activities efficiently (low cost), or of performing activities at comparable cost but in unique ways that create greater buyer value than competitors and, hence, command a premium price (differentiation).

The value chain, shown in figure 2.2, provides a systematic means of displaying and categorizing activities. The activities performed by a firm in any industry can be grouped into the nine generic categories shown. The labels may differ based on industry convention, but every firm performs these basic categories of activities in some way or another. Within each category of activities, a firm typically performs a number of discrete activities which are particular to the industry and to the firm's strategy. In service, for example, firms typically perform such discrete activities as installation, repair, parts distribution, and upgrading.

The generic categories of activities can be grouped into two broad types. Along the bottom are what I call *primary* activities, which are those involved in the physical creation of the product or service, its delivery and marketing to the buyer, and its support after sale. Across the top are what I call *support* activities, which provide inputs or infrastructure that allow the primary activities to take place on an ongoing basis.

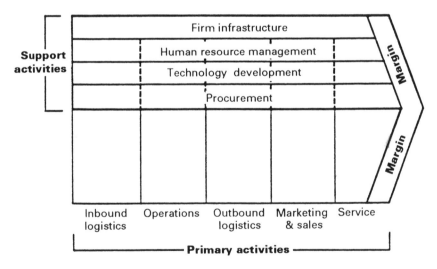

Figure 2.2
The value chain

Procurement is the obtaining of purchased inputs, whether they be raw materials, purchased services, machinery, or so on. Procurement stretches across the entire value chain because it supports every activity—every activity uses purchased inputs of some kind. There are typically many different discrete procurement activities within a firm, often performed by different people. Technology development encompasses the activities involved in designing the product as well as in creating and improving the way the various activities in the value chain are performed. We tend to think of technology in terms of the product or manufacturing process. In fact, every activity a firm performs involves a technology or technologies which may be mundane or sophisticated, and a firm has a stock of know-how about how to perform each activity. Technology development typically involves a variety of different discrete activities, some performed outside the R & D department.

Human resource management is the recruiting, training, and development of personnel. Every activity involves human resources, and thus human resource management activities cut across the entire chain. Finally, firm infrastructure includes activities such as general management, accounting, legal, finance, strategic planning, and all the other activities decoupled from specific primary or support activities but that are essential to enable the entire chain's operation.

Activities in a firm's value chain are not independent, but are connected through what I call linkages. The way one activity is performed frequently affects the cost or effectiveness of other activities. If more is spent on the purchase of a raw material, for example, a firm may lower its cost of fabrication or assembly. There are many linkages that connect activities, not only within the firm but also with the activities of its suppliers, channels, and ultimately its buyers. The firm's value chain resides in a larger stream of activities that I term the value system. Suppliers have value chains that provide the purchased inputs to the firm's chain; channels have value chains through which the firm's product or service passes; buyers have value chains in which the firm's product or service is employed. The connections among activities in this vertical system also become essential to competitive advantage.

A firm important building block in value chain theory, necessary for our purposes here, is the notion of *competitive scope*. Competitive scope is the breadth of activities the firm employs together in competing in an industry. There are four basic dimensions of competitive scope:

• *segment* scope, or the range of segments the firm serves (e.g., product varieties, customer types);

- *industry* scope, or the range of industries the firm competes in with a coordinated strategy;

- *vertical* scope, or what activities are performed by the firm versus suppliers and channels; and

- *geographic* scope, or the geographic regions the firm operates in with a coordinated strategy.

Competitive scope is vital to competitive advantage because it shapes the configuration of the value chain, how activities are performed, and whether activities are shared among units. International strategy is an issue of geographic scope, and can be analyzed quite similarly to the question of whether and how a firm should compete locally, regionally, or nationally within a country. In the international context, government tends to have a greater involvement in competition and there are more significant variations among geographic regions in buyer needs, although these differences are matters of degree.

International Configuration and Coordination of Activities

A firm that competes internationally must decide how to spread the activities in the value chain among countries. A distinction immediately arises between the activities labeled downstream on figure 2.3 and those labeled upstream activities and support activities. The location of downstream activities, those more related to the buyer, is usually tied to where the buyer is located. If a firm is going to sell in Japan, for example, it usually must provide service in Japan and it must have salespeople stationed in Japan. In some industries it is possible to have a single sales force that travels to the buyer's country and back again; some other specific downstream activities such as the production of advertising copy can also sometimes be done centrally. More typically, however, the firm must locate the capability to perform downstream activities in each of the countries in which it operates. Upstream activities and support activities, conversely, can at least conceptually be decoupled from where the buyer is located.

This distinction carries some interesting implications. The first is that downstream activities create competitive advantages that are largely country-specific: a firm's reputation, brand name, and service network in a country grow out of a firm's activities in that country and create entry/ mobility barriers largely in that country alone. Competitive advantage in upstream and support activities often grows more out of the entire system

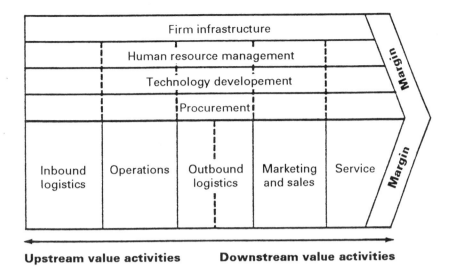

Figure 2.3
Upstream and downstream activities

of countries in which a firm competes than from its position in any one country, however.

A second implication is that in industries where downstream activities or buyer-tied activities are vital to competitive advantage, there tends to be a more multidomestic pattern of international competition. In industries where upstream and support activities (such as technology development and operations) are crucial to competitive advantage, global competition is more common. In global competition, the location and scale of these potentially footloose activities is optimized from a worldwide perspective.[10]

The distinctive issues in international, as contrasted to domestic, strategy can be summarized in two key dimensions of how a firm competes internationally. The first is what I term the *configuration* of a firm's activities worldwide, or where in the world each activity in the value chain is performed, including in how many places. The second dimension is what I term *coordination*, which refers to how like activities performed in different countries are coordinated with each other. If, for example, there are three plants—one in Germany, one in Japan, and one in the U.S.—how do the activities in those plants relate to each other?

A firm faces an array of options in both configuration and coordination for each activity. Configuration options range from concentrated (performing an activity in one location and serving the world from it—e.g., one

R & D lab, one large plant) to dispersed (performing every activity in each country). In the latter case, each country would have a complete value chain. Coordination options range from none to very high. For example, if a firm produces its product in three plants, it could, at one extreme, allow each plant to operate with full autonomy—e.g., different product standards and features, different steps in the production process, different raw materials, different part numbers. At the other extreme, the plants could be tightly coordinated by employing the same information system, the same production process, the same parts, and so forth. Options for coordination in an activity are typically more numerous than the configuration options because there are many possible levels of coordination and many different facets of the way the activity is performed.

Table 2.1 lists some of the configuration issues and coordination issues for several important categories of value activities. In technology development, for example, the configuration issue is where R & D is performed: one location? two locations? and in what countries? The coordination issues have to do with such things as the extent of interchange among R & D centers and the location and sequence of product introduction around the world. There are configuration issues and coordination issues for every activity.

Figure 2.4 is a way of summarizing these basic choices in international strategy on a single diagram, with coordination of activities on the vertical axis and configuration of activities on the horizontal axis. The firm has to make a set of choices for each activity. If a firm employs a very dispersed configuration—placing an entire value chain in every country (or small group of contiguous countries) in which it operates, coordinating little or not at all among them—then the firm is competing with a country-centered strategy. The domestic firm that only operates in one country is the extreme case of a firm with a country-centered strategy. As we move from the lower left-hand corner of the diagram up or to the right, we have strategies that are increasingly global.

Table 2.2 illustrates some of the possible variations in international strategy. The purest global strategy is to concentrate as many activities as possible in one country, serve the world from this home base, and tightly coordinate those activities that must inherently be performed near the buyer. This is the pattern adopted by many Japanese firms in the 1960s and 1970s, such as Toyota. However, figure 2.4 and table 2.2 make it clear that there is no such thing as one global strategy. There are many different kinds of global strategies, depending on a firm's choices about configuration and coordination throughout the value chain. In copiers, for example,

Table 2.1
Configuration and coordination issues by category and activity

Value activity	Configuration issues	Coordination issues
Operations	• Location of production facilities for components and end products	• Networking of international plants • Transferring process technology and production know-how among plants
Marketing and sales	• Product line selection • Country (market) selection	• Commonality of brand name worldwide • Coordination of sales to multinational accounts • Similarity of channels and product positioning worldwide • Coordination of pricing in different countries
Service	• Location of service organization	• Similarity of service standards and procedures worldwide
Technology development	• Number and location of R & D centers	• Interchange among dispersed R & D centers • Developing products responsive to market needs in many countries • Sequence of product introductions around the world
Procurement	• Location of the purchasing function	• Managing suppliers located in different countries • Transferring market knowledge • Coordinating purchases of common items

Xerox has until recently concentrated R & D in the U.S. but dispersed other activities, in some cases using joint-venture partners to perform them. On dispersed activities, however, coordination has been quite high. The Xerox brand, marketing approach, and servicing procedures have been quite standardized worldwide. Canon, on the other hand, has had a much more concentrated configuration of activities and somewhat less coordination of dispersed activities. The vast majority of support activities and manufacturing of copiers has been performed in Japan. Aside from using the Canon brand, however, local marketing subsidiaries have been given quite a bit of latitude in each region of the world.

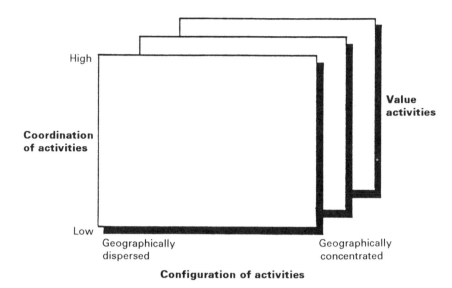

Figure 2.4
The dimensions of international strategy

Table 2.2
Types of international strategy

	Geographically dispersed	Geographically concentrated
High — Coordination of activities	High foreign investment with extensive coordination among subsidiaries	Purest global strategy
Low	Country-centered strategy by multinationals with a number of domestic firms operating in only one country	Export-based strategy with decentralized marketing

Configuration of activities

A global strategy can now be defined more precisely as one in which a firm seeks to gain competitive advantage from its international presence through either concentrating configuration, coordination among dispersed activities, or both. Measuring the presence of a global industry empirically must reflect both dimensions and not just one. Market presence in many countries and some export and import of components and end products are characteristic of most global industries. High levels of foreign investment or the mere presence of multinational firms are not reliable measures, however, because firms may be managing foreign units like a portfolio.

Configuration/Coordination and Competitive Advantage

Understanding the competitive advantages of a global strategy and, in turn, the causes of industry globalization requires specifying the conditions in which concentrating activities globally and coordinating dispersed activities leads to either cost advantage or differentiation. In each case, there are structural characteristics of an industry that work for and against globalization.

The factors that favor concentrating an activity in one or a few locations to serve the world are as follows:

- economies of scale in the activity;
- a proprietary learning curve in the activity;
- comparative advantage in where the activity is performed; and
- coordination advantages of co-locating linked activities such as R & D and production.

The first two factors relate to *how many* sites an activity is performed at, while the last two relate to *where* these sites are. Comparative advantage can apply to any activity, not just production. For example, there may be some locations in the world that are better places than others to do research on medical technology or to perform software development. Government can promote the concentration of activities by providing subsidies or other incentives to use a particular country as an export base, in effect altering comparative advantage—a role many governments are playing today.

There are also structural characteristics that favor dispersion of an activity to many countries, which represent concentration costs. Local product needs may differ, nullifying the advantages of scale or learning from one-site operation of an activity. Locating a range of activities in a country may facilitate marketing in that country by signaling commitment to local buyers and/or providing greater responsiveness. Transport, communication, and storage costs may make it inefficient to concentrate the activity in one location. Government is also frequently a powerful force for dispersing activities. Governments typically want firms to locate the entire value chain in their country, because this creates benefits and spillovers to the country that often go beyond local content. Dispersion is also encouraged by the risks of performing an activity in one place: exchange-rate risks, political risks, and so on. The balance between the advantages of concentrating and dispersing an activity normally differ for each activity (and industry). The best configuration for R & D is different from that for component fabrication, and this is different from that for assembly, installation, advertising, and procurement.[11]

The desirability of coordinating like activities that are dispersed involves a similar balance of structural factors. Coordination potentially allows the sharing of know-how among dispersed activities. If a firm learns how to operate the production process better in Germany, transferring that learning may make the process run better in plants in the United States and Japan. Differing countries, with their inevitably differing conditions, provide a fertile basis for comparison as well as opportunities for arbitraging knowledge obtained in different places about different aspects of the business. Coordination among dispersed activities also potentially improves the ability to reap economies of scale in activities if subtasks are allocated among locations to allow some specialization—e.g., each R & D center has a different area of focus. While there is a fine line between such forms of coordination and what I have termed configuration, it does illustrate how the way a network of foreign locations is managed can have a great influence on the ability to reap the benefits of any given configuration of activities. Viewed another way, close coordination is frequently a partial offset to dispersing an activity.

Coordination may also allow a firm to respond to shifting comparative advantage, where shifts in exchange rates and factor costs are hard to forecast. Incrementally increasing the production volume at the location currently enjoying favorable exchange rates, for example, can lower overall costs. Coordination can reinforce a firm's brand reputation with buyers (and hence lead to differentiation) through ensuring a consistent image and approach to doing business on a worldwide basis. This is particularly likely if buyers are mobile or information about the industry flows freely around the world. Coordination may also differentiate the firm with multinational buyers if it allows the firm to serve them anywhere and in a consistent way.

Coordination (and a global approach to configuration) enhances leverage with local governments if the firm is able to grow or shrink activities in one country at the expense of others. Finally, coordination yields flexibility in responding to competitors, by allowing the firm to differentially respond across countries and to respond in one country to a challenge in another.

Coordination of dispersed activities usually involves costs that differ by form of coordination and industry. Local conditions may vary in ways that may make a common approach across countries suboptimal. If every plant in the world is required to use the same raw material, for example, the firm pays a penalty in countries where the raw material is expensive relative to satisfactory substitutes. Business practices, marketing systems, raw material sources, local infrastructures, and a variety of other factors may differ across countries as well, often in ways that may mitigate the advantages of a common approach or of the sharing of learning. Governments may restrain the flow of information required for coordination or may impose other barriers to it. The transaction costs of coordination, which have recently received increased attention in domestic competition, are vitally important in international strategy.[12] International coordination involves long distances, language problems, and cultural barriers to communication. In some industries, these factors may mean that coordination is not optimal. They also suggest that forms of coordination which involve relatively infrequent decisions will enjoy advantages over forms of coordination involving on-going interchange.

There are also substantial organizational difficulties involved in achieving cooperation among subsidiaries, which are due to the difficulty in aligning subsidiary managers' interests with those of the firm as a whole. The Germans do not necessarily want to tell the Americans about their latest breakthroughs on the production line because it may make it harder for them to outdo the Americans in the annual comparison of operating efficiency among plants. These vexing organizational problems mean that country subsidiaries often view each other more as competitors than collaborators.[13] As with configuration, a firm must make an activity-by-activity choice about where there is net competitive advantage from coordinating in various ways.

Coordination in some activities may be necessary to reap the advantages of configuration in others. The use of common raw materials in each plant, for example, allows worldwide purchasing. Moreover, tailoring some activities to countries may allow concentration and standardization of other activities. For example, tailored marketing in each country may allow the same product to be positioned differently and hence sold successfully in many countries, unlocking possibilities for reaping economies of scale in production and R & D. Thus coordination and configuration interact.

Configuration/Coordination and the Pattern of International Competition

When benefits of configuring and/or coordinating globally exceed the costs, an industry will globalize in a way that reflects the net benefits by value activity. The activities in which global competitors gain competitive advantage will differ correspondingly. Configuration/coordination determines the ongoing competitive advantages of a global strategy which are additive to competitive advantages a firm derives/possesses from its domestic market positions. An initial transfer of knowledge from the home base to subsidiaries is one, but by no means the most important, advantage of a global competitor.[14]

An industry such as commercial aircraft represents an extreme case of a global industry (in the upper right-hand corner of figure 2.4). The three major competitors in this industry—Boeing, McDonnell Douglas, and Airbus—all have global strategies. In activities important to cost and differentiation in the industry, there are compelling net advantages to concentrating most activities and coordinating the dispersed activities extensively.[15] In R & D, there is a large fixed cost of developing an aircraft model ($1 billion or more) which requires worldwide sales to amortize. There are significant economies of scale in production, a steep learning curve in assembly (the learning curve was born out of research in this industry), and apparently significant advantages of locating R & D and production together. Sales of commercial aircraft are infrequent (via a highly skilled sales force), so that even the sales force can be partially concentrated in the home country and travel to buyers.

The costs of a concentrated configuration are relatively low in commercial aircraft. Product needs are homogenous, and there are the low transport costs of delivering the product to the buyer. Finally, worldwide coordination of the one dispersed activity, service, is very important—obviously standardized parts and repair advice have to be available wherever the plane lands.

As in every industry, there are structural features which work against a global strategy in commercial aircraft. These are all related to government, a not atypical circumstance. Government has a particular interest in commercial aircraft because of its large trade potential, the technological sophistication of the industry, its spillover effects to other industries, and its implications for national defense. Government also has an unusual degree of leverage in the industry: in many instances, it is the buyer. Many airlines are government-owned, and a government official or appointee is head of the airline.

The competitive advantages of a global strategy are so great that all the successful aircraft producers have sought to achieve and preserve them. In addition, the power of government to intervene has been mitigated by the fact the there are few viable worldwide competitors and that there are the enormous barriers to entry created in part by the advantages of a global strategy. The result has been that firms have sought to assuage government through procurement. Boeing, for example, is very careful about where it buys components. In countries that are large potential customers, Boeing seeks to develop suppliers. This requires a great deal of extra effort by Boeing both to transfer technology and to work with suppliers to ensure that they meet its standards. Boeing realizes that this is preferable to compromising the competitive advantage of its strongly integrated world-wide strategy. It is willing to employ one value activity (procurement) where the advantages of concentration are modest to help preserve the benefits of concentration in other activities. Recently, commercial aircraft competitors have entered into joint ventures and other coalition arrangements with foreign suppliers to achieve the same effect, as well as to spread the risk of huge development costs.

The extent and location of advantages from a global strategy vary among industries. In some industries, the competitive advantage from a global strategy comes in technology development, although firms gain little advantage in the primary activities so that these are dispersed around the world to minimize concentration costs. In other industries such as cameras or videocassette recorders, a firm cannot succeed without concentrating production to achieve economies of scale, but instead it gives subsidiaries much local autonomy in sales and marketing. In some industries, there is no net advantage to a global strategy and country-centered strategies dominate—the industry is multidomestic.

Segments or stages of an industry frequently vary in their pattern of globalization. In aluminum, the upstream (alumina and ingot) stages of the industry are global businesses. The downstream stage, semifabrication, is a group of multidomestic businesses because product needs vary by country, transport costs are high, and intensive local customer service is required. Scale economies in the value chain are modest. In lubricants, automotive oil tends to be a country-centered business while marine motor oil is a global business. In automotive oil, countries have varying driving standards, weather conditions, and local laws. Production involves blending various kinds of crude oils and additives, and is subject to few economies of scale but high shipping costs. Country-centered competitors such as Castrol and Quaker State are leaders in most countries. In the marine segment, conversely, ships move freely around the world and require the same oil everywhere. Successful competitors are global.

The ultimate leaders in global industries are often first movers—the first firms to perceive the possibilities for a global strategy. Boeing was the first global competitor in aircraft, for example, as was Honda in motorcycles, and Becton Dickinson in disposable syringes. First movers gain scale and learning advantages which are difficult to overcome. First mover effects are particularly important in global industries because of the association between globalization and economies of scale and learning achieved through worldwide configuration/coordination. Global leadership shifts if industry structural change provides opportunities for leapfrogging to new products or new technologies that nullify past leaders' scale and learning—again, the first mover to the new generation/technology often wins.

Global leaders often begin with some advantage at home, whether it be low labor cost or a product or marketing advantage. They use this as a lever to enter foreign markets. Once there, however, the global competitor converts the initial home advantage into competitive advantages that grow out of its overall worldwide system, such as production scale or ability to amortize R & D costs. While the initial advantage may have been hard to sustain, the global strategy creates new advantages which can be much more durable.

International strategy has often been characterized as a choice between worldwide standardization and local tailoring, or as the tension between the economic imperative (large-scale efficient facilities) and the political imperative (local content, local production). It should be clear from the discussion so far that neither characterization captures the richness of a firm's international strategy choices. A firm's choice of international strategy involves a search for competitive advantage from configuration/coordination throughout the value chain. A firm may standardize (concentrate) some activities and tailor (disperse) others. It may also be able to standardize and tailor at the same time through the coordination of dispersed activities, or use local tailoring of some activities (e.g., different product positioning in each country) to allow standardization of others (e.g., production). Similarly, the economic imperative is not always for a global strategy—in some industries a country-centered strategy is the economic imperative. Conversely, the political imperative is to concentrate activities in some industries where governments provide strong export incentives and locational subsidies.

Global Strategy vs. Comparative Advantage

Given the importance of trade theory to the study of international competition, it is useful to pause and reflect on the relationship to the framework I have presented to the notion of comparative advantage. Is there a difference? The traditional concept of comparative advantage is that factor-cost or factor-quality differences among countries lead to production of products in countries with an advantage which export them elsewhere in the world. Competitive advantage in this view, then, grows out of *where* a firm performs activities. The location of activities is clearly one source of potential advantage in a global firm. The global competitor can locate activities wherever comparative advantage lies, decoupling comparative advantage from its home base or country of ownership.

Indeed, the framework presented here suggests that the comparative advantage story is richer than typically told, because it not only involves production activities (the usual focus of discussions) but also applies to other activities in the value chain such as R & D, processing orders, or designing advertisements. Comparative advantage is specific to the *activity* and not the location of the value chain as a whole.[16] One of the potent advantages of the global firm is that it can spread activities among locations to reflect different preferred locations for different activities, something a domestic or country-centered competitor does not do. Thus components can be made in Taiwan, software written in India, and basic R & D performed in Silicon Valley, for example. This international specialization of activities within the firm is made possible by the growing ability to coordinate and configure globally.

At the same time as our framework suggests a richer view of comparative advantage, however, it also suggests that many forms of competitive advantage for the global competitor derive less from *where* the firm performs activities than from *how* it performs them on a worldwide basis; economies of scale, proprietary learning, and differentiation with multinational buyers are not tied to countries but to the configuration and coordination of the firm's worldwide system. Traditional sources of comparative advantage can be very elusive and slippery sources of competitive advantage for an international competitor today, because comparative advantage frequently shifts. A country with the lowest labor cost is overtaken within a few years by some other country—facilities located in the first country then face a disadvantage. Moreover, falling direct labor as a percentage of total costs, increasing global markets for raw materials and other inputs, and freer flowing technology have diminished the role of traditional sources of comparative advantage.

My research on a broad cross-section of industries suggests that the achievement of sustainable world market leadership follows a more complex pattern than the exploitation of comparative advantage per se. A competitor often starts with a comparative advantage-related edge that provides the basis for penetrating foreign markets, but this edge is rapidly translated into a broader array of advantages that arise from a global approach to configuration and coordination as described earlier. Japanese firms, for example, have done a masterful job of converting temporary labor-cost advantages into durable systemwide advantages due to scale and proprietary know-how. Ultimately, the systemwide advantages are further reinforced with country-specific advantages such as brand identity as well as distribution channel access. Many Japanese firms were fortunate enough to make their transitions from country-based comparative advantage to global competitive advantage at a time when nobody paid much attention to them and there was a buoyant world economy. European and American competitors were willing to cede market share in "less desirable" segments such as the low end of the producer line, or so they thought. The Japanese translated these beachheads into world leadership by broadening their lines and reaping advantages in scale and proprietary technology. The Koreans and Taiwanese, the latest low-labor-cost entrants to a number of industries, may have a hard time replicating Japan's success, given slower growth, standardized products, and now alert competitors.

Global Platforms

The interaction of the home-country conditions and competitive advantages from a global strategy that transcend the country suggest a more complex role of the country in firm success than implied by the theory of comparative advantage. To understand this more complex role of the country, I define the concept of a *global platform*. A country is a desirable global platform in an industry if it provides an environment yielding firms domiciled in that country an advantage in competing globally in that particular industry.[17] An essential element of this definition is that it hinges on success *outside* the country, and not merely country conditions which allow firms to successfully master domestic competition. In global competition, a country must be viewed as a platform and not as the place where all a firm's activities are performed.

There are two determinants of a good global platform in an industry, which I have explored in more detail elsewhere.[18] The first is comparative advantage, or the factor endowment of the country as a site to perform particular activities in the industry. Today, simple factors such as low-cost unskilled labor and natural resources are increasingly less important to global competition compared to complex factors such as skilled scientific and technical personnel and advanced infrastructure. Direct labor is a minor proportion of cost in many manufactured goods and automation of non-production activities is shrinking it further, while markets for resources are increasingly global, and technology has widened the number of sources of many resources. A country's factor endowment is partly exogenous and partly the result of attention and investment in the country.

The second determinant of the attractiveness of a country as a global platform in an industry are the characteristics of a country's demand. A country's demand conditions include the size and timing of its demand in an industry, factors recognized as important by authors such as Linder and Vernon.[19] They also conclude the sophistication and power of buyers and channels and the product features and attributes demanded. Local demand conditions provide two potentially powerful sources of competitive advantage to a global competitor based in that country. The first is *first-mover advantages* in perceiving and implementing the appropriate global strategy. Pressing local needs, particularly peculiar ones, lead firms to embark early to solve local problems and gain proprietary know-how. This is then translated into scale and learning advantages as firms move early to compete globally. The other potential benefit of local demand conditions is a baseload of demand for product varieties that will be sought after in international markets. These two roles of the country in the success of a global firm reflect the interaction between conditions of local supply, the composition and timing of country demand, and economies of scale and learning in shaping international success.

The two determinants interact in important and sometimes counterintuitive ways. Local demand and needs frequently influence private and social investment in endogenous factors of production. A nation with oceans as borders and dependence on sea trade, for example, is more prone to have universities and scientific centers dedicated to oceanographic education and research. Similarly, factor endowment seems to influence local demand. The per capita consumption of wine is highest in wine-growing regions, for example.

Comparative disadvantage in some factors of production can be an advantage in global competition when combined with pressing local demand. Poor growing conditions have led Israeli farmers to innovate in irrigation and cultivation techniques, for example. The shrinking role in competition of simple factors of production relative to complex factors such as technical personnel seem to be enhancing the frequency and importance of such circumstances. What is important today is unleashing innovation in the proper direction, instead of passive exploitation of static cost advantages in a country which can shift rapidly and be overcome. International success today is a dynamic process resulting from continued development of products and processes. The forces which guide firms to undertake such activity thus become central to international competition.

A good example of the interplay among these factors is the television set industry. In the U.S., early demand was in large-screen console sets because television sets were initially luxury items kept in the living room. As buyers began to purchase second and third sets, sets became smaller and more portable. They were used increasingly in the bedroom, the kitchen, the car, and elsewhere. As the television set industry matured, table model and portable sets became the universal product variety. Japanese firms, because of the small size of Japanese homes, cut their teeth on small sets. They dedicated most of their R & D to developing small picture tubes and to making sets more compact. In the process of naturally serving the needs of their home market, then, Japanese firms gained early experience and scale in segments of the industry that came to dominate world demand. U.S. firms, conversely, cut their teeth on large-screen console sets with fine furniture cabinets. As the industry matured, the experience base of U.S. firms was in a segment that was small and isolated to a few countries, notably the U.S. Japanese firms were able to penetrate world markets in a segment that was both uninteresting to foreign firms and in which they had initial scale, learning, and labor cost advantages. Ultimately the low-cost advantage disappeared as production was automated, but global scale and learning economies took over as the Japanese advanced product and process technology at a rapid pace.

The two broad determinants of a good global platform rest on the interaction between country characteristics and firms' strategies. The literature on comparative advantage, through focusing on country factor endowments, ignoring the demand side, and suppressing the individual firm, is most appropriate in industries where there are few economies of scale, little proprietary technology or technological change, or few possibilities for product differentiation.[20] While these industry characteristics are those of many traditionally traded goods, they describe few of today's important global industries.

The Evolution of International Competition

Having established a framework for understanding the globalization of industries, we are now in a position to view the phenomenon in historical perspective. If one goes back far enough, relatively few industries were global. Around 1880, most industries were local or regional in scope.[21] The reasons are rather self-evident in the context of our framework. There were few economies of scale in production until fuel-powered machines and assembly-line techniques emerged. There were heterogeneous product needs among regions within countries, much less among countries. There were few if any national media—the *Saturday Evening Post* was the first important national magazine in the U.S. and developed in the teens and twenties. Communicating between regions was difficult before the telegraph and telephone, and transportation was slow until the railroad system became well developed.

These structural conditions created little impetus for the widespread globalization of industry. Those industries that were global reflected classic comparative advantage considerations—goods were simply unavailable in some countries (who then imported them from others) or differences in the availability of land, resources, or skilled labor made some countries desirable suppliers to others. Export of local production was the form of global strategy adapted. There was little role or need for widespread government barriers to international trade during this period, although trade barriers were quite high in some countries for some commodities.

Around the 1880s, however, were the beginnings of what today has blossomed into the globalization of many industries. The first wave of modern global competitiors grew up in the late 1800s and early 1900s. Many industries went from local (or regional) to national in scope, and some began globalizing. Firms such as Ford, Singer, Gillette, National Cash Register, Otis, and Western Electric had commanding world market shares by the teens, and operated with integrated worldwide strategies. Early global competitors were principally American and European companies.

Driving this first wave of modern globalization were rising production scale economies due to advancements in technology that outpaced the growth of the world economy. Product needs also became more homogenized in different countries as knowledge and industrialization diffused. Transport improved, first through the railroad and steamships and later in trucking. Communication became easier with the telegraph then the telephone. At the same time, trade barriers were either modest or overwhelmed by the advantages of the new large-scale firms.

The burst of globalization soon slowed, however. Most of the few industries that were global moved increasingly towards a multidomestic pattern—multinationals remained, but between the 1920s and 1950 they often evolved towards federations of autonomous subsidiaries. The principal reason was a strong wave of nationalism and resulting high tariff barriers, partly caused by the world economic crisis and world wars. Another barrier to global strategies, chronicled by Chandler,[22] was a growing web of cartels and other interfirm contractual agreements. These limited the geographic spread of firms.

The early global competitors began rapidly dispersing their value chains. The situation of Ford Motor Company was no exception. While in 1925 Ford had almost no production outside the U.S., by World War II its overseas production had risen sharply. Firms that became multinationals during the interwar period tended to adopt country-centered strategies. European multinationals, operating in a setting where there were many sovereign countries within a relatively small geographical area, were quick to establish self-contained and quite autonomous subsidiaries in many countries. A more tolerant regulatory environment also encouraged European firms to form cartels and other cooperative agreements among themselves, which limited their foreign market entry.

Between the 1950s and the late 1970s, however, there was a strong reversal of the interwar trends. As figure 2.1 illustrated, there have been very strong underlying forces driving the globalization of industries. The important reasons can be understood using the configuration/coordination dichotomy. The competitive advantage of competing worldwide from concentrated activities rose sharply, while concentration costs fell. There was a renewed rise in scale economies in many activities due to advancing technology. The minimum efficient scale of an auto assembly plant more than tripled between 1960 and 1975, for example, while the average cost of developing a new drug more than quadrupled.[23] The pace of technological change has increased, creating more incentive to amortize R & D costs against worldwide sales.

Product needs have continued to homogenize among countries, as income differences have narrowed, information and communication has flowed more freely around the world, and travel has increased.[24] Growing similarities in business practices and marketing systems (e.g., chain stores) in different countries have also been a facilitating factor in homogenizing needs. Within countries there has been a parallel trend towards greater market segmentation, which some observers see as contradictory to the view that product needs in different countries are becoming similar. However, segments today seem based less on country differences and more on buyer differences that transcend country boundaries, such as demographic, user industry, or income groups. Many firms successfully employ global focus strategies in which they serve a narrow segment of an industry worldwide, as do Daimler-Benz and Rolex.

Another driver of post-World War II globalization has been a sharp reduction in the real costs of transportation. This has occurred through innovations in transportation technology including increasingly large bulk carriers, container ships, and larger, more efficient aircraft. At the same time, government impediments to global configuration/coordination have been falling in the postwar period. Tariff barriers have gone down, international cartels and patent-sharing agreements have disappeared, and regional economic pacts such as the European Community have emerged to facilitate trade and investment, albeit imperfectly.

The ability to coordinate globally has also risen markedly in the postwar period. Perhaps the most striking reason is falling communication costs (in voice and data) and reduced travel time for individuals. The ability to coordinate activities in different countries has also been facilitated by growing similarities among countries in marketing systems, business practices, and infrastructure—country after country has developed supermarkets and mass distributors, television advertising, and so on. Greater international mobility of buyers and information has raised the payout to coordinating how a firm does business around the world. The increasing number of firms who are multinational has created growing possibilities for differentiation by suppliers who are global.

The forces underlying globalization have been self-reinforcing. The globalization of firms' strategies has contributed to the homogenization of buyer needs and business practices. Early global competitors must frequently stimulate the demand for uniform global varieties; for example, as Becton Dickinson did in disposable syringes and Honda did in motorcycles. Similarly, globalization of industries begets globalization of supplier industries—the increasing globalization of automotive component suppliers is a good example. Pioneering global competitors also stimulate the development and growth of international telecommunication infrastructure as well as the creation of global advertising media—e.g., *The Economist* and *The Wall Street Journal*.

Strategic Implications of Globalization

When the pattern of international competition shifts from multidomestic to global, there are many implications for the strategy of international firms. While a full treatment is beyond the scope of this paper, I will sketch some of the implications here.[25]

At the broadest level, globalization casts new light on many issues that have long been of interest to students of international business. In areas such as international finance, marketing, and business-government relations, the emphasis in the literature has been on the unique problems of adapting to local conditions and ways of doing business in a foreign country in a foreign currency. In a global industry, these concerns must be supplemented with an overriding focus on the ways and means of international configuration and coordination. In government relations, for example, the focus must shift from stand-alone negotiations with host countries (appropriate in multidomestic competition) to a recognition that negotiations in one country will both affect other countries and be shaped by possibilities for performing activities in other countries. In finance, measuring the performance of subsidiaries must be modified to reflect the contribution of one subsidiary to another's cost position or differentiation in a global strategy, instead of viewing each subsidiary as a stand-alone unit. In battling with global competitors, it may be appropriate in some countries to accept low profits indefinitely—in multidomestic competition this would be unjustified.[26] In global industries, the overall system matters as much as or more than the country.

Of the many other implications of globalization for the firm, there are two of such significance that they deserve some treatment here. The first is the role of *coalitions* in global strategy. A coalition is a long-term agreement linking firms but falling short of merger. I use the term coalition to encompass a whole variety of arrangements that include joint ventures, licenses, supply agreements, and many other kinds of interfirm relationships. Such interfirm agreements have been receiving more attention in the academic literature, although each form of agreement has been looked at separately and the focus has been largely domestic.[27] International coalitions, linking firms in the same industry based in different countries, have become an even more important part of international strategy in the past decade.

International coalitions are a way of configuring activities in the value chain on a worldwide basis jointly with a partner. International coalitions are proliferating rapidly and are present in many industries.[28] There is a particularly high incidence in automobiles, aircraft, aircraft engines, robotics, consumer electronics, semiconductors, and pharmaceuticals. While international coalitions have long been present, their character has been changing. Historically, a firm from a developed country formed a coalition with a firm in a lesser-developed country to perform marketing activities in that country. Today, we observe more and more coalitions in which two firms from developed countries are teaming up to serve the world, as well as coalitions that extend beyond marketing activities to encompass activities throughout the value chain.[29] Production and R & D coalitions are very common, for example.

Coalitions are a natural consequence of globalization and the need for an integrated worldwide strategy. The same forces that lead to globalization will prompt the formation of coalitions as firms confront the barriers to establishing a global strategy of their own. The difficulties of gaining access to foreign markets and in surmounting scale and learning thresholds in production, technology development, and other activities have led many firms to team up with others. In many industries, coalitions can be a transitional state in the adjustment of firms to globalization, reflecting the need of firms to catch up in technology, cure short-term imbalances between their global production networks and exchange rates, and accelerate the process of foreign market entry. Many coalitions are likely to persist in some form, however.

There are benefits and costs of coalitions as well as difficult implementation problems in making them succeed (which I have discussed elsewhere). How to choose and manage coalitions is among the most interesting questions in international strategy today. When one speaks to managers about coalitions, almost all have tales of disaster which vividly illustrate that coalitions often do not succeed. Also, there is the added burden of coordinating global strategy with a coalition partner because the partner often wants to do things its own way. Yet, in the face of copious corporate experience that coalitions do not work and a growing economics literature on transaction costs and contractual failures, we see a proliferation of coalitions today of the most difficult kind—those between companies in different countries.[30] There is a great need for researching in both the academic community and in the corporate world about coalitions and how to manage them. They are increasingly being forced on firms today by new competitive circumstances.

A second area where globalization carries particular importance is in *organizational structure*. The need to configure and coordinate globally in complex ways creates some obvious organizational challenges.[31] Any organization structure for competing internationally has to balance two dimensions; there has to be a *country* dimension (because some activities are inherently performed in the country) and there has to be a *global* dimension (because the advantages of global configuration coordination must be achieved). In a global industry, the ultimate authority must represent the global dimension if a global strategy is to prevail. However, within any international firm, once it disperses any activities there are tremendous pressures to disperse more. Moreover, forces are unleashed which lead subsidiaries to seek growing autonomy. Local country managers will have a natural tendency to emphasize how different their country is and the consequent need for local tailoring and control over more activities in the value chain. Country managers will be loath to give up control over activities or how they are performed to outside forces. They will also frequently paint an ominous picture of host government concerns about local content and requirements for local presence. Corporate incentive systems frequently encourage such behavior by linking incentives narrowly to subsidiary results.

In successful global competitors, an environment is created in which the local managers seek to exploit similarities across countries rather than emphasize differences. They view the firms's global presence as an advantage to be tapped for their local gain. Adept global competitors often go to great lengths to devise ways of circumventing or adapting to local differences while preserving the advantages of the similarities. A good example is Canon's personal copier. In Japan, the typical paper size is bigger than American legal size and the standard European size. Canon's personal copier will not handle this size—a Japanese company introduced a product that did not meet its home market needs in the world's largest market for small copiers! Canon gathered its marketing managers from around the world and cataloged market needs in each country. They found that capacity to copy the large Japanese paper was only needed in Japan. In consultation with design and manufacturing engineers, it was determined that building this feature into the personal copier would significantly increase its complexity and cost. The decision was made to omit the feature because the price elasticity of demand for the personal copier was judged to be high. But this was not the end of the deliberations. Canon's management then set out to find a way to make the personal copier saleable in Japan. The answer that emerged was to add another feature to the copier—the ability to copy business cards—which both added little cost and was particularly valuable in Japan. This case illustrates the principle of looking for the similarities in needs among countries and in finding ways of creating similarities, not emphasizing the differences.

Such a change in orientation is something that typically occurs only grudgingly in a multinational company, particularly if it has historically operated in a country-centered mode (as has been the case with early U.S. and European multinationals). Achieving such a reorientation requires first that managers recognize that competitive success demands exploiting the advantages of a global strategy. Regular contact and discussion among subsidiary managers seems to be a prerequisite, as are information systems that allow operations in different countries to be compared.[32] This can be followed by programs for exchanging information and sharing know-how and then by more complex forms of coordination. Ultimately, the reconfiguring of activities globally may then be accepted, even though subsidiaries may have to give up control over some activities in the process.

The Future of International Competition

Since the late 1970s, there have been some gradual but significant changes in the pattern of international competition which carry important implications for international strategy. Our framework provides a template with which we can examine these changes and probe their significance. The factors shaping the global configuration of activities by firms are developing in ways which contrast with the trends of the previous thirty years. Homogenization of product needs among countries appears to be continuing, though segmentation within countries is as well. As a result, consumer packaged goods are becoming increasingly prone to globalization, though they have long been characterized by multidomestic competition. There are also signs of globalization in some service industries as the introduction of information technology creates scale economies in support activities and facilitates coordination in primary activities. Global service firms are reaping advantages in hardware and software development as well as procurement.

In many industries, however, limits have been reached in the scale economies that have been driving the concentration of activities. These limits grow out of classic diseconomies of scale that arise in very large facilities, as well as out of new, more flexible technology in manufacturing and other activities that is often not as scale sensitive as previous methods. At the same time, though, flexible manufacturing allows the production of multiple varieties (to serve different countries) in a single plant. This may encourage new movement towards globalization in industries in which product differences among countries have remained significant and have blocked globalization in the past.

There also appear to be some limits to further decline in transport costs, as innovations such as containerization, bulk ships, and larger aircraft have run their course. However, a parallel trend toward smaller, lighter products and components may keep some downward pressure on transport costs. The biggest change in the benefits and costs of concentrated configuration has been the sharp rise in protectionism in recent years and the resulting rise in nontariff-barriers, harkening back to the 1920s. As a group, these factors point to less need and less opportunity for highly concentrated configurations of activities (see figure 2.5).

When we examine the coordination dimension, the picture looks starkly different. Communication and coordination costs are dropping sharply, driven by breathtaking advances in information systems and telecommunication technology. We have just seen the beginning of developments in this area, which are spreading throughout the value chain.[33] Boeing, for example, is employing computer-aided design technology to jointly design components on-line with foreign suppliers. Engineers in different countries are communicating via computer screens. Marketing systems and business practices continue to homogenize, facilitating the coordination of activities in different countries. The mobility of buyers and information is also growing rapidly, greasing the international spread of brand reputations and

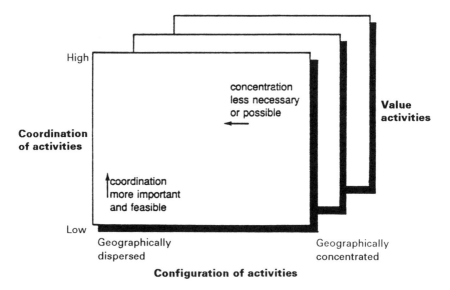

Figure 2.5
Future trends in international competition

enhancing the importance of consistency in the way activities are performed worldwide. Increasing numbers of multinational and global firms are begetting globalization by their suppliers. There is also a sharp rise in the computerization of manufacturing as well as other activities throughout the value chain, which greatly facilitates coordination among dispersed sites.

The imperative of global strategy is shifting, then, in ways that will require a rebalancing of configuration and coordination. Concentrating activities is less necessary in economic terms, and less possible as governments force more dispersion. At the same time, the ability to coordinate globally throughout the value chain is increasing dramatically through modern technology. The need to coordinate is also rising to offset greater dispersion and to respond to buyer needs.

Thus, today's game of global strategy seems increasingly to be a game of coordination—getting more and more dispersed production facilities, R & D laboratories, and marketing activities to truly work together. Yet, widespread coordination is the exception rather than the rule today in many multinationals, as I have noted. The imperative for coordination raises many questions for organizational structure, and is complicated even more when the firm has built its global system using coalitions with independent firms.

Japan has clearly been the winner in the postwar globalization of competition. Japan's firms not only had an initial labor cost advantage but the orientation and skills to translate this into more durable competitive advantages such as scale and proprietary technology. The Japanese context also offered an excellent platform for globalization in many industries, given postwar environmental and technological trends. With home market conditions favoring compactness, a lead in coping with high energy costs, and a national conviction to raise quality, Japan has proved a fertile incubator of global leaders. Japanese multinationals had the advantage of embarking on international strategies in the 1950s and 1960s, when the imperatives for a global approach to strategy were beginning to accelerate, but without the legacy of past international investments and modes of behavior.[34] Japanese firms also had an orientation towards highly concentrated activities that fit the strategic imperative of the time. Most European and American multinationals, conversely, were well established internationally before the war. They had legacies of local subsidiary autonomy that reflected the interwar environment. As Japanese firms spread internationally, they dispersed activities only grudgingly and engaged in extensive global coordination. European and country-centered American companies struggled to rationalize overly dispersed configurations of activities and to boost the level of global coordination among foreign units. They found their decentralized organization structures—so fashionable in the 1960s and 1970s—to be a hindrance to doing so.

As today's international firms contemplate the future, Japanese firms are rapidly dispersing activities, due largely to protectionist pressures but also because of the changing economic factors I have described. They will have to learn the lessons of managing overseas activities that many European and American firms learned long ago. However, Japanese firms enjoy an organizational style that is supportive of coordination and a strong commitment to introducing new technologies such as information systems that facilitate it. European firms must still overcome their country-centered heritage. Many still do not compete with truly global strategies and lack modern technology. Moreover, the large number of coalitions formed by European firms must overcome the barriers to coordination if they are not to prove ultimately limiting. The European advantage may well be in exploiting an acute and well-developed sensitivity to local market conditions as well as a superior ability to work with host governments. By using modern flexible manufacturing technology and computerizing elsewhere in the value chain, European firms may be able to serve global segments and better differentiate products.

Many American firms tend to fall somewhere in between the European and Japanese situations. Their awareness of international competition has risen dramatically in recent years, and efforts at creating global strategies are more widespread. The American challenge is to catch the Japanese in a variety of technologies, as well as to learn how to gain the benefits of coordinating among dispersed units instead of becoming trapped by the myths of decentralization. The changing pattern of international competition is creating an environment in which no competitor can afford to allow country parochialism to impede its ability to turn a worldwide position into a competitive edge.

Notes

1. United Nations Center on Transnational Corporations, *Salient Features and Trends in Foreign Direct Investment* (New York: United Nations, 1984).

2. For a survey, see R. E. Caves and Ronald W. Jones. *World Trade and Payments*, 4th ed. (Boston: Little, Brown, 1985).

3. There are many books on the theory and management of the multinational, which are too numerous to cite here. For an excellent survey of the literature, see

R. E. Caves, *Multinational Enterprise and Economic Analysis* (Cambridge, England: Cambridge University Press, 1982).

4. Raymond Vernon, "International Investment and International Trade in the Product Cycle," *Quarterly Journal of Economics*, Vol. 80 (May 1966): 190–207. Vernon himself, among others, has raised questions about how general the product cycle pattern is today.

5. Michael E. Porter, *Competitive Strategy: Techniques for Analyzing Industries and Competitors* (New York: The Free Press, 1980); Michael E. Porter, "Beyond Comparative Advantage," Working Paper, Harvard Graduate School of Business Administration, August 1985.

6. For a description of this research, see Michael E. Porter, ed., *Competition in Global Industries* (Boston: Harvard Business School Press, forthcoming).

7. The distinction between multidomestic and global competition and some of its strategic implications were described in T. Hout, Michael E. Porter, and E. Rudden, "How Global Companies Win Out," *Harvard Business Review* (September/October 1982), pp. 98–108.

8. Howard V. Perlmutter, "The Tortuous Evolution of the Multinational Corporation," *Columbia Journal of World Business* (January/February 1969), pp. 9–18. Perlmutter's concept of ethnocentric, polycentric, and geocentric multinationals takes the *firm*, not the industry, as the unit of analysis and is decoupled from industry structure. It focuses on management attitudes, the nationality of executives, and other aspects of organization. Perlmutter presents ethnocentric, polycentric, and geocentric as stages of an organization's development as a multinational, with geocentric as the goal. A later paper (Yoram Wind, Susan P. Douglas, and Howard V. Perlmutter, "Guidelines for Developing International Marketing Strategies," *Journal of Marketing*, Vol. 37 (April 1973: 14–23) tempers this conclusion based on the fact that some companies may not have the required sophistication in marketing to attempt a geocentric strategy. Products embedded in the lifestyle or culture of a country are also identified as less susceptible to geocentrism. The Perlmutter et al. view does not link management orientation to industry structure and strategy. International strategy should grow out of the net competitive advantage in a global industry of different types of worldwide coordination. In some industries, a country-centered strategy, roughly analogous to Perlmutter's polycentric idea, may be the best strategy irrespective of company size and international experience. Conversely, a global strategy may be imperative given the competitive advantage that accrues from it. Industry and strategy should define the organization approach, not vice versa.

9. Michael E. Porter, *Competitive Advantage: Creating and Sustaining Superior Performance* (New York: The Free Press, 1985).

10. Buzzell (Robert D. Buzzell, "Can You Standardize Multinational Marketing," *Harvard Business Review* [November/December 1980], pp. 102–113); Pryor (Millard H. Pryor, "Planning in a World-Wide Business," *Harvard Business Review*, Vol. 23 [January/February 1965]); and Wind, Douglas, and Perlmutter (op. cit.) point out

that national differences are in most cases more critical with respect to marketing than to production and finance. This generalization reflects the fact that marketing activities are often inherently country-based. However, this generalization is not reliable because in many industries production and other activities are widely disperse.

11. A number of authors have framed the globalization of industries in terms of the balance between imperatives for global integration and imperatives for national responsiveness, a useful distinction. See C. K. Prahalad, "The Strategic Process in a Multinational Corporation," unpublished DBA dissertation, Harvard Graduate School of Business Administration, 1975; Yves Doz, "National Policies and Multinational Management," an unpublished DBA dissertation, Harvard Graduate School of Business Administration, 1976; and Christopher A. Bartlett, "Multinational Structural Evolution: The Changing Decision Environment in the International Division," unpublished DBA dissertation. Harvard Graduate School of Business Administration, 1979. I link the distinction here to where and how a firm performs the activities in the value chain internationally.

12. See, for example, Oliver Williamson, *Markets and Hierarchies* (New York: The Free Press, 1975). For an international application, see Mark C. Casson, "Transaction Costs and the Theory of the Multinational Enterprise," in Alan Rugman, ed., *New Theories of the Multinational Enterprise* (London: Croom Helm, 1982); David J. Teece, "Transaction Cost Economics and the Multinational Enterprise: An Assessment," *Journal of Economic Behavior and Organization* (forthcoming, 1986).

13. The difficulties in coordinating are internationally parallel to those in coordinating across business units competing in different industries with the diversified firm. See Michael E. Porter, *Competitive Advantage: Creating and Sustaining Superior Performance* (New York: The Free Press, 1985), Chapter 11.

14. Empirical research has found a strong correlation between R & D and advertising intensity and the extent of foreign direct investment (for a survey, see Caves, op. cit.). Both these factors have a place in our model of the determinants of globalization, but for quite different reasons, R & D intensity suggests scale advantages for the global competitor in developing products or processes that are manufactured abroad either due to low production scale economies or government pressures, or which require investments in service infrastructure. Advertising intensity, however, is much closer to the classic transfer of marketing knowledge to foreign subsidiaries. High advertising industries are also frequently those where local tastes differ and manufacturing scale economies are modest, both reasons to disperse many activities.

15. For an interesting description of the industry, see the paper by Michael Yoshino in Porter, ed., op. cit.

16. It has been recognized that comparative advantage in different stages in a vertically integrated industry sector such as aluminum can reside in different countries. Bauxite mining will take place in resource-rich countries, for example, while smelting will take place in countries with low electrical power cost. See R. E. Caves

and Ronald W. Jones, op. cit. The argument here extends this thinking *within* the value chain of any stage and suggests that the optimal location for performing individual activities may vary as well.

17. The firm need not necessarily be owned by investors in the country, but the country is its home base for competing in a particular country.

18. See Porter, op. cit.

19. See S. Linder, *An Essay on Trade and Transformation* (New York, NY: John Wiley, 1961); Vernon, op. cit., (1966); W. Gruber, D. Mehta, and R. Vernon, "R & D Factor in International Trade and International Investment of United States Industries," *Journal of Political Economics*, 76/1 (1967): 20–37.

20. Where it does recognize scale economies, trade theory views them narrowly as arising from production in one country.

21. See Alfred Chandler in Porter, ed., op. cit. for a penetrating history of the origins of the large industrial firm and its expansion abroad, which is consistent with the discussion here.

22. Ibid.

23. For data on auto assembly, see "Note on the World Auto Industry in Transition," Harvard Business School Case Services (#9-382-122).

24. For a supporting view, see Theodore Levitt, "The Globalization of Markets," *Harvard Business Review* (May/June 1983), pp. 92–102.

25. The implications of the shift from multidomestic to global competition were the theme of a series of papers on each functional area of the firm prepared for the Harvard Business School Colloquium on Competition in Global Industries. See Porter, ed., op. cit.

26. For a discussion, see Hout, Porter, and Rudden, op. cit. For a recent treatment, see Gary Hamel and C. K. Prahalad, "Do You Really Have a Global Strategy," *Harvard Business Review* (July/August 1985), pp. 139–148.

27. David J. Teece, "Firm Boundaries, Technological Innovation, and Strategic Planning," in L. G. Thomas, ed., *Economics of Strategic Planning* (Lexington, MA: Lexington Books, 1985).

28. For a treatment of coalitions from this perspective, see Porter, Fuller, and Rawlinson, in Porter, ed., op. cit.

29. Hladik's recent study of international joint ventures provides supporting evidence. See K. Hladik, "International Joint Ventures: An Empirical Investigation into the Characteristics of Recent U.S.-Foreign Joint Venture Partnerships," unpublished doctoral dissertation, Business Economics Program, Harvard University, 1984.

30. For the seminal work on contractual failures, see Williamson, op. cit.

31. For a thorough and sophisticated treatment, see Christopher A. Bartlett's paper in Porter, ed., op. cit.

32. For a good discussion of the mechanisms for facilitating international coordination in operations and technology development, see M. T. Flaherty in Porter, ed., op. cit. Flaherty stresses the importance of information systems and the many dimensions that valuable coordination can take.

33. For a discussion, see Michael E. Porter and Victor Millar, "How Information Gives You Competitive Advantage," *Harvard Business Review* (July/August 1985), pp. 149–160.

34. Prewar international sales enjoyed by Japanese firms were handled largely through trading companies. See Chandler, op. cit.

3

Foreign Direct Investment

J. Saúl Lizondo

Foreign direct investment has long been a subject of interest. This interest has been renewed in recent years for a number of reasons. One of them is the rapid growth in global foreign direct investment flows, which increased from $47 billion in 1985 to $139 billion in 1980.[1] Another reason is the recent sharp increase in foreign direct investment inflows into the United States, which caused some concern about the causes and consequences of such an expansion in foreign ownership. A third reason is the possibility offered by foreign direct investment for channeling resources to developing countries. Although foreign direct investment has not been a significant component of total capital inflows into developing countries, its relative importance may increase now that many of them have quite limited access to other sources of financing.[2]

As a result of the continuous interest in foreign direct investment, a large number of studies have analyzed both the determinants and the effects of such investment. This study reviews the conclusions reached in some of these studies about the determinants of foreign direct investment, and it includes hypotheses that emphasize a variety of factors. Some of these hypotheses use arguments that could also be applied, and in some cases were typically applied, to analyzing portfolio investment. In contrast, other hypotheses stress that to understand foreign direct investment it is essential to take into account the fundamental difference between portfolio investment and direct investment in terms of the control exercised over the operations of the firm.[3]

The structure of this study is based on that employed in the comprehensive survey by Agarwal (1980).[4] It first examines the determinants of

From *Determinants and Systemic Consequences of International Capital Flows*, International Monetary Fund, 1991, pp. 68–82. Reprinted by permission.

foreign direct investment identified in theories that assume perfect markets, which focus on differential rates of return, portfolio diversification, and market size. Then it considers the factors viewed as important in theories that assume imperfect markets and emphasizes the role of industrial organizations, internalization, the product cycle, and oligopolistic reaction. The next sections discuss the theories based on liquidity, currency areas, diversification with barriers to international capital flows, and the Kojima hypothesis and examine some factors that are considered to have an important effect on foreign direct investment, but that sometimes are not included explicitly in the theories mentioned above. Finally, it presents the overall conclusions.

Theories Assuming Perfect Markets

Differential Rates of Return

This approach argues that foreign direct investment is the result of capital flowing from countries with low rates of return to countries with high rates of return. This proposition follows from the idea that, in evaluating their investment decisions firms equate expected marginal returns with the marginal cost of capital. If expected marginal returns are higher abroad than at home, and assuming that the marginal cost of capital is the same for both types of investment, there is an incentive to invest abroad rather than at home.

This theory gained wide acceptance in the late 1950s when U.S. foreign direct investment in manufacturing in Europe increased sharply. At that time, after-tax rates of return of U.S. subsidiaries in manufacturing were consistently above the rate of return on U.S. domestic manufacturing. However, this relationship proved to be unstable. During the 1960s U.S. foreign direct investment in Europe continued to rise, although rates of return for U.S. subsidiaries in Europe were below rates of return on domestic manufacturing.[5]

Empirical tests of this hypothesis proceeded along several lines. Some authors tried to find a positive relationship between the ratio of a firm's foreign direct investment to its domestic investment and the ratio of its foreign profits to its domestic profits. Others tried to relate foreign direct investment and the rate of foreign profits, usually allowing for a certain time lag. Another approach was to examine the relationship between relative rates of returns in several countries and the allocation of foreign direct investment among those countries.

As reported by Agarwal (1980), these empirical studies failed to provide strong supporting evidence, maybe partly owing to the difficulties of measuring expected profits. In the various tests, reported profits were used to represent expected profits. However, reported profits are likely to differ from actual profits, which in turn may differ from expected profits. The main reason for a divergence of reported profits from actual profits is intra-firm pricing for transactions between a subsidiary and the parent firm, and among subsidiaries. Multinational firms may establish intra-firm prices that are different from market prices, for example, to reduce their overall tax burden, or to avoid exchange controls. In turn, actual profits may differ from expected profits owing to unexpected events and the difficulties of using observations for a few years to represent the expected results from an investment with a longer time horizon.

In addition to these inconclusive empirical results, there are certain aspects of foreign direct investment that this theory cannot explain. Since this theory postulates that capital flows from countries with low rates of return to countries with high rates of return, it assumes implicitly that there is a single rate of return across activities within a country. Therefore, this theory is not consistent with some countries experiencing simultaneously inflows and outflows of foreign direct investment. Similarly, it cannot account for the uneven distribution of foreign direct investment among different types of industries. These considerations, as well as the weak empirical results, suggest that the differential rates of return theory does not satisfactorily explain the determinants of foreign direct investment flows.

Portfolio Diversification

Since expected returns did not appear to provide an adequate explanation of foreign direct investment, attention was next focused on the role of risk. In choosing among the various available projects, a firm would presumably be guided by both expected returns and the possibility of reducing risk. Since the returns on activities in different countries are likely to have less than perfect correlation, a firm could reduce its overall risk by undertaking projects in more than one country. Foreign direct investment can therefore be viewed as international portfolio diversification at the corporate level.

Various attempts to test this theory have been made. One approach was to try to explain the share of foreign direct investment going to a group of countries by relating it to the average return on those investments, and to the risk associated with those investments, as measured by the variance of the average returns. A variant of this procedure was to estimate first the optimal geographical distribution of assets of multinational firms based on portfolio considerations, and then to assume that firms gradually adjust their flow of foreign direct investment to obtain that optimal distribution. Another line of inquiry was to ascertain whether large firms with more extensive foreign activities showed smaller fluctuations in global profits and sales.

The results from these tests offered only weak support for the portfolio diversification theory, as documented in Hufbauer (1975) and in Agarwal (1980). In some cases, results that were favorable for a group of countries failed to hold for individual countries. In others, the results were not significant or were more consistent with alternative theories. Although the lack of strong empirical support may be due partly to the difficulties associated with measuring expected profits and risk, there are more basic, theoretical problems with this approach.

The portfolio diversification theory is an improvement over the differential rates of return theory in the sense that, by including the risk factor, it can account for countries experiencing simultaneously inflows and outflows of foreign direct investment. However, it cannot account for the observed differences in the propensities of different industries to invest abroad. In other words, it does not explain why foreign direct investment is more concentrated in some industries than in others.

A more fundamental criticism of this theory has been the argument that in a perfect capital market there is no reason to have firms diversifying activities just to reduce risk for their stockholders. If individual investors want reduced risk, they can obtain it directly by diversifying their individual portfolios. This criticism implies that for the diversification motive to have any explanatory power for foreign direct investment, the assumption of perfect capital markets must be dropped.[6]

Output and Market Size

Two other approaches worth reporting relate foreign direct investment to some measure of output of the multinational firm in the host country. The output approach considers the relevant variable to be output (sales), while the market size approach uses the host country's GNP or GDP, which can be considered as a proxy for potential sales. The relevance of output for foreign direct investment can be derived from models of neoclassical domestic investment theory, whereas the relevance of the host country's market size has generally been postulated rather than derived from a theoretical model. Despite this lack of explicit theoretical backing, the market size model has been very popular, and a variable representing the size of the host country appears in a large number of empirical papers.

These hypotheses have been tested in a variety of ways.[7] One approach was to take models of domestic investment and estimate them using foreign direct investment data to see whether the output of multinational firms in host countries is a significant explanatory variable. Another technique was to see whether the share of foreign direct investment of a given country going to a group of countries was correlated with the income level of the individual host countries. Sometimes, the rate of growth of income in the host country, or the difference between the rate of growth of income in the host and the investing country, were also used as explanatory variables. Some authors distinguished between external and internal determinants of foreign direct investment with market size being an external factor and sales of foreign subsidiaries an internal factor.

These empirical studies support the notion that higher levels of sales by the foreign subsidiary and of the host country's income, or income growth, have been associated with higher foreign direct investment. The broad support for these hypotheses is generally valid across a variety of countries, periods, estimation techniques, and specification of the variables.

This support, however, has to be carefully interpreted (Agarwal, 1980). As mentioned above, proponents of the market size hypothesis have seldom presented an explicit theoretical model from which the estimated relationships are derived. Therefore, the correlation between foreign direct investment and market size may be consistent with various structural models. Also, the size and growth of the host country's market should affect foreign direct investment that is used to produce for the domestic market, not for exports. In most of the empirical studies, however, no distinction is made between the two types of investment. Finally, some evidence suggests that the decisions of firms regarding foreign direct investment may be guided by different considerations depending on whether it is the firm's initial investment in the country. In this case, it would be incorrect to use the same variables to explain all types of foreign direct investment.

Theories Based on Imperfect Markets

The theories outlined in the previous section did not make any specific assumption about market imperfections or market failures. Hymer (1976) was perhaps the first analyst to point out that the structure of the markets and the specific characteristics of firms should play a key role in explaining foreign direct investment.[8] The role of these factors has been analyzed in both a static context, which focuses on issues associated with industrial organization and the internalization of decisions, and in a dynamic framework, which highlights oligopolistic rivalry and product cycle considerations.

Industrial Organization

Hymer (1976) argued that the very existence of multinational firms rests on market imperfections. Two types of market imperfection are of particular importance: structural imperfections and transaction-cost imperfections.[9] Structural imperfections, which help the multinational firm to increase its market power, arise from economies of scale, advantages of knowledge, distribution networks, product diversification, and credit advantages. Transaction costs, on the other hand, make it profitable for the multinational firm to substitute an internal "market" for external transactions. The literature focusing on structural imperfections gave rise to the industrial organization theory of foreign direct investment whereas that focusing on transaction costs led to the internalization theory of foreign direct investment.[10]

The industrial organization approach argues that when a foreign firm establishes a subsidiary in another country, it faces a number of disadvantages when competing with domestic firms. These include the difficulties of managing operations spread out in distant places, and dealing with different languages, cultures, legal systems, technical standards, and customer preferences. If, in spite of those disadvantages, a foreign firm does engage in foreign direct investment, it must have some firm-specific advantages with respect to domestic firms. The advantages of the multinational firm are those associated with brand name, patent-protected superior technology, marketing and managerial skills, cheaper sources of financing, preferential access to markets, and economies of scale.

The industrial organization approach has been used recently by Graham and Krugman (1989) to explain the growth of foreign direct investment in the United States. They argue that 20 years ago U.S. firms had significant advantages over firms from other countries in terms of technology and management skills. U.S. firms were also superior to foreign rivals in producing abroad, as well as at home. As a result, there was not much foreign direct investment in the United States. Since then, U.S. technological and managerial superiority has declined, and foreign firms can therefore compete with U.S. firms in the U.S. market. Thus, the authors interpret the growing inflow of foreign direct investment into the United States as evidence supporting their hypothesis.

The industrial organization theory, in the restrictive sense employed in this paper, is not a complete theory of foreign direct investment. While the existence of some firm-specific advantages explains why a foreign firm can compete successfully in the domestic market, such advantages do not explain why this competition must take the form of foreign direct investment. The foreign firm could just as well export to the domestic market, or license or sell its special skills to domestic firms. The internalization theory and the eclectic approach, discussed below, offer explanations of why firms choose foreign direct investment over the other alternatives.

Internalization

This hypothesis explains the existence of foreign direct investment as the result of firms replacing market transactions with internal transactions. This in turn is seen as a way of avoiding imperfections in the markets for intermediate inputs (see Buckley and Casson, 1976). Modern businesses conduct many activities in addition to the routine production of goods and services. All these activities, including marketing, research and development, and training of labor, are interdependent and are related through flows of intermediate products, mostly in the form of knowledge and expertise. However, market imperfections make it difficult to price some types of intermediate products. For example, it is often hard to design and enforce contractual arrangements that prevent someone who has purchased or leased a technology (such as a computer software program) from passing it on to others without the knowledge of the original producer. This problem provides an incentive to bypass the market and keep the use of the technology within the firm. This produces an incentive for the creation of intrafirm markets.

The internalization theory of foreign direct investment is intimately related to the theory of the firm. The question of why firms exist was first raised by Coase (1937) and later examined by Williamson (1975). They argued that, with certain transaction costs, the firm's internal procedures are better suited than the market to organize transactions. These transaction costs arise when strategic or opportunistic behavior is present among agents to an exchange, the commodities or services traded are ambiguously defined, and contractual obligations extend in time. When these three conditions are present, enforcement and monitoring costs may become prohibitive. Under those circumstances, the firm opts to internalize those transactions. The main feature of this approach therefore is treating markets on the one hand, and firms on the other, as alternative modes of organizing production.[11]

It is the internalization of markets across national boundaries that gives rise to the international enterprise, and thus, to foreign direct investment. This process continues until the benefits from further internalization are outweighed by the costs. As indicated in Agarwal (1980), the benefits include avoidance of time lags, bargaining and buyer uncertainty, minimization of the impact of government intervention through transfer pricing, and the ability to use discriminatory pricing. The costs of internalization include administrative and communication expenses.

The internalization hypothesis is a rather general theory of foreign direct investment. In fact, Rugman (1980) has argued that most, if not all, of the other hypotheses for foreign direct investment are particular cases of this general theory. As a result of this generality, this approach has been accused of being almost tautological, and of having no empirical content. Rugman (1986), however, argues that with a precise specification of additional conditions and restrictions, this approach can be used to generate powerful implications.

The difficulties in formulating appropriate tests for the internalization theory were examined further by Buckley (1988). He agreed that the general theory cannot be tested directly, but argued that it may be sharpened to obtain relevant testable implications. Since much of the argument rests on the incidence of costs in external and internal markets, the specification and measurement of those costs is crucial for any test. Empirical evidence suggests that transaction costs are particularly high in vertically integrated process industries, knowledge-intensive industries, quality-assurance-dependent products, and communication-intensive industries. Therefore, the internalization theory predicts that those will be the industries dominated by multinational firms. Buckley also cited evidence showing that the pattern of foreign direct investment across industries and nationalities, is broadly consistent with the theory's predictions, but he emphasized that tests need to be more precise and rigorous to increase our confidence in the theory.

An Eclectic Approach

Dunning (1977, 1979, 1988) developed an eclectic approach by integrating three strands of the literature on foreign direct investment: the industrial organization theory, the internalization theory, and the location theory. He argued that three conditions must be satisfied if a firm is to engage in foreign direct investment. First, the firm must have some ownership advantages with respect to other firms; these advantages usually arise from the possession of firm-specific intangible assets. Second, it must be more beneficial for the firm to use these advantages rather than to sell or lease them to other independent firms. Finally, it must be more profitable to use these advantages in combination with at least some factor inputs located abroad, otherwise foreign markets would be served exclusively by exports. Thus, for foreign direct investment to take place, the firm must have ownership and internationalization advantages, and a foreign country must have locational advantages over the firm's home country.[12]

The eclectic approach postulates that all foreign direct investment can be explained by reference to the above conditions. It also postulates that the advantages mentioned above are not likely to be uniformly spread among countries, industries, and enterprises and are likely to change over time. The flows of foreign direct investment of a particular country at a particular point in time depend on the ownership and internationalization advantages of the country's firms, and on the locational advantages of the country, at that point in time. Dunning (1979, 1980) used this approach to suggest reasons for differences in the industrial pattern of the outward direct investment of five developed countries, and to evaluate the significance of ownership and location variables in explaining the industrial pattern and geographical distribution of the sales of U.S. affiliates in 14 manufacturing industries in seven countries.

Product Cycle

This hypothesis postulates that most products follow a life cycle, in which they first appear as innovations and ultimately become completely standardized. Foreign direct investment results when firms react to the threat of losing markets as the product matures, by expanding overseas and capturing the remaining rents from development of the product. This hypothesis, developed by Vernon (1966), was mainly intended to explain the expansion of U.S. multinational firms after World War II.

Innovation can be stimulated by the need to respond to more intense competition or to the perception of a new profit opportunity. The new product is developed and produced locally (in the United States) both because it will be designed to satisfy local demand and because it will facilitate the efficient coordination between research, development, and production units. Once the first production unit is established in the home market, any demand that may develop in a foreign market (Europe) would ordinarily be satisfied by exports. However, rival producers will eventually emerge in foreign markets, since they can produce more cheaply (owing to lower distribution costs) than the original innovator. At this stage, the innovator is compelled to examine the possibility of setting up a production unit in the foreign location. If the conditions are considered favorable, the innovator engages in foreign direct investment. Finally, when the product is standardized and its production technique is no longer an exclusive possession of the innovator, he may decide to invest in developing countries to obtain some cost advantages, such as cheaper labor.

Agarwal (1980) describes a number of studies offering support for the product-cycle hypothesis. Those studies generally refer to U.S. foreign direct investment, although they also cover some German and U.K. foreign direct investment.

Despite those favorable results, the explanatory power of the product-cycle hypothesis has declined considerably as a result of changes in the international environment. Vernon (1979) has noted that, since U.S. multilateral firms now have better knowledge of market demands all around the world, they no longer follow the typical geographical sequence of first setting up subsidiaries in the markets with which they are most familiar, such as in Canada and the United Kingdom, and then in less familiar areas, such as Asia and Africa. Therefore, the assumption that U.S. firms receive stimulus for the development of new products only from their home market is no longer tenable. Furthermore, since the income and technological gap between the United States and other industrial countries has declined, it is less defensible to assume that U.S. firms are exposed to a very different home environment from that faced by firms from other countries. Vernon (1979) speculated that the hypothesis is likely to remain important in explaining foreign direct investment carried out by small firms and in developing countries.

Oligopolistic Reaction

Knickerbocker (1973) suggested that, in an oligopolistic environment, foreign direct investment by one firm will trigger similar investments by other leading firms in the industry to maintain their market shares.[13] Using data from a large number of U.S. multinational firms, he calculated an entry concentration index for each industry, which showed the extent to which subsidiaries' entry dates were bunched in time. As indicated in Hufbauer (1975), the entry concentration index was positively correlated with the U.S. industry concentration index, implying that increased industrial concentration caused increased reaction by competitors to reduce the possibility of one rival gaining a significant cost or marketing advantage over the others. The entry concentration index was also positively correlated with market size, implying that the reaction was stronger, the larger the market at stake. The entry concentration index was negatively correlated with the product diversity of the multinational firms and with their expenditure on research and development. This suggested that the reaction of firms was less intense if they had a variety of investment opportunities, or if their relative positions depended on technological considerations. Flowers (1976) tested this hypothesis with data on foreign direct investment by Canadian and European firms in the United States. He found a significant positive correlation between the concentration of foreign direct investment in the United States and the industrial concentration in the source countries.

An implication of this hypothesis is that the process of foreign direct investment by multinational firms is self-limiting, since the invasion of each other's home market will increase competition and thus reduce the intensity of oligopolistic reaction (Agarwal, 1980). However, while foreign direct investment has increased competition in many industries, this has not resulted in a corresponding reduction in foreign direct investment. This hypothesis has also been criticized for not recognizing that foreign direct investment is only one of several methods of servicing foreign markets. In addition, there is no explanation of the reason for the initial investment that starts the foreign investment process.

To examine the factors motivating the initial investment of multinational firms, Yu and Ito (1988) studied one oligopolistic and one competitive industry. Their results suggest that in an oligopolistic industry, foreign direct investment is motivated by the behavior of rivals, as well as host-country-related and firm-related factors; in contrast, in more competitive industries, firms do not generally match their competitors' foreign direct investments. As a result, the authors argued that firms in oligopolistic industries, besides considering their competitors' activities, make their foreign direct investment decisions on the basis of the same economic factors as firms in competitive industries.

Other Theories of Foreign Direct Investment

Liquidity

U.S. multinational firms have traditionally committed only modest amounts of resources to their initial foreign direct investment, and subsequent expansions of their activities were carried out by reinvesting local profits. As a result, it has been postulated that there is a positive relationship between internal cash flows and the investment outlays of subsidiaries of multinational firms. This relationship is said to arise because the cost of internal funds is lower than the cost of external funds.

Agarwal (1980) presented the results of empirical studies, which provided mixed support for this hypothesis. Some studies concluded that there was no evidence that the expansion of subsidiaries was financed only by their retained earnings. Internally generated funds seemed to be allocated between the parent and the subsidiaries to maximize the overall profits of the firm. However, other studies found that the most important sources of funds for the expansion of subsidiaries were undistributed profits and depreciation allowances, although the share of new investment thus financed varied from country to country. In other studies, liquidity-related variables had a higher explanatory power for foreign direct investment than variables based on the accelerator theory of investment.

Some other studies, based on interview data, suggested that small and large international firms may behave differently, with subsidiaries of smaller firms being more dependent on internally generated funds to finance their expansion and therefore behaving more in agreement with the liquidity hypothesis. These studies also suggested that it is important to distinguish between the overall cash flow of the firm and the cash flow of the subsidiary, particularly when examining foreign direct investment in developing countries. Since new investment in developing countries is likely to be only one component of a variety of reinvestment opportunities open to the firm, the overall cash flow of the firm may not be an important determinant in a particular country. Cash flows of the subsidiary, on the other hand, may be important, particularly in countries that place restrictions on repatriation of profits and capital.

Based on the results mentioned above, Agarwal (1980) concludes that the liquidity hypothesis has some empirical support. An expansion of foreign direct investment seems to be partly determined by the subsidiaries' internally generated funds. This factor may be particularly valid for investment in developing countries owing to their restrictions on movements of funds of foreign firms and the lower degree of development of their financial and capital markets.

Currency Area

Aliber (1970, 1971) postulated that the pattern of foreign direct investment can be best explained in terms of the relative strength of the various currencies. The stronger the currency of a certain country, the more likely it is that firms from that country will engage in foreign investment, and the less likely it is that foreign firms will invest in the domestic country. The argument is based on capital market relationships, exchange rate risks, and the market's preference for holding assets in selected currencies.

The crucial assumption of this theory is the existence of a certain bias in the capital market. This bias is assumed to arise because an income stream located in a country with a weak currency has associated with it a certain exchange risk. Investors, however, are less concerned with this exchange risk when the income stream is owned by a firm from a strong currency country than when owned by a firm from a weak currency country. According to Aliber (1971), this could reflect the view that the strong currency firm might be more efficient in hedging the exchange risk or that the strong currency firm can provide the investors with a diversified portfolio at a lower cost than the investor can acquire on his own. Alternatively, investors may take into account exchange risk for a strong currency firm only if a substantial portion of its earnings are from foreign sources.

For any of these reasons, an income stream is capitalized at a higher rate by the market (has a higher price) when it is owned by a strong currency firm than when owned by a weak currency firm. As a result, firms from countries with strong currencies have an advantage in the capital market in acquiring this income stream. Strong currency countries therefore tend to be sources of foreign direct investment, and weak currency countries tend to become host countries.

Most empirical studies have tested the currency area hypothesis by focusing on whether an overvaluation of a currency is associated with foreign direct investment outflows and undervaluation with foreign direct investment inflows. Studies of foreign direct investment in the United States, the United Kingdom, Germany, France, and Canada yielded results that were consistent with the currency area hypothesis (see Agarwal, 1980).

Despite this empirical support, the currency area theory cannot account for cross investment between currency areas, for direct investment in countries in the same currency area, and for the concentration of foreign direct investment in certain types of industries. Furthermore, it is not clear why hedging or a diversification advantage should accrue solely to the strong currency firms, or why investors show persistent ignorance or short-sightedness.

A more elaborate theory based on capital market imperfections, with similar implications to those of the currency area hypothesis, was developed by Froot and Stein (1989). They argued that a low real value of the domestic currency may be associated with foreign direct investment inflows owing to informational imperfections in the capital market that cause firms' external financing to be more expensive than their internal financing. Since the availability of internal funds depends on the level of net worth, a real depreciation of the domestic currency that lowers the wealth of domestic residents and raises that of foreign residents can lead to foreign acquisition of some domestic assets.

Their analysis of U.S. data indicates that foreign direct investment inflows into the United States are negatively correlated with the real value of the dollar. Moreover, other types of capital inflows have not shown a similar negative correlation so that this relationship is a distinctive characteristic of foreign direct investment, as expected from the theory. However, this negative correlation between foreign direct investment inflows and the real value of currency was not evident in three out of the other four countries examined.

Additional evidence regarding the relationship between exchange rate levels and foreign direct investment was presented by Caves (1988). He argued that exchange rates have an impact on foreign direct investment inflows through two channels. First, changes in the real exchange rate modify the attractiveness of foreign investment in the United States by changing a firm's real costs and revenues. The net effect on foreign direct investment is ambiguous, depending on certain characteristics of the firm's activity, such as the share of imported inputs in total costs and the share of output that is exported. The second channel is associated with expected short-run exchange rate movements. A depreciation that is expected to be reversed will encourage foreign direct investment inflows to obtain a capital gain when the domestic currency appreciates.

Caves studied the behavior of foreign direct investment inflows into the United States using panel data from several source countries. The results showed a significant negative correlation between the level cf the exchange rate, both nominal and real, and inflows of foreign direct investment. Despite these empirical results, the theory cannot satisfactorily explain why foreign residents would have an advantage over domestic residents at bidding for a given firm; nor is it clear why expected changes in the exchange rate would lead to direct investment inflows instead of portfolio inflows.

Either owing to the arguments used by the currency area theory, or by other theories with similar implications, there is some evidence that the decline in the real value of the domestic currency encourages inflows and discourages outflows of foreign direct investment. However, neither the theory nor the evidence about this relationship is completely satisfactory.

Diversification with Barriers to International Capital Flows

As noted earlier, there is no reason for firms to carry out diversification activities for their stockholders in perfect capital markets, since any desired diversification could be obtained directly by individual investors. Agmon and Lessar (1977) have argued that for international diversification to be carried out through corporations, two conditions must hold. First, barriers or costs to portfolio flows must exist that are greater than those to foreign direct investment. Second, investors must recognize that multinational firms provide a diversification opportunity that is otherwise not available. After providing some examples that justify assuming that the first condition holds, they postulate a simple model in which the rate of return of a security is a function both of a domestic market factor and of a rest-of-the-world market factor. They tested the proposition that securities prices of firms with relatively large international operations were more closely related to the rest-of-the-world market factor and less to the domestic market factors than shares of firms that are essentially domestic. They obtained favorable results for a sample of data applying to U.S. firms. However, as noted by Adler (1981) and Agmon and Lessard (1981), these results are consistent with the second condition mentioned above but do not support a fully developed theoretical model.

Errunza and Senbet (1981) developed a framework in which both firms and investors face barriers to international capital flows. As a result, individual investors have a demand for diversification services and multinational firms are able to supply diversification services. In equilibrium, individual investors accept lower expected returns on multinational stocks than on domestic stocks in order to obtain diversification benefits. Since the diversification services provided by multinationals are reflected in the price of their stocks, Errunza and Senbet's empirical test is based on a market-value theoretical framework, which is applied to the U.S. capital market over subperiods characterized by differential government control. Their results suggest that a systematic relationship exists between the current degree of international involvement and excess market value. This relationship was stronger during the period characterized by barriers to capital flows in comparison with the period in which no substantial restrictions were in effect.[14]

The Kojima Hypothesis

Kojima (1973, 1975, 1985) was concerned with explaining the differences in the patterns of U.S. and Japanese foreign direct investment in developing countries and the consequences of those differences for the expansion of international trade and global welfare.[15] Foreign direct investment was viewed as providing a means of transferring capital, technology, and managerial skills from the source country to the host country. However, it was argued that there were two types of foreign direct investment: trade-oriented and anti-trade-oriented. Foreign direct investment is trade-oriented if it generates an excess demand for imports and an excess supply of exports at the original terms of trade. The opposite occurs if foreign direct investment is anti-trade-oriented.

Kojima also proposed that trade-oriented foreign direct investment was welfare improving in both source and host countries, while anti-trade-oriented foreign direct investment was welfare reducing. Since trade-oriented foreign direct investment implied investment in industries in which the source country has a comparative disadvantage, it would accelerate trade between the two nations, and promote a beneficial industrial restructuring in both countries. In contrast, anti-trade-oriented foreign direct investment would imply investment in industries in which the source country has a comparative advantage. Thus, international trade would be reduced, and industry would be restructured in a direction opposite to that recommended by comparative advantage considerations. This would reduce welfare in both countries, creating balance of payments problems, the export of jobs, and incentives for trade protectionism in the source country.

It was also argued that Japanese foreign direct investment has been trade-oriented, while U.S. foreign direct investment has been anti-trade-oriented. This reflected the fact that Japanese foreign direct investment was mainly directed toward development of natural resources in which Japan has a comparative disadvantage, and toward some manufacturing sectors in which Japan had been losing its comparative advantage. Japanese investment was also viewed as being more export-oriented, occurring in less sophisticated industries with smaller firms being more labor intensive, and with a higher share of local ownership. In contrast, Kojima suggested that the United States has transferred abroad those industries in which it had a comparative advantage. The reason for this was found in the dualistic structure of the U.S. economy, with a group of innovative and oligopolistic new industries coexisting alongside a group of traditional price-competitive stagnant industries. Only the innovative and oligopolistic industries undertook foreign direct investment, since their rate of return on foreign investment was higher owing to their oligopolistic advantages. Since these were the industries in which the United States had a comparative advantage, such foreign direct investment was anti-trade-oriented.

Kojima therefore concluded that while U.S. foreign direct investment was rational from the multinational firms' point of view, it was damaging to national welfare and economic development. As a result, some policies were needed to modify the characteristics of these investments. These policies could potentially involve selecting the types of industries in which foreign direct investment would be allowed, requiring the use of licensing arrangements instead of foreign direct investment, allowing only joint ventures with local capital instead of wholly owned subsidiaries, and requiring a progressive transfer of ownership to local residents. Kojima viewed his proposed code of behavior for international investment as consistent with comparative advantage and as resulting in a higher level of international welfare.

This hypothesis has been evaluated at two levels. At the empirical level, there is the issue of whether significant differences exist in the patterns of U.S. and Japanese foreign direct investment as implied by the hypothesis. On this score, the evidence is not conclusive. While favorable evidence was presented in Kojima (1985) for investment in a group of Asian developing countries, Lee's (1983) analysis of the Korean experience, and Chou's (1988) discussion of Taiwan Province of China yielded mixed results. In addition, Mason (1980) argued that the existing differences in the pattern of foreign direct investment mainly reflected different stages in the evolution of U.S. and Japanese multinational firms.

At the theoretical level, there is the issue of whether the neoclassical framework adopted by Kojima is appropriate for studying foreign direct investment. According to Dunning (1988), Kojima's approach can neither explain nor evaluate the welfare implications of foreign direct investment prompted by the desire to rationalize international production, since it ignores the essential characteristic of foreign direct investment, that is, the internalization of intermediate product markets. The neoclassical framework of perfect competition used by Kojima does not allow for the possibility of market failure. Furthermore, Lee (1984) argued that Kojima did not succeed in establishing a plausible microeconomic basis for his theory. In summary, although the Kojima hypothesis is consistent with some characteristics of U.S. and Japanese foreign direct investment behavior, the welfare implications and the policy recommendations derived from this approach have not been widely endorsed.

Other Variables

Although political instability, tax policy, and government regulations have in some circumstances been incorporated into the theories reviewed above, their importance justifies a more explicit consideration.

Political Instability

An unstable political and social environment is not conducive to inflows of foreign capital. The fear is that large and unexpected modifications of the legal and fiscal frameworks may drastically change the economic outcome of a given investment. However, empirical tests of this proposition have yielded rather mixed results.

The role of political instability has been examined empirically using both survey data and econometric analysis. Survey studies have employed data collected by contacting multinational firms and inquiring how their investment policies in foreign countries are affected by political risk. Almost all of these studies have concluded that political risk is an important factor in the decisions regarding foreign direct investment. The other type of study has used traditional econometric techniques, such as regression analysis, to test for the effect of political risk on foreign direct investment. While some studies have found a negative relationship between political risk and inflows of foreign direct investment, others fail to find any statistically significant relationship.[16]

These mixed results may reflect a variety of factors. First, it is difficult to measure political risk or political instability. Second, a given political event may give rise to different levels of risk depending on the country of origin of the investment or the type of industry in which the investment was made. Furthermore, some cross-country econometric studies did not allow for lags between the time when a change in risk is perceived and the time when the change in foreign direct investment takes place. Finally, some of the early studies did not include factors, other than political risk, as explanatory variables of foreign direct investment.

More recent studies have addressed some of those problems and offered new evidence on the effects of political risk on foreign direct investment. Nigh (1985) uses pooled, time-series, cross-sectional estimation to examine the role of political risk in affecting foreign direct investment of U.S. multinationals in manufacturing. He distinguishes between industrial and developing host countries, and includes economic as well as political variables. Among the political variables, he distinguishes between intracountry and intercountry conflict and cooperation variables. His empirical results suggested that U.S. multinational firms reacted to both intracountry and intercountry variables when the host country was a developing country, but that they only responded to intercountry variables when the host country was an industrial country. Schneider and Frey (1985) compared the predictive power of four different models in explaining inflows of foreign direct investment for a sample of developing countries. The analyses included (1) a model with only political variables; (2) a model with only economic variables; (3) a model with an explanatory variable that incorporated political and economic factors in a single index; and (4) a model that included in a desegregated fashion both economic and political variables. They conclude that the fourth model provided the best forecasts, indicating that economic variables should also be included in the estimation, and that indices that try to capture simultaneously political and economic effects do not perform well.

Two recent papers have taken a different look at the problem. While the usual approach is to consider the effect of host-country political risk on inflows of foreign direct investment, Tallman (1988) examined whether political risk in the home country had an effect on outward foreign direct investment. Using the United States as the host country and a number of industrial countries as home countries, he examined the effects of international and domestic political and economic events on foreign direct investment. His results indicated that reducing domestic political risk reduced outward foreign direct investment, while improved political relations between countries increased outward foreign direct investment. Chase, Kuhle, and Walther (1988) also examined whether countries with relatively high political risk, as measured by available indices reported in commercial publications, provide higher returns on foreign direct investment. However, their empirical tests did not provide support for this hypothesis. The reasons may be that commercially available indices are not good representations of political risk, that reported returns are different from actual returns owing to intracompany transfer pricing, or that expected returns are not well represented by actual returns.

Tax Policy

Since the net return on foreign direct investment is affected by the tax system of both the home and the host country, tax policies affect the incentives to engage in foreign investment, as well as the way in which that investment is financed.

There are two alternative approaches to avoiding the double taxation of income earned abroad if both the home and the host countries tax a multinational's earnings. Both approaches recognize the primary right of the host country to tax income generated within its jurisdiction, but differ on the portion of tax revenue that accrues to the home country. Under the territorial approach, the home country does not tax income earned abroad. Under the more common residence approach, the home country does tax income earned abroad, but allows for a tax credit on taxes paid to host governments. Furthermore, the home country tax payments can usually be deferred until the income earned abroad is repatriated to the domestic parent. Most analyses of tax effects focus on the residence approach.

A comprehensive theoretical treatment of the effects of taxes on direct investment capital flows has been developed by Jun (1989).[17] In this study, the author identifies three channels through which tax policy affects firms' decisions on foreign direct investment. First, the tax treatment of income generated abroad has a direct effect on the net return on foreign direct investment, which will be influenced by such instruments as the corporate tax rate, the foreign tax credit, and the deferral of home country taxes on unrepatriated income. Second, the tax treatment of income generated at home affects the net profitability of domestic investment, and thus the relative net profitability between domestic and foreign investment. Finally, tax policy can affect the relative net cost of external funds in different countries.

Jun uses an intertemporal optimizing model incorporating these three channels to discuss the effects on foreign direct investment of changes in tax policy. For example, an increase in the domestic corporate tax rate was shown to increase the outflow of foreign direct investment, although the magnitude of the effect depended on whether the marginal source of funds for the subsidiary is retained earnings, transfers from the parent firm, or external funds, and on whether the payment of taxes on unrepatriated income can be deferred. A reduction in the foreign tax credit would reduce foreign direct investment outflows unless the marginal source of financing of the subsidiary is retained earnings. An increase in the domestic investment tax credit, or the elimination of the deferral of tax payments on unrepatriated earnings, would reduce the outflow of foreign direct investment.

The limited empirical literature on this subject has recently been expanded by various studies of U.S. foreign direct investment inflows and outflows, starting with Hartman (1984).[18] This paper examines inflows of foreign direct investment into the United States by first separating investment financed by retained earnings from investment financed by transfer from abroad. For both categories, the paper studies the response of investment to the after-tax rate of return obtained by foreign investors in the United States (as a proxy for expected rate of return for firms considering expansion of current operations), and the overall after-tax rate of return on capital in the United States (as a proxy for expected returns for firms considering acquisition of existing assets). The estimated coefficients had the expected positive sign for both rates of return. However, the model did not explain investments financed by transfers from abroad very satisfactorily. The same type of equations were estimated by Boskin and Gale (1987) and by Young (1988), using expanded samples, revised data, alternative functional forms, and some additional explanatory variables. Although the estimated coefficients differ from those of Hartman (1984), the qualitative, results were similar.

Slemrod (1989) examined the effect of host country and home country tax policy on foreign direct investment in the United States. The estimation results were generally supportive of a negative impact of the U.S. effective rate of taxation on total foreign direct investment, and on transfers of funds, but not on retained earnings. The paper then disaggregated the data by seven major investing countries to test for the effect of home country tax policy on foreign direct investment and did not find it had a significant impact. A different conclusion, however, was reached by Jun (1990), who found that U.S. tax policy toward domestic investment had a significant effect on U.S direct investment outflows by influencing the relative net rate of return between the United States and abroad. The overall conclusion based on the evidence examined above is that both home country and host country tax policies seem to have an effect on foreign direct investment flows. However, the ability of present models to capture those effects is not completely satisfactory.

Government Regulations

A number of factors, in addition to those included in the theories examined above, may have an impact on foreign direct investment decisions. They generally originate from government regulations that modify the risk and expected returns from a given investment project. Those regulations are sometimes implemented to counteract foreign firms' practices that are perceived to be harmful to the host country, such as intrafirm pricing and discriminatory input purchases. In other cases, they are implemented for other policy objectives, such as to favor the development of a particular industrial sector, to reduce regional disparities, or to reduce unemployment.

Independent of their specific policy purpose, however, those regulations are likely to affect decisions on the size, timing, location, and sectoral allocation of foreign direct investment.

The various government regulations can be classified into incentives and disincentives to foreign direct investment, according to whether they tend to increase or to reduce the flow of investment to a given country. Incentives include, in addition to fiscal benefits such as tax credits and tax exemptions, some financial benefits such as grants and subsidized loans. Some countries provide nonfinancial benefits, such as public sector investment on infrastructure aimed at enhancing the profitability of a given foreign investment project, public sector purchasing contracts, and the establishment of free trade zones.

Disincentives include a number of impediments to foreign direct investment which may range from the slow processing of authorizations for foreign investment to the outright prohibition of foreign investment in specified regions or sectors. Most impediments, however, lie between those extremes and take the form of conditions attached to the authorization of foreign direct investment in general, or for certain regions and sectors. Those conditions may include setting a lower limit on the portion of inputs purchased from local sources and on export levels, or a specified relationship between the value of exported output and the value of imported inputs. Other conditions may include requirements regarding levels of employment, transfer of technology, expenditure on research and development, or investment in unrelated areas. In addition, there may be some upper limit on foreign ownership of equity and restrictions on foreign exchange transactions, especially those associated with profit remittances, and repatriation of capital. These regulations are particularly prevalent in developing countries.

The empirical effect of the various incentives and disincentives on the level of foreign direct investment has been examined by a number of authors. The results of those studies are documented in Agarwal (1980) and Organization for Economic Cooperation and Development (1989), which provide similar conclusions. In general, the incentives mentioned above appear to have a limited effect on the level of foreign direct investment. Investors seem to base their decisions on risk and return considerations that are only marginally affected by those incentives. However, this result may be partly due to difficulties that exist in isolating the effect of a given factor when various factors are operating simultaneously. Incentives are seldom granted without conditions; instead, they are usually subject to the compliance of requirements that constitute disincentives to foreign direct investment. Therefore, the empirical results may be capturing the net effect of incentives coupled with disincentives, which in principle can be positive or negative, depending on the strength of each component. If this is so, the weak response to incentives shown by foreign direct investment implies that the benefits of incentives serve primarily to compensate for the additional costs arising from the performance requirements usually attached to those incentives.

Disincentive regulations seem to have a more definite impact on foreign investment than incentive regulations. This is clearly true when a certain type of foreign direct investment is directly prohibited. Also, specific requirements are sometimes imposed as a condition for authorizing the investment, rather than as a condition for receiving special benefits. In this situation, in which disincentives are not accompanied by matching incentives, those requirements may be too costly, and thus prevent the investment project from being undertaken. Furthermore, the existence of a wide range of disincentives may have a negative effect on foreign direct investment beyond the one originating from the additional costs of present regulations. If investors interpret those regulations as an indication of an environment hostile to foreign investment, they may decide against investing because of possible future regulations that would reduce their profits even further.

Conclusions

At present there is no unique, widely accepted theory of foreign direct investment. Instead, there are various hypotheses emphasizing different microeconomic and macroeconomic factors that are likely to affect it. While most of those hypotheses have some empirical support, no single hypothesis is sufficiently supported to cause the others to be rejected.

Theories derived from the industrial organization approach have probably gained the widest acceptance. They seem to provide a better explanation for cross-country, intra-industry investment, and for the uneven concentration of foreign direct investment across industries, than do alternative models.

Regardless of the specific ranking of the various theories according to their explanatory power, it is clear from a review of the literature that in explaining the determination of international capital movements direct investment flows must be distinguished from portfolio flows. The basis for this distinction is that direct investment implies control of the foreign firm, and therefore the usual arguments regarding expected returns and diversification do not provide a satisfactory explanation. Other factors, usually associated with industrial organization and the theory of the firm, become crucial in explaining why residents of a given country would want to keep control of a foreign firm. The different reasons motivating direct investment flows and portfolio flows also imply that those flows do not necessarily move together. As a result, a given pattern of foreign direct investment flows does not necessarily have to be associated with a particular pattern of overall capital flows.

Notes

1. International Monetary Fund, *Balance of Payments Statistics*. Recent studies describing the evolution of foreign direct investment include Thomsen (1989), DeAnne and Thomsen (1989a and b), and Lipsey (1989).

2. Foreign direct investment inflows into net debtor developing countries increased gradually from $2 billion in 1970 to $15 billion in 1981. These inflows then declined, remaining at about $10 billion for a few years, before increasing again to $17 billion in 1988.

3. It is not obvious what constitutes control of a firm. In general, countries classify as direct investment enterprises those in which the percentage of foreign ownership is above a certain limit, usually between 10 and 25 percentage. Although there are no uniform criteria among countries, moderate difference in the percentage used for the classification do not alter significantly the measurement of foreign direct investment, since the share of foreign ownership in firms considered to be foreign affiliates is usually much larger. For discussion of some of these issues, and other methodological and data problems, see Thomsen (1989).

4. There are also alternative ways of organizing the discussion. For example, Boddewyn (1955) groups the theories according to whether they refer to conditions, motivations, or precipitating circumstances for foreign direct investment. Kojima and Ozawa (1984) distinguish between macro- and micromodels of foreign direct investment.

5. See Hufbauer (1975).

6. The discussion of this point is continued in the section on diversification the barriers to international capital flows.

7. See Agarwal (1980).

8. Although Hymer's dissertation was completed in 1960, it was not published until 1976.

9. See Dunning (1981).

10. The concept of "industrial organization theory of foreign direct investment" is not uniformly used in the literature. Sometimes it is used to encompass all the

theories derived from Hymer's work, that is, all the theories included in this section. In this study, the concept is used in its more restrictive sense, to refer to the literature focusing on structural imperfections.

11. This approach also implies that the motivation behind multinational production, and therefore foreign direct investment, may well be the search for efficiency rather than the attempt to profit from monopoly power. This change in focus has important welfare implications. See Dunning and Rugman (1985) and Teece (1985).

12. Dunning (1979) lists the advantages of each of the categories mentioned above.

13. A variant of this "follow the leader" hypothesis is the "exchange of threat" hypothesis, in which intra-industry foreign direct investment results from firms invading each other's home markets owing to oligopolistic rivalry (see Graham, 1978).

14. In Errunza and Senbet (1981), the authors further developed the theoretical basis for their view that indirect portfolio diversification by multinational firms helps complete international capital markets, and they expanded their empirical investigation. Some limitations of this paper are indicated in Bicksker (1984).

15. Kojima's hypothesis is mainly concerned with international economic relationships between industrial and developing countries. This is clear from several passages in his papers and is explicitly stated in Kojima (1975), where he speculates that two-way direct foreign investment between advanced industrial countries may be explained by other theories.

16. Surveys of the two types of studies mentioned above are presented in Agarwal (1980) and in Fatehi-Sedeh and Safizadeh (1989).

17. Other discussions of theoretical issues may be found in Gersovitz (1987) and in Alworth (1988).

18. A summary of previous results can be found in Caves (1982).

References

Adler, Michael, "Investor Recognition of Corporation International Diversification: Comment," *Journal of Finance*, Vol. 36 (March 1981).

Agarwal, Jamuna P., "Determinants of Foreign Direct Investment: A Survey," *Weltwirtshaftliches Archiv*, Vol. 116, Heft 4 (1980).

Agmon, Tamir, and Donald R. Lessard, "Investor Recognition of Corporate International Diversification," *Journal of Finance*, Vol. 32 (September 1977).

Agmon, Tamir, and Donald R. Lessard, "Investor Recognition of Corporate International Diversification: Reply," *Journal of Finance*, Vol. 36 (March 1981).

Aliber, R. Z., "A Theory of Direct Foreign Investment," in *The International Corporation: A Symposium*, ed. by C. P. Kindleberger (Cambridge: MIT Press, 1970).

Aliber, R. Z., "The Multinational Enterprise in a Multiple Currency World," in *The Multinational Enterprise*, ed. by John H. Dunning (London: Allen & Unwin, 1971).

Alworth, Julian, *The Finance, Investment and Taxation Decisions of Multinationals* (Oxford; New York: Basil Blackwell, 1988).

Bicksler, James L., "Discussion," *Journal of Finance*, Vol. 39 (July 1984).

Boddewyn, J. J., "Theories of Foreign Direct Investment and Investment: A Classificatory Note," *Management International Review*, Vol. 25, No. 1 (1985).

Boskin, M., and W. Gale, "New Results on the Effects of Tax Policy on the International Location of Investment," in *The Effects of Taxation on Capital Accumulation*, ed. by Martin S. Feldstein (Chicago: University of Chicago Press, 1987).

Buckley, Peter J., "The Limits of Explanation: Testing the Internalization Theory of the Multinational Enterprise," *Journal of International Business Studies*, Vol. 19 (Summer 1988).

Buckley, Peter J., and Mark Casson, *The Future of the Multinational Enterprise* (London: Macmillan, 1976).

Caves, Richard E., *Multinational Enterprise and Economic Analysis* (Cambridge: Cambridge University Press, 1982).

Caves, Richard E., "Exchange-Rate Movements and Foreign Direct Investment in the United States," Harvard Institute of Economic Research, Discussion Papers Series No. 1383 (May 1988).

Chase, C. D., J. L. Kuhle, and C. H. Walther, "The Relevance of Political Risk in Direct Foreign Investment," *Management International Review*, Vol. 28 (3rd Quarter 1988).

Chou, Tein-Chen, "American and Japanese Direct Foreign Investment in Taiwan: A Comparative Study," *Hitotsubashi Journal of Economics*, Vol. 29 (December 1988).

Coase, R. H., "The Nature of the Firm," *Economica*, Vol. 4 (November 1937).

DeAnne, Julius, and Stephen E. Thomsen, "Explosion of Foreign Direct Investment Among the G-5," Royal Institute of International Affairs, RIIA Discussion Papers, No. 8 (1989a).

DeAnne, Julius, and Stephen E. Thomsen, "Inward Investment and Foreign-Owned Firms in the G-5," Royal Institute of International Affairs, RIIA Discussion Papers, No. 12 (1989a).

Dunning, John H., "Trade, Location of Economic Activity and the MNE: A Search for an Eclectic Approach," in *The International Allocation of Economic Activity*, ed. by Bertil Ohlin, P. O. Hesselborn, and P. J. Wijkman (London: Macmillan, 1977).

Dunning, John H., "Explaining Changing Patterns of International Production: In Defence of the Eclectic Theory," *Oxford Bulletin of Economics and Statistics*, Vol. 41 (November 1979).

Dunning, John H., "Toward an Eclectic Theory of International Production," *Journal of International Business Studies*, Vol. 11 (1980).

Dunning, John H., *International Production and the Multinational Enterprise* (London: Allen & Unwin, 1981).

Dunning, John H., "The Eclectic Paradigm of International Production: A Restatement and Some Possible Extensions," *Journal of International Business Studies,* Vol. 19 (Spring 1988).

Dunning, John H., and Alan M. Rugman, "The Influence of Hymer's Dissertation on the Theory of Foreign Direct Investment," *American Economic Review, Papers and Proceedings,* Vol. 75 (May 1985).

Errunza, Vihang R., and Lemma W. Senbet, "The Effects of International Operations on the Market Value of the Firm: Theory and Evidence," *Journal of Finance,* Vol. 36 (May 1981).

Errunza, Vihang R., and Lemma W. Senbet, "International Corporate Diversification, Market Valuation, and Size-Adjusted Evidence," *Journal of Finance,* Vol. 39 (July 1981).

Fatehi-Sedeh, K., and M. H. Safizadeh, "Association Between Political Instability and Flow of Foreign Direct Investment," *Management International Review,* Vol. 29, No. 4 (1989).

Flowers, Edward B., "Oligopolistic Reactions in European and Canadian Investment in the United States," *Journal of International Business Studies,* Vol. 7 (Fall/Winter 1976).

Froot, Kenneth A., and Jeremy C. Stein. *Exchange Rates and Foreign Direct Investment: An Imperfect Capital Markets Approach,* NBER Working Paper No. 2914 (Cambridge, Mass.: National Bureau of Economic Research, March 1989).

Gersovitz, M., "The Effect of Domestic Taxes on Foreign Private Investment," in *The Theory of Taxation for Developing Countries,* ed. by David Newbery and Nicholas Stern (New York: Oxford University Press, 1987).

Graham, Edward M., "Transatlantic Investment by Multinational Firms: A Rivalistic Phenomenon?" *Journal of Post Keynesian Economics,* Vol. 1 (Fall 1978).

Graham, Edward M., and Paul R. Krugman, *Foreign Direct Investment in the United States* (Washington: Institute for International Economics, 1989).

Hartman, David G., "Tax Policy and Foreign Direct Investment in the United States, *National Tax Journal,* Vol. 37, (December 1984).

Hufbauer, G. C., "The Multinational Corporation and Direct Investment," in *International Trade and Finance: Frontiers for Research,* ed. by Peter B. Kenen (Cambridge: Cambridge University Press, 1975).

Hymer, S. H., "The International Operations of National Firms: A Study of Direct Foreign Investment." Ph.D. dissertation, 1960, Massachusetts Institute of Technology (Cambridge: MIT Press, 1976).

Jun, Joosung, *Tax Policy and International Direct Investment,* NBER Working Paper No. 3048 (Cambridge, Massachusetts: National Bureau of Economic Research, July 1989).

Jun, Joosung, "U.S. Tax Policy and Direct Investment Abroad," in *Taxation in the Global Economy*, ed. by Assaf Razin and Joel Slemrod (Chicago: University of Chicago Press, 1990).

Knickerbocker, Frederick T., *Oligopolistic Reaction and Multinational Enterprise* (Boston: Division of Research, Harvard University Graduate School of Business Administration, 1973).

Kojima, Kiyoshi, "A Macroeconomic Approach to Foreign Direct Investment," *Hitotsubashi Journal of Economics*, Vol. 14 (June 1973).

Kojima, Kiyoshi, "International Trade and Foreign Investment: Substitutes or Complements," *Hitotsubashi Journal of Economics* , Vol. 16 (June 1975).

Kojima, Kiyoshi, "Japanese and American Direct Investment in Asia: A Comparative Analysis," *Hitotsubashi Journal of Economics*, Vol. 26 (June 1985).

Kojima, Kiyoshi, and Terutomo Ozawa, "Micro- and Macroeconomic Models of Direct Foreign Investment: Toward a Synthesis," *Hitotsubashi Journal of Economics*, Vol. 25 (June 1981).

Lee, Chung H., "International Production of the United States and Japan in Korean Manufacturing Industries: A Comparative Study," *Weltwirtschaftliches Archiv*, Vol. 119, Heft 4 (1983).

Lee, Chung H., "On Japanese Macroeconomic Theories of Direct Foreign Investment," *Economic Development and Cultural Change*, Vol. 32 (July 1984).

Lipsey, Robert E, *The Internationalization of Production*, NBER Working Paper No. 2923 (Cambridge, Massachusetts: National Bureau of Economic Research, April 1989).

Mason, R. Hal, "A Comment on Professor Kojima's 'Japanese Type versus American Type of Technology Transfer'," *Hitotsubashi Journal of Economics*, Vol. 20 (February 1980).

Nigh, Douglas, "The Effect of Political Events on United States Direct Foreign Investment: A Pooled Time-Series Cross-Sectional Analysis," *Journal of International Business Studies*, Vol. 16 (Spring 1985).

Organization for Economic Cooperation and Development, *Investment Incentives and Disincentives: Effects on International Direct Investment* (Paris, 1989).

Rugman, Alan M., "Internalization as a General Theory of Foreign Direct Investment: A Re-Appraisal of the Literature," *Weltwirtschaftliches Archiv*, Vol. 116, Heft 2 (1980).

Rugman, Alan M., "New Theories of the Multinational Enterprise: An Assessment of Internalization Theory," *Bulletin of Economic Research*, Vol. 38 (May 1986).

Schneider, Friedrich, and Bruno S. Frey, "Economic and Political Determinants of Foreign Direct Investment," *World Development*, Vol. 13 (February 1985).

Slemrod, Joel, "Tax Effects on Foreign Direct Investment in the U.S.: Evidence from a Cross-Country Comparison," NBER Working Paper No. 3042 (Cambridge, Mass.: National Bureau of Economic Research, July 1989).

Tallman, Stephen B., "Home Country Political Risk and Foreign Direct Investment in the United States," *Journal of International Business Studies*, Vol. 19 (Summer 1988).

Teece, D., "Multinational Enterprise, Internal Governance, and Industrial Organization," *American Economic Review, Papers and Proceedings*, Vol. 75 (May 1985).

Thomsen, Stephen E., "The Growth of American, British, and Japanese Direct Investment in the 1980s," Royal Institute of International Affairs, RIIA Disussion Papers, No. 2 (1989).

Vernon, Raymond, "International Investment and International Trade in the Product Cycle," *Quarterly Journal of Economics*, Vol. 80 (May 1966).

Vernon, Raymond, "The Product Cycle Hypothesis in a New International Environment," *Oxford Bulletin of Economics and Statistics*, Vol. 41 (November 1979).

Williamson, Oliver E., *Markets and Hierarchies, Analysis and Antitrust Implications: A Study in the Economics of Internal Organization* (New York: Free Press, 1975).

Young, Kan H., "Effects of Taxes and Rates of Return on Foreign Direct Investment in the United States," *National Tax Journal*, Vol. 41 (March 1988).

Yu, Chwo-Ming J., and Kiyohiko Ito, "Oligopolistic Reaction and Foreign Direct Investment: The Case of the U.S. Tire and Textiles Industries," *Journal of International Business Studies*, Vol. 19 (Fall 1988).

I Patterns of International Business

Key Terms

- direct foreign investment (DFI)
- source country
- host country
- joint venture
- product cycle
- multidomestic corporation
- global corporation
- hit parade

Questions

1. What are the empirical characteristics of the stocks and flows of direct foreign investment between developed and developing countries? Why might political leaders in the developing countries be concerned about this development?

2. There is usually concern in any country when foreigners acquire a large share of domestic assets; recent Japanese acquisitions of U.S. firms illustrate the point. Should U.S. political leaders be concerned by this development?

3. When firms establish foreign subsidiaries, the concern arises that jobs are being exported. Should U.S. political leaders be concerned by this development?

4. Why have imports in most countries increased as a share of national income?

5. Why have Japanese banks increased their size relative to U.S. banks, and climbed in the hit parade of world banks?

Suggested Readings

Dunning, John H., "Explaining Changing Patterns of International Production: In Defence of the Eclectic Theory," *Oxford Bulletin of Economics and Statistics*, November 1979, pp. 269–295.

Hood, Neil, and Stephen Young, "The Determinants of Direct Foreign Investment," Chapter 2 of *The Economics of Multinational Enterprise*, Longman, 1979, pp. 44–86.

Porter, Michael E., "The Competitive Advantage of Nations," *Harvard Business Review*, March–April 1990, pp. 73–93.

U.S. Department of Commerce, International Trade Administration, *International Direct Investment*, 1988.

II

Multinational Corporate Strategy

Analysts have long debated whether the key proposition of elementary economics textbooks that firms maximize profits is a good description of their behavior, or whether instead firms maximize some other objective, such as market share, shareholder value, assets, stability of income, or the income of managers. Some firms may seek to maximize several of these objectives at the same time, and slight any possible conflict between them. The development of a firm's strategy—how the firm organizes its financial, physical, intellectual, and human resources—is closely linked to the specification of its objectives.

Japanese firms and firms headquartered in a few other countries act as if they were more interested in maximizing market share than in maximizing profits or shareholder value. U.S. firms, in contrast, seem more interested in maximizing profits and, more recently, shareholder value. The distinction may reflect that shareholders who dominate U.S. equity markets have different expectations from the shareholders of Japanese firms.

The first cliché about strategy is that the managers need to recognize the business the firm is in. Was the New York Central a railroad company, a transportation company, or a personal services company? Is United Airlines in the air passenger business or in the transportation business? Is Kubota in tractor production or in precision manufacturing? Is Citicorp in banking, financial services, or information processing? Are ABC, CBS, and NBC in television programming, entertainment, or information processing? These questions represent an attempt to identify the generic essence of a firm's business and to recognize the firm's key competitors. They suggest that the ability of a firm to expand in a profitable way may be handicapped unless the managers of the firm have a clear view of the business the firm is in, and its inherent advantages relative to its competitors. Traditionally firms have been organized around their products rather than the basis of the inherent activity. The New York Central Railroad started on the path to bankruptcy because it failed to realize it was in the transportation business; as a result it was slow to adjust to the changes in technology and in demand for new types of services.

Consider Merck, Ciba-Geigy, and Burroughs-Welcome. These firms are listed in all the hit parades as pharmaceutical firms. Yet they started as producers of basic organic chemicals, and have continually attempted to transform their product lines into higher-value-added activities through research and development. Similarly DuPont is in the chemical business, but many of its products today—and certainly the most profitable ones—were not being produced twenty and thirty years ago.

The significance of considering strategy in the global rather than national context is that a new set of markets becomes relevant for the firm, and a new set of competitors in its traditional industry. The new set of markets raises questions about the types of the firm's products most appropriate for consumers in different countries; how similar are these products to the ones that have been sold successfully in the domestic market? The range-of-products issue is relevant because production for foreign markets provides opportunities for economies of scale and diversification of the sources of income. Consumers in most foreign countries differ from domestic consumers in terms of both the types of products they prefer and the attributes of these products. Moreover, some of the foreign markets may be growing more rapidly than the domestic market, which means that firms that produce for these foreign markets are likely to have high levels of investment in plant and equipment; and rapid growth in sales is likely to be associated with an increase in the ranges of products demanded.

The expansion of the set of competitors to include foreign firms raises questions about their scope and strategies, their inherent advantages in terms of costs, production technologies, manufacturing know-how, and product design—and hence their competitive impacts on domestic firms. The success of Japanese automobile and electronics firms is dramatically evident. The success of German chemical firms and Swiss drug firms is less dramatic—and it's a puzzle that three of the eight largest drug firms in the world should be headquartered in Basel—a city of 350,000. The reasons for the success of these firms in global markets is less evident. The firms headquartered in various foreign countries may have quite different advantages and strategies from those of their U.S. competitors. Thus the Japanese automobile firms have objectives and strategies different from U.S. automobile firms; the Japanese firms seem more interested in increasing market share than in maximizing shareholder value, and they have spent a higher share of their revenues on new product development, even though their profits, on average, are below those of U.S. firms.

The identification of markets where a firm can achieve a rapid increase in its sales is an important aspect of its strategy—if a firm fails to grow as rapidly as its competitors, then the firm may increasingly find itself at a cost disadvantage.

Once a firm has decided on the markets that appear likely to promise rapid growth, the firm must decide on where to produce. The prototypical sourcing question is "Where do we put the plant?" The general form of the answer is to select the number of plants, their sites, and their technology so as to minimize the net costs of production, transportation, and holding inventories, while maintaining flexibility in both production and control to cope with changes in the volume of sales in different national markets. One complication is that the sourcing questions almost always are incremental, so this question frequently becomes "How will the location of new plants fit with the locations of long-established plants." The managers must decide on the make-or-buy decision, which involves how far upstream—how vertically integrated—the firm should become in each of the countries in which it produces.

The answers to the sourcing question for the managers of a multinational firm are more complex because of both current and prospective differences in the relationship among wage rates and labor productivity—and in national rates of growth of demand—in different foreign countries as compared to the United States. Economies of scale frequently are very important.

Wage rates in many foreign countries are lower than in the United States, and as a result, labor costs per unit of output may be lower. In many countries, labor productivity is low, with the consequence that labor costs per unit of output may be higher. But even if productivity in individual foreign countries is sufficiently high so that labor costs per unit of output are below those domestically, production costs in these foreign countries may be higher than production costs in the United States because labor costs may be modest—15 to 30 percent of total production costs. The other components of costs include those associated with the infrastructure, including transportation, electricity, water, insurance, and security.

One reason that the relationship among costs of supply in the United States and different foreign countries may change significantly more rapidly than the relationship among costs of supply in various U.S. regions is that the real exchange rate may change, as a result of monetary shocks and of real or structural shocks. Moreover, the relationship among production costs in different countries will be significantly affected by differences in their rates of economic growth. The more rapid the rate of economic growth within a country, the larger the change in the relationship among the production costs of different types of goods within that country. The production costs of new manufactures are likely to decline if demand for these products is growing rapidly, while the production costs of more traditional manufactures, and of many services, will increase.

Moreover, the attitudes of host governments toward foreign firms may change. And while these changes in attitudes and policies are part of political risk, they affect the location of plants, since placing a plant in a location where the government is less than welcoming is a high-risk activity.

A large number of statements about strategy are sufficiently general so that they apply to every firm in an industry. Yet there are many firm-specific aspects to strategy that reflect (or should reflect) the firm's ranking in the industry's hit parade of sales and profits, the newness of its product line, and whether the firm has a monopoly in certain niches. Consider the problems of Chrysler and Volvo, which have had problems of maintaining market share—are their current problems inevitable, or did they in the past fail to make the most appropriate strategic decisions?

The articles in part 2 cover a firm's strategic management decisions, primarily manufacturing decisions dealing with location and sourcing. No reading is presented on how firms should identify their generic advantage, and modify or alter their product lines to cope with the changes in competitive situation. And no reading is presented which suggests how different firms in the same industry in different countries—the number one firm, the number five firm, the number ten firm—should adapt their products to enhance their competitive position.

"How to Take Your Company to the Global Market" by George S. Yip, Pierre M. Loewe, and Michael Y. Yoshino examines the strategic planning decision by determining whether—and more importantly, how—to globalize a firm's corporate strategy. They consider both external business forces and internal organizational factors. The external "drivers" of firm's potential for globalization include market factors, economic factors, environmental factors, and competitive factors. The internal factors that facilitate a global strategy are organizational structure, management processes, people, and culture.

Sumantra Ghoshal's "Global Strategy: An Organizing Framework," provides a schematic representation of strategic management decisions as a basis for synthesizing different perspectives and prescriptions. He identifies three broad strategic management decisions: (1) production location and sourcing decisions to achieve efficiency; (2) production location and sourcing decisions to manage risk; and (3) organizational decisions to innovate and adapt to future changes. Ghoshal examines three sources of competitive advantage: (1) national differences in input and output markets; (2) economies of scale in production; and (3) economies of scope—or synergies—across activities. The result is a 3 × 3 matrix framework for strategic management decisions. The problems for the managers of firms in various industries differ, depending on whether their firms share in these advantages.

"Making American Manufacturing Competitive" by Elwood S. Buffa focuses on manufacturing strategy, with an emphasis on enhancing productivity. Buffa starts from the premise that U.S. multinationals have traditionally placed too much emphasis on marketing and finance, and not enough on production and productivity.

Bruce Kogut's "Designing Global Strategies: Profiting from Operational Flexibility" asserts that international strategic planning lies less in its content than in creating the operational flexibility to profit from uncertainty over changes in exchange rates, government policy, and competitors' moves. To illustrate the benefits of operational flexibility he specifically examines production shifting, tax minimization, financial arbitrage, information arbitrage, global coordination, and political risk. The common thread through these operating decisions is the capability of managers to coordinate international activities in response to changes in the economic environment.

These articles are generic. They suggest how strategy questions might be approached without regard to the industry that a firm is involved in, the country where a firm is headquartered, and the standing of the firm in its industry's hit parade relative to its domestic and foreign competitors. In this sense, they are more like checklists of factors that the managers should consider when they plan an expansion into a market (or perhaps even when they plan an exit from a foreign market) than models of how decisions should be structured.

4

How to Take Your Company to the Global Market

George S. Yip,
Pierre M. Loewe, and
Michael Y. Yoshino

Most managers have to face the increasing globalization of markets and competition. That fact requires each company to decide whether it must become a worldwide competitor to survive.[1]

This is not an easy decision. Take the division of a multibillion-dollar company, a company that's very sophisticated and has been conducting international business for more than fifty years. The division sells a commodity product, for which it is trying to charge 40% more in Europe than it does in the United States. The price was roughly the same in the United States and in Europe when the dollar was at its all-time high. The company built a European plant which showed a greater return on investment with that European price. But the dollar has fallen and, if the company drops its European price to remain roughly the same as the US price, the return on the plant becomes negative, and some careers are in serious jeopardy. So it is attempting to maintain a 40% European price premium by introducing minor upgrades to the European product.

But its multinational customers will have none of it. They start buying the product in the United States and transshipping it to Europe. When the company tries to prevent them from transshipping, they go to a broker, who does the work for them; they still save money.

The manufacturer doesn't have a choice. It's working in a global market. And it's going to have to come up with a global price. But management is fighting a losing battle because it is unwilling to make the hard strategic and organizational changes necessary to adapt to global market conditions.

European and Japanese corporations also face these kinds of organizational roadblocks. Large European firms, for example, historically have been more multinational than US companies. Their international success is due, in part, to decentralized management. The companies simply repro-

From *Columbia Journal of World Business*, Winter 1988, pp. 37–48. Reprinted by permission.

duced their philosophy and culture everywhere, from India to Australia to Canada. They set up mini-headquarters operations in each country and became truly multinational with executives of different nationalities running them.

Now they are having problems running operations on a worldwide basis because these multinational executives are fighting the global imperative. In one European company, for example, the manager running a Latin American division has built an impenetrable wall around himself and his empire. He's done very well, and everyone has allowed him to do as he pleases. But the company's global strategy requires a new way of looking at Latin America. The organization needs to break down his walls of independence. So far, that's proved next to impossible.

Japanese companies face a different set of problems. On the whole, they have followed a basic, undifferentiated marketing strategy: make small Hondas, and sell them throughout the world. Then make better Hondas, ending up with the $30,000 Honda Acura. It's incremental, and it has worked.

Now, however, the Japanese must create various manufacturing centers around the globe and they're facing many difficulties. They have a coordinated marketing strategy and have built up infrastructures to coordinate marketing, which requires one particular set of skills. But now they've begun to establish three or four major manufacturing operations around the world, and they need a different set of skills to integrate these manufacturing operations. In addition, many Japanese companies are trying to add some elements of a multinational strategy back into their global one.

American multinationals have tended to take a different path. The huge domestic market, combined with cultural isolation, has fostered an "us-them" mentality within organizations. This split has made it difficult to fully adapt to the needs of international business. Until recently, overseas posts have been spurned. A marketing manager for new products in a United States consumer products company told us that running the sizable United Kingdom business would be a step down for him. As a result of others' similar views, many American firms face two conflicting challenges today. They need to complete their internationalization by increasing their adaptation to local needs, while at the same time they need to make their strategies more global.

But some companies are better off not trying to compete globally because of the difficulties of their internal situation. The CEO of one midwest manufacturer decided that his company had to go global to survive. He gave marching orders. And the organization marched. Unfortunately, they started marching over a global cliff. For example, they set up a small operation in Brazil since they had targeted South America as part of their global strategy. But the executives they appointed to run the operation had never been outside the United States before, and the company started losing money. Company analysis found that going global was just too unnatural to its cultural system and that a viable strategic alternative was to stay in the United States and play a niche strategy.

Most international companies have grappled with the types of problems we have been describing, and have tried to find a solution. This paper provides a framework for thinking through this complex and important issue. In particular, the framework addresses the dual challenge of formulating and implementing a global strategy. Readers may find the framework a convenient way to analyze globalization issues.

The Dual Challenge

Managers who want to make their businesses global face two major challenges. First, they need to figure out what a gobal strategy is. Then when they know what to do, they have to get their organizations to make it happen.

Different Ways of Being Global

Developing a global strategy is complicated by the fact that there are at least five major dimensions of globalization. These are:

• Playing big in major markets.
• Standardizing the core product.
• Concentrating value-adding activities in a few countries.
• Adopting a uniform market positioning and marketing mix.
• Integrating competitive strategy across countries.

Each of these can offer significant benefits:

Playing Big in Major Markets

Playing big in major markets—countries that account for a sizable share of worldwide volume or where changes in technology or consumer tastes are most likely to start—brings these benefits:

• Larger volume over which to amortize development efforts and investments in fixed assets.

• Ability to manage countries as one portfolio, including being able to exploit differences in position along the product life cycle.

• Learning from each country.

• Being at the cutting edge of the product category by participating in the one or two major countries that lead development.

Standardizing the Core Product

The local managers of multinational subsidiaries face strong pressures to adapt their offerings to local requirements. This gets the company laudably close to the customer. But the end result can be such great differences among products offered in various countries that the overall business garners few benefits of scale.

The core product can be standardized while customizing more superficial aspects of the offering. McDonald's has done well with this approach. Europeans and Japanese may think they are eating the same hamburgers as Americans, but the ingredients have been adapted for their tastes. A French McDonald's even serves alcohol. But the core formula remains the same.

Concentrating Value-adding Activities in a Few Countries

Instead of repeating every activity in each country, a pure global strategy provides for concentration of activities in just a few countries. For example, fundamental research is conducted in just one country, commercial development in two or three countries, manufacturing in a few countries, and core marketing programs developed at regional centers, while selling and customer service take place in every country in the network. The benefits include gaining economies of scale and leveraging the special skills or strengths of particular countries. For example, the lower wage rates and higher skills in countries such as Malaysia or Hong Kong have encouraged many electronics firms to centralize worldwide assembly operations in these countries.

Adopting a Uniform Market Positioning and Marketing Mix

The more uniform the market positioning and marketing mix, the more the company can save in the cost of developing marketing strategies and

Box 4.1
Example of Global Strategy: Black & Decker

Black & Decker, manufacturer of hand tools, provides an example of a company that is pursuing a global strategy. In the past decade; Black & Decker was threatened by external and internal pressures.: Externally, it faced a powerful Japanese competitor, Makita. Makita's strategy to produce and market standardized products worldwide made it a low-cost producer, and enabled it to increase steadily its share in the world market. Internally, international fiefdoms and nationalist chauvinism at Black & Decker had stifled coordination in product development and new product introductions, resulting in lost opportunities.

In response, Black & Decker decisively moved toward globalization. It embarked on a major program to coordinate new product development worldwide to develop core standardized products that can be marketed worldwide with minimal modification. The streamlining in R & D also offers scale economies and less duplication of effort, and new products can be introduced more quickly. It consolidated worldwide advertising by using two principal agencies, gaining a more consistent image worldwide. Black & Decker also strengthened the functional organization by giving functional managers a larger role in coordinating with the country management. Finally, Black & Decker purchased General Electric's small appliance business to achieve world-scale economies in manufacturing, distribution, and marketing.

The globalization strategy initially met with skepticism and resistance from country management due to entrenched factionalism among country managers. The CEO took a visible leadership role and made some management changes to start the company moving toward globalization. Today, in his words, "Globalization is spreading and now has a life of its own."

programs. As one company told us, "Good ideas are scarce. By taking a uniform approach we can exploit those ideas in the maximum number of countries." Another benefit is internal focus. A company may struggle with numerous brand names and positionings around the world, while its rivals single-mindedly promote just one or two brands. There also are marketing benefits to a common brand name as international travel and cross-border media continue to grow. In consolidating its various names around the world, Exxon rapidly achieved global focus and recognition. Coca-Cola, Levis, and McDonald's are other companies that have successfully used a single-brand strategy. Mercedes, BMW, and Volvo not only use the same brand name throughout the world, but also have consistent images and positionings in different countries.

Integrating Competitive Moves across Countries

Instead of making competitive decisions in a country without regard to
what is happening in other countries, a global competitor can take an
integrated approach. Tyrolia, the Austrian ski-binding manufacturer, at-
tacked Salomon's stronghold position in its biggest market, the United
States. Rather than fighting Tyrolia only in the US, Salomon retaliated in
the countries where Tyrolia generated a large share of its sales and profits
—Germany and Austria. Taking a global perspective, Salomon viewed the
whole world—not just one country—as its competitive battleground.

Another benefit of integrating competitive strategy is the ability of a
company to cross-subsidize. This involves utilizing cash generated in a
profitable, high-market-share country to invest aggressively in a strategically important but low-market-share country. The purpose is, of course, to
optimize results worldwide.

Industry Drivers of Globalization

How can a company decide whether it should globalize a particular business? What sort of global strategy should it pursue? Managers should look
first to the business's industry. An industry's potential for globalization is
driven by market, economic, environmental, and competitive factors (see
Figure 4.1).[2] Market forces determine the customers' receptivity to a global
product; economic factors determine whether pursuing a global strategy
can provide a cost advantage; environmental factors show whether the
necessary supporting infrastructure is there; and competitive factors provide a spur to action.

The automotive industry provides a good example of all four forces.
People in the industry now talk of "world cars." A number of *market
factors* are pushing the industry toward globalization, including a mature
market, similar demand trends across countries (such as quality/reliability
and fuel efficiency), shortening product life cycles (e.g., twelve years for the
Renault 5; eight for the Renault 18, and five each for the Renault 11 and
Renault 9), and worldwide image-building. Similarly, *economic factors* are
pushing the automotive industry toward globalization. For example, economies of scale, particularly on engines and transmissions, are very important, and few country markets provide enough volume to get full benefits
of these economies of scale. Similarly, many car manufacturers have now
moved to worldwide sourcing. In the *environmental* area, converging regulations (safety, emissions) and rapid technological evolution (new materials,

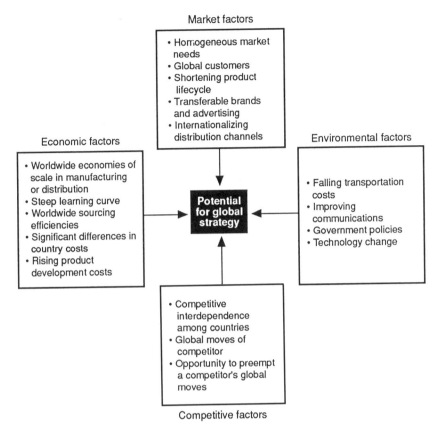

Figure 4.1
External drives of industry potential for globalization

electronics, robotics), all requiring heavy investment in R & D and plant and equipment, also are moving the industry inexorably toward globalization. Finally, *competitive* factors are contributing to globalization. Witness the increasing number of cooperative ventures among manufacturers— Toyota-GM, Toyo Kogyo-Ford, Chrysler-Mitsubishi. These ventures are putting pressure on all automotive manufacturers to go global.

In summary, managers wrestling with globalization issues should first analyze the four sets of industry forces to determine whether they compete in an industry that is global or globalizing. Next, they need to assess how global their companies are, and how global their competitors are, along the five dimensions defined previously. This step—which is illustrated in the Appendix—helps define the broad direction of the strategic moves needed to change their company's global competitive posture. A very difficult part remains: assessing whether the organization has the capacity to go global.

Organizational Factors in Globalization

Organizational factors can support or undercut a business's attempt to globalize.[3] Therefore, taking a close look at how the organization will affect the relative difficulty of globalization is essential. Four factors affect the ability of an organization to develop and implement global strategy: organization structure, management processes, people, and culture (see figure 4.2). Each of these aspects of organization operates powerfully in different ways. A common mistake, in implementing *any* strategy, is to ignore one or more of them, particularly the less tangible ones such as culture.

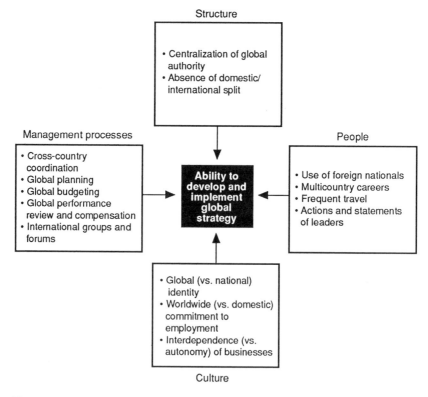

Figure 4.2
Internal factors that facilitate a global strategy

Organization Structure

• *Centralization of global authority.* One of the most effective ways to develop and implement a global strategy is to centralize authority, so all units of the business around the world report to a common sector head. Surprisingly few companies do this. Instead, they are tied for historical reasons to a strong country-based organization where the main line of authority runs by country rather than by business. In a company pursuing a global strategy, the business focus should dominate the country focus. It's difficult, but necessary.

• *Domestic/international split.* A common structural barrier to global strategy is an organizational split between domestic and international divisions. The international division oversees a group of highly autonomous country subsidiaries, each of which manages several distinct businesses. A global strategy for any one of these businesses can then be coordinated only at the CEO level. This split is very common among US firms, partly for historical reasons and partly because of the enormous size of the US market. Ironically, some European multinationals with small domestic markets have separated out not their home market but the US market. As a result they find it difficult to get their US subsidiaries to cooperate in the development and implementation of global strategy. In one European company we know, the heads of worldwide business sectors go hat in hand to New York to solicit support for their worldwide strategies.

Management Processes

While organization structure has a very direct effect on management behavior, it is management processes that power the system. The appropriate processes can even substitute to some extent for the appropriate structure.

• *Cross-country coordination.* Providing cross-country coordination is a common way to make up for the lack of a direct reporting structure. Some consumer packaged goods companies are beginning to appoint European brand managers to coordinate strategy across countries.

• *Global planning.* Too often strategic plans are developed separately for each country and are not aggregated globally for each business across all countries. This makes it difficult to understand the business's competitive position worldwide and to develop an integrated strategy against competitors who plan on a global basis.

• *Global budgeting.* Similarly, country budgets need to be consolidated into a global total for each product line to aid the allocation of resources across product lines. Surprisingly few companies do this.

• *Global performance review and compensation.* Rewards, especially bonuses, need to be set in a way that reinforces the company's global objectives. An electronics manufacturer, for example, decided to start penetrating the international market by introducing a new product through its strongest division. The division head's bonus was based on current year's worldwide sales, with no distinction between domestic and international sales. Because increasing his domestic sales was easier—and had a much quicker pay-off—than trying to open new international markets, the division head didn't worry much about his international sales. Predictably, the firm's market penetration strategy failed.

• *International groups and forums.* Holding international forums allows exchange of information and building of relationships across countries. This, in turn, makes it easier for country nationals to gain an understanding of whether the differences they perceive between their home country and others are real or imagined. It also facilitates the development of common products and the coordination of marketing approaches. For example, a French manufacturer of security devices uses councils of country managers, with different countries taking the lead on different products. While this approach is time-consuming, the company has found that this reliance on line managers makes it easier for various countries to accept the input of other countries, and thus for global approaches to be pursued by all.

People

Being truly global also involves using people in a different way from that of a multinational firm.

• *Use foreign nationals.* High-potential foreign nationals need to gain experience not only in their home country, but also at headquarters and in other countries. This practice has three benefits: broadening the pool of talent available for executive positions; demonstrating the commitment of top management to internationalization; and giving talented individuals an irreplaceable development opportunity. US companies have been slow to do this, particularly at the most senior ranks.

Promoting foreigners, and using staff from various countries, has often paid off. In the 1970s, an ailing NCR vaulted William S. Anderson, the British head of their Asian business, to the top job. Anderson is widely credited with turning around NCR. A French packaged goods manufacturer undertook seven years ago to move its European staff from country to country. Today, of fifteen staff members working at headquarters, seven are French, three are English, three are German and two are Italian. The company credits this practice—among others—for its remarkable turnaround.

• *Require multicountry careers.* Making work experience in different countries necessary for progression, rather than a hindrance, is another step that helps a company become truly global. One electronics manufacturer decided to make a major push into Japan, but an executive offered a transfer there was loath to take it. He was unsure a job would remain for him when he came back. As he put it, "The road to the executive suite lies through Chicago, not Osaka."

• *Travel frequently.* Senior managers must spend a large amount of time in foreign countries. The CEO of a large grocery products company we have worked with spends half his time outside the United States—a visible demonstration of the importance and commitment of the company to its international operations.

• *State global intentions.* The senior management of a company that wants to go global needs to constantly restate that intention and to act accordingly. Otherwise, the rank and file won't believe that the globalization strategy is real. One test among many is the prominence given to international operations in formal communications such as the chairman's letter in the annual report and statements to stock analysts.

Culture

Culture is the most subtle aspect of organization, but, as shown below, it can play a formidable role in helping or hindering a global strategy.

• *Global (vs. national) identity.* Does the company have a strong national identity? This can hinder the willingness and ability to design global products and programs. It can also create a "them and us" split among employees. One firm was making a strong global push, and yet many of its corporate executives wore national flag pins! European companies are generally well in advance of both American and Japanese firms in adopting a global identity.

• *Worldwide (vs. domestic) commitment to employment.* Many American companies view their domestic employees as more important than their overseas employees and are much more committed to preserving domestic employment than to developing employment regardless of location. This often leads them to decide to keep expensive manufacturing operations in the United States, rather than relocate them to lower-cost countries. This puts them at a competitive cost disadvantage and threatens their overall competitive position.

• *Interdependence (vs. autonomy) of businesses.* A high level of autonomy for local business can also be a barrier to globalization.

In sum, the four internal factors of organization—structure, management processes, people, and culture—play a key role in a company's move toward globalization.

For example, a company with a strong structural split between domestic and international activities, management processes that are country— rather than business—driven, people who work primarily in their home countries, and a parochial culture is likely to have difficulty implementing integrated competitive strategies. If the analysis of external drivers has shown that such strategies are necessary for market, competitive, environmental, or economic reasons, top management needs to either adapt the internal environment to the strategic moves the company needs to make —or decide that the profound organizational changes needed are too risky. In the latter case, the company should avoid globalization and compete based on its existing organizational strengths.

Conclusion

There are many was to pursue a global strategy. Industry forces play a major role in determining whether going global makes sense. An analysis of a company's competitive position against the five dimensions of globalization—major market participation, product standardization, activity specialization, uniform market positioning, and integrated competitive strategy—helps define the appropriate approach for a globalization strategy. Finally, and very importantly, the ability of the organization to implement the different elements of global strategy needs to be considered.

Matching the external and internal imperatives is critical. For example, we have worked with a company whose culture included the following characteristics:

• A high degree of responsiveness to customers' requests for product tailoring.

- A strong emphasis on letting every business and every country be highly autonomous.
- A desire for 100% control over foreign operations.
- A commitment to preserving domestic employment.

The difficulty the company found in pursuing a globalization strategy is illustrated in the strategy/culture fit matrix in Figure 4.3. The matrix helped management articulate the pros and cons of the three major options they could pursue: a pure global strategy with an organizational revolution; a series of incremental changes in both strategy and organization, leading to a mixed strategy of globalization/national responsiveness; and an explicit rejection of globalization, accompanied with a conscious decision to build on the company's existing organizational and cultural characteristics to develop a pure national responsiveness strategy. This enabled them to make fundamental and realistic choices rather than assuming the unavoid-

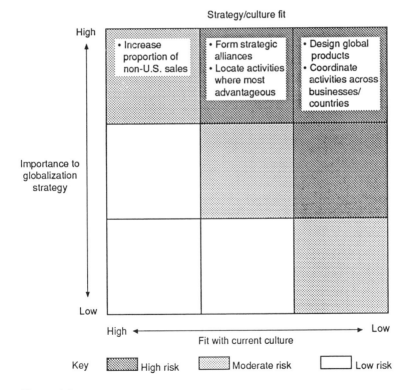

Figure 4.3
Identification of high-risk areas in implementing a global strategy

able dominance of strategy over organization and of globalization over national responsiveness.

Competing globally is tough. It requires a clear vision of the firm as a global competitor, a long-term time horizon, a concerted effort to match strategy and organization changes, a cosmopolitan view and a substantial commitment from the top. But the result can be the opportunity to gain significant competitive advantage through cost, focus, and concentration, and improved response to customers' needs and preferences.

Appendix

To illustrate use of the global strategy framework, or global strategy audit, we summarize here the experiences of two companies, both of them multibillion-dollar multinationals. One company, disguised as "TransElectronics," is a US-based concern operating in many aspects of electronics. The other company, disguised as "Persona," is a European-based manufacturer and marketer of consumer packaged goods. The two companies provide different views of the challenge of global strategy. TransElectronics is still developing as a fully multinational company and faces the challenge of accelerating that process to become a global competitor. Persona, on the other hand, has long been thoroughly multinational, with many highly autonomous companies operating around the world. Its challenge is to temper some aspects of that multinational autonomy to compete more effectively on a global basis.

TransElectronics

Step 1—Identify Business Unit
All six TransElectronics business sectors faced pressing issues of global competition. The Communications Sector had one division, Electron, based in the United States, that sold what we will call "transcramblers" against fierce European and Japanese competition. A major market, Japan, closed until recently to foreign competition, was beginning to open through a combination of TransElectronics' efforts and US government pressure on Japanese trade barriers. So developing a global strategy for transcramblers was a high priority for TransElectronics. A complication was that Electron was not a stand-alone business unit—other units had related responsibilities. As we will describe, this split of responsibilities was one of the major barriers to Electron's implementation of a global strategy.

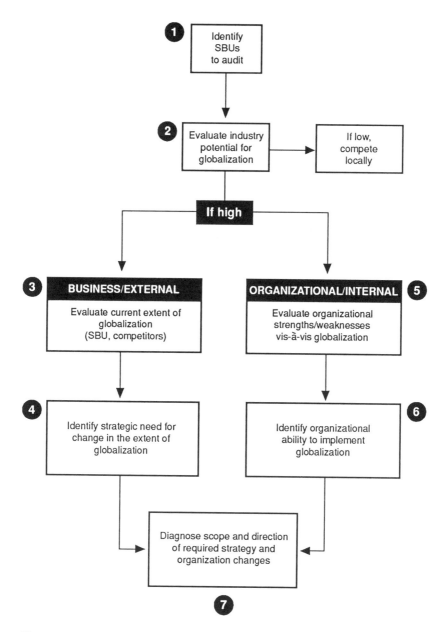

Figure 4.4
The steps of the global strategy audit

Step 2—Evaluate Industry Potential for Globalization
Market factors pushed for globalization: there were few differences among countries in what they wanted from transcramblers. On the other hand, few global customers existed because of strong national boundaries between public sector customers (PTTs), who accounted for a large share of the market.

Economic factors strongly pushed for globalization. There were substantial scale economies and learning effects, sourcing efficiencies could be gained by consolidating manufacturing, and Electron's labor costs—a significant part of the product's total cost—were much lower in Puerto Rico and Taiwan than they were in the United States.

Environmental factors also pushed for globalization. The privatization of some national PTTs was opening up previously closed markets, and products were becoming more standardized in Europe around a common format. An offsetting factor was local content requirements in many countries.

Competitive forces were also in line. Electron's major competitors (European and Japanese) took a global product approach with fewer price levels and minimum product customization. They also had largely centralized their manufacturing activities in just one or two countries each.

In conclusion, strong external forces pushed the transcrambler industry toward globalization. Not only was globalization already high, it was likely to continue increasing.

Step 3—Evaluate Current Extent of Globalization
Market participation. Electron was quite global in its market participation. Its sales split among countries closely matched that of the industry.
Product standardization. Electron's product line was highly standardized—in fact, more so than its executives realized. They initially thought that their product was not standard across countries because 40% of the product cost was in a decoder that was different in each country. But digging deeper, however, they discovered that within the decoder only the software was unique. Furthermore, the software was embodied in purchased parts (masked ROMs). Therefore, there was no difference in the manufacturing process, only in the inventory to be kept. Also, the cost of developing the unique software was amortized over a large sales base. As a result, what initially appeared to be 40% nonstandard turned out to be 3% nonstandard.
Activity concentration. Electron's R & D and purchasing activities were specialized in the US, but much of their manufacturing was dispersed across the US, Puerto Rico, Taiwan, and Europe. Marketing was primarily done in

the US. Selling, distribution, and service were by necessity done locally but were not coordinated across countries. Electron's competitors were all much more centralized and coordinated.

Marketing uniformity. The product positioning of transcramblers was consistent across countries, as was that of Electron's competitors. If anything, TransElectronics' marketing policies were too uniform, given a rigid pricing policy that did not allow Electron to adapt to the wide variations in price across countries. As a result, Electron did not use price as a strategic weapon.

Integration of competitive moves. Electron did not integrate its competitive moves across countries, nor did its competitors.

Step 4—Identify Strategic Need for Change in the Extent of Globalization

From the previous analyses, Electron concluded that its extent of globalization was significantly lower than the industry potential, and lower than its competitors' globalization. Furthermore, the industry potential for globalization was steadily increasing. It was clear that Electron had a strong need to develop a more global strategy. The next issue was whether Electron would be able to implement such a strategy.

Step 5—Evaluate Organization Factors

Structure. TransElectronics' structure worked in two major ways against a global strategy. First, TransElectronics operated with a strong domestic/international split within each sector. Second, worldwide responsibilities for Electron's business were scattered throughout the organization. The Electron division itself had responsibility for some product development, some manufacturing, and some marketing. Other divisions in the US and overseas shared these responsibilities. Selling was the responsibility of both local non-US countries, and in the US, of a totally separate distribution group for the entire communications sector. In effect, there was no one manager below the sector head who had global authority over transcramblers.

Management processes. The budget process worked against a global approach. The Electron division budgeted only a total number for overseas sales, without country targets. The International Group in the Communications Sector set country quotas for the entire sector, without product quotas or product-by-country quotas. The strategic planning process did not help either. The Electron division and the International Group developed separate plans simultaneously. There were no international components in the bonus for domestic managers.

People. TransElectronics' employee practices worked against a global approach. There were few foreign nationals in the US at either corporate or divisional levels. There were many foreign nationals overseas, but these were mostly in their home countries, and there was little movement between international and domestic jobs. In particular, the US divisions were reluctant to give up people, and overseas assignments were not seen as being part of a desirable career track.

Culture. TransElectronics' corporate culture worked against a global view in both obvious and subtle ways. At the obvious level, TransElectronics was very much an American company with a "them-us" mentality. Indeed, the chairman had made speeches calling for increased trade barriers against Japanese firms. More subtly, TransElectronics had a very strong culture of being responsive to customer requests for product tailoring, born of a heritage of selling exclusively to a very small number of automotive customers. This culture worked strongly against attempts to standardize globally.

Step 6—Identify Organizational Ability to Implement Globalization
TransElectronics clearly had a very low organizational ability to develop a global strategy for transcramblers. They had certainly experienced many difficulties in their fitful attempts at doing so.

Step 7—Diagnose Scope and Direction of Required Changes
In summary, the most important business changes that Electron had to make were to exploit more opportunities for product standardization and to specialize somewhat more where different activities (particularly manufacturing) were conducted.

More widespread changes were needed in terms of management and organization. While many aspects of these needed to change, the most implementable change was in terms of management process. TransElectronics adopted for the transcrambler business a global strategic planning process and globally based evaluation and compensation. These relatively modest changes would pave the way for future acceptance of the more radical changes needed in organization structure, people, and culture.

Persona

Step 1—Identify Business Unit
As in the case of Electron, there were difficulties in defining the relevant business unit. Persona had operating companies around the world that sold

many kinds of personal-care as well as other household products. The global strategy audit was conducted for one particular product, "hairfloss," that was sold around the world.

Step 2—Evaluate Industry Potential for Globalization
Market factors pushed strongly for globalization: market needs were very much the same around the world within income categories—higher-income countries were earlier users of the new variants and ingredients that were introduced every few years. Brand names and advertising were also widely transferable—some competitors used just one major brand name and essentially the same advertising campaign around the world.

Economic factors were less important, given that product costs were only about 25% of total costs, economies of scale were low and price was not a major basis of competition. Also the low value-to-weight ratio of hairfloss made it uneconomical to ship far. Nonetheless, there was some centralized manufacturing on a multicountry regional basis, e.g., parts of Western Europe, Southeast Asia, and Africa.

Environmental factors did not particularly favor globalization. In Western Europe, however, the increasing importance of multicountry media, particularly satellite television with wide reception, and of the European Economic Community, pushed for regional, if not global, approaches.

Competitive behavior was the major force pushing the industry to globalization. Persona faced three major worldwide competitors, multinationals like itself. Two of these competitors took a much more standardized approach than Persona—they concentrated their resources behind the same one or two brands of hairfloss in each. In contrast, Persona tended to market three or four brands in each country, and these brands were different among major countries. Persona's competitors also were quick to transfer successful innovations from one country to the next, while Persona's brand fragmentation hindered its efforts. This global fragmentation seemed to be a major reason behind Persona's slipping market share and profitability.

Persona concluded that there were strong external forces pushing the hairfloss industry toward globalization—at least to the extent of coordinated regional operations—and this push toward globalization was likely to increase in the future.

Step 3—Evaluate Current Extent of Globalization
Market participation. Persona participated in markets that accounted for almost 90% of worldwide (excluding communist countries) hairfloss volume. The largest competitor, not Persona, participated in almost 100%.

Product standardization. Persona's hairfloss product line was quite highly standardized around half a dozen variants. Persona generally marketed a large number of variants in wealthier countries, but the variants were still basically the same across countries.

Activity concentration. Like most consumer packaged goods multinationals, Persona practiced very little specialization by country. Persona fielded a full business operation in most countries.

Marketing uniformity. On this dimension of globalization Persona was severely lacking because of its multiple brands, multiple product positionings and multiple advertising campaigns.

Integration of competitive moves. Persona did not do much to integrate its competitive moves across countries, although it had begun recently to experiment with such attempts.

Overall, Persona's actual extent of globalization was somewhat lower than that of its competitors.

Step 4—Identify Strategic Need for Change in the Extent of Globalization
In conclusion, while Persona's worldwide hairfloss strategy was quite global in some respects, the lack of marketing uniformity was the biggest problem. The key variables that Persona could manipulate were brand name and positioning. First, to increase local marketing muscle, Persona needed to reduce the number of brands in each country to two. Second, to achieve the benefits of global market uniformity, they had three broad alternatives:

1. A different brand but common positioning for each product variant in each country.

2. A common regional brand and positioning.

3. A common global brand and positioning.

Because Persona already had strong brand names around the world that it did not want to abandon, and because a common positioning would achieve most of the benefits of uniformity, the company concluded that the second alternative was best. The next issue was whether Persona would be able to implement such a strategy.

Step 5—Evaluate Organizational Factors
Structure. Persona's structure made it difficult to develop and implement a global strategy. Persona operated with a strong geographic structure that was overlaid with a worldwide product direction function at corporate.

This function, however, had advisory rather than direct authority over the individual country businesses. Furthermore, the direction function did not include the U.S.

Management processes. The budget and compensation systems worked against global strategy. These were done on a strictly local basis, although aggregated geographically. But there was no mechanism to encourage local participation in a worldwide effort. A strategic plan was developed globally, but local acceptance was voluntary.

People. On this score, Persona was very capable of implementing a global strategy. Its managers were drawn from all over the world, and transfers both among countries and to and from corporate were common.

Culture. Culture was the biggest barrier. Persona had a very strong culture of giving autonomy to its local managers. Although corporate leaders increasingly wanted to give direct orders on strategy, they were loath to risk the possible loss of local accountability and commitment.

Step 6—Identify Organizational Ability to Implement Globalization
Like TransElectronics, Persona also had a low organizational capacity for global strategy but for somewhat different reasons.

Step 7—Diagnose Scope and Direction of Required Changes
In summary, the most important business changes that Persona had to make in hairfloss were to reduce its number of brands in each country and to develop a common brand by region and common positioning for each major product variant.

Organizationally, changing the structure would create too much disruption. What was needed was a greater willingness by corporate to push countries to adopt a global approach. A first step was a directive that all countries should launch the new "high-gloss" variant within a six-month period. Persona hoped that a successful experience of common action would start moving the culture toward greater acceptance of global strategies.

Further Steps
A global strategy audit provides four concrete outputs:

• An assessment of how global the industry is today and is likely to become in the future.

• An understanding of how global the firm's approach is today and how it compares to its competitors and to the industry potential for further globalization.

• An identification of the organizational factors that will facilitate or hinder a move toward globalization.

• A broad action plan, specifying strategic and organizational change priorities.

The audit, in and of itself, does not provide the details of a competitive strategy. If its output has shown that adopting some form of global strategy is indeed desirable, the audit needs to be followed by another effort aimed at developing a detailed global strategy. Among the decisions that will need to be made are the definition of a competitive posture in various countries (i.e., in what part of the world should we compete on our own, and in what part should we form alliances?); the articulation of specific functional strategies (manufacturing, marketing, financial, etc.) and, for each function, of the appropriate balance between global and local approaches (for example, all elements of manufacturing could be global, while some elements of marketing, such as sales promotion, might remain local); and the adoption of organizational mechanisms aimed at reinforcing the strategic objectives sought.

However, the audit provides a relatively simple and quick way to get answers to some of the most complicated questions facing corporate management today. It also greatly facilitates the undertaking of the strategy development phase that follows, because it has identified the major thrusts that are needed. Furthermore, it has the potential for avoiding major errors —such as a move toward globalization when none is warranted. Finally, it sensitizes the organization to the issues and to the commitments needed if it really decides to compete globally.

Notes

1. See Theodore Levitt's arguments in "The Globalization of Markets," *Harvard Business Review*, May–June 1983, pp. 92–102. For a counterargument, see Susan P. Douglas and Yoram Wind, "The Myth of Globalization," *Columbia Journal of World Business*, Winter: 1987, pp. 19–29.

2. For related frameworks on the role of industry forces in global strategy, see Thomas Hout, Michael E. Porter, and Eileen Rudden, "How Global Companies Win Out," *Harvard Business Review*, September–October 1982, pp. 98–109. Also Porter, "Changing the Patterns of Interntional Competition," *California Management Review*, Winter 1986, pp. 9–40; and Porter, editor, *Competition in Global Industries*, Boston: Harvard Business School Press, 1986. Bruce Kogut takes a somewhat different view in "Designing Global Strategies," *Sloan Management Review*, Summer 1985, pp. 15–38, and Fall 1985, pp. 27–38.

3. For a discussion of organizational issues in global strategy, see Christopher A. Bartlett, "MNCs: Get Off the Reorganization Merry-Go-Round." *Harvard Business Review*, March–April 1983, pp. 138–146; Christopher A. Bartlett and Sumantra Goshal, "Tap Your Subsidiaries for Global Reach," *Harvard Business Review*, November–December 1986, pp. 87–94. Also Gary Hamel and C. K. Prahalad, "Do You Really Have a Global Strategy?" *Harvard Business Review*, July–August 1985, pp. 139–148; and C. K. Prahalad and Yves L. Doz, *The Multinational Mission: Balancing Local Demands and Global Vision*, New York: The Free Press, 1987.

4. For global marketing strategy, see John A. Quelch and Edward J. Hoff, "Customizing Global Marketing," *Harvard Business Review*, May–June 1986, pp. 59–68.

5. For a discussion of different types of global strategic planning, see Balaji S. Chakravarthy and Howard V. Perlmutter, "Strategic Planning for a Global Business," *Columbia Journal of World Business*, Summer 1985, pp. 3–10; and David C. Shanks, "Strategic Planning for Global Competition," *Journal of Business Strategy*, Winter 1985, pp. 80–89.

6. See John J. Dyment's discussion of global budgeting in "Strategies and Management Controls for Global Corporations," *Journal of Business Strategy*, Spring 1987, pp. 20–26.

5

Global Strategy: An Organizing Framework

Sumantra Ghoshal

Over the past few years the concept of global strategy has taken the world of multinational corporations (MNCs) by storm. Scores of articles in the *Harvard Business Review, Fortune, The Economist,* and other popular journals have urged multinationals to "go global" in their strategies. The topic has clearly captured the attention of MNC managers. Conferences on global strategy, whether organized by the Conference Board in New York, *The Financial Times* in London, or Nomura Securities in Tokyo, have invariably attracted enthusiastic corporate support and sizeable audiences. Even in the relatively slow-moving world of academe the issue of globalization of industries and companies has emerged as a new bandwagon, as manifest in the large number of papers on the topic presented at recent meetings of the Academy of Management, the Academy of International Business, and the Strategic Management Society. "Manage globally" appears to be the latest battlecry in the world of international business.

Multiple Perspectives, Many Prescriptions

This enthusiasm notwithstanding, there is a great deal of conceptual ambiguity about what a "global" strategy really means. As pointed out by Hamel and Prahalad (1985), the distinction among a global industry, a global firm, and a global strategy is somewhat blurred in the literature. According to Hout, Porter, and Rudden (1982), a global strategy is appropriate for global industries which are defined as those in which a firm's competitive position in one national market is significantly affected by its competitive position in other national markets. Such interactions between a firm's positions in different markets may arise from scale benefits or from the potential of synergies or sharing of costs and resoures across markets.

From *Strategic Management Journal,* Volume 8, 1987, pp. 425–440. Reprinted by permission.

However, as argued by Bartlett (1985), Kogut (1984), and many others, those scale and synergy benefits may often be created by strategic actions of individual firms and may not be "given" in any a priori sense. For some industries, such as aeroframes or aeroengines, the economies of scale may be large enough to make the need for global integration of activities obvious. However, in a large number of cases industries may not be born global but may have globalness thrust upon them by the entrepreneurship of a company such as Yoshida Kagyo KK (YKK) or Procter and Gamble. In such cases the global industry–global strategy link may be more useful for ex-post explanation of outcomes than for ex-ante predictions or strategizing.

Further, the concept of a global strategy is not as new as some of the recent authors on the topic have assumed it to be. It was stated quite explicitly about 20 years ago by Perlmutter (1969) when he distinguished between the geocentric, polycentric, and ethnocentric approaches to multinational management. The starting point for Perlmutter's categorization scheme was the worldview of a firm, which was seen as the driving force behind its management processes and the way it structured its world-wide activities (see Robinson, 1978, and Rutenberg, 1982, for detailed reviews and expositions). In much of the current literature, in contrast, the focus has been narrowed and the concept of global strategy has been linked almost exclusively with how the firm structures the flow of tasks within its world-wide value-adding system. The more integrated and rationalized the flow of tasks appears to be, the more global the firm's strategy is assumed to be (e.g. Leontiades, 1984). On the one hand, this focus has led to improved understanding of the fact that different tasks offer different degrees of advantages from global integration and national differentiation and that, optimally, a firm must configure its value chain to obtain the best possible advantages from both (Porter, 1984). But, on the other hand, it has also led to certain dysfunctional simplifications. The complexities of managing large, world-wide organizations have been obscured by creating polar alternatives between centralization and decentralization, or between global and multidomestic strategies (e.g. Hout et al., 1982). Complex management tasks have been seen as composites of simple global and local components. By emphasizing the importance of rationalizing the flow of components and final products within a multinational system, the importance of internal flows of people, technology, information, and values has been de-emphasized.

Differences among authors writing on the topic of global strategy are not limited to concepts and perspectives. Their prescriptions on how to manage globally have also been very different, and often contradictory.

1. Levitt (1983) has argued that effective global strategy is not a bag of many tricks but the successful practice of just one: product standardization. According to him, the core of a global strategy lies in developing a standardized product to be produced and sold the same way throughout the world.

2. According to Hout et al. (1982), on the other hand, effective global strategy requires the approach not of a hedgehog, who knows only one trick, but that of a fox, who knows many. Exploiting economies of scale through global volume, taking pre-emptive positions through quick and large investments, and managing interdependently to achieve synergies across different activities are, according to these authors, some of the more important moves that a winning global strategist must muster.

3. Hamel and Prahalad's (1985) prescription for a global strategy contradicts that of Levitt (1983) even more sharply. Instead of a single standardized product, they recommend a broad product portfolio, with many product varieties, so that investments on technologies and distribution channels can be shared. Cross-subsidization across products and markets, and the development of a strong world-wide distribution system, are the two moves that find the pride of place in these authors' views on how to succeed in the game of global chess.

4. If Hout et al.'s (1982) global strategist is the heavyweight champion who knocks out opponents with scale and pre-emptive investments, Kogut's (1985b) global strategist is the nimble-footed athelete who wins through flexibility and arbitrage. He creates options so as to turn the uncertainties of an increasingly volatile global economy to his own advantage. Multiple sourcing, production shifting to benefit from changing factor costs and exchange rates, and arbitrage to exploit imperfections in financial and information markets are, according to Kogut, some of the hallmarks of a superior global strategy.

These are only a few of the many prescriptions available to MNC managers about how to build a global strategy for their firms. All these suggestions have been derived from rich and insightful analyses of real-life situations. They are all reasonable and intuitively appealing, but their managerial implications are not easy to reconcile.

The Need for an Organizing Framework

The difficulty for both practitioners and researchers in dealing with the small but rich literature on global strategies is that there is no organizing framework within which the different perspectives and prescriptions can be assimilated. An unfortunate fact of corporate life is that any particular strategic action is rarely an unmixed blessing. Corporate objectives are multidimensional, and often mutually contradictory. Contrary to received wisdom, it is also usually difficult to prioritize them. Actions to achieve a particular objective often impede another equally important objective. Each of these prescriptions is aimed at achieving certain objectives of a global strategy. An overall framework can be particularly useful in identifying the trade-offs between those objectives and therefore in understanding not only the benefits but also the potential costs associated with the different strategic alternatives.

The objective of this paper is to suggest such an organizing framework which may help managers and academics in formulating the various issues that arise in global strategic management. The underlying premise is that simple categorization schemes such as the distinction between global and multidomestic strategies are not very helpful in understanding the complexities of corporate-level strategy in large multinational corporations. Instead, what may be more useful is to understand what the key strategic objectives of an MNC are, and the tools that it possesses for achieving them. An integrated analysis of the different means and the different ends can help both managers and researchers in formulating, describing, classifying, and analyzing the content of global strategies. Besides, such a framework can relate academic research, which is often partial, to the totality of real life that managers must deal with.

The Framework: Mapping Means and Ends

The proposed framework is shown in table 5.1. While the specific construct may be new, the conceptual foundation on which it is built is derived from a synthesis of existing literature.

The basic argument is simple. The goals of a multinational—as indeed of any organization—can be classified into three broad categories. The firm must achieve efficiency in its current activities; it must manage the risks that it assumes in carrying out those activities; and it must develop internal learning capabilities so as to be able to innovate and adapt to future changes. Competitive advantage is developed by taking strategic actions that optimize the firm's achievement of these different and, at times. conflicting goals.

A multinational has three sets of tools for developing such competitive advantage. It can exploit the differences in input and output markets

Table 5.1
Global strategy: an organizing framework

	Sources of competitive advantage		
Strategic objectives	National differences	Scale economies	Scope economies
Achieving efficiency in current operations	Benefiting from differences in factor costs—wages and cost of capital	Expanding and exploiting potential scale economies in each activity	Sharing of investments and costs across products, markets, and businesses
Managing risks	Managing different kinds of risks arising from market or policy-induced changes in comparative advantages of different countries	Balancing scale with strategic and operational flexibility	Portfolio diversification of risks and creation of options and side-bets
Innovation, learning, and adaptation	Learning from societal differences in organizational and managerial processes and systems	Benefiting from experience—cost reduction and innovation	Shared learning across organizational components in different products, markets, or businesses

among the many countries in which it operates. It can benefit from scale economies in its different activities. It can also exploit synergies or economies of scope that may be available because of the diversity of its activities and organization.

The strategic task of managing globally is to use all three sources of competitive advantage to optimize efficiency, risk, and learning simultaneously in a world-wide business. The key to a successful global strategy is to manage the interactions between these different goals and means. That, in essence, is the organizing framework. Viewing the tasks of global strategy this way can be helpful to both managers and academics in a number of ways. For example, it can help managers in generating a comprehensive checklist of factors and issues that must be considered in reviewing different strategic alternatives. Such a checklist can serve as a basis for mapping the overall strategies of their own companies and those of their competitors so as to understand the comparative strengths and vulnerabilities of both. Table 5.1 shows some illustrative examples of factors that must be considered while carrying out such comprehensive strategic audits.

Another practical utility of the framework is that it can highlight the contradictions between the different goals and between the different means, and thereby make salient the strategic dilemmas that may otherwise get resolved through omission.

In the next two sections the framework is explained more fully by describing the two dimensions of its construct, viz. the strategic objectives of the firm and the sources of competitive advantage available to a multinational corporation. Subsequent sections show how selected articles contribute to the literature and fit within the overall framework. The paper concludes with a brief discussion of the tradeoffs that are implicit in some of the more recent prescriptions on global strategic management.

The Goals: Strategic Objectives

Achieving Efficiency

A general premise in the literature on strategic management is that the concept of strategy is relevant only when the actions of one firm can affect the actions or performance of another. Firms competing in imperfect markets earn different "efficiency rents" from the use of their resources (Caves, 1980). The objective of strategy, given this perspective, is to enhance such efficiency rents.

Viewing a firm broadly as an input-output system, the overall efficiency of the firm can be defined as the ratio of the value of its outputs to the costs of all its inputs. It is by maximizing this ratio that the firm obtains the surplus resources required to secure its own future. Thus it differentiates its products to enhance the exchange value of its outputs, and seeks low cost factors to minimize the costs of its inputs. It also tries to enhance the efficiency of its throughput processes by achieving higher scale economies or by finding more efficient production processes.

The field of strategic management is currently dominated by this efficiency perspective. The generic strategies of Porter (1980), different versions of the portfolio model, as well as overall strategic management frameworks such as those proposed by Hofer and Schendel (1978) and Hax and Majluf (1984) are all based on the underlying notion of maximizing efficiency rents of the different resources available to the firm.

In the field of global strategy this efficiency perspective has been reflected in the widespread use of the integration-responsiveness framework originally proposed by Prahalad (1975) and subsequently developed and applied by a number of authors including Doz, Bartlett, and Prahalad

(1981) and Porter (1984). In essence, the framework is a conceptual lens for visualizing the cost advantages of global integration of certain tasks vis-á-vis the differentiation benefits of responding to national differences in tastes, industry structures, distribution systems, and government regulations. As suggested by Bartlett (1985), the same framework can be used to understand differences in the benefits of integration and responsiveness at the aggregate level of industries, at the level of individual companies within an industry, or even at the level of different functions within a company (see figure 5.1, reproduced from Bartlett, 1985). Thus the consumer electronics industry may be characterized by low differentiation benefits and high integration advantages, while the position of the packaged foods industry may be quite the opposite. In the telecommunications switching industry, in contrast, both local and global forces may be strong, while in the automobile industry both may be of moderate and comparable importance.

Within an industry (say, automobile), the strategy of one firm (such as Toyota) may be based on exploiting the advantages of global integration through centralized production and decision-making, while that of another (such as Fiat) may aim at exploiting the benefits of national differentiation by creating integrated and autonomous subsidiaries which can exploit strong links with local stakeholders to defend themselves against more efficient global competitors. Within a firm, research may offer greater efficiency benefits of integration, while sales and service may provide greater differentiation advantages. One can, as illustrated in figure 5.1, apply the framework to even lower levels of analysis, right down to the level of individual tasks. Based on such analysis, a multinational firm can determine the optimum way to configure its value chain so as to achieve the highest overall efficiency in the use of its resources (Porter, 1984).

However, while efficiency is clearly an important strategic objective, it is not the only one. As argued recently by a number of authors, the broader objective of strategic management is to create value which is determined not only by the returns that specific assets are expected to generate, but also by the risks that are assumed in the process (see Woo and Cool, 1985, for a review). This leads to the second strategic objective of firms—that of managing risks.[1]

Managing Risks

A multinational corporation faces many different kinds of risks, some of which are endemic to all firms and some others are unique to organizations

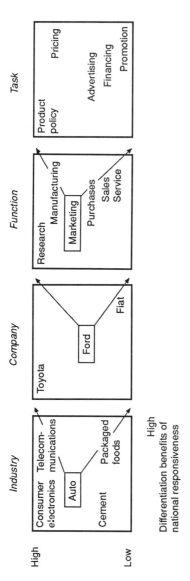

Figure 5.1
The integration-responsiveness framework (reproduced from Barlett, 1985)

operating across national boundaries. For analytical simplicity these different kinds of risks may be collapsed into four broad categories.

First, an MNC faces certain *macroeconomic risks* which are completely outside its control. These include cataclysmic events such as wars and natural calamities, and also equilibrium-seeking or even random movements in wage rates, interest rates, exchange rates, commodity prices, and so on.

Second, the MNC faces what is usually referred to in the literature as political risks but may be more appropriately called *policy risks* to emphasize that they arise from policy actions of national governments and not from either long-term equilibrium-seeking forces of global markets, nor from short-term random fluctuations in economic variables arising out of stickiness or unpredictability of market mechanisms. The net effect of such policy actions may often be indistinguishable from the effect of macroeconomic forces; for example, both may lead to changes in the exchange rate of a particular currency. But from a management perspective the two must be distinguished, since the former is uncontrollable but the latter is at least partially controllable.

Third, a firm also faces certain *competitive risks* arising from the uncertainties of competitors' responses to its own strategies (including the strategy of doing nothing and trying to maintain the status quo). While all companies face such risks to varying extents (since both monopolies and perfect competition are rare), their implications are particularly complex in the context of global strategies since the responses of competitors may take place in many different forms and in many different markets. Further, technological risk can also be considered as a part of competitive risk since a new technology can adversely affect a firm only when it is adopted by a competitor, and not otherwise.[2]

Finally, a firm also faces what may be called *resource risks*. These are the risks that the adopted strategy will require resources that the firm does not have, cannot acquire, or cannot spare. A key scarce resource for most firms is managerial talent. But resource risks can also arise from lack of appropriate technology, or even capital (if managers, for reasons of control, do not want to use capital markets, or if the market is less efficient than finance theorists would have us believe).

One important issue with regard to risks is that they change over time. Vernon (1977) has highlighted this issue in the context of policy risks, but the same is true of the others. Consider resource risks as an example. Often the strategy of a multinational will assume that appropriate resources will be acquired as the strategy unfolds. Yet the initial conditions on which the plans for on-going resource acquisition and development have been based may change over time. Nissan, for instance, based its aggressive internationalization strategy on the expectation of developing technological, financial, and managerial resources out of its home base. Changing competitive positions among local car manufacturers in Japan have affected these resource development plans of the company, and its internationalizing strategy has been threatened significantly. A more careful analysis of alternative competitive scenarios, and of their effects on the resource allocation plans of the company, may have led Nissan to either a slower pace of internationalization, or to a more aggressive process of resource acquisition at an earlier stage of implementing its strategy.

The strategic task, with regard to management of risks, is to consider these different kinds of risks *jointly* in the context of particular strategic decisions. However, not all forms of risk are strategic since some risks can be easily diversified, shifted, or shared through routine market transactions. It is only those risks which cannot be diversified through a readily available external market that are of concern at the strategic level.

As an example, consider the case of currency risks. These can be classified as contractual, semi-contractual and operating risks (Lessard and Lightstone, 1983). Contractual risks arise when a firm enters into a contract for which costs and revenues are expected to be generated in different currencies: for example a Japanese firm entering into a contract for supplying an item to be made in Japan to an American customer at a price fixed in dollars. Semi-contractual risks are assumed when a firm offers an option denominated in foreign currencies, such as a British company quoting a firm rate in guilders. Operating risks, on the other hand, refer to exchange rate-related changes in the firm's competitiveness arising out of long-term commitments of revenues or costs in different currencies. For example, to compete with a Korean firm, an American firm may set up production facilities in Singapore for supplying its customers in the United States and Europe. A gradual strengthening of the Singapore dollar, in comparison with the Korean won, can erode the overall competitiveness of the Singapore plant.

Both contractual and semi-contractual currency risks can be easily shifted or diversified, at relatively low cost, through various hedging mechanisms. If a firm does not so hedge these risks, it is essentially operating as a currency speculator and the risks must be associated with the speculation business and not to its productmarket operations. Operating risks, on the other hand, cannot be hedged so easily,[3] and must be considered at the strategic rather than the operational level.

Analysis of strategic risks will have significant implications for a firm's decisions regarding the structures and locations of its cost and revenue streams. It will lead to more explicit analysis of the effects of environmental uncertainties on the configuration of its value chain. There may be a shift from ownership to rental of resources: from fixed to variable costs. Output and activity distributions may be broadened to achieve the benefits of diversification. Incrementalism and opportunism may be given greater emphasis in its strategy in comparison to pre-emptive resource commitments and long-term planning. Overall strategies may be formulated in more general and flexible terms, so as to be robust to different environmental scenarios. In addition, side-bets may be laid to cover contingencies and to create strategic options which may or may not be exercised in the future (see Kogut, 1985b; Aaker and Mascarenhas, 1984: and Mascarenhas, 1982).

Innovation, Learning, and Adaptation

Most existing theories of the multinational corporation view it as an instrument to extract additional rents from capabilities internalized by the firm (see Calvet, 1981, for a review). A firm goes abroad to make more profits by exploiting its technology, or brand name, or management capabilities in different countries around the world. It is assumed that the key competencies of the multinational always reside at the center.

While the search for additional profits or the desire to protect existing revenues may explain why multinationals come to exist, they may not provide an equally complete explanation of why some of them continue to grow and flourish. An alternative view may well be that a key asset of the multinational is the diversity of environments in which it operates. This diversity exposes it to multiple stimuli, allows it to develop diverse capabilities, and provides it with a broader learning opportunity than is available to a purely domestic firm. The enhanced organizational learning that results from the diversity internalized by the multinational may be a key explanator of its ongoing success, while its initial stock of knowledge may well be the strength that allows it to create such organizational diversity in the first place (Bartlett and Ghoshal, 1985).

Internal diversity may lead to strategic advantages for a firm in many different ways. In an unpredictable environment it may not be possible, ex ante, to predict the competencies that will be required in the future. Diversity of internal capabilities, following the logic of population ecologists (e.g. Hannan and Freeman, 1977; Aldrich, 1979), will enhance the probability of the firm's survival by enhancing the chances that it will be in possession of the capabilities required to cope with an uncertain future state. Similarly, diversity of resources and competencies may also enhance the firm's ability to create joint innovations, and to exploit them in multiple locations. One example of such benefits of diversity was recently described in the *Wall Street Journal* (April 29, 1985):

> P & G [Procter and Gamble Co.] recently introduced its new Liquid Tide, but the product has a distinctly international heritage. A new ingredient that helps suspend dirt in wash water came from the company's research center near P & G's Cincinnati headquarters. But the formula for Liquid Tide's surfactants, or cleaning agents, was developed by P & G technicians in Japan. The ingredients that fight mineral salts present in hard water came from P & G's scientists in Brussels.

As discussed in the same *WSJ* article, P & G's research center in Brussels has developed a special capability in water softening technology due, in part, to the fact that water in Europe contains more than twice the level of mineral content compared to wash water available in the United States. Similarly, surfactant technology is particularly advanced in Japan because Japanese consumers wash their clothes in colder waters compared to consumers in the US or Europe, and this makes greater demands on the cleaning ability of the surfactants. The advantage of P & G as a multinational is that it is exposed to these different operating environments and has learned, in each environment, the skills and knowledge that coping with that environment specially requires. Liquid Tide is an example of the strategic advantages that accrue from such diverse learning.

The mere existence of diversity, however, does not enhance learning. It only creates the potential for learning. To exploit this potential, the organization must consider learning as an explicit objective, and must create mechanisms and systems for such learning to take place. In the absence of explicit intention and appropriate mechanisms, the learning potential may be lost. In some companies, where all organizational resources are centralized and where the national subsidiaries are seen as mere delivery pipelines to supply the organization's value-added to different countries, diverse learning may not take place either because the subsidiaries may not possess appropriate sensing, analyzing, and responding capabilities to learn from their local environments, or because the centralized decision processes may be insensitive to knowledge accumulated outside the corporate headquarters. Other companies, in which the subsidiaries may, enjoy very high levels of local resources and autonomy, may similarly fail to exploit global learning benefits because of their inability to transfer and synthesize knowledge and expertise developed in different organizational components. Lo-

cal loyalties, turf protection, and the "not invented here" (NIH) syndrome
—the three handmaidens of decentralization—may restrict internal flow of
information across national boundaries which is essential for global learning to occur. In other words, both centralization and decentralization may
impede learning.

The Means: Sources of Competitive Advantage

Most recent articles on global strategy have been aimed at identifying
generic strategies (such as global cost leadership, focus, or niche) and advo-
cating particular strategic moves (such as cross-subsidy or pre-emptive
investments). Underlying these concepts, however, are three fundamental
tools for building global competitive advantage: exploiting differences in
input and output markets in different countries, exploiting economies of
scale, and exploiting economies of scope (Porter, 1985).

National Differences

The comparative advantage of locations in terms of differences in factor
costs is perhaps the most discussed, and also the best understood, source of
competitive advantage in international business.

Different nations have different factor endowments, and in the absence
of efficient markets this leads to inter-country differences in factor costs.
Different activities of the firm, such as R & D, production, marketing, etc.,
have different factor intensities. A firm can therefore gain cost advantages
by configuring its value-chain so that each activity is located in the country
which has the least cost for the factor that the activity uses most intensely.
This is the core concept of comparative advantage-based competitive advantage—a concept for which highly developed analytical tools are available from the discipline of international economics. Kogut (1985a) provides
an excellent managerial overview of this concept.

National differences may also exist in output markets. Customer tastes
and preferences may be different in different countries, as may be distribution systems, government regulations applicable to the concerned product-
markets, or the effectiveness of different promotion strategies and other
marketing techniques. A firm can augment the exchange value of its ouput
by tailoring its offerings to fit the unique requirements in each national
market. This, in essence, is the strategy of national differentiation, and it lies
at the core of what has come to be referred to as the multidomestic approach in multinational management (Hout et al., 1982).

From a strategic perspective, however, this static and purely economic view of national differences may not be adequate. What may be more useful is to take a dynamic view of comparative advantage and to broaden the concept to include both societal and economic factors.

In the traditional economics view, comparative advantages of countries are determined by their relative factor endowments and they do not change. However, in reality one lesson of the past four decades is that comparative advantages change and a prime objective of the industrial policies of many nations is to effect such changes. Thus, for any nation, the availability and cost of capital change, as do the availability of technical manpower and the wages of skilled and unskilled labor. Such changes take place, in the long run, to accommodate different levels of economic and social performance of nations, and in the short run they occur in response to specific policies and regulations of governments.

This dynamic aspect of comparative advantages adds considerable complexity to the strategic considerations of the firm. There is a first-order effect of such changes—such as possible increases in wage rates, interest rates or currency exchange rates for particular countries that can affect future viability of a strategy that has been based on the current levels of these economic variables. There can also be a more intriguing second-order effect. If an activity is located in an economically inefficient environment, and if the firm is able to achieve a higher level of efficiency in its own operations compared to the rest of the local economy, its competitive advantage may actually increase as the local economy slips lower and lower. This is because the macroeconomic variables such as wage or exchange rates may change to reflect the overall performance of the economy relative to the rest of the world and, to the extent that the firm's performance is better than this national aggregate, it may benefit from these macro-level changes (Kiechel, 1981).

Consistent with the discipline that gave birth to the concept, the usual view of comparative advantage is limited to factors that an economist admits into the production function, such as the costs of labor and capital. However, from a managerial perspective it may be more appropriate to take a broader view of societal comparative advantages to include "all the relative advantages conferred on a society by the quality, quantity and configuration of its material, human and institutional resources, including "soft" resources such as inter-organizational linkages, the nature of its educational system, and organizational and managerial know-how" (Westney, 1985: 4). As argued by Westney, these "soft" societal factors, if absorbed in the overall organizational system, can provide benefits as real to a multinational as those provided by such economic factors as cheap labor or low-cost capital.

While the concept of comparative advantage is quite clear, available evidence of its actual effect on the overall competitiveness of firms is weak and conflicting. For example, it has often been claimed that one source of competitive advantage for Japanese firms is the lower cost of capital in Japan (Hatsopoulos, 1983). However, more systematic studies have shown that there is practically no difference in the risk-adjusted cost of capital in the United States and Japan, and that capital cost advantages of Japanese firms, if any, arise from complex interactions between government subsidies and corporate ownership structures (Flaherty and Itami, 1984). Similarly, relatively low wage rates in Japan have been suggested by some authors as the primary reason for the success of Japanese companies in the US market (Itami, 1978). However, recently, companies such as Honda and Nissan have commissioned plants in the USA and have been able to retain practically the same levels of cost advantages over US manufacturers as they had for their production in Japan (Allen, 1985). Overall, there is increasing evidence that while comparative advantages of countries can provide competitive advantages to firms, the realization of such benefits is not automatic but depends on complex organizational factors and processes.

Scale Economies

Scale economies, again, is a fairly well established concept, and its implications for competitive advantage are quite well understood. Microeconomic theory provides a strong theoretical and empirical basis for evaluating the effect of scale on cost reduction, and the use of scale as a competitive tool is common in practice. Its primary implication for strategy is that a firm must expand the volume of its output so as to achieve available scale benefits. Otherwise a competitor who can achieve such volume can build cost advantages, and this can lead to a vicious cycle in which the low-volume firm can progressively lose its competitive viability.

While scale, by itself, is a static concept, there may be dynamic benefits of scale through what has been variously described as the experience or learning effect. The higher volume that helps a firm to exploit scale benefits also allows it to accumulate learning, and this leads to progressive cost reduction as the firm moves down its learning curve.

The concept of the value-added chain recently popularized by Porter (1985) adds considerable richness to the analysis of scale as a source of competitive advantage. This conceptual apparatus allows a disaggregated analysis of scale benefits in different value-creating activities of the firm. The efficient scale may vary widely by activity—being higher for component production, say, than for assembly. In contrast to a unitary view of scale, this disaggregated view permits the firm to configure different elements of its value chain to attain optimum scale economies in each.

Traditionally, scale has been seen as an unmixed blessing—something that always helps and never hurts. Recently, however, many researchers have argued otherwise (e.g. Evans, 1982). It has been suggested that scale efficiencies are obtained through increased specialization and through creation of dedicated assets and systems. The same processes cause inflexibilities and limit the firm's ability to cope with change. As environmental turbulence has increased, so has the need for strategic and operational flexibility (Mascarenhas, 1982). At the extreme, this line of argument has led to predictions of a re-emergence of the craft form of production to replace the scale-dominated assembly form (Piore and Sabel, 1984). A more typical argument has been to emphasize the need to balance scale and flexibility, through the use of modern technologies such as CAD/CAM and flexible manufacturing systems (Gold, 1982).

Scope Economies

Relatively speaking, the concept of scope economies is both new and not very well understood. It is based on the notion that certain economies arise from the fact that the cost of the joint production of two or more products can be less than the cost of producing them separately. Such cost reductions can take place due to many reasons—for example resources such as information or technologies, once acquired for use in producing one item, may be available costlessly for production of other items (Baumol, Panzer, and Willig, 1982).

The strategic importance of scope economies arises from a diversified firm's ability to share investments and costs across the same or different value chains that competitors, not possessing such internal and external diversity, cannot. Such sharing can take place across segments, products, or markets (Porter, 1985) and may involve joint use of different kinds of assets (see table 5.2).

A diversified firm may share physical assets such as production equipment, cash, or brand names across different businesses and markets. Flexible manufacturing systems using robots, which can be used for production of different items, are one example of how a firm can exploit such scope

Table 5.2
Scope economies in product and market diversification

| | Sources of scope economies | |
	Product diversification	Market diversification
Shared physical assets	Factory automation with flexibility to produce multiple products (Ford)	Global brand name (Coca-Cola)
Shared external relations	Using common distribution channel for multiple products (Matsushita)	Servicing multinational customers world-wide (Citibank)
Shared learning	Sharing R & D in computer and communications businesses (NEC)	Pooling knowledge developed in different markets (Procter and Gamble)

benefits. Cross-subsidization of markets and exploitation of a global brand name is another example of sharing a tangible asset across different components of a firm's product and market portfolios.

A second important source of scope economies is shared external relations: with customers, suppliers, distributors, governments, and other institutions. A multinational bank like Citibank can provide relatively more effective service to a multinational customer than can a bank that operates in a single country (see Terpstra, 1982). Similarly, as argued by Hamel and Prahalad (1985), companies such as Matsushita have benefited considerably from their ability to market a diverse range of products through the same distribution channel. In another variation, Japanese trading companies have expanded into new businesses to meet different requirements of their existing customers.

Finally, shared knowledge is the third important component of scope economies. The fundamental thrust of NEC's global strategy is "C & C"— computers and communication. The company firmly believes that its even strengths in the two technologies and resulting capabilities of merging them in-house to create new products gives it a competitive edge over global giants such as IBM and AT & T, who have technological strength in only one of these two areas. Another example of the scope advantages of shared learning is the case of Liquid Tide described earlier in this paper.

Even scope economies, however, may not be costless. Different segments, products, or markets of a diversified company face different environmental demands. To succeed, a firm needs to differentiate its management systems and processes so that each of its activities can develop *external consistency* with the requirments of its own environment. The search for scope economies, on the other hand, is a search for *internal consistencies* within the firm and across its different activities. The effort to create such synergies may invariably result in some compromise with the objective of external consistency in each activity.

Further, the search for internal synergies also enhances the complexities in a firm's management processes. In the extreme, such complexities can overwhelm the organization, as they did in the case of EMI, the U.K.-based music, electronics, and leisure products company which attempted to manage its new CT scanner business within the framework of its existing organizational structure and processes (see EMI and the CT scanner. ICCH case 9-383-194). Certain parts of a company's portfolio of businesses or markets may be inherently very different from some others, and it may be best not to look for economies of scope across them. For example, in the soft drinks industry, bottling and distribution are intensely local in scope, while the tasks of creating and maintaining a brand image, or that of designing efficient bottling plants, may offer significant benefits from global integration. Carrying out both these sets of functions in-house would clearly lead to internalizing enormous differences within the company with regard to the organizing, coordinating, and controlling tasks. Instead of trying to cope with these complexities, Coca-Cola has externalized those functions which are purely local in scope (in all but some key strategic markets). In a variation of the same theme, IBM has "externalized" the PC business by setting up an almost stand-alone organization, instead of trying to exploit scope benefits by integrating this business within the structure of its existing organization (for a more detailed discussion on multinational scope economies and on the conflicts between internal and external consistencies, see Lorange, Scott Morton, and Ghoshal, 1986).

Prescriptions in Perspective

Existing literature on global strategy offers analytical insights and helpful prescriptions for almost all the different issues indicated in table 5.1. Table 5.3 shows a selective list of relevant publications, categorized on the basis of issues that, according to this author's interpretations, the pieces primarily focus on.[4]

Pigeon-holing academic contributions into different parts of a conceptual framework tends to be unfair to their authors. In highlighting what the authors focus on, such categorization often amounts to an implicit criticism for what they did not write. Besides, most publications cover a broader range of issues and ideas than can be reflected in any such categorization

Table 5.3
Selected references for further reading

	Sources of competitive advantage		
Strategic objectives	National differences	Scale economies	Scope economies
Achieving efficiency in current operations	Kogut (1985a); Itami (1978); Okimoto, Sugano, and Weinstein (1984)	Hout, Porter, and Rudden (1982); Levitt (1983); Doz (1978); Leontiades (1984); Gluck (1983)	Hamel and Prahalad (1985); Hout, Porter, and Rudden (1982); Porter (1985); Ohmae (1985)
Managing risks	Kiechel (1981); Kobrin (1982); Poynter (1985); Lessard and Lightstone (1983); Srinivasulu (1981); Herring (1983)	Evans (1982); Piore and Sabel (1984); Gold (1982); Aaker and Mascarenhas (1984)	Kogut (1985b); Lorange, Scott Morton, and Ghoshal (1986)
Innovation, learning, and adaptation	Westney (1985); Terpstra (1977); Ronstadt and Krammer (1982)	Boston Consulting Group (1982); Rapp (1973)	Bartlett and Ghoshal (1985)

scheme. Table 5.3 suffers from all these deficiencies. At the same time, however, it suggests how the proposed framework can be helpful in integrating the literature and in relating the individual pieces to each other.

From Parts to the Whole

For managers, the advantage of such synthesis is that it allows them to combine a set of insightful but often partial analyses to address the totality of a multidimensional and complex phenomenon. Consider, for example, a topic that has been the staple for academics interested in international management: explaining and drawing normative conclusions from the global successes of many Japanese companies. Based on detailed comparisons across a set of matched pairs of US and Japanese firms, Itami concludes that the relative successes of the Japanese firms can be wholly explained as due to the advantages of lower wage rates and higher labor productivity. In the context of a specific industry, on the other hand, Toder (1978) shows that manufacturing scale is the single most important source of the Japanese competitive advantage. In the small car business, for example, the minimum efficient scale requires an annual production level of about 400,000 units. In the late 1970s no US auto manufacturer produced even 200,000 units of any subcompact configuration vehicle, while Toyota produced around 500,000 Corollas and Nissan produced between 300,000 and 400,000 B210s per year. Toder estimates that US manufacturers suffered a cost disadvantage of between 9 and 17 percent on account of inefficient scale alone. Add to it the effects of wage rate differentials and exchange rate movements, and Japanese success in the US auto market may not require any further explanation. Yet process-orientated scholars such as Hamel and Prahalad suggest a much more complex explanation of the Japanese tidal wave. They see it as arising out of a dynamic process of strategic evolution that exploits scope economies as a crucial weapon in the final stages. All these authors provide compelling arguments to support their own explanations, but do not consider or refute each other's hypotheses.

This multiplicity of explanations only shows the complexity of global strategic management. However, though different, these explanations and prescriptions are not always mutually exclusive. The manager's task is to find how these insights can be combined to build a multidimensional and flexible strategy that is robust to the different assumptions and explanations.

The Strategic Trade-offs

This, however, is not always possible because there are certain inherent contradictions between the different strategic objectives and between the different sources of competitive advantage. Consider, for instance, the popular distinction between a global and a multidomestic strategy described by Hout et al. (1982). A global strategy requires that the firm should carefully separate different value elements, and should locate each activity at the most efficient level of scale in the location where the activity can be carried out at the cheapest cost. Each activity should then be integrated and managed interdependently so as to exploit available scope economies. In essence, it is a strategy to maximize efficiency of current operations.

Such a strategy may, however, increase both endogenous and exogenous risks for the firm. Global scale of certain activities such as R & D and manufacturing may result in the firm's costs being concentrated in a few countries, while its revenues accrue globally, from sales in many different countries. This increases the operating exposure of the firm to the vicissitudes of exchange rate movements because of the mismatch between the currencies in which revenues are obtained and those in which costs are incurred. Similarly, the search for efficiency in a global business may lead to greater amounts of intra-company, but inter-country, flows of goods, capital, information, and other resources. These flows are visible, salient, and tend to attract policy interventions from different host governments. Organizationally, such an integrated system requires a high degree of coordination, which enhances the risks of management failures. These are lessons that many Japanese companies have learned well recently.

Similarly, consideration of the learning objective will again contradict some of the proclaimed benefits of a global strategy. The implementation of a global strategy tends to enhance the forces of centralization and to shift organizational power from the subsidiaries to the headquarters. This may result in demotivation of subsidiary managers and may erode one key asset of the MNC—the potential for learning from its many environments. The experiences of Caterpillar is a case in point. An exemplary practioner of global strategy, Cat has recently spilled a lot of red ink on its balance sheet and has lost ground steadily to its archrival, Komatsu. Many factors contributed to Caterpillar's woes, not the least of which was the inability of its centralized management processes to benefit from the experiences of its foreign subsidiaries.

On the flip side of the coin, strategies aimed at optimizing risk or learning may compromise current efficiency. Poynter (1985) has recommended "upgrade", i.e. increasing commitment of technology and resources in subsidiaries, as a way to overcome risk of policy interventions by host governments. Kogut (1985b), Mascarenhas (1982), and many others have suggested creating strategic and operational flexibility as a mechanism for coping with macroenvironmental risks. Bartlett and Ghoshal (1985) have proposed the differentiated network model of multinational organizations as a way to operationalize the benefits of global learning. All these recommendations carry certain efficiency penalties, which the authors have ignored.

Similar trade-offs exist between the different sources of competitive advantages. Trying to make the most of factor cost economies may prevent scale efficiency, and may impede benefiting from synergies across products or functions. Trying to benefit from scope through product diversification may affect scale, and so on. In effect, these contradictions between the different strategic objectives, and between the different means for achieving them, lead to trade-offs between each cell in the framework and practically all the others.

These trade-offs imply that to formulate and implement a global strategy, MNC managers must consider all the issues suggested in table 5.1, and must evaluate the implications of different strategic alternatives on each of these issues. Under a particular set of circumstances a particular strategic objective may dominate and a particular source of competitive advantage may play a more important role than the others (Fayerweather, 1981). The complexity of global strategic management arises from the need to understand those situational contingencies, and to adopt a strategy after evaluating the trade-offs it implies. Existing prescriptions can sensitize MNC managers to the different factors they must consider, but cannot provide ready-made and standardized solutions for them to adopt.

Conclusion

This paper has proposed a framework that can help MNC managers in reviewing and analyzing the strategies of their firms. It is not a blueprint for formulating strategies; it is a road map for reviewing them. Irrespective of whether strategies are analytically formulated or organizationally formed (Mintzberg, 1978), every firm has a realized strategy. To the extent that the realized strategy may differ from the intended one, managers need to review what the strategies of their firms really are. The paper suggests a scheme for such a review which can be an effective instrument for exercising strategic control.

Three arguments underlie the construct of the framework. First, in the global strategy literature, a kind of industry determinism has come to prevail not unlike the technological determinism that dominated management literature in the 1960s. The structures of industries may often have important influences on the appropriateness of corporate strategy, but they are only one of many such influences. Besides, corporate strategy may influence industry structure just as much as be influenced by it.

Second, simple schemes for categorizing strategies of firms under different labels tend to hide more than they reveal. A map for more detailed comparison of the content of strategies can be more helpful to managers in understanding and improving the competitive positions of their companies.

Third, the issues of risk and learning have not been given adequate importance in the strategy literature in general, and in the area of global strategies in particular. Both these are important strategic objectives and must be explicitly considered while evaluating or reviewing the strategic positions of companies.

The proposed framework is not a replacement of existing analytical tools but an enhancement that incorporates these beliefs. It does not present any new concepts or solutions, but only a synthesis of existing ideas and techniques. The benefit of such a synthesis is that it can help managers in integrating an array of strategic moves into an overall strategic thrust by revealing the consistencies and contradictions among those moves.

For academics, this brief view of the existing literature on global strategy will clearly reveal the need for more empirically grounded and systematic research to test and validate the hypotheses which currently appear in the literature as prescriptions and research conclusions. For partial analyses to lead to valid conclusions, excluded variables must be controlled for, and rival hypotheses must be considered and eliminated. The existing body of descriptive and normative research is rich enough to allow future researchers to adopt a more rigorous and systematic approach to enhance the reliability and validity of their findings and suggestions. The proposed framework, it is hoped, may be of value to some researchers in thinking about appropriate research issues and designs for furthering the field of global strategic management.

Acknowledgments

The ideas presented in this paper emerged in the course of discussions with many friends and colleagues. Don Lessard, Eleanor Westney, Bruce Kogut, Chris Bartlett, and Nitin Nohria were particularly helpful. I also benefited greatly from the comments and suggestions of the two anonymous referees from the *Strategic Management Journal*.

Notes

1. In the interest of simplicity the distinction between risk and uncertainty is ignored, as is the distinction between systematic and unsystematic risks.

2. This assumes that the firm has defined its business correctly and has identified as competitors all the firms whose offerings are aimed at meeting the same set of market needs that the firm meets.

3. Some market mechanisms such as long-term currency swaps are now available which can allow at least partial hedging of operating risks.

4. From an academic point of view, strategy of the multinational corporation is a specialized and highly applied field of study. It is built on the broader field of business policy and strategy which, in turn, rests on the foundation of a number of academic disciplines such as economics, organization theory, finance theory, operations research, etc. A number of publications in those underlying disciplines, and a significant body of research carried out in the field of strategy, in general, provide interesting insights on the different issues highlighted in table 5.1. However, given the objective of suggesting a limited list of further readings that *managers* may find useful, such publications have not been included in table 5.3. Further, even for the more applied and prescriptive literature on global strategy, the list is only illustrative and not exhaustive.

References

Aaker, D. A., and B. Mascarenhas. "The need for strategic flexibility," *Journal of Business Strategy*, 5(2), Fall 1984, pp. 74–82.

Aldrich, H. E. *Organizations and Environments*, Prentice-Hall. Englewood Cliffs. NJ, 1979.

Allen, M. K. "Japanese companies in the United States: the success of Nissan and Honda," unpublished manuscript, Sloan School of Management, MIT, November 1985.

Bartlett, C. A. "Global competition and MNC managers," ICCH Note No. 0-385-287, Harvard Business School, Boston, 1985.

Bartlett, C. A., and S. Ghoshal. "The new global organization: differentiated roles and dispersed responsibilities," Working Paper No. 9-786-013, Harvard Business School, Boston, October 1985.

Baumol, W. J., J. C. Panzer, and R. D. Willig. *Contestable Markets and the Theory of Industry Structure*, Harcourt, Brace, Jovanovich, New York, 1982.

Boston Consulting Group. *Perspectives on Experience*, BCG, Boston, 1982.

Calvet, A. L. "A synthesis of foreign direct investment theories and theories of the multinational firm," *Journal of International Business Studies*, Spring-Summer 1981, pp. 43–60.

Caves, R. E. "Industrial organization, corporate strategy and structure," *Journal of Economic Literature*, XVIII, March 1980, pp. 64–92.

Doz, Y. L. "Managing manufacturing rationalization within multinational companies," *Columbia Journal of World Business*, Fall 1978, pp. 82–94.

Doz, Y. L., C. A. Bartlett, and C. K. Prahalad. "Global competitive pressures and host country demands: managing tensions in MNC's." *California Management Review*, Spring 1981, pp. 63–74.

Evans, J. S. *Strategic Flexibility in Business*, Report No. 678. SRI International, December 1982.

Fayerweather, J. "Four winning strategies for the international corporation," *Journal of Business Strategy*, Fall 1981, pp. 25–36.

Flaherty, M. T., and H. Itami. "Finance," in Okimoto, D. I., T. Sugano, and F. B. Weinstein (eds), *Competitive Edge*, Stanford University Press, Stanford, CA, 1984.

Gluck, F. "Global competition in the 1980's." *Journal of Business Strategy*, Spring 1983, pp. 22–27.

Gold, B. "Robotics, programmable automation, and international competitiveness," *IEEE Transactions on Engineering Management*, November 1982.

Hamel, G., and C. K. Prahalad. "Do you really have a global strategy?" *Harvard Business Review*, July-August 1985, pp. 139–148.

Hannan, M. T., and J. Freeman. "The population ecology of organizations," *American Journal of Sociology*, 82, 1977, pp. 929–964.

Hatsopoulos, G. N. "High cost of capital: handicap of American industry," report sponsored by the American Business Conference and Thermo-Electron Corporation, April 1983.

Hax, A. C., and N. S. Majluf. *Strategic Management: An Integrative Perspective*, Prentice-Hall, Englewood Cliffs, NJ, 1984.

Herring, R. J. (ed.), *Managing International Risk*, Cambridge University Press, Cambridge, 1983.

Hofer, C. W., and D. Schendel. *Strategy Formulation: Analytical Concepts*, West Publishing Co., St. Paul, MN, 1978.

Hout, T., M. E. Porter and E. Rudden. "How global companies win out," *Harvard Business Review*, September-October 1982, pp. 98–108.

Itami, H. "Japanese-U.S. comparison of managerial productivity," *Japanese Economic Studies*, Fall 1978.

Kiechel, W. "Playing the global game," *Fortune*, November 16, 1981, pp. 111–126.

Kobrin, S. J. *Managing Political Risk Assessment*, University of California Press, Los Angeles, 1982.

Kogut, B. "Normative observations on the international value-added chain and strategic groups," *Journal of International Business Studies*, Fall 1984, pp. 151–167.

Kogut, B. "Designing global strategies: comparative and competitive value added chains," *Sloan Management Review*, 26(4), Summer 1985a, pp. 15–28.

Kogut, B. "Designing global strategies: profiting from operational flexibility," *Sloan Management Review*, Fall 1985b, pp. 27–38.

Leontiades. J. "Market share and corporate strategy in international industries," *Journal of Business Strategy*, 5(1), Summer 1984, pp. 30–37.

Lessard, D., and J. Lightstone. "The impact of exchange rates on operating profits: new business and financial responses," mimeo, Lightstone-Lessard Associates, 1983.

Levitt, T. "The globalization of markets," *Harvard Business Review*, May-June 1983, pp. 92–102.

Lorange, P., M. S. Scott Morton, and S. Ghoshal. *Strategic Control*, West Publishing Co., St. Paul, MN, 1986.

Mascarenhas, B. "Coping with uncertainty in inter-national business," *Journal of International Business Studies*, Fall 1982, pp. 87–98.

Mintzberg, H. "Patterns in strategic formation," *Management Science*, 24, 1978, pp. 934–948.

Ohmae, K. *Triad Power: The Coming Shape of Global Competition*, Free Press, New York, 1985.

Okimoto, D. I., T. Sugano, and F. B. Weinstein (eds). *Competitive Edge*, Stanford University Press, Stanford, CA, 1984.

Perlmutter, H. V. "The tortuous evolution of the multinational corporation," *Columbia Journal of World Business*, January-February 1969, pp. 9–18.

Piore, M. J., and C. Sabel. *The Second Industrial Divide: Possibilities and Prospects*, Basic Books, New York, 1984.

Porter, M. E. *Competitive Strategy*, Basic Books, New York, 1980.

Porter, M. E. "Competition in global industries: a conceptual framework," paper presented to the Colloquium on Competition in Global Industries, Harvard Business School, Boston 1984.

Porter, M. E. *Competitive Advantage*, Free Press, New York, 1985.

Poynter, T. A. *International Enterprises and Government Intervention*, Croom Helm, London, 1985.

Prahalad, C. K. "The Strategic process in a multinational corporation," unpublished doctoral dissertation, Graduate School of Business Administration, Harvard University, 1975.

Rapp, W. V. "Strategy formulation and international competition," *Columbia Journal of World Business*, Summer 1983, pp. 98–112.

Robinson, R. D. *International Business Management: A Guide to Decision Making*, Dryden Press, Hinsdale, Illinois, 1978.

Ronstadt, R., and R. J. Krammer. "Getting the most out of innovations abroad." *Harvard Business Review*, March-April 1982, pp. 94–99.

Rutenberg, D. P. *Multinational Management*. Little, Brown, Boston, 1982.

Srinivasula, S. "Strategic response to foreign exchange risks," *Columbia Journal of World Business*, Spring 1981, pp. 13–23.

Terpstra, V. "International product policy: the role of foreign R & D," *Columbia Journal of World Business*, Winter 1977, pp. 24–32.

Terpstra, V. *International Dimensions of Marketing*, Kent, Boston, 1982.

Toder, E. J. *Trade Policy and the U.S. Automobile Industry*, Praeger Special Studies, New York, 1978.

Vernon, R. *Storm over the Multinationals*. Harvard University Press. Cambridge, MA, 1977.

Wall Street Journal, April 29, 1985, p. 1.

Westney, D. E. "International dimensions of information and communications technology," unpublished manuscript, Sloan School of Management, MIT, 1985.

Woo, C. Y., and K. O. Cool. "The impact of strategic management of systematic risk," mimeo, Krannert Graduate School of Management, Purdue University, 1985.

6

Making American
Manufacturing
Competitive

Elwood S. Buffa

A great contest is changing the industrial foundations of the world economy—and America is losing. Once the chief industrial state, the United
States is ceding its supremacy—at least in industrial competiveness—to
Japan and West Germany and a flock of other sovereignties on down to the
city-state of Singapore. The decline in American industrial productivity
is both absolute and relative and is not attributable in any fundamental
sense to the 1981–1983 world recession. Cheaper labor and low tariffs are
factors, but so are hard work and skill and ingenuity. America is losing to
professional superiority. It is reliably estimated that Japanese automobile
companies produce cars for $2,000–$2,500 less than American companies.
Even allowing for cheaper wage rates in Japan, the true difference in favor
of Japan is still at least $2,000. In confirmation, American producers have
freely admitted that the quality of Japanese autos has been consistently
better than American autos for several years. The American disadvantage
is not limited to automobile and steel production—the list of industries
extends to consumer electronics, farm equipment, machine tools, room
airconditioners, and many more. These are only the most visible examples
of a competitive industrial inferiority that has few limits in its implications—in living standards, in general economic performance, in education
and research, in our defense and foreign affairs. The decline in American
industrial competitiveness is at the center of our security and national
well-being.

An announcement by General Motors reported in the *Wall Street Journal*
stated that they would "solve" the problem of producing a subcompact car
for the American market by joining with Toyota to produce a Toyota-
designed car (a version of the Corolla) in Fremont, California.[1] This humili-
ating admission that GM cannot do the job alone emphasizes the malaise

---

From *California Management Review*, Spring 1984, pp. 29–46. Reprinted by permission.

within the industry. To complete the embarrassment, GM and Toyota have agreed to give the final operational authority to Toyota.[2] Toyota will select the new venture's chief executive officer, apparently have the final say in all the operational decisions of the joint venture, and also rely heavily on Japanese assembly and management techniques. Chrysler has sued to prevent the combination of the two auto giants.

Toyota has apparently agreed that the work force will be organized by the United Auto Workers. About half the new car's parts will come from U.S. sources and the rest from Japan, including the engine and transmission, both critical components that GM has always considered to be "captive," that is, not candidates for manufacture by outside suppliers. Of course, both Ford and Chrysler have already resorted to the solution of hiring their arch rivals in Japan to build their small cars for them.

High costs may be Detroit's single most important problem with small cars. American auto workers not only are paid more than their Japanese counterparts—about $8 more per hour in wages and benefits—but it also takes them considerably longer to build a car. According to James Harbour, an automotive consultant in Detroit, better factory layouts and more flexible use of workers enables Japanese automakers to assemble a small car with, approximately 15 man-hours of labor, compared with as much as 30 hours for American producers.[3] Considering the entire production process —from iron ore to finished vehicles—Mr. Harbour estimates that the average Japanese car contains slightly more than 100 man-hours of labor, while U.S. cars require an average of 190 hours. Along with a host of other advantages, such as superior inventory controls, this accounts for the Japanese cost edge over U.S. manufacturers.

However, it seems that the disease of high cost and poor quality extends to any car built in the United States. Volkswagen invested more than $250 million during the 1970s in a New Stanton, Pennsylvania, plant to build VWs. Now they seem to face the same problems of high cost and questionable quality that have plagued American car makers. "A moderately equipped Honda Civic hatchback sells for $7,340, a similarly equipped Rabbit for $9,116 ... VW acknowledges that it is losing money on every U.S.-made Rabbit it sells."[4] Therefore, as with American manufacturers, there appears to be roughly a $2,000 difference in manufacturing cost between the Rabbit and the Honda Civic. Part of the difference may be accounted for by the $8 per hour labor-cost difference, but that is not the whole difference. The VW body shop is not automated: the stamping plant is four hours away in West Virginia and bodies must be trucked to the New Stanton plant. Finally, American VW also seems to have quality problems not shared by the Japanese. "Various measures of auto quality consistently place Honda and Toyota at the top of the list for reliability and for so-called fit and finish."[5]

Cost and quality are the responsibility of the manufacturing function. Should we therefore jump to the conclusion that we are simply witnessing the failure of that function? While production cannot escape some of the responsibility, the burden for the failure seems to be at the highest levels of American manufacturing management. Top management has ignored the production function since the end of World War II and has not taken it into account in overall enterprise strategy formulation. This fact was first recognized by Wickham Skinner in a 1969 article in the *Harvard Business Review*,[6] but management has been slow to give concrete recognition to the idea that they may be missing something important. Management's attention was riveted on marketing in the 1960s, followed by a preoccupation with finance in the 1970s. The question is whether or not international competition will force managers to develop manufacturing strategies as an integral part of competitive strategy. Will managers refocus on what they produce, its cost, its quality, its availablity, and on the required service/flexibility of the production system in relation to the market needs? All these critical factors are related to system productivity and competitiveness.

The Marketing and Finance Eras

Management has not always neglected production. In the 100 years from 1870 to 1970, productivity in America increased ten-fold. During and immediately following World War II, we were the world masters of production. American products set the world standards for both quality and cost. We may not have been quite as good as we thought we were, however, because we faced no global competition of consequence. The European and Japanese economies were destroyed by the war, and Japan had not been a world-class competitor anyway. Perhaps American managers felt that the production problem was "solved," and they could turn their attention to more important matters. At any rate, they did turn their attention away from production.

In the 1960s, they turned to marketing. Television provided a new medium that could bring a marketing message to a mass audience, and the techniques of market segmentation and consumer behavior brought marketing to the forefront. Marketing strategy became central to enterprise strategy. In fact, many academicians seem to think that competitive strategy and marketing strategy are synonymous terms. It worked for a long time and was reinforced as top managers, including CEOs, were recruited from the ranks of marketing managers. But if the product is a piece of junk, its marketing and promotion are soon discovered to be a fraud. The consumer movement, and Ralph Nader's influence, developed as shoddy products became common. Part of the campus unrest of the 1960s was directed against the quality of American manufactured products.

We should have paid closer attention to these protests, but we were too busy reaping the profits, and foreign competitive alternatives were not yet gaining dominance. We were too easily swept into the finance era of the 1970s, where fortunes could be made seemingly without the hard work of producing anything.

Get rid of the dogs,
milk the cows,
kick the problem children in the ass,
and make them into stars.

This statement summarizes the philosophy of the CEO of a prominent conglomerate in a 1970 memo to his top aides. This use of the Boston Consulting Group's growth/share matrix for classifying the company's "portfolio" of companies might have made even BCG wince. However, it shows where the CEO's attention was focused. There is no recognition of any fundamental role of the businesses and the products that these businesses produced, how they were related if at all, and whether or not synergy between the businesses existed or was even considered important. It was strictly a financial portfolio concept. The CEO might just as well have been selecting stocks from the New York Stock Exchange.

Conglomeration has been proceeding at a breakneck pace. By 1972, 33 percent of the employees of America's manufacturing companies were involved in lines of business totally unrelated to the primary businesses of their companies. In 1977, American companies spent $22 billion acquiring one another. In 1979, they spent $43.5 billion—paper entrepreneurialism has replaced product entrepreneurialism as the most dynamic and innovative occupation in the American economy. Paper entrepreneurs produce nothing of tangible use. For an economy to maintain its health, entrepreneurial rewards should flow primarily to products, not paper.[7]

Who really cares about cost and quality under such conditions?

A business organization must have a reason for being. It must produce something of economic value to justify its existence. Is it important to examine characteristics of synergy and the fundamental role of an organization if it is a candidate for either merger or liquidation? The merger or acquisition of companies that are high-cost producers of inferior merchandise may only produce another noncompetitive but larger business unit. The entire idea of a "portfolio" of companies is disjointed, if there is no other rationale. Yet merger mania with no better rationale than that has been the preoccupation of managers in the 1970s and the early 1980s.

For example, the attempt at merger or "take over" between Bendix Corporation and Martin Marietta, that finally also involved United Technologies and Allied Corporation in 1982, resulted in no net addition of economic output for the resulting corporate combination. Yet it is estimated that $1.5 billion of stockholders' funds were spent in the battle. To fend off Bendix, and to keep its independence, Martin Marietta borrowed about $900 million. Martin Marietta bought back most of the stock tendered to Bendix, and Bendix was finally taken over by Allied. "Allied's chairman, Edward Hennessey, has predicted it could take seven years to straighten out Martin Marietta's finances. The company's new borrowings pushed long-term debt to $1.34 billion. At the same time, shareholder equity was cut by more than half to $564.4 million as the repurchased shares were put in the company treasury."[8]

In addition, a Martin Marietta shareholder has sued the company's board of directors, charging that a defensive tender offer by Martin Marietta directors was made to "perpetuate themselves in office against the interest of Martin Marietta's shareholders."[9] How much top management time and attention will be used up before the issues generated will be solved?

The Productivity Record

In 1764, James Watt made improvements on the steam engine which produced a practical power source. As a result, energy systems began to replace muscle power in industry. The sources of the productivity increases through 1920, shown in figure 6.1, were probably dominated by the substitution of machine power for man power and the application of the concept of division of labor. But late in this era, the seeds were being sown for dramatic changes. Just before the turn of the century, Frederick W. Taylor set in motion a managerial philosophy which he called "Scientific Management." Taylor propounded a new philosophy which stated, essentially, that the scientific method could and should be applied to all managerial problems. He urged that the methods by which work was accomplished should be determined by management through scientific investigation.

The effects of the scientific management period can be seen in the dramatic rate of increase in productivity that developed during and after

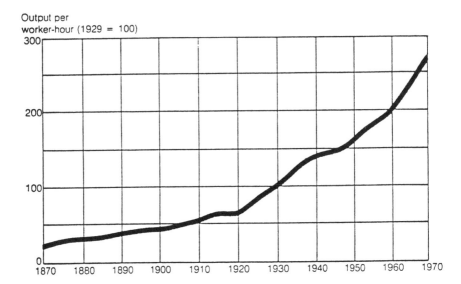

Figure 6.1
One hundred years of productivity growth. Output per worker-hour in United States
manufacturing, 1870–1972
Sources: J.W. Kendrick, *Productivity Trends in the United States* (Princeton, NJ: Princeton
University Press, 1961): and the Bureau of Labor Statistics.

World War I (see figure 6.1). Although the scientific management period
produced great controversy, its results were to revolutionize managerial
thought and practice.

The modern era is characterized by an acceleration of the substitution of
machine power for man power and the use of machines and computers for
computation and control. The concept of production has been broadened
—encompassing the entire material flow system—and the specialization
concept has been extended and applied at all levels including specialization
within organizations and within industries. The average annual rate of productivity increase during the modern era until 1970 was about 5 percent.
However, this average rate was not maintained during the 1973–1975
recession, nor in the period following—the 1981–1983 recession. This
indicates a malaise that is of great concern to American managers.

The Productivity Crisis

Figure 6.1 presents a record of which any nation could be proud. However,
figure 6.1 ends in 1970 and so does the rate of increase in the productivity

Making

Table 6.1
Changes in manufacturing productivity, 1960–1980 (annual changes in percent)

Year	United States	Canada	Japan	France	West Germany	United Kingdom
Output per year						
1960–80	2.7	3.8	9.4	5.6	5.4	3.6
1960–73	3.0	4.5	10.7	6.0	5.5	4.3
1973–80	1.7	2.2	6.8	4.9	4.8	1.9
1974	−2.4	1.6	2.4	3.5	6.0	0.8
1975	2.9	−2.6	3.9	3.1	4.8	−2.0
1976	4.4	4.9	9.4	8.2	6.3	4.0
1977	2.4	5.1	7.2	5.1	5.3	1.6
1978	0.9	3.1	7.9	5.3	3.8	3.2
1979	1.1	1.2	8.0	5.4	6.3	3.3
1980	−0.3	−1.4	6.2	0.6	−0.7	0.3

Source: P. Capdevielle and D. Alvarez, "International Comparisons of Trends in Productivity and Labor Costs," *Monthly Labor Review* (December 1981), pp. 14–20.

record. Even after recovery from the 1973–75 recession, U.S. productivity leveled off.

Table 6.1 provides a comparative record of productivity statistics for 6 countries during the recent period of 1960 to 1980. During that period, United States productivity averaged only 2.7 percent, ending with an actual decline in productivity in 1980 (−0.3 percent). During the same period, Japan had an average productivity increase of 9.4 percent, and France and West Germany had productivity increases of 5.6 and 5.4 percent respectively.

Table 6.2 shows the effect of both productivity and hourly compensation on unit labor costs for the same six countries during the same 1960 to 1980 period. While the net cost effects were greater in Japan than in the United States during the earlier period of 1960 to 1973, the most recent period of 1973 to 1980 is of great concern because unit costs increased by 7.5 percent in the U.S. versus only 3.4 percent in Japan, culminating in a 1980 increase of 11.0 percent versus only 0.8 percent in Japan. When exchange rates are taken into account, these figures are expressed in U.S. dollars in the bottom half of table 6.2. We see that the 1980 increase in unit labor costs was 11.0 percent for the U.S. versus an actual decline in unit labor costs of 2.5 percent in Japan.

Updating the U.S. figures for 1981 and 1982 is not encouraging. Manufacturing productivity increased 2.8 percent in 1981, but fell one percent

Table 6.2
Changes in manufacturing unit cost in 6 countries, 1960–1980 (annual changes in percent)

Year	United States	Canada	Japan	France	West Germany	United Kingdom
Unit labor costs						
1960–80	3.8	4.7	5.3	5.9	4.7	8.8
1960–73	1.9	1.8	3.5	3.1	3.7	4.1
1973–80	7.5	9.5	3.4	9.9	4.7	17.2
1974	13.3	13.2	28.1	16.2	8.7	24.1
1975	8.8	17.8	12.6	16.1	7.5	32.5
1976	3.4	9.0	− 2.5	5.6	0.9	12.7
1977	5.7	7.3	2.4	8.6	4.4	10.7
1978	7.3	4.3	− 1.8	7.3	4.6	12.8
1979	8.6	8.6	− 1.3	8.1	2.7	15.4
1980	11.0	10.9	0.8	14.3	8.7	23.3
Unit labor cost in U.S. dollar						
1960–80	3.8	4.4	8.0	6.5	9.3	6.6
1960–73	1.9	1.9	4.9	2.8	6.1	2.6
1973–80	7.5	6.4	8.3	10.9	11.2	15.3
1974	13.3	15.8	19.0	7.2	11.5	18.5
1975	8.8	13.3	10.7	30.3	13.1	25.8
1976	3.4	12.5	− 2.4	− 5.3	− 1.6	− 8.5
1977	5.7	− 0.4	13.3	5.5	13.1	7.0
1978	7.3	− 2.8	26.2	17.1	21.0	24.0
1979	8.6	5.7	− 5.7	14.3	12.4	27.7
1980	11.0	11.1	− 2.5	15.3	9.8	35.1

Note: Rates of change computed from the least squares trend of the logarithms of the index numbers.
Source: P. Capdevielle and D. Alvarez, "International Comparisons of Trends in Productivity and Labor Costs," *Monthly Labor Review* (December 1981), pp. 14–20.

for 1982, due to the recession to some extent, but most observers feel that this poor performance is more deeply rooted in a fundamental decline in our manufacturing management capability.[10]

Manufacturing productivity increased by a brisk annual rate of 8.0 percent during the first quarter of 1983, and 8.9 percent during the second quarter.[11] But we must not be lulled into a sense of false security, for such increases are expected following a recession, as we put idle resources back to work. The fundamental problem still exists. Both Japan and West Germany can deliver steel in the U.S. at prices which the U.S. producers cannot meet. Toyota and other Japanese automakers have taken 25 percent of the U.S. auto market, while our domestic auto producers seem unable to compete not only on price, but also on the basis of the design of the product demanded and its quality.

The data in tables 6.1 and 6.2 are alarming and their implications are creating an inferiority complex among U.S. producers concerning their ability to compete. It is important to put these data in perspective with comparative absolute productivity figures. These data represent productivity *changes* during the periods stated. However, on an absolute basis, U.S. productivity is by all odds the highest in the world by a substantial margin. If agriculture is included, the margin is even greater. Therefore, the concern is that the United States is losing its *advantage*, although it has, of course, already lost its lead in certain industries. Figure 6.2 shows the comparison between United States and several other countries in terms of real Gross Domestic Product per employee for 1950, 1960, and 1977. While the U.S. lead is substantial, it is falling rapidly, particularly in comparison to Japan, West Germany, and France. Where Japan's relative productivity was only 16 percent of the U.S. in 1950, it was 63 percent in 1977, a gain of 47 percentage points in just 17 years. Canada enjoys productivity that has been relatively close to ours, and is improving.

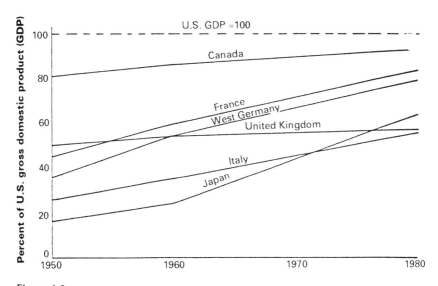

Figure 6.2
Gross Domestic Product (GDP) per employee for several countries, 1950, 1960, and 1977
Source: U.S. Bureau of Labor Statistics.

Why We Have a Crisis

The reasons for the decline in both the United States' productivity growth
and its ability to compete internationally are many and complex. One
factor is the contrast between work-ethic values in the U.S. and those in
Japan and West Germany. Another factor is U.S. government policies. Part
of the cause may also be that we in the U.S. have made conscious social
decisions that adversely affect productivity but improve such things as
air quality, noise levels, and employee safety. Nations that ignore these
factors may find that they will have to make similar social decisions at some
point, which would tend to equalize this dimension of the U.S. productivity disadvantage. On the other hand, our major global competitors have
also made equivalent expenditures to meet both environmental and safety
regulations.

During the 1970s, the U.S. Steel industry spent an average of $365 million annu-
ally to reduce pollution and improve worker safety—about 17 percent of its
annual capital investment during the decade. Of this cost, 48 percent was subsidized by state and local governments through industrial-development bonds.
Spending by European steelmakers was of an equal magnitude. During the same
period, Japanese steel manufacturers spent substantially more for these purposes.
Safety regulations also add some costs to operations, but the reduction in accidents
has meant savings in time and expense that go far to offset these extra costs.
Overall, capital expenditures on pollution control and safety combined have never
exceeded 6 percent of industrial investment, and can be blamed for at most around
a tenth of the slowdown in productivity.[12]

Other explanations that have been put forth for the decline in productivity are inadequate capital formation and a fall in research and development
expenditures. Investment in domestic manufacturing as a percent of total
output of goods actually increased from 10.8 percent between 1960 and
1964 to 14.8 percent between 1973 and 1978—a level not significantly
less than those of our foreign competitors. However, U.S. investment in
R & D declined from 3 percent of GNP to 2 percent during the 1970s—a
slowdown that has fundamental implications for future competitiveness.
The blame cannot be put on higher energy prices, since they affected all
countries, with Japan and Germany being even more dependent on OPEC
than the U.S.

Robert Reich advances the theory that our decline is rooted in a fundamental change in the structure of world competition, noting that by 1980,
more than 70 percent of all the goods produced in America had to compete
with equivalent goods made abroad. These products are largely those from

high-volume standardized production systems (the bastion of our previous competitive strength) where skills are low and so are wages. Eighty-five percent of the 36 million people who enter the world-wide labor force annually are from third world nations, which put them to work producing high-volume standardized products at a cost lower than can be matched here in the U.S. We will therefore remain exposed to foreign advantage in this regard. Reich suggests that our comparative advantage will be in flexible production systems that produce to order whatever the customer wants, since these systems require higher skills and education that are not yet easily duplicated by developing nations.

Recognition of the Need for Change

There is already considerable evidence that top management now sees both the effects of the past emphasis on marketing and finance and the result of ignoring the manufacturing function. While mergers continue at an unprecedented pace, conglomeritis is being considered for what it is—a disease. For example, by the end of the 1970s, Ralston Purina "was running a Colorado resort, breeding shrimp in Panama, growing mushrooms in California, fishing for tuna in the Pacific and Atlantic oceans, and operating its own canneries (one of which was in distant Pago Pago)."[13] This assembly of activities was far afield from the humble beginnings of Ralston as an animal feed store in St. Louis. Apparently, new CEO William P. Stirtz thought that it was *too* far, and he has decided to jettison much of the smorgasbord that has characterized Ralston's recent portfolio. He has already dumped the tuna-catching, mushroom-raising, and European-based pet food businesses. "Our future growth," he says, "will come primarily through aggressive new product development in our core businesses."

In his comprehensive study of diversified companies, *Strategy, Structure, and Economic Performance*, Richard Rumelt found that companies that stick to their core businesses substantially outperform those that go far afield.[14] This does not mean that there should be no diversification, but rather that diversification should have a relationship to the dominant activity, or that there should be close relationships between businesses, even though different technologies may be involved. The value of sticking to one's core business was underlined in the recent best-selling book, *In Search of Excellence*, where Peters and Waterman devote a full chapter to this factor as one of the important lessons to be learned from America's best run companies.[15]

Labor has now recognized a problem that management has been concerned about for a long time—i.e., work rules that adversely affect productivity. Perhaps it is only because of the recession, but labor has now been agreeing to important work-rule changes that have an effect on competitiveness. There is a new concern for efficiency.

Some experts see such changes as part of a major change in the way corporations view their role as managers. Top management is finally getting around to noticing that it had better be concerned about how efficiently they produce things.[16]

The recognition that change is needed has also finally trickled back into the curricula of schools of business administration and management. A course in production and operations management is now required at most schools.

But how is top management in America going to provide emphasis to operating problems? It is interesting to compare the composition of boards of directors in Japan, where manufacturing industries are competitive, with those in the U.S., where the competitiveness is questionable.

More than 65 percent of all seats on the boards of Japanese manufacturing companies are occupied by people who are trained as engineers. Roughly the same percentage of seats on American boards is taken by people trained in law, finance, or accountancy. Thus in Japan, many problems that arise in business are viewed as problems of engineering or science, for which technical solutions can be found. In present-day America, the same problems are apt to be viewed as problems of law or finance, to be dodged through clever manipulation of rules or numbers.[17]

A recent study of board compensation and composition by Korn/Ferry International,[18] the nation's largest executive search firm, indicates that there is a movement towards having more executives on boards with strong operating experience, and away from investment bankers and attorneys, neither of whom could presume to provide either operating experience or insight into operating problems. But in this survey, the presence of investment bankers and attorneys is still very strong. Korn/Ferry asked 1,000 U.S. companies if they had at least one person in various categories on their boards. The 1973 and 1982 results for investment bankers and attorneys are shown in table 6.3.

Individuals with operating experience serving on boards were not identified separately in the Korn/Ferry survey, so it is difficult to see the extent of the new emphasis.

We can no longer ignore the fact that a major reason for the productivity decline is simply that we have poor or uncoordinated manufacturing strategy that culminates in a poor match between our manufacturing sys-

Table 6.3

	1973	1982
Investment banker	37.3%	23.7%
Attorney (provides legal services to the company)	51.7	28.2
Attorney (does not provide legal services to the company)	NA	33.7

tem capability and markets and our non-competitive production techniques
—that is, we have failure of managerial competence. To reverse the decline
in the U.S. position, we must place new emphasis on the manufacturing
function and on all the factors that contribute to productivity and quality
improvement. We must train people in the art and science of managing
productive systems. Professional managers of productive systems are at a
premium today, and we now know that their skills are essential if we are to
regain our competitive position with high-quality, low-cost products and
services. We must reward manufacturing executives in ways that give
recognition to their roles in strategy formulation and in achieving goals in
competitive strategy. But most important of all, we must learn more about
manufacturing strategy and policy. We must elevate it to a level where it
can have an impact on competitive strategy and it can relate to all elements of strategy. We must understand it and all its implications and
incorporate it as an integral part of the overall competitive strategy of our
companies.

If manufacturing strategy is carefully developed and coordinated with
company strategy, then the foundation is laid for more detailed policies
and procedures necessary to achieve improved productivity and quality.
But leadership must come from the top of the organization.

The Future Direction

With competitiveness as the imperative, the central focus for the 1980s
should therefore be on how to develop manufacturing strategy and policy
in the context of overall company strategy. There are many questions that
we must address. How can manufacturing strategy make a difference? How
can we improve productivity and reduce costs? Is it solely labor productivity that is our concern? Is capital as productive as it should be in American
industry? Do we get the inventory turnovers of the Japanese manufacturer?
The answer is that we do not, but what is different about Japanese practice?

American manufacturers have learned to position products and promotional campaigns with respect to markets, but are their manufacturing systems well positioned to meet the needs of those markets? Do we use manufacturing technology in ways that support manufacturing strategy and maintain our competitive position? What future labor-management relationship is required if we are to remain competitive? How do we deal with suppliers? What are crucial successful strategies for capacity expansion and its location?

What is it really that the Japanese do to make their production systems tick? Is it only the result of east-west cultural differences, or is there something fundamentally superior about the way they manage their systems that can be imitated or applied in the U.S.? Is it possible that they have established a corporate culture, a value set, that integrates pride of workmanship, producing at low cost and high quality, minimizing inventories— a production oriented culture?

Competitive Strategy

Manufacturing strategy cannot go off on an independent course any more than can marketing or finance. Through an analysis of the basic competitive forces in each industry, growth/share relationships, the experience curve, and the value added at various stages of the overall process, we can determine the key areas of advantage and disadvantage for ourselves and our competitors, and attempt to chart a winning course.

Based on such industry analysis, the general practice has been to choose a fundamental competitive strategy and simply assume the continued performance of the production system, which is seldom involved in the strategy formulation process. It remains possible to develop competitive strategies without coordinating manufacturing strategy. This uncoordinated approach is what we have been doing all along, yet we do not like the results.

Manufacturing Strategy

Put simplistically, the basic manufacturing strategies are the minimum-cost/high-availability strategy and the highest-quality–flexibility strategy. These are the two extremes and the choice of options in between is the positioning issue. These strategies are crucial to the implementation of the overall company strategy. If company and manufacturing strategies are not carefully coordinated, the company can expect to be non-competitive.

A manufacturing policy that is of strategic significance is the decision to manufacture to-stock or to-order. Such a decision needs to be coordinated with the positioning of the producing system with respect to the market. A to-order policy would be difficult to implement if the basic market strategy was directed toward low-cost/high-volume standardized products.

The experience curve provides an important concept that has been used in strategy formulation. But the concept is largely one involving the manufacturing function. The benefits of the experience curve may not "just happen" unless the strategy supports the achievement of lower costs with the required investment in process technology, and an appropriate organization structure.

It is interesting to note which markets the Japanese have chosen for intense competition. Surprisingly, they are mostly in the "cash cow" category: autos, steel, motorcycles, cameras, small appliances, and so on. These are products for which there were already established markets with existing market leaders who had substantial experience. Yet the Japanese manufacturers were able to break in. How were they able to do it? How could they match the cost position of established market leaders, and in most instances beat it? The answer seems to be superior Japanese manufacturing strategies and techniques. While Japanese finance and marketing have also been very good, they did not create the low-cost/high-quality position that makes them competitive.

James C. Abegglen, a consultant who has operated in Japan for a number of years, states that the products with which Japanese manufacturers have deeply penetrated U.S. markets share certain characteristics.[19] First, the products are invariably ones for which there have been large markets in Japan and for which domestic demand is peaking. Therefore, these are products with which the Japanese have accumulated substantial experience. Second, the Japanese have significant advantages in factor costs, particularly in wage costs in autos and steel, and in labor productivity, particularly in industries with complex manufacturing operations that require a high degree of coordination. When these characteristics of successful Japanese exports are compared with the list of actual exports, there is a high correlation.

Perhaps the superior Japanese manufacturing strategy and technique are shown most clearly in the U.S. steel industry, which must be classified as a mature, even declining industry. A conglomerate with a U.S. steel company in its portfolio would surely classify it as a "dog." Kaiser Steel, once a giant in the industry has announced that it will phase out its steel-finishing and production operations by the end of 1983 or early 1984.[20] Established producers such as U.S. Steel and Bethlehem Steel had much greater experience than the Japanese and Germans and should have been far down the cost-experience curve and almost unbeatable on a cost basis.

Almost 200 U.S. steel producing facilities have already been closed. We still make a substantial proportion of our steel in inefficient open-hearth furnaces, but virtually all the steel made in Japan and Europe is done in oxygen and electric furnaces. U.S. steelmakers have been slow to convert to continuous casting—a process that improves product yield, cuts energy use, and improves labor productivity. Only 26 percent of the steel produced in the U.S. is continuously cast versus 86 percent in Japan and 61 percent in Europe.

The American Iron & Steel Institute estimates that the industry will have to spend $60 billion (in 1982 dollars) over the next decade to bring its facilities up to world-class levels. But last year, U.S. steelmakers spent just $2.2 billion for modernization, and this year they will that cut to about $1.7 billion.[21]

The Six Basics of Manufacturing Strategy

All activities in the line of material flow from suppliers—from fabrication and assembly to product distribution—must be integrated for manufacturing strategy formulation. Leaving out any part can lead to uncoordinated strategies. In addition to the material inputs, other crucial inputs of labor, job design, and technology must be a part of the integrated strategy. The crucial decisions of capacity and location must also be included. Finally, there are aspects of operating decisions that have strategic significance and must be included.

The six basics of manufacturing strategy are:

• Positioning the Production System
• Capacity/Location Decisions
• Product and Process Technology
• The Work Force and Job Design
• Strategic Implications of Operation Decisions
• Suppliers and Vertical Integration

There is a wide range of managerial choice available in each of these basic components which affects the long-term competitive position of the firm by impacting cost, quality, product availability, and flexibility/service.

Positioning the Production System

As the product goes through its life cycle, the production system should follow with a process life cycle of its own. The proper match between the two is a matter for careful strategic choice. If a manager chooses to compete in terms of cost and product availability, the system must have certain design and organizational characteristics. On the other hand, if the chosen market niche is for the highest quality and flexibility, then the system must have quite different design and organizational characteristics. How do we measure competence in the operations function? What are the advantages of achieving focus in operations?

Capacity/Location Decisions

We must become more sophisticated in making capacity decisions from a strategic perspective. What are the economics of capacity added in large or small increments? When is a preemptive capacity decision warranted? What are the differences in capacity expansion for established products versus new and risky products? What are the effects of excess capacity in an industry, or in a given company? How are the issues of capacity and its location interrelated from a strategic point of view? How should strategically important alternatives be evaluated?

Product and Process Technology

In the 1890s, manufacturers must place heavier emphasis on computer aided design and manufacturing (*CAD/CAM*), robotics, and automation and on the relationships of these techniques to manufacturing strategy. Still, we must consider whether or not these technologies are as applicable to the U.S. with its labor surplus as to Japan which has a labor shortage. Products must, in the first place, be designed for producibility and low cost. One of our most significant problems is that engineers are taught how to design circuits and mechanical marvels, *but are not taught how these items might be manufactured.* Consequently, the cost of manufacture is usually a result rather than a criterion for a good design. Are the Japanese gearing up to compete with our stars as well as our cash cows? There is some evidence that they are. For example, while machine tools are considered to be a mature industry, the Japanese are leaders in computer-controlled tools, which represent the industry of the future.

The Work Force and Job Design

We must give greater consideration to the role of the work force in productivity, the impact of long-term commitments to employment, and the results of giving up competitive strength through extraordinarily high wages. Both the steel and auto industries made wage concessions in the 1970s that were fundamentally out of line with global competition in their industries. A short-term gain of labor peace was traded off for a devastating long-term competitive disadvantage, and the final result has not been good for labor, management, or the American economy.

One of the most important advantages that the Japanese have is in the flexibility of their work rules, which allow workers to perform a much wider variety of tasks. American management has agreed to restrictive work rules, which represents another trade-off of short-term advantage for a long-term serious cost disadvantage in future competitiveness.

In the future, we must more closely examine the nature of the labor-management relationship and its role in manufacturing strategy and policy. We are becoming a "high-tech" society with "low-tech" education. This situation is in contrast to both Japan and West Germany, where mathematics and science are more highly emphasized in primary and secondary education. If high-volume standardized products are made in developing countries in the future while we in the U.S. concentrate on products that require flexible systems, higher skills, and information processing, how will we achieve this more advanced level of labor skills? If we are successful in finding and developing the necessary personnel, can we achieve competitiveness without redefining the labor-management relationship to recognize the enhanced role of these more highly trained people?

Strategic Implications of Operating Decisions

Many operating decisions have strategic significance, though upper levels of management tend to ignore them. Are our systems of production planning and scheduling and aggregate inventory control systems more complex than they need to be? How can we maintain quality and what supporting organization structures are required? What are the effects of the Japanese emphasis on low process set-up time for their Just-In-Time systems, Kanban systems, total quality control systems, and quality circles? Who should have the responsiblity for quality? A recent book, *Japanese Manufacturing Techniques*, by Richard Schonberger, shows clearly that there is little mystery in the Japanese success in manufacturing.[22] Rather, they have created simple, effective operating systems that have strategic significance in reducing costs and controlling quality.

Strategies Regarding Suppliers

U.S. manufacturers maintain a leverage over their suppliers by various strategic policies, such as posing the threat of vertical integration. Such policies are in direct contrast with the Japanese Just-In-Time Purchasing System, which creates a close relationship with suppliers, together with agreements that reduce purchasing costs, increase supply frequency, and reduce inventories. Conversely, U.S. manufacturers must always guard against the threat of forward integration from powerful suppliers.

The distribution system is a part of the overall material flow, and manufacturers must think of it as a part of the operations function. The distribution system involves a series of processing steps, and the relationship between the plant locations and distribution points is important in production-distribution strategy.

If America is losing its competitive edge, it is not because we do not know how to market and promote products. It is not because we cannot finance the capital requirements necessary to compete. It *is* because we sometimes produce the wrong product for the market at a noncompetitive price, or produce a product of less than competitive quality, or even simply because we do not have a particular product available in the competitive marketplace. In short, we have not learned how to develop manufacturing strategy to support the grand strategic plans of the enterprise.

The Time Is Ripe

All the indicators show that we are losing our competitive advantage. That does not mean that we have lost. It *does* mean that we must do something or we will lose. We can catch up by recognizing again that a manufacturer has a fundamental reason for existence—to produce a product that has economic value. If we turn our backs on this fundamental value, competitive forces will ultimately foreclose. We must refocus our attention on the broadly defined manufacturing function and learn how to use it in a strategic way. The Japanese have become competitive largely through their superior production systems, by producing a quality product at a low cost. Their production systems are the difference.

It is important to point out that we do have many extremely well-managed manufacturing companies in the U.S., which clearly shows that we *do* have the knowledge and skill to improve productivity and quality. We need to train more managers with these capabilities and use such companies as models for the economy.

What happens if we do not change? How long it will take to be in Great Britain's position, simply managing our economic decline or mere survival? Can we catch up?

Notes

1. "U.S. Car Industry Has Full-Sized Problems in Subcompact Market," *Wall Street Journal,* January 7, 1983.

2. "GM-Toyota Plan Said to Give Japan Firm Authority to Pick U.S. Joint-Venture Chief," *Wall Street Journal,* February 9, 1983.

3. "Small Car War: U.S. Volkswagen Has Problems with Price. Quality and Japanese," *Wall Street Journal.* February 7, 1983.

4. Ibid.

5. Ibid.

6. W. Skinner, "Manufacturing—Missing Link in Corporate Strategy," *Harvard Business Review* (May/June 1969), p. 136.

7. Robert B. Reich. "The Next American Frontier," *Atlantic Monthly* (March 1983), pp. 43–58.

8. "Martin Marietta Looks for Ways to Reduce Its Large Debt but Shuns 'Fire Sale' of Assets," *Wall Street Journal,* January 11, 1983.

9. "Marietta Holder Sues Board over Its Defense against Bendix Offer," *Wall Street Journal,* January 11, 1983.

10. "Productivity Grew at the Rate of 2.7% in Fourth Quarter," *Wall Street Journal,* January 29, 1983.

11. *Employment and Earnings,* U.S. Department of Labor Statistics, (August 1983).

12. Robert B. Reich, "The Next American Frontier,"*The Atlantic Monthly* (March 1983), pp. 43–58.

13. "Ralston Purina: Dumping Products That Led it Away from Checkerboard Square." *Business Week,* January 31, 1983.

14. Richard Rumelt, *Strategy, Structure, and Economic Performance,* (Boston: Division of Research, Harvard Business School, 1974).

15. Thomas J. Peters and Robert H. Waterman, *In Search of Excellence* (New York: Harper & Row, 1982).

16. "Work-Rule Changes Quietly Spread as Firms Try to Raise Productivity," *Wall Street Journal,* January 25, 1983.

17. Robert B. Reich, "The Next American Frontier," *The Atlantic Monthly* (March 1983), pp. 43–58.

18. Betsy Bauer, "Directors: More Money, Power," *USA Today*, March 15, 1983.

19. James C. Abegglen, "How to Defend Your Business Against Japan,'" *Business Week*, August 15, 1983, p. 14.

20. "Kaiser Steel to Close Steelmaking Group unless a Buyer or Partner Can Be Found," *Wall Street Journal*, March 7, 1983.

21. "Time Runs Out for Steel," *Business Week*, June 13, 1983.

22. Richard J. Schonberger, *Japanese Manufacturing Techniques: Nine Hidden Lessons in Simplicity* (New York: The Free Press 1982).

7

Designing Global Strategies: Profiting from Operational Flexibility

Bruce Kogut

.... Comparative advantage is driven by differences in the costs of inputs (e.g., unskilled and skilled workers or capital equipment) among countries.[1] Competitive advantage is driven by differences among firms in their abilities to transform these inputs into goods and services at maximum profit. The outstanding feature of global competition is the uncertainty over these advantages. This uncertainty stems from three factors:

1. The world economy is undergoing a fundamental shift in terms of the comparative advantages of countries. This shift is manifested in changes in the *intersectoral* allocation of world industry and trends toward protectionism.

2. Global competition consists of firms which differ radically in the constellation of bets they have placed along the value-added chain and on different sourcing and marketing sites.

3. Global competition is often characterized by a lack of historical rules for industry competition. As a result, there is uncertainty over the initial moves and competitive reactions in terms of pricing and market penetration.

From this perspective, the thesis is developed that the unique content of a *global* versus a purely domestic strategy lies less in the methods to design long-term strategic plans than in the construction of flexibility which permits a firm to exploit the uncertainty over future changes in exchange rates, competitive moves, or government policy. This flexibility can be attained, for example, by building excess capacity into dispersed sourcing platforms or by arbitraging between different tax regimes. In short, flexibility is gained by decreasing the firm's dependence on assets already in place.

A largely neglected question is whether firms have indeed developed the organizational structures and incentives to profit from changes in the

From *Sloan Management Review*, Fall 1985, pp. 27–38. Reprinted by permission.

environment and coordinate an international response. The question is more than a matter of whether subsidiaries are integrated into the headquarters' strategic plans or whether they report data which reflects their contribution to these plans. Rather, the question is whether there exists either a centralized organizational unit which is responsible, for example, for the shifting of production schedules and the transshipment of goods or a decentralized system which provides the proper incentives to subsidiaries to respond to changes in exchange rates and relative price movements. The exercise of strategic flexibility is a moot question unless the organizational wherewithal exists to coordinate activities internationally.

This article explores the creation of the operational flexibility of the multinational corporation in order to benefit from being global. There are many sources of environmental volatility, such as new product entries, new government policies, or new international competitors, to which firms can respond and exploit to their advantage. The first section examines only one of these sources, namely, fluctuations in exchange rates and the impact on the real cost of labor. The second section continues to examine exchange rate fluctuations, but this time in terms of the impact upon the decision of where to source and how much risk should be borne. The third section of the article widens the analysis to look more broadly at the kinds of strategic flexibility that the multinational corporation can exercise. Two kinds of flexibility are described, one is the arbitrage of market imperfections, the second is leverage, by which a firm's position in one national market is enhanced by its position in a second. A key question is whether firms recognize and have created organizational structures to respond proactively to these opportunities. This question is expanded further in the fourth section to a consideration of integrative systems that promote flexibility by managerial incentives.

Volatility in International Markets

Volatility in world markets affects both the firm's cost structure and its choice of technology along the value-added chains. When applied to the study of international strategies, the concept of the value-added chain pinpoints two methods with which to analyze the implications of this uncertainty. The first involves tracing out the current and future cost advantages of competitors under different assumptions regarding factor payments and technologies. The second involves determining the demand characteristics of different national markets and designing tailored marketing programs that exploit economies of scale and scope in upstream links.

The value-added chain exercise outlined above does not appear to be greatly different if conducted in an international or national setting with regional differences in wage rates and market prices. Yet, there is a critical difference that cannot be underestimated, and that is the tremendous variability of macroeconomic parameters between countries. Though southern parts of the United States tend toward lower wage rates than the North, this differential will not be strongly affected by fluctuating exchange rates or by changes in other macroeconomic parameters, such as interest rates.[2] On the other hand, the international economy is rocked to a much greater extent by the variability of exchange rates and movements in the relative factor costs between countries.

The extent of this variability can be suggested by considering, first, movements in wage rates between sourcing platforms over time and, second, movements in real (i.e., inflation-adjusted) exchange rates over time. The impact on profitability because of unexpected movements in exchange rates can be naively illustrated by considering the decision of an American firm to source in Singapore in the mid-1970s. The success of such a venture is dependent upon what happens to the Singapore wage rates over time relative to the location decisions of competitors. Data on wage rates in dollar terms are given in table 7.1 for Singapore and Sri Lanka. Clearly, the firm's competitive position would have deteriorated had it invested in Singapore and relied on the expectation that the wage rate differential vis-á-vis Sri Lanka (where its competitors sourced) would remain the same over time.

Table 7.1
Hourly wage rates in manufacturing (in U.S. dollars)

	Sri Lanka	Singapore
1973	.13	.36
1974	.16	.45
1975	.16	.50
1976	.14	.54
1977	.11	.56
1978	.15	.61
1979	.12	.88
1980	.11	.80
1981	.11	1.05
1982	.14	1.17

Source: Compiled from *Yearbook of Labour Statistics*, 1983, ILO; *International Financial Statistics*, IMF.

The quintessential element of volatility in international markets, however, is the fluctuation in exchange rates. One theory which explains the determination of exchange rates is that of purchasing power parity (PPP). Stated with unabashed simplicity, PPP claims that the price of foreign goods sold in their home markets should be equal to the price of these goods at home, adjusted for exchange rates and transportation costs. Based on this supposition, and holding transportation costs constant, it proposes that changes in observed or nominal exchange rates must, therefore, be linked to changes in the prices of goods in one country relative to prices in another country. Exchange rate movements should reflect, then, differences in inflation between countries. The relevance of PPP for our purposes is that deviations from the predicted value of an exchange rate under this theory imply that there has been a change in *real* economic variables between countries, such as wage rates adjusted for inflation.

Because exchange rates are no longer pegged, a major source of uncertainty is the impact of exchange rate fluctuations precisely on these

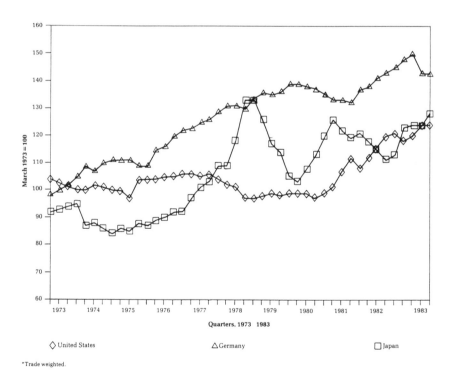

Figure 7.1
Fluctuations in nominal exchange rates

real economic variables. Figure 7.1 graphs nominal exchange rates for Germany, Japan, and the United States against a basket of currencies weighted by the significance of the trade with the country of issuance. Clearly, the German mark and Japanese yen appreciated in nominal terms against the currencies of their trading partners throughout the 1970s, whereas the dollar's value is fairly stable until its rapid rise beginning in 1982. Curiously, the Japanese yen appears to evidence the greatest volatility, fluctuating dramatically between 1978 and 1983.

The impact of these changes on competitive positions becomes more transparent when the effect of movements in real exchange rates on nominal wages is isolated. In table 7.2, manufacturing wages for Germany, Japan, and the United States are listed. All wages are calculated in dollars. The wages have been calculated in two ways, the first showing nominal wages calculated using the prevailing exchange rate for each year, the second showing wages if purchasing power parity had held. (Under PPP, changes in exchange rates would only reflect differences in inflation rates between the United States and its trading partners, Germany and Japan.) As seen in the PPP-adjusted rates, if PPP had held, the wage bill paid by German and Japanese firms in the 1970s would have tracked more closely that of their American competitors. In nominal terms, the wage increases for Japan and Germany are even more impressive, but when compared to the PPP-adjusted wage estimates, a substantial portion of this increase can

Table 7.2
Changes in nominal and PPP-adjusted wage rates (in U.S. dollar)

	U.S.	Germany		Japan	
	Nominal	Nominal	PPP-adjusted	Nominal	PPP-adjusted
1973	100	100	100	100	100
1974	108	123	116	115	114
1975	118	128	129	133	124
1976	128	153	140	157	134
1977	139	177	153	200	143
1978	151	199	168	246	158
1979	164	218	189	209	180
1980	178	214	218	274	204
1981	195	216	240	295	228
1982	208	227	254	302	244

Source: Compiled from *Yearbook of Labour Statistics*, 1983, ILO; *International Financial Statistics*, various years, IMF.
Calculated at purchasing-power-parity exchange rates by consumer price index.

be attributed to the *real* appreciation of the yen and deutsche mark against the dollar throughout the 1970s. Because of the real appreciation of the dollar between 1980 and 1982, this pattern was reversed. American wages rose 17 percent, whereas German and Japanese nominal wages calculated in dollars rose only 6.1 percent and 10.2 percent respectively.

Changes in real economic variables are difficult to forecast for the very reason that they are affected by both nominal fluctuations in foreign exchange rates and by structural shifts in the economy. Because these variables cannot be perfectly forecasted, firms bear the risk of their fluctuations whenever a contract is signed or an investment is made. There are no financial markets where the risk of real foreign exchange rate fluctuations can be shifted.

Risk Profiles and Investment Decisions

The absence of financial markets to lay off this risk does not mean, though, that firms cannot affect their risk profiles in reference to these variables. On the contrary, sourcing policy can radically influence the risk borne. There are three types of risk profile policies, namely, the speculative, the hedged, and the flexible.

The speculative consists of betting on one sourcing site. Such a strategy is warranted when advantages stemming from economies of scale override the costs attached to the risk that relative factor costs may change drastically. Without economies of scale, an investment in a single site is a bet, albeit perhaps an informed one, that the relative factor cost advantage will persist in the future.

Like all risky bets, however, the potential return is highly variable. In part, this captures the phenomenal success of Japanese firms, who bet consistently through the 1970s and early 1980s that the increasing costs of home wages could be offset by new home investments and an ensuant rise in labor productivity.[3] For Germany, the United States, and the United Kingdom, less than 30 percent of their foreign direct investment stock is in services, the remainder consists of extractive and manufacturing operations. For Japan, approximately 45 percent is in services, commonly in the form of sales offices of trading companies. Moreover, Japanese overseas operations are generally not sourcing platforms for intermediate components. On the contrary, the overseas operations are dependent on components manufactured by the Japanese firms. Whereas only 6 percent of the production of Japanese overseas affiliates is exported back to

Japan, some 47 percent of the procurements by these same affiliates originated in Japan.[4]

This trend appears to contravene strongly the tendency of American firms to source overseas component manufacture or assembly of goods that are later sold in the United States. The Japanese strategy suggests, therefore, the gamble that exchange rates might move back to long-term parity or that new investments in technology might overcome the higher labor costs. The first gamble represents a bet on the comparative advantage of Japan; the second, a bet on the competitive advantage of the firm.

In the absence of large economies of scale or technological advantages, a firm can reduce its risk exposure by sourcing from multiple locations. An example of this strategy is illustrated by Volkswagen, which suffered large losses in the early 1970s as the real cost of German wages rose relative to its competitors in its principal export markets. This experience led to investments in plants in Mexico and Brazil for its low end of the line cars, in the United States for its middle line, and a concentration of mid and upper lines in Germany. The logic of the policy was that by keeping the top of the line production in Germany, Volkswagen was able to "pass through" the impact of exchange rate movements to foreign and domestic consumers who are less sensitive to price increases of the higher quality cars. On the other hand, placing plants in Mexico, Brazil, and the United States for primarily local sales reflected the greater restraint on a complete pass through in the case of the lower line of cars. Thus, by matching the exchange exposure on the cost side to that on the revenue side, Volkswagen hedged a considerable portion of its operating margin against exchange rate fluctuations. That this hedged strategy did not meet expectations in the United States can be attributed partly to the fact that the Japanese speculative bet paid off in the American market.

A hedged position can lead, though, to a flexible strategy which permits the firm to exploit valuable options. One option is to invest in excess capacity in plants in multiple countries. In response to a movement in real exchange rates, a firm can shift production between sites to the extent that labor can work overtime or be placed on shortened schedules. Another option is to invest in flexible technologies that increase capital leverage but permit firms to tailor products to other markets in response to competitive in-roads caused by shifts in real economic variables between countries.[5] Though such options incur costs in terms of loss of scale economies, their distinctive feature is that they become more valuable the greater the unpredictability of the environment. Under this strategy, variance implies greater profit opportunities.

Identifying and Managing Global Opportunities

The value of these opportunities depends on the answer to three questions: the first is a strategic issue, the second, cognitive, and the third, organizational.

• Are the benefits sufficient to justify the costs attached to the loss of scale economies in production or to the organizational support systems?

• Do managers perceive and identify potential options generated by being multinational?

• Are there organizational mechanisms that permit the coordination of the international activities essential to the exploitation of flexibility?

Based on a series of interviews with managers from American and European multinational corporations, I found that firms vary widely in the recognition of, and their organizational capabilities to capitalize on, these opportunities. Some firms have failed to exercise these options as a result of cognitive factors, namely, the tendency to extend the historical organization to overseas operations or to treat each subsidiary as an individual business.[6] In part, these styles reflect the salient features of the relevant environment. It is not surprising that American firms, given the size of the home market, should resist having the international tail of their operations wag the dog. Nor is it surprising that European firms, many of whom developed multinational operations during a period of extensive tariff barriers, tended toward loose headquarters/subsidiary relations in order to establish an identity as a collection of national companies. Running a truly global company is costly, and a policy of home organization extension or local market adaptation may be the most cost-effective choice in many environments.

Whatever these cost trade-offs may have been, though, several elements have increased the benefits of developing organizational structures along global lines. These elements are, principally, the continual reduction of tariffs since 1950; a greater similarity in incomes in developed countries; a reputed convergence in cultures and consumer tastes; and a growth in the economies of scale of production in some industries such as steel, auto components, and television tubes. Evidence from numerous case and cross-sectional studies over the past decade and more have shown a remarkable trend toward organizational structures better suited to a global orientation.[7] These structures include the creation of world product lines, divisions along regions—with the United States being one or part of North America—and matrix structures.

This transformation notwithstanding, multinational corporations appear to vary substantially in the coordination of their international activities and response to the market place. In part, the coordination of a global strategy is constrained by the imposition of governments demanding local content or performance requirements. Yet, even here, concessions and bargaining positions can be coordinated in terms of the larger strategic considerations of maintaining global cost economies in the relevant links of the value-added chain.

From the perspective of managing the strategic flexibility embedded in the multinational corporation, there are six tasks that need to be centralized in order to benefit from being global. Four of these tasks concern the exercise of *arbitrage* opportunities. The other two concern the identification of points of *leverage* to enhance the strategic gaming position of the international firm vis-á-vis competitors and governments.

Arbitrage Opportunities

1.   Production Shifting

As discussed above, production shifting permits the firm to respond to movements in exchange rates. The exercise of such an option is character-ized minimally by two features. First, the loss in economies of scale must be less than the value of the option to shift production and the added cost of holding excess capacity.[8] Thus, in industries where economies of scale are significant, the cost of building two plants with excess capacity may be unjustified, especially if real exchange rates do not fluctuate greatly. Sec-ond, the value of shifting of production rests on the ability of firms to capitalize on differences in variable costs between plants located in separate countries because of fluctuations in exchange rates. The most relevant of these variable costs are locally sourced inputs that are not priced on world markets, the best example being labor. Yet, the degree to which labor is a fixed or variable cost will differ greatly between countries in terms of layoff and overtime constraints. As a result, the successful exercise of this option requires that, one, industrial relations be included in the investment deci-sion and, two, that overtime provisions be made a central feature of labor contracts.[9]

As a result of the interaction between investments and strategic flexi-bility, the decision of where to locate a plant is frequently centralized. The extent to which corporations have adopted a policy of *internal flexible sourcing* by establishing a central committee to monitor exchange rates and costs and shift production in response to exchange rate movements is less clear. For many corporations, this decision cannot be left to divisions, for plants can often be shared between different product lines or areas. A major problem, as reported by a few interviewed firms, is the lack of incentives for divisions to cooperate in production shifting. This problem is treated in the next section.

2. Tax Minimization

One of the more touted features of the multinational corporation is its ability to minimize its tax bill through thoughtful adjustments of transfer prices and choice of remittance channels. The issue of transfer prices is sufficiently well known to warrant only a short discussion. When operating in two countries with different rates of taxation on corporate income, a multinational corporation can, unlike the entirely domestic firm, adjust its mark-up on intracompany sales of goods in order to realize profits in the low tax jurisdiction. Given the tremendous contribution transfer pricing can make to after-tax income, the administration of intra-firm prices for the purpose of income reporting is invariably centralized.

A more subtle form of tax minimization involves establishing multiple channels for income remittance.[10] In many countries, dividends, royalties, fees, and interest payments are taxed at differential rates. To a significant extent, a multinational corporation has the flexibility of choosing to transfer intangibles, such as technology or brand labels, to its subsidiaries in the form of a capitalized equity investment, a sale financed by corporate debt, or as a license. By under- or overevaluating the transferred intangibles, a firm can shift reported profits to subsidiaries in low-tax countries. Similarly, interest payments and royalties can be adjusted to minimize taxes on remitted income. Finally, a firm has some discretion over the timing of remittances, and can, thus, choose to remit according to its tax situation. All of these potential tax benefits stem from the attributes of being a multinational corporation.

3. Financial Markets

The above two cases represent factor market and institutional arbitrage. Arbitrage in financial markets represents a combination of the two, for it is often the imposition of government barriers or subsidies which creates riskless profit opportunities. For example, domestic credit rationing and cross-border capital flows are commonly imposed by governments seeking to equilibrate the balance of payments. A multinational corporation, often in cooperation with an international bank, can circumvent many of these restrictions by its transfer price and remittance policy and also by innovative financial products, such as parallel loans and back-to-back loans. By similar mechanisms, a multinational corporation can often benefit from subsidized loans intended for local investment, but, in fact, transfer the loans outside a country by its remittance, transfer pricing, and financing flexibility.

Often, however, governments cooperate to provide financial incentives for multinational corporations. To this extent, governments by policy intention create arbitrage incentives. For example, export credits have been a heated point of competition between western governments in recent years. Among some developed, and a considerable number of developing countries, competition has centered around investment incentives such as tax holidays, duty relief on imported components, and guaranteed loans. As a result, some corporations centralize the decision of where to locate export activity in order to benefit from the best package of export credit and investment incentive programs.

4.   Information Arbitrage

The final arbitrage opportunity for the multinational corporation concerns information. This information may concern scanning world markets to match sellers and buyers. An increasing characteristic of world trade is the growth of countertrade demands by governments. Estimates of countertrade vary substantially, with some corporations reporting that as much as 25 percent of their world business is in this form. The export firm is dramatically hindered in its ability to absorb the countertraded goods and use them externally or trade them on world markets. On the contrary, a number of large American firms, following a Japanese and, to a lesser extent, European tradition, have created world trade divisions that exploit profitably their multinational subsidiary network for the location of potential buyers for the traded goods. These trading services also reflect arbitrage benefits in terms of avoiding capital constraints on trade as well as tariffs imposed on the monetary value of the traded goods.

In addition to arbitraging informational imperfections in product markets, the multinational corporation can also benefit by transferring new product and process developments from one location to the next. For example, innovations are often stochastic in nature. With differences in expenditures on research and development between nations growing smaller, it is often necessary to monitor multiple national markets in order to exploit potential innovations. In some industries, the impetus to being global consists largely of scanning innovations in foreign markets. For this reason, it has been a common practice for firms in technologically advanced industries to set up research and development offices in the United States, and similar trends are apparent for American firms regarding monitoring the Japanese market.

Leverage Opportunities

1. Global Coordination

Unlike arbitrage, leverage reflects not the exploitation of differences in the price of an asset, product, or factor of production between markets, but rather, the creation of market or bargaining power because of the global position of the firm. One of the more important sources of this power for the international firm is the ability to differentiate prices according to its world competitive posture. For example, in response to Michelin's entry into North America, Goodyear dropped its prices on tires in Europe, forcing the family-held French company to slow its investment program and, eventually, to issue outside equity. Much like the reputed benefits embedded in portfolio models that encourage firms to diversify in order to cross-subsidize between product lines, a benefit of global activity is the possibility of carrying out an aggressive price cutting strategy in one region by relying on profits gained in other regions of the world. Of course, laws, as well as political pressures in the form of government retaliatory policies, limit the extent to which prices can be cut.

Global coordination can take forms other than price differentiation. A multinational firm can build overseas coalitions between suppliers or between a group of competitors in order to exercise leverage on the behavior of a rival firm. Boeing's subcontracting and recent Japanese joint ventures are examples of moves to preempt Airbus. Thus, Boeing's advances toward multinationality are almost entirely promoted by the benefits of acquiring competitive leverage.

Centralization policy varies according to the context and type of strategic decision. Pricing coordination is easily centralized when the firm is organized along global product or area lines. It becomes more difficult under a structure that includes a weak international division, for external pricing then often becomes entangled in the complex issue of establishing the transfer price between divisions. Centralization of joint-venture and long-term supply decisions appears to vary substantially between firms. A few of the firms interviewed for this study delegated these decisions without specifying its place in the long-term plan. Another firm had a central office to oversee the joint venture policy, but its posture was more reactive to local government policy than proactive in the sense of coalition building.

The benefits of coalition building need to be balanced by a clear understanding of the costs. It is unlikely a firm will have the resources to compete in every regional market without adjusting its entry strategy. Because some assets are not transferable between countries, such as distribution or, to a lesser extent, marketing research, a trend in several industries, such as telecommunications, has been to form joint ventures with local firms that provide the distribution and marketing. In many industries, these ventures offer low-cost entry into a market, achieve upstream economies, and leave local competition to firms who have established market positions. Yet, if joint ventures permit firms to concentrate their resources in upstream links, they also have the disadvantage of constraining the firm's ability to respond to the volatility of the global marketplace. An extensive strategy of joint ventures can lead not only to a division of profits between partners, but also to a potential reduction in profitability because of the loss of valuable options. Joint ventures are, thus, no panacea, but raise the fundamental issue in any strategy: namely, what price is the firm willing to pay in order to lay off some of the risk and forego flexibility?

2.   Political Risk

The final point of leverage gained by being global is the bargaining power captured by operating dispersed operations. The key to this power is the leverage that different links of the international value-added chain exercise on enforcing equity claims or contracts in national markets. The classic case has been the petroleum industry. When the industry norms broke down and competition increased between the majors in terms of marketing, the OPEC countries nationalized the upstream production in order to sell the oil to the highest bidder. In many cases, however, the leverage is weighted toward the multinational corporation. Expropriations have been less frequent in high-technology industries since the value of the local subsidiaries depends on future technology flows.

Creating Compatible Incentives

The benefits of flexibility depend upon the extent to which the firm creates the organizational resources to exploit these arbitrage and leverage opportunities. Whether the costs of centralizing the above tasks are warranted will vary according to the uncertainty confronting the individual firms. But firms that have centralized these functions still confront a formidable challenge in terms of creating the appropriate incentive system. Consider the following cases. A large European multinational corporation continued to pour new investments into a hyperinflationary Latin American country and only realized its competitive position had consistently deteriorated subsequent to a long overdue devaluation of the local currency. A large American corporation was pleased at headquarters that one of its subsidiaries in Asia had won a major order, eventually to learn that the only significant competition was its Japanese subsidiary. A division of another large American corporation recently agreed to an overseas joint venture to offset its perceived weakness in international marketing, despite the fact that a second division in the corporation had several decades of experience selling to the targeted market segments.

The multinational corporation faces, therefore, a fundamental dilemma. On the one hand, its multinationality creates valuable opportunities to arbitrage markets and to exercise competitive leverage. The exploitation of these opportunities rests on the efficiency of the organization to coordinate its overseas operations and subsidiaries. On the other hand, the centralized coordination of these activities entails significant fixed costs and variable costs in communicating information from subsidiaries to corporate headquarters. Changes in environmental and competitive conditions may only be evident at the local subsidiary level. As a result, the subsidiaries often possess the best knowledge concerning the country environment and the know-how for local adaptation.

Because of the limits on centralization and the need to maintain local adaptation, the realization of global benefits is significantly dependent upon the formalization of *integrative systems* to decentralize some of the responsibility for effective exploitation of these opportunities. Two of the most important systems are human resource management and planning and control. Curiously, there have been few studies which have linked these systems to decentralized mechanisms to enhance the strategic flexibility of the multinational corporation.

To the extent that studies have been carried out, the results have tended to show a surprising conflict between the corporate strategy and the embedded incentives of the two systems. Planning and control systems for American firms have tended to export the home organization overseas.[11] Recently, a number of firms have tried to tackle the problem of setting targets and monitoring performance in a multiple currency world.

Very few firms have appeared to develop sophisticated systems that decouple the measurement of subsidiary from managerial performance. Yet, without such a decoupling, local managers are, for example, penalized for shifting production to plants in other countries. Furthermore, they are held responsible for exogenous shifts in exchange rates which affect the *competitive* position of the subsidiary but which are beyond their immediate control. A prerequisite to a planning and control system which provides incentives compatible with the overall strategy is the decoupling of exogenously caused competitive effects on the subsidiary from the measurement of managerial performance.[12] Only with such a decoupling can the inherent flexibility of the MNC be exploited without excessive centralization.

Another system to link managerial performance to strategy is human resource management. A few studies have found a tendency for career paths to be tied to frequent international reassignment when the effective deployment of strategies depended strongly on local subsidiaries.[13] Generally, though, evidence for American firms has tended to show significant failure rates for expatriate managers and the frequent use of local nationals.[14]

Conclusion

Global strategies . . . rest on the interplay of the competitive advantage of firms and the comparative advantage of countries. The decision of where to invest along a firm's value-added chain is a question of competitive advantage. The decision of where to place these activities internationally constitutes a question of comparative advantage. Except for trivial and uninteresting exceptions, these decisions are based upon considerable uncertainty over future costs, market developments, and technologies. They are also influenced by the willingness of firms to bear the risk of betting on a single sourcing platform, product market, or technology.

No matter what the risk profile, the firm that is able to exploit this volatility possesses a competitive advantage gained by its ownership of a global network. This advantage may be in the form of arbitraging markets. In the case of American multinational corporations, this arbitrage might potentially consist of production shifting. For a Japanese trading company, it might consist of the ability to respond quickly to new information due to its ownership of an international purchasing and sales organization coupled with an extensive logistics capability. An advantage of being global also includes an enhanced leverage in local marketplaces or in negotiations with governments.

The capability to exercise these arbitrage and leverage opportunities rests on the existence of centralized task groups responsible for the coordination of the international activities of the firm. However, centralization is constrained by the need to maintain a careful balance between local subsidiary responsiveness and the coordination of these global benefits. From this perspective, the *structural* configuration of dispersed investment location and market penetration is a prerequisite to, but no less important than, the *operational* flexibility of the firm to respond to changes in the international environment.

For many firms, the failure to develop systems tied to the global strategy of the firm may well reflect the significant costs attached to a sophisticated information system that supports the management of planning and control and human resources. One suspects, however, that the benefits of such a system have not been fully specified in terms of balancing the centralized coordination of the multinational network against the maintenance of local subsidiary responsiveness. Where this balancing is critical, the enhancement of integrative systems is invariably an integral element in the exploitation of the benefits gained by the global activities of the multinational corporation.

Notes

Research for this paper has been funded by the Reginald H. Jones Center of The Wharton School. The author thanks Laurent Jacque and Louis Wells for their comments.

1. Comparative advantage can also be defined in terms of the availability or abundance of factors of production. Thus, a country can be seen to have a comparative advantage in skilled workers by reason of their relative abundance, even though skilled wages may be the same for all countries.

2. Even here, though, a qualification must be added, for changes in exchange rates may attract the migration of foreign labor and interest rates may affect economic growth, the first affecting the supply, the second the demand of labor. Certainly, though, these second-order effects are less strong than the immediate impact that exchange rate movements have on international competitiveness.

3. It would be wrong, however, to deduce from this single trend any conclusion on differences in risk tolerances between countries. The Japanese pattern might well reflect the avoidance of risk attached to operating overseas subsidiaries, or the

problems in transferring culturally bound practices and technologies to foreign countries. Our point here is that, in terms of exchange rate exposure only, an export strategy is a high risk bet in the face of global competition.

4. The procurement patterns of Japanese overseas affiliates given in Ministry of International Trade and Industry are Survey, 1980. K. Haberich kindly brought these data to my attention.

5. This latter option is suited also to a purely domestic setting. It has been argued, in fact, that the frontier of new technologies and industries is characterized by smaller-scale or flexible manufacturing that is particularly well suited to the purported higher variance of the current marketplace. This argument is given by B. Kogut in the case of steel mini-mills, and, for flexible technologies, cursorily by K. Ohmae and at length in the impressive study by M. Piore and C. Sabel. See B. Kogut, "Steel and the European Economic Community," working paper, Sloan School of Management, MIT, 1980; K. Ohmae, *The Mind of the Strategist: Business Planning for Competitive Advantage* (New York: McGraw-Hill, 1982): and M. Piore and C. Sabel, *The Second Industrial Divide* (New York: Basic Books, 1985).

6. H. Perlmutter in a seminal work remarked upon several different cognitive orientations, naming them ethnocentric, polycentric, and geocentric. The first one refers to the condition of exporting the home organization; the second, to the treatment of each subsidiary separately; and the third, to the development of a global or cosmopolitan style. We develop the third cognitive orientation below. See H. Perlmutter, "The Tortuous Evolution of the Multinational Corporation," *Columbia Journal of World Business*, 1969.

7. Of the many works, the book by Stopford and Wells was one of the earliest and remains one of the best studies of the transformation of American multinational corporations. Franko shows a similar trend for European firms toward more global structures. Root develops the notion of the multinational corporation as a network, which parallels our discussion below. See J. Stopford and L. Wells, *Managing the Multinational Enterprise* (New York: Basic Books, 1974); L. Franko, *The European Multinationals* (Stamford, CT: Greylock, 1977); and F. Root, *International Trade and Investment* (Cincinnati, OH: Southwestern Publishing Co., 1984).

8. A discussion of valuation of such an option can be found in B. Kogut, "Foreign Direct Investment as a Sequential Process," in *The Multinational Corporation in the 1980s*, ed. C. P. Kindleberger and D. P. Audretsch (Cambridge: MIT Press, 1983) and is the subject of current work.

9. For a discussion on the management of international and interdependent manufacturing operations, see B. Mascarenhas, "Coordination of Manufacturing Interdependence in MNCs," *Journal of International Business Studies*, 1984.

10. The following discussion on remittance channels and financial market arbitrage draws substantially from work by D. Lessard. See his articles "Transfer Prices, Taxes and Financial Markets: Implications of Internal Financial Transfers within the Multinational Firm," in *Economic Issues of Multinational Firms*, ed. R. B. Hawkins (Greenwich, CT: JAI Press, 1979) and "Finance and Global Competition," paper

prepared for colloquium on Competition in Global Industries (Harvard University, April 26–27, 1984).

11. M. McInnes, "Financial Control Systems for Multinational Operations: An Empirical Investigation," *Journal of International Business Studies*, 1971. Swedish studies show that weak control systems, true to the European pattern of loose headquarter/subsidiary ties, tend to prevail for Swedish multinational corporations. See G. Hedlund and P. Aman, *Managing Relationships with Foreign Subsidiaries: Organization and Control in Swedish MNCs* (Stockholm: Sveriges Mekanforbun, 1983).

12. Some recent work suggests possible ways to achieve this decoupling: D. Lessard and D. Sharp, "Measuring the Performance of Operations Subject to Fluctuating Exchange Rates," *Midland Corporate Journal*, 1984. L. Jacque and P. Lorange, "Hyperinflation and Global Strategic Management," *Columbia Journal of World Business*, 1984; and L. Jacque and B. Kogut, "The International Control Conundrum: A Multivariate Variance Smoothing Model," mimeo, The Wharton School, 1984.

13. See A. Edstrom and J. Galbraith, "International Transfer of Managers: Some Important Policy Considerations," *Columbia Journal of World Business*, 1976, and Y. L. Doz and C. K. Prahalad, "Headquarters Influence and Strategic Control in MNCs," *Sloan Management Review*, Fall 1981, pp. 15–29.

14. See R. Tung, "Selection and Training of Personnel for Overseas Assignments," *Columbia Journal of World Business*, 1982.

II Multinational Corporate Strategy

Key Terms

- economies of scale
- economies of scope
- synergy
- manufacturing strategy
- organizational flexibility
- production shifting
- strategic planning decisions

Questions

1. What are some of the key strategic decisions?

2. Why are the strategic decisions in a global context different from those in a domestic context?

3. Why have Japanese firms increased their ranking in the hit parade of their industries?

4. How might a firm improve its standing in the hit parade of its industry?

5. Why is it difficult for firms to improve their standing in their industry?

Suggested Readings

Bartlett, Christopher A., and Sumantra Ghoshal, "Organizing for Worldwide Effectiveness," *California Management Review*, Fall 1988, pp. 54–74.

Chakravarthy, Balaji S., and Howard V. Perlmutter, "Strategic Planning for a Global Business," *Columbia Journal of World Business*, Summer 1985, pp. 3–10.

Kogut, Bruce, "Designing Global Strategies: Comparative and Competitive Value-Added Chains," *Sloan Management Review*, Summer 1985, pp. 15–28.

Starr, Martin K., "Global Production and Operations Strategy," *Columbia Journal of World Business*, Winter 1984, pp. 17–22.

Tung, Rosalie L., "Strategic Management of Human Resources in the Multinational Enterprise," *Human Resource Management*, Summer 1984, pp. 129–143.

Yip, George S., "Global Strategy ... in a World of Nations?" *Sloan Management Review*, Fall 1989, pp. 29–41.

III

International Marketing

In Great Britain and Japan, traffic drives on the left side of the road; the Japanese adopted the practice from the British, and the British set this convention following the practice of their railroads. In the United States and much of the rest of the world, traffic drives on the right side of the road.

All the automobiles produced in Japan and exported to the United States have the steering wheels on the left to conform to the U.S. practice. Thus far, none of the automobiles produced by U.S. firms and exported to Japan has had a steering wheel on the right—and obviously the market share is insignificant. General Motors and Ford are caught up in the proverbial chicken and egg problem—they won't move the steering wheel to conform to the Japanese practice until their sales increase substantially, but the Japanese market share will remain small until they move the steering wheel. Imagine the growth of Japanese auto sales in the United States if the steering wheels followed the Tokyo convention.

Inevitably the firms that are successful in increasing their sales at a rapid rate will begin to outgrow their domestic market because the ratio of their sales to domestic sales will become increasingly large; if these firms are to avoid a sharp reduction in the rate of growth of their sales, they must expand their sales in various foreign markets. Expanding sales in foreign markets is difficult; foreigners usually aren't like us. Firms must identify and rank the foreign markets in terms of the potential for the increase in their sales and their profits, and they must select the marketing strategy most appropriate for each of these foreign markets, for various groups of countries, or for all countries as a group.

The tautological answer to the question, "how to select the countries to enter abroad?" is "In terms of ease of entry" or "In terms of anticipated profitability." Ease of entry means low-cost entry. And entry into some foreign markets may cost less than entry into others because of geographic proximity ("It's the closest foreign market"), or cultural proximity ("They have the same tastes" or "They speak the same language") or economic proximity ("Their per capita incomes are similar to ours"). U.S. firms find it natural (i.e., easy) to first expand into Canada, and then into Great Britain and Australia—these foreign countries aren't very foreign. Similarly Canadian firms are likely to expand their sales abroad in the United States before they seek to expand in most other foreign countries.

The ease of entry into different foreign markets is a function of the size of these markets, the scope or extent of the protective policies followed by the governments in the various foreign countries, and whether the foreign market is fragmented into several regional markets. Entry into the U.S.

market for foreign firms is much easier than the entry into foreign markets for U.S. firms, because the U.S. market is larger, fragmented geographically, and less extensively protected. Japanese firms find it much easier to enter the U.S. market than almost any other foreign market. On the other hand, U.S. firms find it much more difficult to enter the Japanese market than Japanese firms do to enter the U.S. market—the Japanese market is smaller, highly protected, and extremely crowded with Japanese firms. Korean firms also find it much harder to expand their sales in the Japanese market than in the U.S. market—the Japanese and the Koreans do not have fond memories of each other.

The derivative question involves the choice of a marketing program for each foreign country. Consider the alternatives. The marketing program for each foreign country might be identical to the domestic marketing program, with the exception of the modest changes of language. Or there might be a separate marketing program for each foreign country or for each large foreign country, because the consumers in these countries are so different from domestic consumers. And a third possibility is that a new marketing program might be developed that is more or less the same for all countries; hence, "globalization" may be achieved. Moreover, these choices may change over time and as the ratio of the foreign sales of the firm increase relative to its domestic sales.

A marketing program involves decisions about the product, the package, the promotion, and the distribution. The firm may standardize these variables, and ignore the national differences in consumer incomes, tastes, and preferences—or it may adapt these variables to fit each national market. Some of these factors may be adapted while others are standardized; thus the firm might adapt the distribution arrangements to the local market while selling the standard product.

The significance of the marketing decision is that, for some consumer products, marketing costs may exceed production costs. To the extent there are economies of scale in these marketing activities, there may be savings from using the same marketing program for several countries—which means that more can be spent on promotion.

The articles in part 3 examine the basic international decisions: product design decisions, packaging decisions, pricing decisions, and promotion decisions.

"Evolution of Global Marketing Strategy: Scale, Scope, and Synergy" by Susan P. Douglas and C. Samuel Craig examines the development of international marketing programs by accounting for the extent of a firm's experience overseas and the stage in its international evolution. They identify three phases: (1) initial foreign market entry, (2) expansion and adaptation to individual national markets, and (3) rationalization of individual national marketing activities into a coherent international program. Movement from one phase to the next is achieved by managing at each stage the key international "levers"— the variables under management control— in response to external and internal "triggers"—particular events which stimulate the managers to seek new solutions.

The second article is Theodore Levitt's classic, "The Globalization of Markets." Levitt asserts that the best-managed companies have moved from dependence on items customized for individual national markets toward offering globally standardized products that are technologically advanced and low-priced. These companies are positioned to achieve long-term success by concentrating on the emerging similarity of demands; as Levitt says, "the earth is flat." The assumption that is implicit in Levitt's argument is that the additional funds realized from standardizing the marketing program are better spent on promotion, which leads to a larger increase in sales and profits, than on tailoring the marketing program to the incomes and preferences of each national market.

John A. Quelch and Edward J. Hoff provide a counterbalance in "Customizing Global Marketing." They examine first the problems of global marketing, and then the separate marketing decisions on a continuum from globalization/standardization to customization. They suggest that a company's approach to international marketing depends upon its overall business strategy. Firms will centralize marketing only after manufacturing, finance, and research and development are centralized because marketing effectiveness is hard to measure from headquarters. Quelch and Hoff also link the firm's product to economies of scale and worldwide cultural acceptance; products that enjoy large economies of scale and are not highly "culture-bound" are easier to market globally than others. Focusing on the elements of the marketing program, they address two questions: "How far should the company go in globalization?" and "How can the company get there?" For most products, the scope of globalization varies from one element of the marketing program to another. Strategic elements, like product positioning, are more easily standardized than execution-sensitive elements like sales promotion. Finally, Quelch and Hoff examine the transition to globalization on a continuum from "informing" subsidiaries and undertaking "patient persuasion" to "directing" subsidiaries through fiat. The appropriate way to achieve globalization depends on the relationship of headquarters to its subsidiaries, but, in general, informing and persuading will alienate managers in the subsidiaries the least.

Is there one answer to the debate between Levitt and his critics? Probably not. The answers are likely to be firm-specific, and perhaps even specific to a range of products. There are a few consumer goods—low-cost, repetitive purchases—for which the Levitt approach may be optimal. For most products, however, some form of adaption of the elements in the marketing mix is likely to be profit-enhancing.

8

Evolution of Global
Marketing Strategy:
Scale, Scope, and Synergy

Susan P. Douglas and
C. Samuel Craig

In recent years, issues relating to international marketing strategy have stirred increasing interest. To date, however, much of the discussion has focused on specific decisions rather than broader strategic issues. The inherent complexity and dynamic aspects of strategy formulation in international markets have frequently been ignored. Yet, a firm's strategic thrust and key decisions will change as it expands its operations overseas. The process of internationalization thus involves a firm moving through successive phases, each characterized by new strategic challenges and decision priorities.

Previous discussion of international marketing strategy has, however, tended to focus on the initial stage of entry into international markets. Often the perspective of a novice in international markets is adopted. Consequently, attention has centered on decisions such as the choice of countries to enter, the mode of operation to adopt or the extent to which products or positioning can be standardized, or must be adapted for different country markets.[1] This latter issue in particular has attracted considerable attention and has been the source of much controversy in recent years.[2]

Emphasis on initial international market entry and issues of standardization were appropriate in the 1960s and early 1970s, when many companies, whether of U.S. or other national origin, had only limited experience in international markets. Today, however, many companies already have operations in a number of countries. Consequently, the issues they face are infinitely more complex than those faced by companies contemplating initial foreign market entry. In determining the direction for future growth, the costs of expansion into new countries have to be weighed with those of expansion within the existing matrix of country operations. The extent

From *Columbia Journal of World Business*, Fall 1989, pp. 47–59. Reprinted by permission.

to which operations are coordinated and integrated across countries and product divisions must also be determined in order to optimize the transfer of knowledge and experience, and take advantage of potential synergies arising from the multinational character of operations.

The key issues and strategic imperatives facing the firm will vary depending on the degree of experience and the nature of operations in international markets. In the initial phase of entry into international markets, a key objective is the geographic expansion of operations to identify markets overseas for existing products and services and to leverage potential economies of scale in production and marketing. Once an initial beachhead has been established, emphasis shifts to developing local markets and exploiting potential economies of scope, building upon the existing geographic base. In the third phase, attention shifts to consolidation of overseas expansion initiatives, and improved coordination and integration of operations to take advantage of potential synergies in multinational operations.

The purpose of this article is to examine each of these phases, together with their underlying dynamics, and the forces which trigger movement from one phase to another. The key issues and levers which characterize each phase are highlighted, and the implications for the formulation of global marketing strategy are discussed.

Strategy Formulation in International Markets

An evolutionary perspective of internationalization of the firm has been adopted by a number of authors in the areas of international economics and international management. The theory of the international product life cycle, propounded by Vernon and others,[3] identifies a number of phases in the internationalization process based on the location of production. In the initial phase, a firm exports to overseas markets from a domestic production base. As market potential builds up, overseas production facilities are established. Low-cost local competition then enters the market, and ultimately exports to the home market of the initial entrant, thus challenging its international market position.

A number of empirical studies examining this theory have been conducted.[4] These suggest that the theory provides an adequate explanation of U.S. foreign direct investment in the 1960s and 1970s. More recent developments, such as the emergence of global competition and integration of markets, suggest, however, a considerably more complex pattern of internationalization.

In-depth studies of the internationalization process of several firms have also been conducted, focusing on their acquisition and use of knowledge about foreign markets and the growth of involvement overseas.[5] These studies suggest that the internationalization process is gradual, involving incremental commitments to overseas markets rather than major foreign production investments at a single point in time. These studies tend however, to focus on the early stages of internationalization, and on the relation between information acquisition and market commitment, rather than issues related to strategy formulation.

The EPRG framework developed by Perlmutter[6] also identifies four stages in the evolution of the multinational corporation, each characterized by different management attitudes and orientations. In the first stage, ethnocentrism, overseas operations are viewed as subordinate to domestic operations, and domestic performance standards are applied to overseas subsidiaries. The polycentric or host country orientation emphasizes local cultural differences, and evaluation and control procedures are established locally, with little communication between headquarters and subsidiaries. A regiocentric orientation focuses on regional organization of authority and communication flows, while a geocentric or global orientation aims for collaboration between headquarters and subsidiaries to identify standards and procedures which meet both worldwide and local goals and objectives. While this approach has been linked to different organizational structures and policies, it provides few explicit guidelines for strategy formulation and implementation.

Formulating strategy explicitly with regard to international markets is crucial for a number of reasons. Initial forays into international markets are often unsystematic and somewhat haphazard, resulting from an unsolicited export order from a foreign buyer, an order from a domestic customer for his overseas operations or interest expressed by an importer or potential business partner in a foreign market. Consequently, it is important to establish objectives with regard to international market operations, especially in terms of the level of involvement and degree of risk, as part of a systematic evaluation of opportunities worldwide. Otherwise, international activities will lack direction, resulting from creeping commitment and sporadic efforts, and will not necessarily be targeted to the most attractive opportunities for the firm in world markets.

Strategy formulation in international markets involves a number of key parameters whose nature and impact will depend on the phase in the internationalization process. These are shown diagramatically in Figure 8.1. At

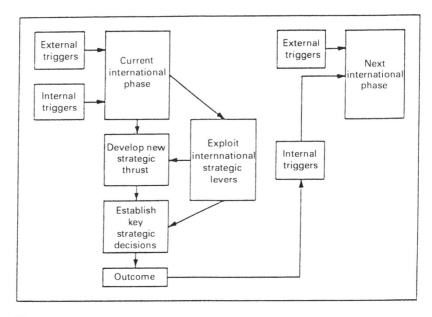

Figure 8.1
The dynamics of global strategy development

each phase a number of triggers will prompt movement into a new phase, stimulating generation of a new strategic thrust. The direction of these is channelled by the key international levers associated with each phase. Together these will define investment and resource allocation priorities, thus establishing the key strategic decisions and expected outcomes.

The Triggers

The triggers which prompt a firm to move from one phase to the next are both external and internal. External triggers, such as environmental factors, industry trends or competitive pressures, cause the firm to reassess its current strategy. Internal triggers, on the other hand, are caused by factors such as internal sales and profits or management initiatives. Certain internal triggers, for example, declining sales volume, may be the result of external factors, such as increased competition from foreign firms. Also, firms may respond differently to the same set of external factors. Internal and external triggers may thus combine to generate the development of a new strategic thrust.

The Strategic Thrust

The strategic thrust determines the direction the firm will pursue and defines the arena in which the firm will compete, as well as its strategic priorities.

In international markets, defining the geographic extent of operations and direction for expansion is of critical importance. As noted above, this varies with the phase of internationalization. In the initial phase, emphasis is placed on geographic expansion, and hence the specific countries to be targeted must be determined. The subsequent phase is one of geographic consolidation, and hence growth within each country centers around expansion of product lines. This leads to rationalization of product lines across country boundaries, and the transfer of product ideas and lines, so that the concept of a domestic market disappears, and planning is formulated on a global basis.

Key International Levers

The key strategic levers aid in further redefining the direction of the firm's efforts and determining the decision and investment priorities at each successive stage of internationalization. In the intial phase, lacking experience or familiarity with overseas markets, a firm will seek to leverage its domestic position internationally, thus achieving economies of scale. This might, for example, be grounded in superior product quality or technological expertise, cost efficiency, mass-merchandising expertise or a strong corporate or brand image. As familiarity with the local market environment increases, and a marketing and distribution infrastructure and contacts with local distributors and other organizations are developed, a firm will seek to leverage these across a broader range of products and services in order to achieve economies of scope. In the final phase, a firm will try to leverage both internal skills and environment-related experience, transferring learning across national boundaries, so as to take maximum advantage from potential synergies in multinational operations.

Strategic Decisions

The firm's strategic thrust and the levers to internationalization together determine key strategic decisions at each phase of internationalization. In the initial phase, the key decisions center on the choice of countries to

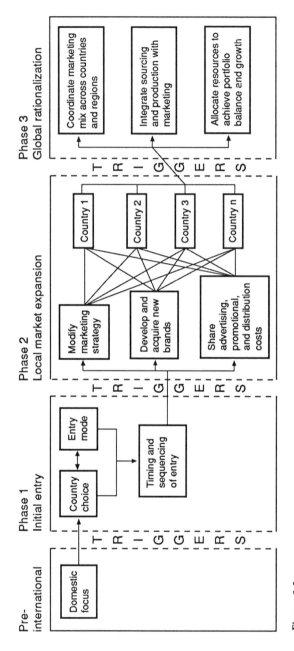

Figure 8.2
Phases in global marketing evolution

enter, the mode of operation and the timing and sequencing of entry. Once initial entry has been successfully achieved, decisions at the next phase center around the development of local market potential through product modification, product line extension, and development of new products tailored to specific local market needs. This typically results in the creation of a patchwork of local operations, and hence leads to the need to improve efficiency, and to establish mechanisms to coordinate and integrate strategy across national markets, allowing for the transfer and exchange of learning and experience, and leading eventually to the establishment of strategy relative to regional and global rather than multi-domestic markets.

Thus, in international markets, the strategic thrust, the key decisions and levers evolve with the degree of experience and stage of involvement in overseas operations. This is analogous to the product life cycle concept[7] where the key strategic imperatives vary with the stage of its evolution. While in practice this evolution is a continuous process, for the purposes of analytical simplicity, three phases may be identified, in addition to a preliminary phase of pre-internationalization: (1) initial foreign market entry; (2) local or national market expansion; and (3) globalization. (See Figure 8.2, which depicts the relation between the different stages.)

Phases of International Market Development

Pre-Internationalization

Prior to entry into international markets, the domestic market is the focal point of strategy development and defines the boundaries of operations. Strategy is designed and developed based on information relating to customer needs and interests, industry trends, and economic, socio-cultural and technological trends likely to influence demand for the firm's products and services in the domestic market. Similarly, attention is centered on the strategies of domestic competitors viewed as major threats to the firm.

Although in some cases a firm may deliberately decide *not* to enter international markets, and concentrate instead on serving its domestic market, a domestically oriented firm is likely to be inwardly focused, with limited interest or concern for events outside its immediate sphere of operation. Often such a firm will be characterized by a certain lethargy and lack of dynamism, content to supply its traditional customer base with existing technology through established marketing channels. Such an attitude may well be tinged with a certain complacency, satisfaction with present performance, and few ambitions to tackle new frontiers.

A domestic orientation may lead to lack of attention to changes taking place in the global marketplace such as new life-styles or target segments, new customer needs, growth of new competition, and the restructuring of market forces worldwide. A firm may thus be vulnerable to the emergence of new technology or the advent of foreign competition armed with a superior product or an aggressive marketing strategy. Such competitors may be quicker to respond to new challenges and opportunities in the marketplace. The failure of the U.S. TV manufacturers to monitor developments in the Japanese TV market in the 1960s and 1970s, and to respond to the entry of low-cost Japanese TV sets into the U.S. market by moving to low-cost offshore production locations led to their ultimate demise.[8] As a result, Zenith is the sole U.S. manufacturer with a significant share (12% of the U.S. market) in the industry.[9]

Triggers to Internationalization

A variety of factors may prompt the domestically-oriented firm to re-examine its position. (See table 8.1 for a summary of typical events.) Trends within the industry or product market, in terms of demand and supply conditions, competitive developments, or other discrete events may all

Table 8.1
Triggers to each stage of internationalization

Initial market entry	Local market	Globalization
1. Saturation of domestic market duplication of efforts	1. Local market growth	1. Cost inefficiencies and duplication of efforts between countries
2. Movement overseas of domestic customers	2. Meeting local competition	2. Learning via transfer of ideas and experience
3. Diversification of risk	3. Local management initiative and motivation	3. Emergence of global customers
4. Sourcing opportunities in overseas markets	4. Desire to utilize local assets more effectively	4. Emergence of global competition
5. Entry of foreign competition in home market	5. Natural market boundaries	5. Development of global marketing infrastructure
6. Desire to keep abreast of technological changes		
7. Government incentives to export		
8. Advances in communications technology and marketing infrastructure		

open up new opportunities in markets abroad. Each of these factors, alone or in concert, may provide impetus for the firm to venture into overseas markets.

These include:

• *Saturation of the domestic market* resulting from slackening rates of growth or limited potential for expansion;

• *Movement of customers overseas*, stimulating interest in following suit in order to retain the account and supply customers more cost-effectively;

• *Desire to diversify risk* across a range of countries and product markets;

• *Identification of advantageous sourcing opportunities*, i.e., lower labor or production costs in other countries;

• *Retaliation to the entry of foreign competition* into the firm's domestic market;

• *Concern over keeping abreast of technological change* in world markets;

• *Government incentives* such as information, credit insurance, tax exemptions;

• *Advances in transportation and communications technology*, such as the growth of international telephone linkages, fax systems, satellite networks, containerization, etc.

Any one or a combination of these factors may stimulate investigation of developments in markets overseas, and of opportunities for sourcing and/or marketing products and services in other countries and may trigger initial entry into international markets.

Phase 1.   Initial International Market Entry

The decision to move into international markets constitutes a bold step forward. It opens up new opportunities in a multitude of countries throughout the world and new horizons for expansion and growth. At the same time, lack of experience in and of familiarity with conditions in overseas markets creates a considerable strain on management to acquire the knowledge and skills necessary to operate effectively in these markets. Information relating to differences in environmental conditions, market demand and the degree of competition will therefore be needed in order to select the most attractive country markets, and to develop a strategy to guide the firm's thrust into international markets.

This step is especially crucial, since a false move at this stage may result in withdrawal or retreat from international markets. Mistakes made in initial entry can damage a firm's reputation, and be difficult to surmount. Renault's efforts to penetrate the U.S. compact car market have, for example, been haunted by its early mistakes with the Renault Dauphine. Careful formulation of initial entry strategy is thus crucial in shaping the pattern of international market evolution.

Key Strategic Thrust

The firm's efforts are therefore directed toward identifying the most attractive market opportunities overseas for its existing (i.e., domestic) products and services. Attention is centered on pinpointing the closest match between the firm's current offerings and market conditions overseas so that minimal adaptation of products or marketing strategies is required. The guiding principle is to extend the geographic base of operations without incurring major incremental marketing or production costs, other than those required to obtain distribution.

International Levers

The firm therefore seeks to leverage its domestic competitive position and core competency internationally so as to extend economies of scale by establishing a presence in multiple markets (see Figure 8.3a). Given the firm's lack of experience and knowledge in overseas markets, it will focus on product- or skill-related assets which can be leveraged internationally. These might include innovative or high-quality products, a patented process, a brand name, or other proprietary assets.[10] In industries such as computers and medical equipment, the success of many firms has been contingent on the introduction of products new to these markets. High-quality price ratios, the outgrowth of superior production skills, have also been a key element in the penetration of world markets for consumer electronics and compact cars by Japanese companies. Patented processes may also be leveraged internationally, as in the expansion of Xerox and Polaroid into world markets in the 1960s. In consumer markets, well-known brand names, such as Coca-Cola, Levis or Kelloggs, are often an important proprietary asset which can be exploited in overseas markets. Process skills such as mastery of mass-merchandising techniques and expertise in managing distribution channels may also be exploited in foreign markets. Such skills have enabled companies such as P & G and Colgate to outpace competitors in markets throughout the world, but are typically more difficult to leverage directly, especially in the initial stages

a. Scale economies

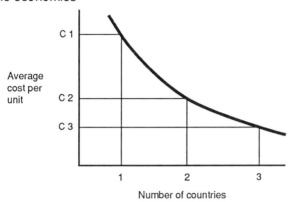

b. Scope economies

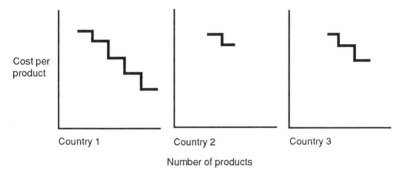

c. Synergies

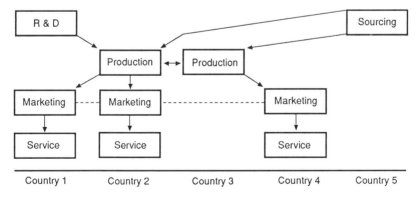

Figure 8.3
Levers underlying global marketing development

of entry. Furthermore, they may require some degree of adaptation to local market conditions, and hence are less likely to be susceptible to scale economies.

Benetton, the Italian manufacturer of casual clothing, has been highly successful in leveraging its brand image worldwide. In 1978, the company realized $78 million in sales, 98% in Italy. By 1987, the company grossed $830 million, with profits of $86.9 million throughout its worldwide network of over 4,000 independently owned retail outlets, in sixty countries, of which 1,500 are in Italy, and 600 in the US. Not only is the Benetton image projected worldwide through the uniform design format of their clear, open-shelved stores, and the use of the bright green Benetton logo, but also through uniform advertising campaigns such as the award-winning "United Colors of Benetton" campaign.

Key Decisions

In the phase of initial entry, the key decisions relate to (1) the choice of countries to enter, (2) the timing of entry, and (3) how operations are to be conducted in these countries.

While each of these decisions is discussed separately here, they are, nonetheless, highly interrelated. The mode of operation or entry, as well as the timing of entry will depend on perceived opportunities and risks in a given country. Similarly, the timing of entry may affect the choice of mode of entry.

Choice of Countries

In choosing which countries to enter, risk and opportunities need to be evaluated relative to both the general business climate of a country and the specific product or service. The stability and rate of economic growth of a country have to be examined as well as the political, financial, and legal risks of entry. Similarly, the size and growth of market potential have to be considered relative to the level of competition and costs of market entry. Often a trade-off has to be made between risk and return. Countries with high growth potential frequently also entail high competitive or country risks or entry costs.

For the novice in international markets, the degree of familiarity or knowledge about a foreign market and its perceived similarity are often key factors in influencing choice. Countries which are perceived as similar in terms of language, culture, education, business practices, or industrial development are viewed as lower in risk and likely to offer a more favorable climate for entry than those where the psychic distance is large.[11] In examining foreign investment patterns of U.S. firms, one study found that close to two-thirds chose to enter Canada first and then the U.K., though such choices were clearly not warranted by country size and growth potential relative to other countries such as West Germany or France. Similarly, Australia ranked considerably higher in investment priorities than its size would suggest.

Knowledge and familiarity with a country is often an important factor influencing perceived risk and uncertainty of market entry. Both objective information and experiential knowledge affect this uncertainty. Thus, proximity and prior contact or experience in a country will influence market choice. Swedish companies have, for example, been found to enter neighboring countries such as Denmark, Norway and Finland first, and more distant countries such as Brazil, Argentina and Australia last.[12]

Timing of Entry

An important issue is whether to enter a number of country markets simultaneously, or alternatively, enter one country first, and then building on this experience, enter other country markets sequentially.[13] A major consideration in this decision is the level of resource commitment required to enter a given market overseas. Given the lack of familiarity and experience in operating in overseas market environments, financial, managerial and other resource requirements may be significant, especially where an overseas sales organization and/or production facilities are to be established. On the other hand, simultaneous entry will enable the firm to preempt competition by establishing a beachhead in all potential markets, limiting opportunities for imitation. Potential scale economies arising from multiple market entry and interdependence of country markets may also be realized.[14]

Mode of Entry

The decision concerning how to operate in a foreign market is closely interrelated with the evaluation of market potential and country risk.[15] A wide variety of modes of operating in foreign markets may be adopted, ranging from exporting, licensing and contract manufacturing, to joint ventures and wholly owned subsidiaries.[16] These vary in terms of the level of resource or equity commitment to overseas markets. Companies can thus limit their equity exposure by adopting low-commitment modes such as licensing, contract manufacturing, or minority joint ventures in high-risk countries or those which are perceived as socio-culturally different, and, hence, unfamiliar operating environments.[17]

In the latter case, a company may prefer to enter a country in a joint venture with a local partner, who can provide knowledge and contacts with the local market. This strategy has often been adopted by foreign companies entering the Japanese market. For example, Wella, the German manufacturer of hair care products, initially entered the Japanese market in a joint venture with a manufacturer of beauty salon chairs. Subsequently, as it acquired greater familiarity with and understanding of the market, Wella bought out the Japanese company.

Another important element in the choice of mode of operation is the desired degree of control and perceived significance of international operations.[18] Non-equity modes such as licensing or contract manufacturing entail minimal risk and commitment, but at the same time afford little control and limited returns.[19] Joint ventures and wholly owned subsidiaries provide greater control and potential returns. Thus, companies which desired to retain a high degree of control over operations in entering the Japanese markets, for example, P & G, Scott, Bristol-Meyers and Ore-Ida, have typically done so through establishing wholly owned subsidiaries rather than joint ventures. Companies with limited experience and expectations with regard to overseas markets may also prefer low commitment modes.[20]

The decision of how to enter a foreign market will also depend on the size of the market and its growth potential, as well as the existence of potential economies of scale and other cost-related factors such as local production costs, shipping costs, and tariff and other barriers. Markets of limited size surrounded by tariff barriers may be supplied most cost effectively via licensing or contract manufacturing. Where there are potential economies of scale, exporting may, however, be preferred. Then, as local market potential builds up and the minimum economic size is reached, a local production and marketing subsidiary may be established.

A firm may also benefit from certain scale economies and other advantages by internalizing or controlling overseas operations rather than contracting them out. These may occur not only in centralization of production, but also in sourcing, R & D, finance, capital asset management, etc. A firm with operations in two or more countries may, for example, be better able to establish large-scale distribution networks and achieve economies in transportation as well as in balancing production scheduling, thus diversifying risk.[21]

The decision with regard to the mode of operation is thus often a key factor in determining the rate of international growth. It not only determines the commitment of resources, and hence risk exposure, in different countries and markets, but also the degree of control exercised over operations and strategy in overseas markets, the flexibility to adjust to changes in market conditions, and the evolution of operations in these markets.

Triggers to Overseas Market Expansion

Once the firm has investigated opportunities overseas and started to establish operations in a number of markets, various factors will trigger a shift in emphasis toward the development of local market potential. The need to develop effective strategies to combat competition in these markets will result in reliance on local market know-how and expertise in local market conditions. The focus thus swings away from foreign opportunity assessment to local market development.

Some of the factors which may underlie this shift are:

• *Concern with increasing market penetration,* and hence adapting or developing new products for the local market;

• *Need to meet local competition,* and to respond to local competitive initiatives in pricing and promotion;

• *Desire to foster local management initiative and motivation;*

• *Concern for more effective utilization of local assets,* i.e., the sales organization and distribution infrastructure, or contacts with local organizations;

• *Constraints imposed by natural market boundaries and barriers* such as transportation systems, media networks, distribution systems and financial and other institutions.

Such pressures lead to adoption of a nationally oriented focus in strategy development. Planning again becomes organized on a domestic or national market basis, though this time in the form of a series of multidomestic markets or businesses.

Phase 2.   Local Market Expansion

Once the firm has firmly established a beachhead in a number of foreign markets, it will begin to seek new directions for growth and expansion, thus moving into the second phase of internationalization. Here, attention is centered on fueling growth in each overseas market and identifying new opportunities within countries where a base of operations has already been established. The expansion effort is, therefore, often directed by local management overseas in each country rather than from corporate headquarters.

The focus shifts toward penetrating local markets more fully, and building on knowledge, experience, and contacts established in the initial phase of entry into overseas markets. Often local management is recruited, and responsibility for strategy development as well as day-to-day operations is shifted to the local subsidiaries, on the grounds that local managers are best qualified to understand the local market environment and to run country operations.[22]

Key Strategic Thrust

The driving force underlying this phase is thus market expansion within countries entered in the initial phase, rather than entering additional markets. Attention is directed to making product and strategy modifications in each country which will broaden the local market base and tap new segments. Product line extensions and new product variants may be considered as well as development of new products and services geared to specific local preferences. The emphasis shifts from "export" of strategy, and its direction from the domestic market base, to development of strategy on a country-by-country basis.

Internationalization Lever

The major lever for effective expansion in this phase is to build strategy based on the organizational structure established in each country, in order to achieve economies of scope and to leverage assets and core competencies so as to foster local market growth. Attention centers on identifying opportunities for shared marketing expenditures, and joint utilization of production and distribution facilities across product lines and product businesses.[23] Administrative overheads may thus be spread across a higher sales volume, reducing unit operating costs. (See Figure 8.3b.) These may include not only sharing of physical assets such as production facilities, or a distribution network, but also intangible assets such as R & D knowledge or market familiarity.[24] The latter may be a particularly critical factor in this phase of operations. Often, the costs associated with initial entry into a country may be substantial, as, for example, in developing familiarity with market conditions and competition, and establishing relations with distributors, agents or regulatory bodies and officials. Consequently, it may be advantageous to amortize such costs across a broad range of products.

In addition to leveraging the organizational structure in each country, proprietary assets such as brand names, and specific skills such as technological expertise, may also be leveraged to expand the product line. The benefits accruing from a well-known brand name or company image may, for example, be further exploited by marketing new products or product variants under the same brand or company names. Swatch, the Swiss fashion watch manufacturer, has leveraged its "chic" image in marketing a range of other products such as sunglasses, casual sweaters and clothing under the Swatch name. Similarly, its well-known company name and its reputation for product quality, reliability and service, may be leveraged in the promotion of new products and product lines, either to end customers or to distributors.

Technological expertise and R & D skills may be applied to the development of new products geared to specific local market needs. P & G has leveraged its expertise in surfactant technology to develop liquid heavy-duty detergents such as Vizir and liquid Ariel adapted to hard-water conditions in Europe. Similarly, marketing and mass-merchandising skills may be spread over a broader range of product or product lines, or applied to the development of new product businesses. In some cases, brands or product businesses may be acquired from local companies. Thus, the firm may be able to capitalize on the "goodwill" or customer franchise associated with an established local brand or local company, while at the same time applying its management expertise and marketing skills to operations management.

Key Decisions

Concern with local market growth implies that the key decisions center around the development of products, product lines and product businesses which offer promise of market growth in each country, as well as strategies to market them effectively in each context. This will, therefore, include not only adaptation and modification of products, but also the development and acquisition of new products and brands. Following the strategic thrust and growth levers, the key criteria in making these decisions are the potential for local market development and the realization of economies of scope.

Product modification and adaptation in order to expand the potential market base, for example, may be examined. In developing countries, machine tool manufacturers may consider streamlining and simplifying their products as well as rendering their use and maintenance easier so as to tap less-sophisticated customer segments. Nabisco reduced the salt content of its snack products and increased the sugar content of its cookies to meet local tastes in Japan. Similarly, Kentucky Fried Chicken reduced the amount of sugar content in its coleslaw, and added fish to its menu in Japan.

Opportunities for developing product variants, extending the product line or developing new products specifically adapted to local market preferences may also be considered. Canada Dry has added a range of different flavors such as melon in the Far East, orange, pineapple and bitter orange in the U.K., and strong ginger in Japan. Heinz developed a special line of rice-based baby foods for the Chinese market, and a fruit-based drink for children called Frutsi for Mexico, which was subsequently rolled out in a number of other Latin American markets. Coca-Cola has also developed a number of products specifically for the Japanese market, including "Georgia," a highly successful canned cold coffee drink, and Real Gold, an isotonic drink. Nabisco has developed "Parfait," thumb-sized chocolate cupcakes for the Japanese markets, as well as Chipstar, a Pringles-type potato chip packaged in a tall can in two flavors, natural and seaweed.

Based on the economies-of-scope criterion, additions of new products or product variants within a country are especially attractive if they enable more effective utilization of the existing operational structure as, for example, administrative capabilities, the distribution network or the sales force, or if they capitalize on experience acquired in operating in a specific market environment, or contacts and relations established with distributors, advertising agencies and other external organizations. As noted previously, such economies are likely to be particularly marked where there are substantial initial investment or set-up costs in establishing contact with distributors, or developing goodwill among the trade in entering a country. In line with the strategic thrust, marketing strategies, including advertising, sales promotion to trade and end users, pricing and distribution channels are geared to local market development. Adaptation of advertising copy and development of new themes should thus be undertaken whenever the costs are outweighed by the potential increase in sales. Similarly, pricing decisions should be designed to stimulate local market penetration. This may, therefore, imply greater attention to pricing based on evaluation of price elasticities in local markets and prices of competing and substitute products rather than on a cost-plus basis.

Triggers to Global Rationalization

The country-by-country orientation associated with this phase, while enabling the consolidation of operations within countries will, however, tend to result in market fragmentation worldwide. Overseas operations functioning as independent profit centers evolve into a patchwork of diverse national businesses. Each national business markets a range of different products and services targeted to different customer segments, utilizing different marketing strategies with little or no coordination of operations between countries. The inefficiencies generated by this system, as well as the external forces integrating markets worldwide, will thus create pressures toward improved coordination across countries.

Some of the factors which may trigger this trend include:

• *Cost inefficiencies and duplication of effort* between country organizations;

• *Opportunities for the transfer of products, brands, and other ideas* and of learning from experience in one country to other countries;

• *Emergence of global customers* in both consumer and industrial markets;

• *Emergence of competition* on a global scale;

• *Improved linkages* between national marketing infrastructures leading to the development of a global marketing infrastructure.

Thus, once again, both internal factors and changes in the external environment will trigger a shift in orientation and create pressures toward global nationalization. Attention will thus center on the elimination of inefficiencies generated by a multiplicity of domestic businesses, and improved coordination and integration of strategy across national boundaries, moving toward the development of strategy on a global rather than a country-by-country basis. (It should, however, be noted that this does not necessarily imply standardization of products, promotion, etc., worldwide, but rather adoption of a global rather than a multi-domestic perspective in designing strategy.)

Phase 3.   Global Rationalization

In the final phase of internationalization, the firm moves toward the adoption of a global orientation in strategy development and implementation. Attention focuses on improving the efficiency of operations worldwide and developing mechanisms for improved transnational coordination of operations and for integrating strategy across countries. Direction shifts toward development of strategy and resource allocation on a global basis. The national orientation thus disappears, and markets are viewed as a set of interrelated, interdependent entities which are becoming increasingly integrated and interlinked worldwide.

Key Strategic Thrust

In this phase, the firm seeks to capitalize on potential synergies arising from operating on a global scale, and seeks to take maximum advantage of the multinational character of its operations. Attention, therefore, centers on optimal allocation of resources across countries, product markets, target segments and marketing strategies so as to maximize profits on a global basis rather than on a country-by-country basis.[24]

A dual thrust is thus adopted, combining a drive to improve the efficiency of operations worldwide with a search for opportunities for global expansion and growth. Greater efficiency may be sought through improved coordination and integration of operations across countries. This includes not only marketing activities such as product development, advertising, distribution and pricing, but also production, sourcing and management. Standardization of product lines across countries, for example, may facilitate improved coordination of production, global sourcing and the establishment of a global production and logistical system, thus resulting in greater cost efficiencies.

At the same time, development on a global scale becomes a key principle guiding strategy formulation. Opportunities for transferring products, brand names, successful marketing ideas or specific skills and expertise acquired or developed in one country to operations in other countries are explored. Global and regional market segments or target customers are also identified, and products and services developed and marketed on a worldwide basis.

Internationalization Levers

In this phase, the key levers lie in exploitation of potential synergies arising from operating on a global scale. Skills or assets which are transferable across national boundaries such as production technology, management expertise and brand or company image, for example, may be leveraged globally. (See figure 8.3c.) While a similar type of leverage occurs in the initial phase from the domestic market to an overseas market, leverage across multiple markets has a synergistic effect.

Improved coordination and integration of marketing strategy across countries may also facilitate realization of potential economies of scale in production and logistics as well as the employment of skills and expertise which would not otherwise be feasible. Leverage may also be achieved through the transfer of experiences, skills and resources from one country or product business to another. Products or promotional campaigns successful in one country may, for example, be transferred to another, just as cash or profits from one business or country may be used to grow a business or compete aggressively in another country.[25]

Key Decisions

Following the dual strategic thrust, key decisions focus on (a) improving the efficiency of operations worldwide and (b) developing a global strategy.

Improving Efficiency
Efficiency may be increased by improved coordination and rationalization of operations across countries and between different functional areas. This may result in consolidation or centralization of R & D, production, sourcing or other activities, thus eliminating duplication of effort as well as allowing for realization of potential economies of scale.

For example, in 1982 Black and Decker operated 25 plants in 13 countries on six continents. Overseas operations were organized into three operating groups, below which were individual companies which operated autonomously in more than 50 countries with little or no communication between them.[26] This led to considerable duplication of effort. For example, its eight design centers produced 260 different motor sizes. A global restructuring of operations reduced this number to ten.

Similarly, in preparation for 1992, Suchard, the Swiss packaged goods manufacturer, is rationalizing production operations on a Europe-wide scale. Production of individual brands is being consolidated in specific factories to gain manufacturing economies of scale. A plant outside Stuttgart and one in Paris were recently closed, and production transferred to plants outside Basel and Strasbourg. Other factories have been modernized and equipped with state-of-the-art automation and flexible manufacturing systems to drive costs down further.[27] Similarly, Electrolux has either closed or focused every factory it has acquired over the past ten years. It now manufactures all front-loading washing machines in Pordenone, Italy, all top-loaders in Revin, France, and all microwave ovens in Luton, England.

Scott Paper has also developed a pan-European approach for 1992, which encompasses not only production and logistics, but also marketing and financial operations. Plants in the U.K., France, Spain, Italy and Belgium still supply predominantly local markets, since tissue and paper towels are high volume/low price items where transportation costs outweigh gains from a high degree production centralization. Brand names such as Scottex are, however, used throughout Europe (with the exception of the U.K.) and experience in product launches, brand positioning and advertising in one market are applied in others. Three new plants are being constructed in France, Italy and Spain, and will all use the same technology, thus allowing for the sharing and transfer of experience in plant management. Capital is now being borrowed globally, rather than being raised locally on a country-by-country basis.

In fact, opportunities for rationalization of production, sourcing and logistical systems are enhanced by product standardization across countries. Moves toward greater product standardization thus open up possibilities for increased rationalization upstream.[28] The Stanley Works, for example, decided to effect a compromise between French preferences for handsaws with plastic handles and "soft" teeth and British preferences for handsaws with wooden handles and "hard" teeth, by producing a plastic-handled saw with "hard" teeth. The objective was thus to consolidate production for the two markets and realize substantial economies of scale.

Improved coordination of marketing strategies, such as brand names, advertising themes across countries and standardization of products and product lines, can be facilitated by the establishment of coordinating mechanisms between country management groups. These may take the form of coordinating committees which facilitate transfer of information and ideas across groups and are responsible for coordinating and integrating their activities, or the widely publicized Eurobrand teams developed by P & G, or regional marketing or sales organizations such as that established by Ford of Europe to direct activities within the region.

Global Strategy Development
In addition to improving the efficiency of existing operations, a global strategy should be established to guide the direction of the firm's efforts, and the allocation of resources across countries, product businesses, target segments and modes of operation worldwide. This should combine global vision and the integration of activities across national boundaries with responsiveness to local market conditions and demand.

A global strategy should determine the customers and segments to be targeted, as well as their specific needs and interest, and the geographic configuration of segments and their needs. As markets for both industrial and consumer products become increasingly international, opportunities for identifying segments which are regional or global rather than national in scope are on the increase. Thus, for example, Bodyshop targets its shampoos and body oils to those concerned with ecology and animal rights, desiring natural-based products not tested on animals, as is generally the case. In the advertising industry, Saatchi and Saatchi targets corporations with multinational operations, supplying services and meeting their needs worldwide.

Marketing programs to meet the specified needs of these regional and global target segments also must be established. This will require putting into place the organization to implement the program. In some instances, this requires establishing an organizational infrastructure which matches that of potential customers. Companies servicing the needs of multinational corporations may establish a system of account executives, with an executive specifically responsible for ensuring that the needs of a given client are satisfied worldwide.

Citibank, for example, instituted a Global Account Management System to coordinate world relations with large multinational corporations and develop its international business. Prior to this reorganization, clients were serviced on a geographic basis, i.e., by the country office for the country in which they were located. Each country branch had responsibility for operations within its area, including both local companies and subsidiaries of multinational corporations, and acted as a local profit center. This led to a number of problems, as local country management often preferred to lend to a local borrower rather than the subsidiary of a multinational corporation, as "spreads," and hence profitability, were perceived to be higher and more likely to generate additional business. In addition, internal communications were fraught with difficulties, as client account managers in the U.S., were not in contact or often even aware of their counterparts handling the client's subsidiaries in a foreign country.

Another decision is the appropriate mix of product businesses worldwide. Here, their complementarity in meeting production, resource or cashflow requirements on an international basis needs to be considered. Thus, for example, Thomson has retained a semiconductor business in France in order to supply its consumer electronics businesses worldwide. Similarly, BiTicino uses profits from its protected domestic light switch business to finance R & D for the development of its global fiber-optics business.

Effective implementation of a global rationalization strategy thus necessitates establishment of mechanisms to coordinate and control activities and flows of information and resources, both across national boundaries and product businesses.[29] In addition, coordination with other functional areas such as production, logistics and finance, will need to be achieved.

Thus, in some cases, a radical restructuring of the organizational structure and management system, including lines of responsibility and communication, may be required to achieve globalization.

Conclusions

Strategy formulation in international markets is thus an evolutionary process, in which the dominant strategic thrust, the international levers and, consequently, the key decisions vary at each successive phase of involvement in international operations. The major strategic challenges facing the firm, how to transfer strategies and skills developed in response to local market conditions to markets overseas; how to acquire and build on local market knowledge and experience; and how to take advantage of potential synergies of multinational operations, will thus differ in each phase.

The dynamic character of international operations thus implies that strategic priorities should be tailored to the stage of evolution in international markets. Thus, rather than assuming, as is commonly the case, that the basic parameters underlying strategy formulation and specifically the key decisions will be the same for all firms, recognition that these will depend on the nature and evolution of international operations is imperative. Strategy should thus be formulated in the light of the firm's current position overseas, and geared to its vision of growth and future position in markets worldwide. The pattern of strategy evolution in international markets suggests a number of prescriptions for the successful formulation of global strategy.

In the first place, strategy should be tailored to the degree of experience in overseas markets. Thus, in the initial phase of international market entry, the firm's key strength is likely to lie in its existing (domestic) product line and attention should be focused on acquiring experience in marketing that line overseas. As this experience builds up, emphasis should shift to new product development geared to overseas market needs. Only in the final stages, once experience in both marketing and new product development for international markets has been acquired, should the more complex issue of strategy integration and coordination across country markets be addressed.

Secondly, potential economies of scale and scope should be maximized. Economies of scale may be realized through attention to opportunities for marketing existing product lines on a broader geographic scale, while centralizing production and sourcing operations, and extending management and logistical systems. Economies of scope, on the other hand, will be achieved through identification of opportunities for shared production, marketing and distribution facilities, and utilization of the same management and logistical systems by different product lines or product businesses.

Thirdly, marketing strategy, especially relating to product line decisions and product standardization, should be closely coordinated with production and sourcing operations. This establishes guidelines for the design of management, information and logistical systems to direct these operations. Effective coordination of key strategy components becomes especially crucial as the scope and complexity of international operations expand and improved global rationalization of strategy is achieved.

Finally, the ultimate goal of global strategy should be to achieve optimal integration and rationalization of operations and decision systems on a global scale. Potential synergies arising from coordination and integration of strategy and of decision systems across country and product markets will thus be captured, and maximal efficiency in the allocation of resources worldwide achieved. Focus on the unique advantages provided by the multinational character of operations is thus the key to the formulation of a successful strategy in a global marketplace.

Notes

1. Cavusgil and Nevin, 1981; Keegan, 1969; Hill and Still, 1984.

2. Levitt, 1983; Douglas and Craig, 1986; Douglas and Wind, 1987; Walters, 1986.

3. Vernon, 1966; Wells, 1972.

4. Davidson, 1983; Hirsh, 1967.

5. Johanson and Vahlue, 1977; Johanson and Wiedershein-Paul, 1975; Wiedershein-Paul, Olson and Welch 1978; Cavusgil, 1980.

6. Perlmutter, 1969.

7. Day, 1981.

8. Rapp, 1973.

9. *Business Week*, May 15, 1989.

10. Caves, 1982.

11. Davidson, 1980.

12. Johanson and Wiedershein-Paul, 1975.

13. Doyle and Gidengil, 1976; Davidson, 1980, 1982.

14. Ayal and Zif, 1979.

15. Goodnow and Hanz, 1972.

16. Root, 1982.

17. Anderson and Gatignon, 1986; Gatignon and Anderson 1987; Root, 1982.

18. Anderson and Gatignon, 1986.

19. Contractor, 1985.

20. Bilkey, 1978.

21. Aliber, 1970.

22. Perlmutter, 1969.

23. Teece, 1980, 1983.

24. Wind and Douglas, 1981.

25. Hamel and Prahalad, 1985.

26. Saporito, 1984.

27. Friberg, 1989.

28. Takeuchi and Porter, 1986.

29. Ghoshal, 1987; Bartlett and Ghoshal, 1986.

References

Abegglen, James G., and George Stalk, Jr., "The Japanese Corporation as Competition." *California Management Review*, 28, Spring, pp. 9–27, 1986.

"Alain Gomez, France's High Tech Warrior." *Business Week*, May 15, 1989, pp. 100–106.

Aliber, Robert Z., "A Theory of Direct Foreign Investment," in Charles P. Kindleberger (ed.), *The International Corporation: A Symposium*, Cambridge, Mass., 1970, pp. 17–34.

Anderson, Erin, and Hubert Gatignon. "Modes of Foreign Entry: Transaction Cost Analysis and Propositions," *Journal of International Business Studies*, 11, Fall, 1986, pp. 1–26.

Ayal, Igal, and Jehiel Zif, "Market Expansion Strategies in Multinational Marketing," *Journal of Marketing*, 43, Spring, 1979, pp. 84–94.

Bartlett, Christopher A., and Sumantra Ghoshal, "Tap Your Subsidiaries for Global Reach," *Harvard Business Review*, November-December, 1986, pp. 87–94.

Bilkey, Warren J., "An attempted Integration of the Literature on the Export Behavior of Firms," *Journal of International Business Studies*, 9, Spring-Summer, 1978, pp. 33–46.

Caves, Richard E., *Multinational Enterprise and Economic Analysis*, Cambridge: Cambridge University Press, 1982.

Cavusgil, S. Tamer, "On the Internationalization Process of Firms," *European Research*, 8, November, 1980, pp. 273–281.

Cavusgil, S. Tamer, and John R. Nevin, "State-of-the-Art in International Marketing: An Assessment," *Review of Marketing 1981*, Ben M. Enis and Kenneth J. Roering (eds.), Chicago: American Marketing Association, 1981, pp. 195–216.

Contractor, Farok, *Licensing in International Strategy: A Guide for Planning and Negotiation*, Westport, CT: Greenwood Press, Quorum Books, 1985.

Davidson, William H., "Marketing Similarity and Market Selection: Implications for International Market Strategy," *Journal of Business Research*, 11, December, 1983, pp. 439–456.

Davidson, William H., *Global Strategic Management*, New York: John Wiley and Sons, 1982.

Davidson, William H., "The Location of Foreign Direct Investment Activity: Country Characteristics and Experience Effects," *Journal of International Business Studies*, 3, Spring, 1980, pp. 33–50.

Day, George, "The Product Life Cycle: Analysis and Application Issues," *Journal of Marketing*, 45, Fall, 1981, pp. 60–67.

Douglas, Susan P., and C. Samuel Craig, "Global Marketing Myopia," *Journal of Marketing Management*, 2. Winter, 1986, pp. 155–169.

Douglas, Susan P., and Yoram Wind, "The Myth of Globalization," *Columbia Journal of World Business*, Winter, 1987, pp. 19–29.

Doyle, Peter, and Zeki Gidengil, "A Strategic Approach for International Market Selection," *Proceedings of the European Academy for Advanced Research in Marketing*, Copenhagen, 1976.

Friberg, Erin, "1992: Moves Europeans Are Making," *Harvard Business Review*, May-June, 1989, pp. 85–89.

Gatignon, Hubert, and Erin Anderson, "The Multinational Corporation's Degree of Control over Foreign Subsidiaries: An Empirical Test of a Transaction Cost Explanation," MSI Report No. 87-103, October, 1987, pp. 1–41.

Ghoshal, Sumantra, "Global Strategy: An Organizing Framework," *Strategic Management Journal*, 8, 1987, pp. 425–440.

Goodnow, James D., and James E. Hanz, "Environmental Determinants of Overseas Market Entry Strategies," *Journal of International Business Studies*, 3, Spring, 1972, pp. 33–50.

Hamel, Gary, and C. K. Prahalad, "Do You Really Have a Global Strategy?" *Harvard Business Review*, July-August, 1985, pp. 139–144.

Hill, J. S., and R. R. Still, "Adapting Products to LDC Tastes," *Harvard Business Review*, 62, March-April, 1984, pp. 92–101.

Hirsh, Sev, *Location of Industry and International Competitiveness*, Oxford: Clarendon Press, 1967.

Johanson, Jan, and Finn Wiedershein-Paul, "The Internationalization of the Firm—
Four Swedish Cases," *Journal of Management Studies*, October, 1975, pp. 305–322.

Johanson, Jan, and Jan-Erik Vahlue, "The Internationalization Process of the Firm
—A Model of Knowledge Development and Increasing Foreign Market Commitments," *Journal of International Business Studies*, Spring/Summer, 1977, pp. 47–
58.

Keegan, Warren J., "Multinational Product Planning: Strategic Alternatives," *Journal of Marketing*, January, 1969, pp. 58–62.

Levitt, T., "The Globalization of Markets," *Harvard Business Review*, May-June
1983, pp. 92–102.

Perlmutter, Howard, "The Tortuous Evolution of the Multinational Corporation,"
Columbia Journal of World Business, January-February, 1969.

Prahalad, C. K., and Yves Doz, *The Multinational Mission*, New York: The Free
Press, 1987.

Rapp, W. V. "Strategy Formulation and International Competition," *Columbia Journal of World Business*, Summer, 1973, pp. 98–112.

Root, Franklin J., *Foreign Market Entry Strategies*, New York: AMACON, 1982.

Saporito, Bill, "Black and Decker's Gamble on Globalization," *Fortune*, May 14,
1984.

Takeuchi, H., and M. E. Porter, "The Strategic Role of International Marketing:
Managing the Nature and Extent of Worldwide Coordination," in Michael E.
Porter (ed.), *Competition in Global Industries*, Boston: Harvard Graduate School of
Business Administration, 1986.

Teece, David J., "Economies of Scope and the Scope of the Enterprise," *Journal of
Economic Behavior and Organization*, 1, 1980, pp. 233–247.

Teece, David J., "Technological and Organizational Factors in the Theory of the
Multinational Enterprise," in Mark Casson (ed.), *The Growth of International Business*, New York: George Allen and Irwin, 1983, pp. 51–62.

Vernon, Raymond, "International Investment and International Trade in the Product Cycle." *Quarterly Journal of Economics*, May 1966, pp. 190–207.

Walters, Peter G. P., "International Marketing Policy: A Discussion of the Standardization Construct and Its Relevance for Corporate Policy," *Journal of International Business Studies*, Summer, 1986, pp. 55–69.

Wells, Louis T., *The Product Life-Cycle and International Trade*, Boston: Division of
Research, Harvard Graduate School of Business Administration, 1972.

Wiedershein-Paul, Finn, Haus G. Olson and Lawrence S. Welch, "Pre-Export Activity: the First in Internationalization," *Journal of International Business Studies*, Spring/
Summer, 1978, pp. 47–58.

Wind, Y., and S. Douglas, "International Portfolio Analysis and Strategy: The
Challenge of the 1980s," *Journal of International Business Studies*, Special Issue, Fall,
1981.

9   The Globalization of Markets

Theodore Levitt

A powerful force drives the world toward a converging commonality, and that force is technology. It has proletarianized communication, transport, and travel. It has made isolated places and impoverished peoples eager for modernity's allurements. Almost everyone everywhere wants all the things they have heard about, seen, or experienced via the new technologies.

The result is a new commercial reality—the emergence of global markets for standardized consumer products on a previously unimagined scale of magnitude. Corporations geared to this new reality benefit from enormous economies of scale in production, distribution, marketing, and management. By translating these benefits into reduced world prices, they can decimate competitors that still live in the disabling grip of old assumptions about how the world works.

Gone are accustomed differences in national or regional preference. Gone are the days when a company could sell last year's models—or lesser versions of advanced products—in the less-developed world. And gone are the days when prices, margins, and profits abroad were generally higher than at home.

The globalization of markets is at hand. With that, the multinational commercial world nears its end, and so does the multinational corporation.

The multinational corporation and the global corporation are not the same thing. The multinational corporation operates in a number of countries, and adjusts its products and practices in each—at high relative costs. The global corporation operates with resolute constancy—at low relative cost —as if the entire world (or major regions of it) were a single entity; it sells the same things in the same way everywhere.

Which strategy is better is not a matter of opinion but of necessity. Worldwide communications carry everywhere the constant drumbeat of

From *Harvard Business Review*, May/June 1983, pp. 92–102. Reprinted by permission.

modern possibilities to lighten and enhance work, raise living standards, divert, and entertain. The same countries that ask the world to recognize and respect the individuality of their cultures insist on the wholesale transfer to them of modern goods, services, and technologies. Modernity is not just a wish but also a widespread practice among those who cling, with unyielding passion or religious fervor, to ancient attitudes and heritages.

Who can forget the televised scenes during the 1979 Iranian uprisings of young men in fashionable French-cut trousers and silky body shirts thirsting with raised modern weapons for blood in the name of Islamic fundamentalism?

In Brazil, thousands swarm daily from pre-industrial Bahian darkness into exploding coastal cities, there quickly to install television sets in crowded corrugated huts and, next to battered Volkswagens, make sacrificial offerings of fruit and fresh-killed chickens to Macumban spirits by candlelight.

During Biafra's fratricidal war against the Ibos, daily televised reports showed soldiers carrying bloodstained swords and listening to transistor radios while drinking Coca-Cola.

In the isolated Siberian city of Krasnoyarsk, with no paved streets and censored news, occasional Western travelers are stealthily propositioned for cigarettes, digital watches, and even the clothes off their backs.

The organized smuggling of electronic equipment, used automobiles, Western clothing, cosmetics, and pirated movies into primitive places exceeds even the thriving underground trade in modern weapons and their military mercenaries.

A thousand suggestive ways attest to the ubiquity of the desire for the most advanced things that the world makes and sells—goods of the best quality and reliability at the lowest price. The world's needs and desires have been irrevocably homogenized. This makes the multinational corporation obsolete and the global corporation absolute.

Living in the Republic of Technology

Daniel J. Boorstin, author of the monumental trilogy *The Americans*, characterized our age as driven by "the Republic of Technology [whose] supreme law ... is convergence, the tendency for everything to become more like everything else."

In business, this trend has pushed markets toward global commonality. Corporations sell standardized products in the same way everywhere —autos, steel, chemicals, petroleum, cement, agricultural commodities and equipment, industrial and commercial construction, banking and insurance services, computers, semiconductors, transport, electronic instruments, pharmaceuticals, and telecommunications, to mention some of the obvious.

Nor is the sweeping gale of globalization confined to these raw-material or high-tech products, where the universal language of customers and users facilitates standardization. The transforming winds whipped up by the proletarianization of communication and travel enter every crevice of life.

Commercially, nothing confirms this as much as the success of McDonald's from the Champs Elysées to the Ginza, of Coca-Cola in Bahrain and Pepsi-Cola in Moscow, and of rock music, Greek salad, Hollywood movies, Revlon cosmetics, Sony televisions, and Levi jeans everywhere. "High-touch" products are as ubiquitous as high-tech.

Starting from opposing sides, the high-tech and the high-touch ends of the commercial spectrum gradually consume the undistributed middle in their cosmopolitan orbit. No one is exempt and nothing can stop the process. Everywhere everything gets more and more like everything else as the world's preference structure is relentlessly homogenized.

Consider the cases of Coca-Cola and Pepsi-Cola, which are globally standardized products sold everywhere and welcomed by everyone. Both successfully cross multitudes of national, regional, and ethnic taste buds trained to a variety of deeply ingrained local preferences of taste, flavor, consistency, effervescence, and aftertaste. Everywhere both sell well. Cigarettes, too, especially American-made, make year-to-year global inroads on territories previously held in the firm grip of other, mostly local, blends.

These are not exceptional examples. (Indeed their global reach would be even greater were it not for artificial trade barriers.) They exemplify a general drift toward the homogenization of the world and how companies distribute, finance, and price products.[1] Nothing is exempt. The products and methods of the industrialized world play a single tune for all the world, and all the world eagerly dances to it.

Ancient differences in national tastes or modes of doing business disappear. The commonality of preference leads inescapably to the standardization of products, manufacturing, and the institutions of trade and commerce. Small nation-based markets transmogrify and expand. Success in world competition turns on efficiency in production, distribution, marketing, and management, and inevitably becomes focused on price.

The most effective world competitors incorporate superior quality and reliability into their cost structures. They sell in all national markets the same kind of products sold at home or in their largest export market. They compete on the basis of appropriate value—the best combinations of price, quality, reliability, and delivery for products that are globally identical with respect to design, function, and even fashion.

That, and little else, explains the surging success of Japanese companies dealing worldwide in a vast variety of products—both tangible products like steel, cars, motorcyles, hi-fi equipment, farm machinery, robots, microprocessors, carbon fibers, and now even textiles, and intangibles like banking, shipping, general contracting, and soon computer software. Nor are high-quality and low-cost operations incompatible, as a host of consulting organizations and data engineers argue with vigorous vacuity. The reported data are incomplete, wrongly analyzed, and contradictory. The truth is that low-cost operations are the hallmark of corporate cultures that require and produce quality in all that they do. High quality and low costs are not opposing postures. They are compatible, twin identities of superior practice.[2]

To say that Japan's companies are not global because they export cars with left-side drives to the United States and the European continent, while those in Japan have right-side drives, or because they sell office machines through distributors in the United States but directly at home, or speak Portuguese in Brazil is to mistake a difference for a distinction. The same is true of Safeway and Southland retail chains operating effectively in the Middle East, and to not only native but also imported populations from Korea, the Philippines, Pakistan, India, Thailand, Britain, and the United States. National rules of the road differ, and so do distribution channels and languages. Japan's distinction is its unrelenting push for economy and value enhancement. That translates into a drive for standardization at high quality levels.

Vindication of the Model T

If a company forces costs and prices down and pushes quality and reliability up—while maintaining reasonable concern for suitability—customers will prefer its world-standardized products. The theory holds, at this stage in the evolution of globalization, no matter what conventional market research and even common sense may suggest about different national and regional tastes, preferences, needs, and institutions. The Japanese have repeatedly vindicated this theory, as did Henry Ford with the Model T. Most important, so have their imitators, including companies from South Korea (television sets and heavy construction), Malaysia (personal calculators and microcomputers), Brazil (auto parts and tools), Colombia (apparel), Singapore (optical equipment), and yes, even from the United States (office copiers, computers, bicycles, castings), Western Europe (automatic washing machines), Rumania (housewares), Hungary (apparel), Yugoslavia (furniture), and Israel (pagination equipment).

Of course, large companies operating in a single nation or even a single city don't standardize everything they make, sell, or do. They have product lines instead of a single-product version, and multiple distribution channels. There are neighborhood, local, regional, ethnic, and institutional differences, even within metropolitan areas. But although companies customize products for particular market segments, they know that success in a world with homogenized demand requires a search for sales opportunities in similar segments across the globe in order to achieve the economies of scale necessary to compete.

Such a search works because a market segment in one country is seldom unique; it has close cousins everywhere precisely because technology has homogenized the globe. Even small local segments have their global equivalents everywhere and become subject to global competition, especially on price.

The global competitor will seek constantly to standardize his offering everywhere. He will digress from this standardization only after exhausting all possibilities to retain it, and he will push for reinstatement of standardization whenever digression and divergence have occurred. He will never assume that the customer is a king who knows his own wishes.

Trouble increasingly stalks companies that lack clarified global focus and remain inattentive to the economics of simplicity and standardization. The most endangered companies in the rapidly evolving world tend to be those that dominate rather small domestic markets with high value-added products for which there are smaller markets elsewhere. With transportation costs proportionately low, distant competitors will enter the now-sheltered markets of those companies with goods produced more cheaply under scale-efficient conditions. Global competition spells the end of domestic territoriality, no matter how diminutive the territory may be.

When the global producer offers his lower costs internationally, his patronage expands exponentially. He not only reaches into distant markets, but also attracts customers who previously held to local preferences and now capitulate to the attractions of lesser prices. The strategy of standardization not only responds to worldwide homogenized markets but also expands those markets with aggressive low pricing. The new technological juggernaut taps an ancient motivation—to make one's money go as far as possible. This is universal—not simply a motivation but actually a need.

Box 9.1
Economies of Scope

One argument that opposes globalization says that flexible factory automation will enable plants of massive size to change products and product features quickly, without stopping the manufacturing process. These factories of the future could thus produce broad lines of customized products without sacrificing the scale economies that come from long production runs of standardized items. Computer-aided design and manufacturing (CAD/CAM), combined with robotics, will create a new equipment and process technology (EPT) that will make small plants located close to their markets as efficient as large ones located distantly. Economies of scale will not dominate, but rather economies of scope—the ability of either large or small plants to produce great varieties of relatively customized products at remarkably low costs. If that happens, customers will have no need to abandon special preferences.

I will not deny the power of these possibilities. But possibilities do not make probabilities. There is no conceivable way in which flexible factory automation can achieve the scale economies of a modernized plant dedicated to mass production of standardized lines. The new digitized equipment and process technologies are available to all. Manufacturers with minimal customization and narrow product-line breadth will have costs far below those with more customization and wider lines.

The Hedgehog Knows

The difference between the hedgehog and the fox, wrote Sir Isaiah Berlin in distinguishing between Dostoevski and Tolstoy, is that the fox knows a lot about a great many things, but the hedgehog knows everything about one great thing. The multinational corporation knows a lot about a great many countries and congenially adapts to supposed differences. It willingly accepts vestigial national differences, not questioning the possibility of their transformation, not recognizing how the world is ready and eager for the benefit of modernity, especially when the price is right. The multinational corporation's accommodating mode to visible national differences is medieval.

By contrast, the global corporation knows everything about one great thing. It knows about the absolute need to be competitive on a worldwide basis as well as nationally and seeks constantly to drive down prices by standardizing what it sells and how it operates. It treats the world as composed of few standardized markets rather than many customized markets. It actively seeks and vigorously works toward global convergence. Its mission is modernity and its mode, price competition, even when it sells top-of-the-line, high-end products. It knows about the one great thing all nations and people have in common: scarcity.

Nobody takes scarcity lying down; everyone wants more. This in part explains division of labor and specialization of production. They enable people and nations to optimize their conditions through trade. The medium is usually money.

Experience teaches that money has three special qualities: scarcity, difficulty of acquisition, and transience. People understandably treat it with respect. Everyone in the increasingly homogenized world market wants products and features that everybody else wants. If the price is low enough, they will take highly standardized world products, even if these aren't exactly what mother said was suitable, what immemorial custom decreed was right, or what market-research fabulists asserted was preferred.

The implacable truth of all modern production—whether of tangible or intangible goods—is that large-scale production of standardized items is generally cheaper within a wide range of volume than small-scale production. Some argue that CAD/CAM will allow companies to manufacture customized products on a small scale—but cheaply. But the argument misses the point. (For a more detailed discussion, see the insert, "Economies of Scope.") If a company treats the world as one or two distinctive product markets, it can serve the world more economically than if it treats it as three, four, or five product markets.

Why Remaining Differences?

Different cultural preferences, national tastes and standards, and business institutions are vestiges of the past. Some inheritances die gradually; others prosper and expand into mainstream global preferences. So-called ethnic markets are a good example. Chinese food, pita bread, country and western music, pizza, and jazz are everywhere. They are market segments that exist in worldwide proportions. They don't deny or contradict global homogenization but confirm it.

Many of today's differences among nations as to products and their features actually reflect the respectful accommodation of multinational corporations to what they believe are fixed local preferences. They *believe* preferences are fixed, not because they are but because of rigid habits of thinking about what actually is. Most executives in multinational corporations are thoughtlessly accommodating. They falsely presume that marketing means giving the customer what he says he wants rather than trying to understand exactly what he'd like. So they persist with high-cost, customized multinational products and practices instead of pressing hard and pressing properly for global standardization.

I do not advocate the systematic disregard of local or national differences. But a company's sensitivity to such differences does not require that it ignore the possibilities of doing things differently or better.

There are, for example, enormous differences among Middle Eastern countries. Some are socialist, some monarchies, some republics. Some take their legal heritage from the Napoleonic Code, some from the Ottoman Empire, and some from the British common law; except for Israel, all are influenced by Islam. Doing business means personalizing the business relationship in an obsessively intimate fashion. During the month of Ramadan, business discussions can start only after 10 o'clock at night, when people are tired and full of food after a day of fasting. A company must almost certainly have a local partner; a local lawyer is required (as, say, in New York), and irrevocable letters of credit are essential. Yet, as Coca-Cola's Senior Vice President Sam Ayoub noted, "Arabs are much more capable of making distinctions between cultural and religious purposes on the one hand and economic realities on the other than is generally assumed. Islam is compatible with science and modern times."

Barriers to globalization are not confined to the Middle East. The free transfer of technology and data across the boundaries of the European Common Market countries are hampered by legal and financial impediments. And there is resistance to radio and television interference ("pollution") among neighboring European countries.

But the past is a good guide to the future. With persistence and appropriate means, barriers against superior technologies and economics have always fallen. There is no recorded exception where reasonable effort has been made to overcome them. It is very much a matter of time and effort.

A Failure in Global Imagination

Many companies have tried to standardize world practice by exporting domestic products and processes without accommodation or change—and have failed miserably. Their deficiencies have been seized on as evidence of bovine stupidity in the face of abject impossibility. Advocates of global standardization see them as examples of failures in execution.

In fact, poor execution is often an important cause. More important, however, is failure of nerve—failure of imagination.

Consider the case for the introduction of fully automatic home laundry equipment in Western Europe at a time when few homes had even semiautomatic machines. Hoover, Ltd., whose parent company was headquartered in North Canton, Ohio, had a prominent presence in Britain as a producer of vacuum cleaners and washing machines. Due to insufficient demand in the home market and low exports to the European continent, the large washing machine plant in England operated far below capacity. The company needed to sell more of its semiautomatic or automatic machines.

Because it had a "proper" marketing orientation, Hoover conducted consumer preference studies in Britain and each major continental country. The results showed feature preferences clearly enough among several countries (see table 9.1).

The incremental unit variable costs (in pounds sterling) of customizing to meet just a few of the national preferences are shown in table 9.2. Considerable plant investment was needed to meet other preferences.

The lowest retail prices (in pounds sterling) of leading locally produced brands in the various countries are shown in table 9.3.

Product customization in each country would have put Hoover in a poor competitive position on the basis of price, mostly due to the higher manufacturing costs incurred by short production runs for separate features. Because Common Market tariff reduction programs were then incomplete, Hoover also paid tariff duties in each continental country.

How to Make a Creative Analysis

In the Hoover case, an imaginative analysis of automatic washing machine sales in each country would have revealed that:

1. Italian automatics, small in capacity and size, low-powered, without built-in heaters, with porcelain enamel tubs, were priced aggressively low and were gaining large market shares in all countries, including West Germany.

2. The best-selling automatics in West Germany were heavily advertised (three times more than the next most promoted brand), were ideally suited to national tastes, and were also by far the highest priced machines available in that country.

3. Italy, with the lowest penetration of washing machines of any kind (manual, semiautomatic, or automatic) was rapidly going directly to automatics, skipping the pattern of first buying hand-wringer, manually assisted machines and then semiautomatics.

4. Detergent manufacturers were just beginning to promote the technique of cold-water and tepid-water laundering then used in the United States.

Table 9.1
Consumer preferences as to automatic washing machine features in the 1960s

Features	Great Britain	Italy	West Germany	France	Sweden
Shell dimensions[a]	34" and narrow	Low and narrow	34" and wide	34" and narrow	34" and wide
Drum material	Enamel	Enamel	Stainless steel	Enamel	Stainless steel
Loading	Top	Front	Front	Front	Front
Front porthole	Yes/no	Yes	Yes	Yes	Yes
Capacity	5 kilos	4 kilos	6 kilos	5 kilos	6 kilos
Spin speed	700 rpm	400 rpm	850 rpm	600 rpm	800 rpm
Water-heating system	No[b]	Yes	Yes[c]	Yes	No[b]
Washing action	Agitator	Tumble	Tumble	Agitator	Tumble
Styling features	Inconspicuous appearance	Brightly colored	Indestructible appearance	Elegant appearance	Strong appearance

a. 34" height was (in the process of being adopted as) a standard work-surface height in Europe.
b. Most British and Swedish homes had centrally heated hot water.
c. West Germans preferred to launder at temperatures higher than generally provided centrally.

Table 9.2
Incremental unit variable costs of laundry equipment

	£	s.	d.
Stainless steel vs. enamel drum	1	0	0
Porthole window		10	0
Spin speed of 800 rpm vs. 700 rpm		15	0
Water heater	2	15	0
6 vs. 5 kilos capacity	1	10	0
Total	£6	10s	0d
	$18.20 at the exchange rate of that time.		

Source: Hoover Ltd.

Table 9.3
Lowest retail prices of washing machines

U.K.	£110
France	114
West Germany	113
Sweden	134
Italy	57

The growing success of small, low-powered, low-speed, low-capacity, low-priced Italian machines, even against the preferred but highly priced and highly promoted brand in West Germany, was significant. It contained a powerful message that was lost on managers confidently wedded to a distorted version of the marketing concept according to which you give the customer what he says he wants. In fact the customers *said* they wanted certain features, but their behavior demonstrated they'd take other features provided the price and the promotion were right.

In this case it was obvious that, under prevailing conditions, people preferred a low-priced automatic over any kind of manual or semiautomatic machine and certainly over higher-priced automatics, even though the low-priced automatics failed to fulfill all their expressed preferences. The supposedly meticulous and demanding German consumers violated all expectations by buying the simple, low-priced Italian machines.

It was equally clear that people were profoundly influenced by promotions of automatic washers; in West Germany, the most heavily promoted ideal machine also had the largest market share despite its high price. Two things clearly influenced customers to buy: low price regardless of feature preferences and heavy promotion regardless of price. Both factors helped homemakers get what they most wanted—the superior benefits bestowed by fully automatic machines.

Hoover should have aggressively sold a simple, standardized high-quality machine at a low price (afforded by the 17% variable cost reduction that the elimination of £6-10-0 worth of extra features made possible). The suggested retail prices could have been somewhat less than £100. The extra funds "saved" by avoiding unnecessary plant modifications would have supported an extended service network and aggressive media promotions.

Hoover's media message should have been *this* is the machine that you, the homemaker, *deserve* to have to reduce the repetitive heavy daily household burdens, so that *you* may have more constructive time to spend with your children and your husband. The promotion should also have targeted the husband to give him, preferably in the presence of his wife, a sense of obligation to provide an automatic washer for her even before he bought an automobile for himself. An aggressively low price, combined with heavy promotion of this kind, would have overcome previously expressed preferences for particular features.

The Hoover case illustrates how the perverse practice of the marketing concept and the absence of any kind of marketing imagination let multinational attitudes survive when customers actually want the benefits of global standardization. The whole project got off on the wrong foot. It asked people what features they wanted in a washing machine rather than what they wanted out of life. Selling a line of products individually tailored to each nation is thoughtless. Managers who took pride in practicing the marketing concept to the fullest did not, in fact, practice it at all. Hoover asked the wrong questions, then applied neither thought nor imagination to the answers. Such companies are like the geocentrists in the Middle Ages who saw with everyday clarity the sun revolving around the earth and offered it as Truth. With no additional data but a more searching mind, Copernicus, like the hedgehog, interpreted a more compelling and accurate reality. Data do not yield information except with the intervention of the mind. Information does not yield meaning except with the intervention of imagination.

Accepting the Inevitable

The global corporation accepts for better or for worse that technology drives consumers relentlessly toward the same common goals—alleviation of life's burdens and the expansion of discretionary time and spending power. Its role is profoundly different from what it has been for the ordinary corporation during its brief, turbulent, and remarkably protean history. It orchestrates the twin vectors of technology and globalization for the world's benefit. Neither fate, nor nature, nor God but rather the necessity of commerce created this role.

In the United States two industries became global long before they were consciously aware of it. After over a generation of persistent and acrimonious labor shutdowns, the United Steelworkers of America have not called an industrywide strike since 1959; the United Auto Workers have not shut down General Motors since 1970. Both unions realize that they have become global—shutting down all or most of U.S. manufacturing would not shut out U.S. customers. Overseas suppliers are there to supply the market.

Cracking the Code of Western Markets

Since the theory of the marketing concept emerged a quarter of a century ago, the more managerially advanced corporations have been eager to offer what customers clearly wanted rather than what was merely convenient. They have created marketing departments supported by professional market researchers of awesome and often costly proportions. And they have proliferated extraordinary numbers of operations and product lines— highly tailored products and delivery systems for many different markets, market segments, and nations.

Significantly, Japanese companies operate almost entirely without marketing departments or market research of the kind so prevalent in the West. Yet, in the colorful words of General Electric's chairman, John F. Welch, Jr., the Japanese, coming from a small cluster of resource-poor islands, with an entirely alien culture and an almost impenetrably complex language, have cracked the code of Western markets. They have done it not by looking with mechanistic thoroughness at the way markets are different but rather by searching for meaning with a deeper wisdom. They have discovered the one great thing all markets have in common—an overwhelming desire for dependable, world-standard modernity in all things, at aggressively low prices. In response, they deliver irresistible value everywhere, attracting people with products that market-research technocrats described with superficial certainty as being unsuitable and uncompetitive.

The wider a company's global reach, the greater the number of regional and national preferences it will encounter for certain product features, distribution systems, or promotional media. There will always need to be some accommodation to differences. But the widely prevailing and often unthinking belief in the immutability of these differences is generally mistaken. Evidence of business failure because of lack of accommodation is often evidence of other shortcomings.

Take the case of Revlon in Japan. The company unnecessarily alienated retailers and confused customers by selling world-standardized cosmetics only in elite outlets; then it tried to recover with low-priced world-standardized products in broader distribution, followed by a change in the company president and cutbacks in distribution as costs rose faster than sales. The problem was not that Revlon didn't understand the Japanese market; it didn't do the job right, wavered in its programs, and was impatient to boot.

By contrast, the Outboard Marine Corporation, with imagination, push, and persistence, collapsed long-established three-tiered distribution channels in Europe into a more focused and controllable two-step system—and did so despite the vociferous warnings of local trade groups. It also reduced the number and types of retail outlets. The result was greater improvement in credit and product-installation service to customers, major cost reductions, and sales advances.

In its highly successful introduction of Contac 600 (the timed-release decongestant) into Japan, SmithKline Corporation used 35 wholesalers instead of the 1,000-plus that established practice required. Daily contacts with the wholesalers and key retailers, also in violation of established practice, supplemented the plan, and it worked.

Denied access to established distribution institutions in the United States, Komatsu, the Japanese manufacturer of lightweight farm machinery, entered the market through over-the-road construction equipment dealers in rural areas of the Sunbelt, where farms are smaller, and the soil sandier and easier to work. Here inexperienced distributors were able to attract customers on the basis of Komatsu's product and price appropriateness.

In cases of successful challenge to prevailing institutions and practices, a combination of product reliability and quality, strong and sustained support systems, aggressively low prices, and sales-compensation packages, as well as audacity and implacability, circumvented, shattered, and transformed very different distribution systems. Instead of resentment, there was admiration.

Still, some differences between nations are unyielding, even in a world of microprocessors. In the United States almost all manufacturers of microprocessors check them for reliability through a so-called parallel system of testing. Japan prefers the totally different sequential testing system. So

Teradyne Corporation, the world's largest producer of microprocessor test equipment, makes one line for the United States and one for Japan. That's easy.

What's not so easy for Teradyne is to know how best to organize and manage, in this instance, its marketing effort. Companies can organize by product, region, function, or by using some combination of these. A company can have separate marketing organizations for Japan and for the United States, or it can have separate product groups, one working largely in Japan and the other in the United States. A single manufacturing facility or marketing operation might service both markets, or a company might use separate marketing operations for each.

Questions arise if the company organizes by product. In the case of Teradyne, should the group handling the parallel system, whose major market is the United States, sell in Japan and compete with the group focused on the Japanese market? If the company organizes regionally, how do regional groups divide their efforts between promoting the parallel vs. the sequential system? If the company organizes in terms of function, how does it get commitment in marketing, for example, for one line instead of the other?

There is no one reliably right answer—no one formula by which to get it. There isn't even a satisfactory contingent answer.[3] What works well for one company or one place may fail for another in precisely the same place, depending on the capabilities, histories, reputations, resources, and even the cultures of both.

The Earth Is Flat

The differences that persist throughout the world despite its globalization affirm an ancient dictum of economics—that things are driven by what happens at the margin, not at the core. Thus, in ordinary competitive analysis, what's important is not the average price but the marginal price; what happens not in the usual case but at the interface of newly erupting conditions. What counts in commercial affairs is what happens at the cutting edge. What is most striking today is the underlying similarities of what is happening now to national preferences at the margin. These similarities at the cutting edge cumulatively form an overwhelming, predominant commonality everywhere.

To refer to the persistence of economic nationalism (protective and subsidized trade practices, special tax aids, or restrictions for home market producers) as a barrier to the globalization of markets is to make a valid

Theodore Levitt 264

point. Economic nationalism does have a powerful persistence. But, as with the present, almost totally smooth, internationalization of investment capital, the past alone does not shape or predict the future. (For reflections on the internationalization of capital, see the insert, "The Shortening of Japanese Horizons.")

Reality is not a fixed paradigm, dominated by immemorial customs and derived attitudes, heedless of powerful and abundant new forces. The world is becoming increasingly informed about the liberating and enhancing possibilities of modernity. The persistence of the inherited varieties of national preferences rests uneasily on increasing evidence of, and restlessness regarding, their inefficiency, costliness, and confinement. The historic past and the national differences respecting commerce and industry it spawned and fostered everywhere are now subject to relatively easy transformation.

Cosmopolitanism is no longer the monopoly of the intellectual and leisure classes; it is becoming the established property and defining characteristic of all sectors everywhere in the world. Gradually and irresistibly it breaks down the walls of economic insularity, nationalism, and chauvinism. What we see today as escalating commercial nationalism is simply the last, violent death rattle of an obsolete institution.

Companies that adapt to and capitalize on economic convergence can still make distinctions and adjustments in different markets. Persistent differences in the world are consistent with fundamental underlying commonalities; they often complement rather than oppose each other—in business as they do in physics. There is, in physics, simultaneously matter and antimatter working in symbiotic harmony.

The earth is round, but for most purposes it's sensible to treat it as flat. Space is curved, but not much for everyday life here on earth.

Divergence from established practice happens all the time. But the multinational mind, warped into circumspection and timidity by years of stumbles and transnational troubles, now rarely challenges existing overseas practices. More often it considers any departure from inherited domestic routines as mindless, disrespectful, or impossible. It is the mind of a bygone day.

The successful global corporation does not abjure customization or differentiation for the requirements of markets that differ in product preferences, spending patterns, shopping preferences, and institutional or legal arrangements. But the global corporation accepts and adjusts to these differences only reluctantly, only after relentlessly testing their immutability, after trying in various ways to circumvent and reshape them as we

Box 9.2
The Shortening of Japanese Horizons

One of the most powerful yet least celebrated forces driving commerce toward global standardization is the monetary system, along with the international investment process.

Today money is simply electronic impulses. With the speed of light it moves effortlessly between distant centers (and even lesser places). A change of ten basis points in the price of a bond causes an instant and massive shift of money from London to Tokyo. The system has profound impact on the way companies operate throughout the world.

The Japan, where high debt-to-equity balance sheets are "guaranteed" by various societal presumptions about the virtue of "a long view," or by government policy in other ways. Even here, upward shifts in interest rates in other parts of the world attract capital out of the country in powerful proportions. In recent years more and more Japanese global corporations have gone to the world's equity markets for funds. Debt is too remunerative in high-yielding countries to keep capital at home to feed the Japanese need. As interest rates rise, equity becomes a more attractive option for the issuer.

The long-term impact on Japanese enterprise will be transforming. As the equity proportion of Japanese corporate capitalization rises, companies will respond to the shorter-term investment horizons of the equity markets. Thus the much-vaunted Japanese corporate practice to taking the long view will gradually disappear.

saw in the cases of Outboard Marine in Europe, SmithKline in Japan, and Komatsu in the United States.

There is only one significant respect in which a company's activities around the world are important, and this is in what it produces and how it sells. Everything else derives from, and is subsidiary to, these activities.

The purpose of business is to get and keep a customer. Or, to use Peter Drucker's more refined construction, to *create* and keep a customer. A company must be wedded to the ideal of innovation—offering better or more preferred products in such combinations of ways, means, places, and at such prices that prospects *prefer* doing business with the company rather than with others.

Preferences are constantly shaped and reshaped. Within our global commonality enormous variety constantly asserts itself and thrives, as can be seen within the world's single largest domestic market, the United States. But in the process of world homogenization, modern markets expand to reach cost-reducing global proportions. With better and cheaper communication and transport, even small local market segments hitherto protected from distant competitors now feel the pressure of their presence. Nobody is safe from global reach and the irresistible economies of scale.

Two vectors shape the world—technology and globalization. The first helps determine human preferences; the second, economic realities. Regardless of how much preferences evolve and diverge, they also gradually converge and form markets where economies of scale lead to reduction of costs and prices.

The modern global corporation contrasts powerfully with the aging multinational corporation. Instead of adapting to superficial and even entrenched differences within and between nations, it will seek sensibly to force suitably standardized products and practices on the entire globe. They are exactly what the world will take, if they come also with low prices, high quality, and blessed reliability. The global company will operate, in this regard, precisely as Henry Kissinger wrote in *Years of Upheaval* about the continuing Japanese economic success—"voracious in its collection of information, impervious to pressure, and implacable in execution."

Given what is everywhere the purpose of commerce, the global company will shape the vectors of technology and globalization into its great strategic fecundity. It will systematically push these vectors toward their own convergence, offering everyone simultaneously high-quality, more or less standardized products at optimally low prices, thereby achieving for itself vastly expanded markets and profits. Companies that do not adapt to the new global realities will become victims of those that do.

Notes

1. In a landmark article, Robert D. Buzzell pointed out the rapidity with which barriers to standardization were falling. In all cases they succumbed to more and cheaper advanced ways of doing things. See "Can You Standardize Multinational Marketing?" *Harvard Business Review*, November-December 1968, p. 102.

2. There is powerful new evidence for this, even though the opposite has been urged by analysts of PIMS data for nearly a decade. See "Product Quality: Cost Production and Business Performance—A Test of Some Key Hypotheses" by Lynn W. Phillips, Dae Chang, and Robert D. Buzzell, Harvard Business School Working Paper No. 83-13.

3. For a discussion of multinational reorganization, see Christopher A. Bartlett, "MNCs: Get Off the Reorganization Merry-Go-Round," *Harvard Business Review*, March-April 1983, p. 138.

10   Customizing Global Marketing

John A. Quelch and Edward J. Hoff

In the best of all possible worlds, marketers would only have to come up with a great product and a convincing marketing program and they would have a worldwide winner. But despite the obvious economies and efficiencies they could gain with a standard product and program, many managers fear that global marketing, as popularly defined, is too extreme to be practical. Because customers and competitive conditions differ across countries or because powerful local managers will not stand for centralized decision making, they argue, global marketing just won't work.

Of course, global marketing has its pitfalls, but it can also yield impressive advantages. Standardizing products can lower operating costs. Even more important, effective coordination can exploit a company's best product and marketing ideas.

Too often, executives view global marketing as an either/or proposition —either full standardization or local control. But when a global approach can fall anywhere on a spectrum from tight worldwide coordination on programming details to loose agreement on a product idea, why the extreme view? In applying the global marketing concept and making it work, flexibility is essential. Managers need to tailor the approach they use to each element of the business system and marketing program. For example, a manufacturer might market the same product under different brand names in different countries or market the same brands using different product formulas.

The big issue today is not whether to go global but how to tailor the global marketing concept to fit each business and how to make it work. In this article, we'll first provide a framework to help managers think about how they should structure the different areas of the marketing function as the business shifts to a global approach. We will then show how

From *Harvard Business Review*, May/June 1986, pp. 59–68. Reprinted by permission.

companies we have studied are tackling the implementation challenges of global marketing.

How Far to Go

How far a company can move toward global marketing depends a lot on its evolution and traditions. Consider these two examples:

• Although the Coca-Cola Company had conducted some international business before 1940, it gained true global recognition during World War II, as Coke bottling plants followed the march of U.S. troops around the world. Management in Atlanta made all strategic decisions then—and still does now, as Coca-Cola applies global marketing principles, for example, to the worldwide introduction of Diet Coke. The brand name, concentrate formula, positioning, and advertising theme are virtually standard worldwide, but the artificial sweetener and packaging differ across countries. Local managers are responsible for sales and distribution programs, which they run in conjunction with local bottlers.

• The Nestlé approach also has its roots in history. To avoid distribution disruptions caused by wars in Europe, to ease rapid worldwide expansion, and to respond to local consumer needs, Nestlé granted its local managers considerable autonomy from the outset. While the local managers still retain much of that decision-making power today, Nestlé headquarters at Vevey has grown in importance. Nestlé has transferred to its central marketing staff many former local managers who had succeeded in their local Nestlé businesses and who now influence country executives to accept standard new product and marketing ideas. The trend seems to be toward tighter marketing coordination.

To conclude that Coca-Cola is a global marketer and Nestlé is not would be simplistic. In table 10.1, we assess program adaptation or standardization levels for each company's business functions, products, marketing mix elements, and countries. Each company has tailored its individual approach. Furthermore, as table 10.1 can't show, the situations aren't static. Readers can themselves evaluate their own *current* and *desired* levels of program adaptation or standardization on these four dimensions. The gap between the two levels is the implementation challenge. The size of the gap—and the urgency with which it must be closed—will depend on a company's strategy and financial performance, competitive pressures, technological change, and converging consumer values.

Four Dimensions of Global Marketing

Now let's look at the issues that arise when executives consider the four dimensions shown in table 10.1 in light of the degree of standardization or adaptation that is appropriate.

Business Functions
A company's approach to global marketing depends, first, on its overall business strategy. In many multinationals, some functional areas have greater program standardization than others. Headquarters often controls manufacturing, finance, and R & D, while the local managers make the marketing decisions. Marketing is usually one of the last functions to be centrally directed. Partly because product quality and accounting data are easier to measure than marketing effectiveness, standardization can be greater in production and finance.

Products
Products that enjoy high scale economies or efficiencies and are not highly culture-bound are easier to market globally than others.

1. Economies or efficiencies. Manufacturing and R & D scale economies can result in a price spread between the global and the local product that is too great for even the most culture-bound consumer to resist. In addition, management often has neither the time nor the R & D resources to adapt products to each country. The markets for high-tech products like computers are not only very competitive but also affected by rapid technological change.

Most packaged consumer goods are less susceptible than durable goods like televisions and cars to manufacturing or even R & D economies. Coca-Cola's global policy and Nestlé's interest in tighter marketing coordination are driven largely by a desire to capitalize on the marketing ideas their managers around the world generate rather than by potential scale economies. Nestlé, for example, manufactures its packaged soups in dozens of locally managed plants around the world, with some transference of engineering know-how through a headquarters staff. Products and marketing programs are also locally managed, but new ideas are aggressively transferred, with local managers encouraged—or even prodded—to adapt and use them in their own markets. For Nestlé, global marketing does not so much yield high manufacturing economies as high efficiency in using scarce new ideas.

Table 10.1
Global marketing planning matrix: how far to go

	Adaptation		Standardization	
	Full	Partial	Partial	Full
Business function				
Research and development			× × × × ×	○○○○○ ○○
Finance and accounting			× × × × ×	○○○○○ ○○
Manufacturing		× × × × × ×	○○○○○	
Procurement	× × × × × ×		○○○○○	
Marketing		× × × × × ×		
Products				
Low cultural grounding / High economies or efficiencies				○○○○○ ○○
Low cultural grounding / Low economies or efficiencies				○○○○○ ○○
High cultural grounding / High economies or efficiencies	× × × × × ×			
High cultural grounding / Low economies or efficiencies		× × × × × ×		
Marketing mix elements				
Product design			× × × × × ×	○○○○○ ○○
Brand name			× × × × × ×	○○○○○ ○
Product positioning		× × × × × ×		
Packaging			× × ×	○○○○

	Advertising theme	Pricing	Advertising copy	Distribution	Sales promotion	Customer service
Countries						
Region 1						
Country A	× ○	× ○	×	×	×	×
Country B	× ○	× ○	×	×	×	×
Region 2						
Country C	○	○	×	×	×	×
Country D	○	○	×	×	×	×
Country E	○	○	× ○	×	×	×

× × × × × Nestlé   ○ ○ ○ ○ ○ Coca-Cola

2. Cultural grounding. Consumer products used in the home—like Nestlé's soups and frozen foods—are often more culture-bound than products used outside the home such as automobiles and credit cards, and industrial products are inherently less culture-bound than consumer products. (Products like personal computers, for example, are often marketed on the basis of performance benefits that share a common technical language worldwide.) Experience also suggests that products will be less culture-bound if they are used by young people whose cultural norms are not ingrained, people who travel in different countries, and ego-driven consumers who can be appealed to through myths and fantasies shared across cultures.

Table 10.1 lists four combinations of the scale economy and cultural grounding variables in order of their susceptibility to global marketing. Managers shouldn't be bound by any matrix, however; they should find creative ways to prepare a product for global marketing. If a manufacturer develops a new version of a seemingly culture-bound product that is based on new capital-intensive technology and generates superior performance benefits, it may well be possible to introduce it on a standard basis worldwide. Procter & Gamble developed Pampers disposable diapers as a global brand in a product category that intuition would say was culturebound.

Marketing Mix Elements
Few consumer goods companies go so far as to market the same products using the same marketing program worldwide. And those that do, like Lego, the Danish manufacturer of construction toys, often distribute their products through sales companies rather than full-fledged marketing subsidiaries.

For most products, the appropriate degree of standardization varies from one element of the marketing mix to another. Strategic elements like product positioning are more easily standardized than execution-sensitive elements like sales promotion. In addition, when headquarters believes it has identified a superior marketing idea, whether it be a package design, a brand name, or an advertising copy concept, the pressure to standardize increases.

Marketing can usually contribute to scale economies most significantly by creating a standard product design that will sell worldwide, permitting savings through globalized production. In addition, scale economies in marketing programming can be achieved through standard commercial executions and copy concepts. McCann-Erickson claims to have saved $90 million in production costs over 20 years by producing worldwide Coca-Cola commercials. To ensure that they have enough attention-getting power to overcome their foreign origins, however, marketers often have to make worldwide commercials expensive productions.

To compensate local management for having to accept a standard product and to fit the core product to each local market, some companies allow local managers to adapt those marketing mix elements that aren't subject to significant scale economies. On the other hand, local managers are more likely to accept a standard concept for those elements of the marketing mix that are less important and, ironically, often not susceptible to scale economies. Overall, then, the driving factor in moving toward global marketing should be the efficient worldwide use of good marketing ideas rather than any scale economies from standardization.

In judging how far to go in standardizing elements of the marketing mix, managers must also be mindful of the interactions among them. For example, when a product with the same brand name is sold in different countries, it can be difficult and sometimes impossible to sell them at different prices.

Countries
How far a decentralized multinational wishes to pursue global marketing will often vary from one country to another. Naturally, headquarters is likely to become more involved in marketing decisions in countries where performance is poor. But performance aside, small markets depend more on headquarters assistance than large markets. Because a standard marketing program is superior in quality to what local executives, even with the benefit of local market knowledge, could develop themselves, they may welcome it.

Large markets with strong local managements are less willing to accept global programs. Yet these are the markets that often account for most of the company's investment. To secure their acceptance, headquarters should make standard marketing programs reflect the needs of large rather than small markets. Small markets, being more tolerant of deviations from what would be locally appropriate, are less likely to resist a standard program.

As we've seen, Coca-Cola takes the same approach in all markets. Nestlé varies its approach in different countries, depending on the strength of its market presence and each country's need for assistance. In completing the table 10.1 planning matrix, management may decide that it can sensibly group countries by region or by stage of market development.

Too Far Too Fast

Once managers have decided how global they want their marketing program to be, they must make the transition. Debates over the size of the gap between present and desired positions and the speed with which it must be closed will often pit the field against headquarters. Such conflict is most likely to arise in companies where the reason for change is not apparent or the country managers have had a lot of autonomy. Casualties can occur on both sides:

• Because Black & Decker dominated the European consumer power tool market, many of the company's European managers could not see that a more centrally directed global marketing approach was needed as a defense against imminent Japanese competition. To make his point, the CEO had to replace several key European executives.

• In 1982, the Parker Pen Company, forced by competition and a weakening financial position to lower costs, more than halved its number of plants and pen styles worldwide. Parker's overseas subsidiary managers accepted these changes but, when pressed to implement standardized advertising and packaging, they dug in their heels. In 1985, Parker ended its much heralded global marketing campaign. Several senior headquarters managers left the company.

If management is not careful, moving too far too fast toward global marketing can trigger painful consequences. First, subsidiary managers who joined the company because of its apparent commitment to local autonomy and to adapting its products to the local environment may become disenchanted. When poorly implemented, global marketing can make the local country manager's job less strategic. Second, disenchantment may reinforce not-invented-here attitudes that lead to game playing. For instance, some local managers may try bargaining with headquarters, trading the speed with which they will accept and implement the standard programs for additional budget assistance. In addition, local managers competing for resources and autonomy may devote too much attention to second-guessing headquarters' "hot buttons." Eventually the good managers may leave, and less competent people who lack the initiative of their predecessors may replace them.

A vicious circle can develop. Feeling compelled to review local performance more closely, headquarters may tighten its controls and reduce resources without adjusting its expectations of local managers. Meanwhile, local managers trying to gain approval of applications for deviations from standard marketing programs are being frustrated. The expanding head-quarters bureaucracy and associated overhead costs reduce the speed with which the locals can respond to local opportunities and competitive actions. Slow response time is an especially serious problem with products for which barriers to entry for local competitors are low.

In this kind of system, weak, insecure local managers can become dependent on headquarters for operational assistance. They'll want headquarters to assume the financial risks for new product launches, and they welcome the prepackaged marketing programs. If performance falls short of head-quarters' expectations, the local management can always blame the failure on the quality of operational assistance or on the standard marketing program. The local manager who has clear autonomy and profit-and-loss responsibility cannot hide behind such excuses.

If headquarters or regions assume much of the strategic burden, managers in overseas subsidiaries may think only about short-term sales. This focus will diminish their ability to monitor and communicate to head-quarters any changes in local competitors' strategic directions. When their responsibilities shift from strategy to execution, their ideas will become less exciting. If the field has traditionally been as important a source of new product ideas as the central R & D laboratory, the company may find itself short of the grass-roots creative thinking and marketing research information that R & D needs. The fruitful dialogue that characterizes a relationship between equal partners will no longer flourish.

How to Get There

When thinking about closing the gap between present and desired positions, most executives of decentralized multinationals want to accommodate their current organizational structures. They rightly view their subsidiaries and the managers who run them as important competitive strengths. They generally do not wish to transform these organizations into mere sales and distribution agencies.

How then in moving toward global marketing can headquarters build rather than jeopardize relationships, stimulate rather than demoralize local managers? The answer is to focus on means as much as ends, to examine the relationship between the home office and the field, and to ask what level of headquarters intervention for each business function, product, marketing mix element, and country is necessary to close the gap in each.

As table 10.2 indicates, headquarters can intervene at five points, ranging from informing to directing. The five intervention levels are cumula-

Table 10.2
Global marketing planning matrix: how to get there

		Informing	Persuading	Coordinating	Approving	Directing
Business functions	Research and development	○○○○○ ×××× ×	○○○○○ ×××× ×	○○○○○ ×××× ×	○○○○○ ×××× ×	○×○× ○×○× ○×○× ○×○× ○×○×
	Finance and accounting	○○○○○ ×××× ×	○○○○○ ×××× ×	○○○○○ ×××× ×	○○○○○ ×××× ×	○×○× ○×○× ○×○× ○×○× ○×○×
	Manufacturing	○○○○○ ×××× ×	○○○○○ ××× ×	○○○○○ ××××	○○○○○	
	Procurement	○○○○○ ×××× ×	○○○○○	○○○○○	○○○○○	
	Marketing	○○○○○ ×××× ×	○○○○○ ××× ×	○○○○○ ××× × ×	○○○○○	○○○○○
Products	Low cultural grounding High economies or efficiencies	○○○○○	○○○○○	○○○○○	○○○○○	○○○○○
	Low cultural grounding Low economies or efficiencies					
	High cultural ground High economies or efficiencies	×××××	×××××	×××××		
	High cultural grounding Low economies or efficiencies					
Marketing mix elements	Product design	○○○○○ ×××× ×	○○○○○ ×××× ×	○○○○○ ×××× ×	○○○○○ ×××× ×	○○○○○

Marketing element	Country A (Countries)	Country B (Region 1)	Country C (Region 1)	Country D (Region 2)	Country E (Region 2)
Brand name	O	O x	O x	O	O
Product positioning	O	O x	O x	O	O
Packaging	O	O x	O x	O	O
Advertising theme	O	O x	O x	O	O
Pricing	O	O x	O x	O	O
Advertising copy	O	O x	O x	O	O
Distribution	O	O x	O	O	O
Sales promotion	O	O	O		
Customer service	O	O	O		

Legend:
O O O O O Coca-Cola
x x x x x Nestlé

tive; for headquarters to direct, it must also inform, persuade, coordinate, and approve. Table 10.2 shows the approaches Atlanta and Vevey have taken. Moving from left to right on table 10.2, the reader can see that things are done increasingly by fiat rather than patient persuasion, through discipline rather than education. At the far right, local subsidiaries can't choose whether to opt in or out of a marketing program, and headquarters views its country managers as subordinates rather than customers.

When the local managers tightly control marketing efforts, multinational managers face three critical issues. In the sections that follow, we'll take a look at how decentralized multinationals are working to correct the three problems as they move along the spectrum from informing to directing.

1. **Inconsistent brand identities.** If head quarters gives country managers total control of their product lines, it cannot leverage the opportunities that multinational status gives it. The increasing degree to which consumers in one country are exposed to the company's products in another won't enhance the corporate image or brand development in the consumers' home country.

2. **Limited product focus.** In the decentralized multinational, the field line manager's ambition is to become a country manager, which means acquiring multiproduct and multifunction experience. Yet as the pace of technological innovation increases and the likelihood of global competition grows, multinationals need worldwide product specialists as well as executives willing to transfer to other countries. Nowhere is the need for headquarters guidance on innovative organizational approaches more evident than in the area of product policy.

3. **Slow new product launches.** As global competition grows, so does the need for rapid worldwide rollouts of new products. The decentralized multinational that permits country managers to proceed at their own pace on new product introductions may be at a competitive disadvantage in this new environment.

Word of Mouth

The least threatening, loosest, and therefore easiest approach to global marketing is for headquarters to encourage the transfer of information between it and its country managers. Since good ideas are often a company's scarcest resource, headquarters efforts to encourage and reward their generation, dissemination, and application in the field will build both relationships and profits. Here are two examples:

• Nestlé publishes quarterly marketing newsletters that report recent product introductions and programming innovations. In this way, each subsidiary can learn quickly about and assess the ideas of others. (The best newsletters are written as if country organizations were talking to each other rather than as if headquarters were talking down to the field.)

• Johnson Wax holds periodic meetings of all marketing directors at corporate headquarters twice a year to build global esprit de corps and to encourage the sharing of new ideas.

By making the transfer of information easy, a multinational leverages the ideas of its staff and spreads organizational values. Headquarters has to be careful, however, that the information it's passing on is useful. It may focus on updating local managers about new products, when what they mainly want is information on the most tactical and country-specific elements of the marketing mix. For example, the concentration of the grocery trade is much higher in the United Kingdom and Canada than it is in the United States. In this case, managers in the United States can learn from British and Canadian country managers about how to deal with the pressures for extra merchandising support that result when a few powerful retailers control a large percentage of sales. Likewise, marketers in countries with restrictions on mass-media advertising have developed sophisticated point-of-purchase merchandising skills that could be useful to managers in other countries.

By itself, however, information sharing is often insufficient to help local executives meet the competitive challenges of global marketing.

Friendly Persuasion

Persuasion is a first step managers can take to deal with the three problems we've outlined. Any systematic headquarters effort to influence local managers to apply standardized approaches or introduce new global products while the latter retain their decision-making authority is a persuasion approach.

Unilever and CPC International, for example, employ world-class advertising and marketing research staff at headquarters. Not critics but coaches, these specialists review the subsidiaries' work and try to upgrade the technical skills of local marketing departments. They frequently visit the field to disseminate new concepts, frameworks, and techniques, and to respond to problems that local management raises. (It helps to build trust if headquarters can send out the same staff specialists for several years.)

Often, when the headquarters of a decentralized multinational identifies or develops a new product, it has to persuade the country manager in a so-called prime-mover market to invest in the launch. A successful launch in the prime-mover market will, in turn, persuade other country managers to introduce the product. The prime-mover market is usually selected according to criteria including the commitment of local management, the probabilities of success, the credibility with which a success would be regarded by managers in other countries, and its perceived transferability.

Persuasion, however, has its limitations. Two problems recur with the prime-mover approach. First, by adopting a wait-and-see attitude, country managers can easily turn down requests to be prime-mover markets on the grounds of insufficient resources. Since the country managers in the prime-mover markets have to risk their resources to launch the new products, they're likely to tailor the product and marketing programs to their own markets rather than to global markets. Second, if there are more new products waiting to be launched than there are prime-mover markets to launch them, headquarters product specialists are likely to give in to a country manager's demands for local tailoring. But because of the need for re-adaptation in each case, the tailoring may delay rollouts in other markets and allow competitors to preempt the product. In the end, management may sacrifice long-term worldwide profits to maximize short-term profits in a few countries.

Marketing to the Same Drummer

To overcome the limits of persuasion, many multinationals are coordinating their marketing programs, whereby headquarters has a structured role in both decision making and performance evaluation that is far more influential than person-to-person persuasion. Often using a matrix or team approach, headquarters shares with country managers the responsibility and authority for programming and personnel decisions.

Nestlé locates product directors as well as support groups at headquarters. Together they develop long-term strategies for each product category on a worldwide basis, coordinate worldwide market research, spot new product opportunities, spark the field launch of new products, advise the field on how headquarters will evaluate new product proposals, and spread the word on new products' performance so that other countries will be motivated to launch them. Even though the product directors are staff executives with no line authority, because they have all been successful line managers in the field, they have great credibility and influence.

Country managers who cooperate with a product director can quickly become heroes if they successfully implement a new idea. On the other hand, while a country manager can reject a product director's advice, headquarters will closely monitor his or her performance with an alternative program. In addition, within the product category in which they specialize, the directors have influence on line management appointments in the field. Local managers thus have to be concerned about their relationships with headquarters.

Some companies assign promising local managers to other countries and require would-be local managers to take a tour of duty at headquarters. But such personnel transfer programs may run into barriers. First, many capable local nationals may not be interested in working outside their countries of origin. Second, powerful local managers are often unwilling to give up their best people to other country assignments. Third, immigration regulations and foreign service relocation costs are burdensome. Fourth, if transferees from the field have to take a demotion to work at headquarters, the costs in ill will often exceed any gains in cross-fertilization of ideas. If management can resolve these problems, however, it will find that creating an international career path is one of the most effective ways to develop a global perspective in local managers.

To enable their regional general managers to work alongside the worldwide product directors, several companies have moved them from the field to the head office. More and more companies require regional managers to reach sales and profit targets for each product as well as for each country within their regions. In the field, regional managers often focus on representing the views of individual countries to headquarters, but at headquarters they become more concerned with ensuring that the country managers are correctly implementing corporatewide policies.

Recently, Fiat and Philips N.V., among others, consolidated their worldwide advertising into a single agency. Their objectives are to make each product's advertising more consistent around the world and to make it easier to transfer ideas and information among local agency offices, country organizations, and headquarters. Use of a single agency (especially one that bills all advertising expenditures worldwide) also symbolizes a commitment to global marketing and more centralized control. Multinationals shouldn't, however, use their agencies as Trojan horses for greater standardization. An undercover operation is likely to jeopardize agency-client relations at the country level.

While working to achieve global coordination, some companies are also trying to tighten coordination in particular regions:

• Kodak recently experimented by consolidating 17 worldwide product line managers at corporate headquarters. In addition, the company made marketing directors in some countries responsible for a line of business in a region as well as for sales of all Kodak products in their own countries. Despite these new appointments, country managers still retain profit-and-loss responsibility for their own markets.

Whether a matrix approach such as this broadens perspectives rather than increases tension and confusion depends heavily on the corporation's cohesiveness. Such an organizational change can clearly communicate top management's strategic direction, but headquarters needs to do a persuasive selling job to the field if it is to succeed.

• Procter & Gamble has established so-called Euro Brand teams that analyze opportunities for greater product and marketing program standardization. Chaired by the brand manager from a "lead country," each team includes brand managers from other European subsidiaries that market the brand, managers from P & G's European technical center, and one of P & G's three European division managers, each of whom is responsible for a portfolio of brands as well as for a group of countries. Concerns that the larger subsidiaries would dominate the teams and that decision making would either be paralyzed or produce "lowest common denominator" results have proved groundless.

Stamped and Approved

By coordinating programs with the field, headquarters can balance the company's local and global perspectives. Even a decentralized multinational may decide, however, that to protect or exploit some corporate asset, the center of gravity for certain elements of the marketing program should be at headquarters. In such cases, management has two options: it can send clear directives to its local managers or permit them to develop their own programs within specified parameters and subject to headquarters approval. With a properly managed approval process, a multinational can exert effective control without unduly dampening the country manager's decision-making responsibility and creativity.

Procter & Gamble recently developed a new sanitary napkin, and P & G International designated certain countries in different geographic regions as test markets. The product, brand name, positioning, and package design were standardized globally. P & G International did, however, invite local managers to suggest how the global program could be improved and how the nonglobal elements of the marketing program should be adapted in their markets. It approved changes in several markets. Moreover, local managers developed valuable ideas on such programming specifics as sampling and couponing techniques that were used in all other countries, including the United States.

Nestlé views its brand names as a major corporate asset. As a result, it requires all brands sold in all countries to be registered in the home country of Switzerland. While the ostensible reason for this requirement is legal protection, the effect is that any product developed in the field has to be approved by Vevey. The head office has also developed detailed guidelines that suggest rather than mandate how brand names and logos should appear on packaging and in advertising worldwide (with exceptions subject to its approval). Thus the country manager's control over the content of advertising is not compromised, and the company achieves a reasonably consistent presentation of its names and logos worldwide.

Doing It the Headquarters Way

Multinationals that direct local managers' marketing programs usually do so out of a sense of urgency. The motive may be to ensure either that a new product is introduced rapidly around the world before the competition can respond or that every manager fully and faithfully exploits a valuable marketing idea. Sometimes direction is needed to prove that global marketing can work. Once management makes the point, a more participative approach is feasible.

In 1979, one of Henkel's worldwide marketing directors wanted to extend the successful Sista line of do-it-yourself sealants from Germany to other European countries where the markets were underdeveloped and disorganized as had once been the case in Germany. A European headquarters project team visited the markets and then developed a standard marketing program. The country managers, however, objected. Since the market potential in each country was small, they said, they did not have the time or resources to launch Sista.

The project team countered that by capitalizing on potential scale economies, its pan-European marketing and manufacturing programs would be superior to any programs the subsidiaries could develop by themselves. Furthermore, it maintained, the already developed pan-European program was available off the shelf. The European sales manager, who was a project team member, discovered that the salespeople as well as tradespeople in the target countries were much more enthusiastic about the proposed program than the field marketing managers. So management devised a special lure for the managers. The project team offered to subsidize the first-year advertising and promotion expenditures of countries launching Sista. Six countries agreed. To ensure their commitment now that their financial risk had been reduced, the sales manager invited each accepting country manager to nominate a member to the project team to develop the final program details.

By 1982, the Sista line was sold in 52 countries using a standard marketing program. The Sista launch was especially challenging because it involved the extension of a product and program already developed for a single market. The success of the Sista launch made Henkel's field managers much more receptive to global marketing programs for subsequent new products.

Motivating the Field

Taking into account the nature of their products and markets, their organizational structures, and their cultures and traditions, multinationals have to decide which approach or combination of approaches, from informing to directing, will best answer their strategic objectives. Multinational managers must realize, however, that local managers are likely to resist any precipitate move toward increased headquarters direction. A quick shift could lower their motivation and performance.

Any erosion in marketing decision making associated with global marketing will probably be less upsetting for country managers who have not risen through the line marketing function. For example, John Deere's European headquarters has developed advertising for its European country managers for more than a decade. The country managers have not objected. Most are not marketing specialists and do not see advertising as key to the success of their operations. But for country managers who view control of marketing decision making as central to their operational success, the transition will often be harder. Headquarters needs to give the field time to adjust to the new decision-making processes that multicountry brand teams and other new organizational structures require. Yet management must recognize that even with a one- or two-year transition period, some turnover among field personnel is inevitable. As one German headquarters executive commented, "Those managers in the field who can't adapt to a more global approach will have to leave and run local breweries."

Here are five suggestions on how to motivate and retain talented country managers when making the shift to global marketing:

1. Encourage field managers to generate ideas. This is especially important when R & D efforts are centrally directed. Use the best ideas from the field in global marketing programs (and give recognition to the local managers who came up with them). Unilever's South African subsidiary developed Impulse body spray, now a global brand. R. J. Reynolds revitalized Camel as a global brand after the German subsidiary came up with a successful and transferable positioning and copy strategy.

2. Ensure that the field participates in the development of the marketing strategies and programs for global brands. A bottom-up rather than top-down approach will foster greater commitment and produce superior program execution at the country level. As we've seen, when P & G International introduced its sanitary napkin as a global brand, it permitted local managers to make some adjustments in areas that were not seen as core to the program, such as couponing and sales promotion. More important, it encouraged them to suggest changes in features of the core global program.

3. Maintain a product portfolio that includes, where scale economies permit, local as well as regional and global brands. While Philip Morris's and Seagram's country managers and their local advertising agencies are required to implement standard programs for each company's global brands, the managers retain full responsibility for the marketing programs of their locally distributed brands. Seagram motivates its country managers to stay interested in the global brands by allocating development funds to support local marketing efforts on these brands and by circulating monthly reports that summarize market performance data by brand and country.

4. Allow country managers continued control of their marketing budgets so they can respond to local consumer needs and counter local competition. When British Airways headquarters launched its £13 million global advertising campaign, it left intact the £18 million worth of tactical advertising budgets that country managers used to promote fares, destinations, and tour packages specific to their markets. Because most of the country managers had exhausted their previous year's tactical budgets and were anxious for further advertising support, they were receptive to the global campaign even though it was centrally directed.

5. Emphasize the general management responsibilities of country managers that extend beyond the marketing function. Country managers who

have risen through the line-marketing function often don't spend enough time on local manufacturing operations, industrial relations, and government affairs. Global marketing programs can free them to focus on and develop their skills in these other areas.

III International Marketing

Key Terms

- global marketing
- standardization
- economies of scope
- market entry
- promotion decisions
- rationalization
- product adaptation

Questions

1. What are the requirements for successful standardized international marketing?

2. What are the stages of development of an international marketing program?

3. When is customized international marketing likely to be more successful?

4. Which aspects of the marketing program—product, price, promotion, and place—are most likely to be standardized and which are most likely to be customized?

5. Which national markets are most likely to be grouped for standardized marketing?

6. Which national markets are most likely to be customized?

Suggested Readings

Douglas, Susan P., and Yoram Wind, "The Myth of Globalization," *Columbia Journal of World Business*, Winter 1987, pp. 19–29.

Huszagh, Sandra M., Richard J. Fox, and Ellen Day, "Global Marketing: An Empirical Investigation," *Columbia Journal of World Business*, Winter 1985, pp. 31–43.

Jain, Subhash C., "Standardization of International Marketing Strategy: Some Research Hypotheses," *Journal of Marketing*, January 1989, pp. 70–79.

Onkvisit, Sak, and John J. Shaw, "Standard International Advertising: A Review and Critical Evaluation of the Theoretical and Empirical Evidence," *Columbia Journal of World Business*, Fall 1987, pp. 43–55.

IV   Multinational Corporate Finance

Assume you have just won one of the largest lottery prizes ever—$100 million. You have an immediate investment decision—should you buy securities denominated in the U.S. dollar, the Canadian dollar, the British pound, the German mark, or the Japanese yen? Interest rates on short-term securities denominated in most of these foreign currencies are higher than interest rates on comparable securities denominated in the U.S. dollar.

There are three dominant answers to this question.

1. Buy only U.S. dollar securities because the additional interest income on the foreign securities is too small to compensate for the likelihood of depreciation of the foreign currencies and the associated risk of this loss.

2. Buy only the foreign securities because the additional interest income on the foreign securities is more than adequate to compensate for the likelihood of depreciation of the foreign currencies and the associated risk of this loss.

3. Buy both U.S. dollar securities and securities denominated in various currencies because differences in interest rates more or less reflect the anticipated changes in the price of the U.S. dollar in terms of these various foreign currencies.

The inference from the currency denomination of the securities in the portfolios of most U.S. investors—the mutual funds, the pension funds, the life insurance companies—is that they believe the first statement. Investors headquartered in virtually every other country also own primarily securities denominated in their domestic currency. Although these investors preach and practice diversification, diversification slows or stalls at the water's edge.

The key feature of international finance in the 1970s and the 1980s has been the large amplitude of movement in the foreign exchange value of the U.S. dollar. The changes in the real exchange rates—the nominal price of the U.S. dollar adjusted by the difference between the U.S. inflation rate and the inflation rate in a particular foreign country, such as Germany or Japan—have been nearly as large as the changes in the nominal or market exchange rates. These large changes in price-level-adjusted exchange rates have had dramatic consequences for the competitive position of plants producing in different countries; thus, when the U.S. dollar appreciated sharply in the 1979–1985 period, the competitive position of the U.S. plants of both U.S. and foreign firms declined very sharply. Conversely, when the U.S. dollar depreciated extensively in the late 1980s, there was a sharp improvement in the competitive position of the U.S. plants of both U.S. and foreign firms.

A second major feature of this period has been the volatile changes in the real interest rates—the nominal or market interest rate adjusted by the past or anticipated inflation rate—on comparable securities denominated in different currencies. The 1970s was a decade of accelerating inflation, and of volatile and declining real interest rates, especially in the United States; in contrast, the 1980s was a decade of stable and high real interest rates. In the late 1970s real interest rates on U.S. dollar securities were declining, and approached zero or were negative; and were below real interest rates on comparable securities denominated in the German mark and the Japanese yen.

As a result of the Federal Reserve's move to a very contractive monetary policy in October 1979, nominal interest rates on U.S. dollar securities increased sharply, and the U.S. inflation rate soon began to decline. Real interest rates on U.S. dollar securities surged, and for most of the 1980s were higher than real interest rates on comparable securities denominated in the German mark and the Japanese yen.

The changes in real exchange rates were a response to the changes in the differentials between real interest rates in the United States and in various foreign countries. Investors tend to shift funds to a country as real interest rates on securities denominated in its currency increase relative to real interest rates on securities denominated in other currencies. And the changes in real interest rates appear to follow changes in anticipated inflation rates, because changes in nominal interest rates appear to lag changes in the actual inflation rate in a systematic way.

The managers of the finance function of the multinational firm must make the same decisions about capital budgeting, capital structure, and cash management in the global economy—in the context of changes in exchange rates and changes in the relationship between real interest rates on comparable securities denominated in different currencies—that they make in the domestic economy. The basic data for these decisions are those on interest rates on comparable securities denominated in different currencies and the anticipated changes in exchange rates. The managers of the finance function also must estimate the firm's exposure to exchange risk as a result of its operating activities, and how the firm can best cope with this risk—whether the firm should hedge its foreign exchange exposure or whether instead the firm should carry this exposure. This decision involves integration of the data on the cost of hedging this risk, the risk of maintaining exposed positions in foreign exchange, and the significance of exchange losses to the income, net worth, and market value of the firm. The finance decision for multinational firms differs from other international business decisions in that a systematic approach is facilitated by a large data base.

The debt denomination decision (which is the mirror of the portfolio decision) can be managed to reduce the firm's exposure to foreign exchange risk—although at the possible cost of a significant increase in the firm's interest payments and hence a reduction in its operating profits. If interest rate differentials and changes in exchange rates were offsetting, then real interest rates would not differ significantly across countries and real exchange rates would not change, and these financial decisions in the global economy would not differ significantly from those in the domestic economy. The data suggest that interest rate differentials do not fully offset realized changes in exchange rates in the long run or in the short run, and hence these decisions are more complex in the global economy.

The readings in part 4 address three international financial decisions: the debt denomination decision, foreign exchange exposure evaluation, and the international capital budgeting decision. The multinational firms are likely to structure the mix of debt and equity in their various foreign subsidiaries to minimize tax burdens (or more precisely, to maximize after-tax income), and so the capital structures of their subsidiaries complement the capital structure of their parent, and hence differ from the capital structures of the firms headquartered in the countries in which the subsidiaries are located.

"The Debt Denomination Decision" by Robert Z. Aliber examines the key issue of international financing: Should the firm issue debt denominated in its domestic currency or in a foreign currency? Aliber's argument is based on what he believes is an empirical regularity in the international financial data—in the long run the difference in interest rates on comparable securities denominated in different currencies is modestly larger than the realized changes in exchange rates, which is consistent with the view that investors in low-interest-rate countries seek to be reimbursed for undertaking the cross-border risks associated with acquiring securities denominated in the currency of a high-interest-rate country. There are two key elements to consider in the debt denomination decision: the market factors, such as interest rates and the expected rate of change in the price of foreign currencies in the foreign exchange market, and the firm-specific factors, especially the firm's operating foreign exchange exposure and the managers' attitudes toward various risks including exchange risk. Firms that seek to minimize net interest costs are likely to remain exposed to losses from changes in exchange rates. Conversely, firms that seek to minimize foreign exchange exposure are likely to have higher net interest costs as a result of borrowing in the foreign countries where operations are located.

Evaluation of foreign exchange exposure is the subject of "Volatile Exchange Rates Can Put Operations at Risk" by Donald R. Lessard and John B. Lightstone. Lessard and Lightstone highlight the impact of changes in exchange rates on profits per unit of sales and on the quantity of sales. They suggest that firms can reduce their foreign exchange exposure (1) by selecting relatively unexposed locations, (2) by developing a diversified portfolio of projects, and (3) by building in the flexibility to shift production from one country to another in response to changes in exchange rates.

Alan Shapiro's "International Capital Budgeting" provides a concise look at the analytical tools required in assessing projects in different countries. The article surveys discounted cash flow and the basic issues involved in assessing foreign projects; in particular, he addresses project-versus-parent cash flow and economic and political risks. Shapiro also examines the cost of capital for foreign investments and the relationship between international capital budgeting and corporate strategy.

11

The Debt Denomination Decision

Robert Z. Aliber

The key decision in international financial management is the debt denomination decision. When borrowing, managers of firms must decide whether to sell new debt and bank loans denominated in their domestic currency or in a foreign currency. Domestic currency, for all practical purposes, is the currency in which the firm reports its income to its stockholders, or to its owners. For most purposes the relevant foreign currency is either the currency of one of the foreign countries in which the firm sells or produces, or the currency of one of the small number of countries in which the firm can borrow readily. The choice of currency for the denomination of debt and bank loans affects both the level and the variability of the firm's income because it impacts on net interest payments and foreign exchange gains and losses.

The key elements in the debt denomination decision can be grouped into two sets. First, the market-factor set includes the interest rates on bonds and bank loans denominated in the domestic currency, the interest rates on comparable bonds and bank loans denominated in one of several foreign currencies, and the anticipated change in the exchange rate for each of these foreign currencies in terms of domestic currency. Second, the firm-specific factor set includes the foreign exchange exposure associated with the various components of the firm's income statement and its balance sheet, the risk associated with individual foreign currencies, the risk of a portfolio of various foreign currencies, and the relation between the firm's total income and capital gain (or loss) from a change in the exchange rate at a time when the firm has a foreign exchange exposure.

The central decision for the firm is whether the currency denomination of its debt and its bank loans should be managed to reduce or fully neutral-

From *The Handbook of International Financial Management*, Dow Jones-Irwin, 1989, pp. 435–451. Reprinted by permission.

ize the foreign exchange exposure of its income statement, or whether the currency denomination of its debt and bank loans should be managed to increase its net income, either by reducing its borrowing costs, or by increasing its foreign exchange gains—at least in an anticipated sense. The inputs to this decision include both the market factors—the relation between the interest rates on comparable bonds denominated in different currencies and the anticipated change in exchange rates—and the firm-specific factors—the firm's attitude toward risk and the relation between the income associated with changes in the firm's foreign exchange exposure and its total income. An individual firm might, and should, have different postures toward maintaining foreign exchange exposures in different groups of currencies, because the market factors associated with each of these groups of currencies might differ. Two firms involved with the same group of foreign currencies may follow quite different policies when making the debt denomination decision because of differences in their attitudes toward risk.

The debt denomination decision for the firm is the mirror image of the portfolio decision of the investor. The key elements in the portfolio decision are all present in the debt denomination decision—the interest rates on comparable assets denominated in various foreign currencies and in domestic currency, the anticipated change in the exchange rate for each of these currencies in terms of domestic currency, the investor's attitude toward risk, and the risk associated with a portfolio of foreign currencies. The debt denomination decision has one element not usually associated with the portfolio decision—the firm may have revenues and costs in individual foreign currencies, and hence income or profits in these currencies. Similarly, to the extent that the firm's profits on its domestic production or sales are sensitive to changes in exchange rates, the firm has an income-statement exposure. Paradoxically the firm may have an income-statement exposure even though it is not engaged in importing or exporting or any other international activities.

The measurement of the exposure of the firm's income statement is discussed in the next section of this chapter. Then the market factors are analyzed; the techniques for altering the foreign exchange exposure of the firm's balance sheet, and the comparative costs of each technique are reviewed. Next the firm-specific factors are evaluated. Each of several strategies that a firm might adopt toward its foreign-exchange exposure are evaluated.

The Foreign Exchange Exposure of the Firm's Income Statement

The key question for the firm involves whether the currency denomination of debt and bank loans should be managed to neutralize the foreign exchange exposure of the income statement. Hence, the first element in the debt denomination decision involves estimating the exposure of several components of its income statement and the sensitivity of the firm's income in domestic currency to changes in exchange rates. Changes in exchange rates may lead to changes in the domestic income associated with royalties and license fees from foreign firms and the firm's foreign subsidiaries, the domestic income equivalent of the profits of the firm's various foreign subsidiaries as reported in the currencies of the countries in which these subsidiaries are organized, and the domestic income on its export activities. Similarly changes in exchange rates may lead to changes in the domestic income of its domestic production and sales. Moreover the profits of the firm's foreign subsidiaries—as reported in the currencies of the countries where they are organized—may be significantly affected by changes in exchange rates.

The measurement of the foreign exchange exposure of these several activities is considered in turn. Consider the foreign exchange exposure of the firm's royalty and licensing income, initially under the assumption that the payment of royalties and license fees is in the domestic currency and subsequently in a foreign currency. If the firm contracts to be paid royalty and licensing income in its domestic currency, it might seem that the firm does not have a foreign currency exposure—instead, the payor has the foreign-exchange exposure. If however, the change in the exchange rate would cause the payor to go bankrupt or to become financially distressed so that it could not make its contractual payments, then the firm has a foreign-exchange exposure.[1] If the firm contracts instead to receive payment in a foreign currency, then the domestic currency equivalent of the scheduled receipts in the foreign currency will change whenever the exchange rate changes. The foreign exchange exposure of a projected stream of receipts in each of several foreign currencies can be measured as the discounted present value of the anticipated receipts in each of these foreign currencies.[2]

Consider the exposure of the income on exports to various foreign countries. These export sales may be invoiced in the currency of the buyer or the currency of the seller. If the exports are invoiced in the currency of the buyer and the buyer's currency depreciates, the firm incurs a foreign exchange loss and the domestic income attached to export sales declines. As a result, the unit volume of exports may decline as the price of these goods in the buyer's currency is increased relative to the price of similar or competitive goods produced in the buyer's country or the profits per unit of export sales decline because the price in the buyer's currency is not increased by as much in percentage terms as the change in the exchange rate. In most cases, both export volume and profits per unit of export decline. Indeed, the firm has a foreign exposure on its exports unless the firm is able to increase its selling price in the foreign country by the same percentage amount as the change in the exchange rate and still maintain the volume of its sales. And the economic condition for being able to raise selling prices is that the firm has no effective competitors in the various foreign countries to which it exports.

If export sales are denominated in the firm's currency, it might seem that the firm does not have a foreign exchange exposure on these sales, but that the importer has the foreign exchange exposure. However, the volume of the importer's purchases is likely to decline as the importer has to pay a higher price in its own currency for imports; the importer's sales may decline and its profits per unit of sales also may decline. Hence the factors that lead to a foreign exchange exposure when the exports are denominated in the firm's currency are the same as those when the exports are denominated in the importer's currency. In both cases, the exporter's exposure is the anticipated revenues in the foreign currency discounted to the present.[3]

The firm's foreign-exchange exposure on its export sales is the anticipated revenues in the foreign currency, or more precisely, the discounted present value of these revenues.[4] The appropriate interest rate is the market interest rate in the country in which the exports are sold.

Consider the exposure of the projected income of the firm's foreign subsidiaries. Initially, this income is estimated in the currency of the country in which the subsidiary is located, and then the domestic currency equivalent is determined on the basis of the anticipated exchange rate. If the foreign currency depreciates more rapidly than anticipated, the domestic currency equivalent of the subsidiary's income is smaller than anticipated. The anticipated income of these subsidiaries can be estimated under a number of assumptions about exchange rates at various future dates: the firm's exposure in each of these foreign currencies is the present value of the anticipated income in these currencies. The exposure of the income of the foreign subsidiaries differs from the exposure of royalty and licensing income in foreign currencies of the parent in one significant way—the income in each of the foreign currencies may vary as the foreign exchange value of the currencies of the countries in which the subsidiaries are located varies. Thus, each of the foreign subsidiaries has its own foreign exchange exposure and its income is sensitive to changes in the exchange rate.[5] The firm's exposure in each currency is the domestic currency equivalent of the anticipated profits of each of the foreign subsidiaries.

The firm may have an exposure on its income statement even though the firm does not participate in international trade. The income statement is exposed if profits on domestic sales are sensitive to changes in exchange rates, perhaps because the firm's products are competitive with imported goods or because one of the components to domestic production is imported. Changes in the exchange rates might lead to changes in the volume of domestic sales or to changes in the price and, hence, unit profits of domestic sales. The foreign exchange exposure of export sales provides this analogy: if one or several foreign currencies should depreciate, then the domestic demand for imports may increase, and the firm may lose sales in its domestic market. If the firm responds to the loss of its market share by cutting prices, then its profits per unit of sales decline. The foreign exchange exposure of domestic sales and revenues is measured as the foreign currency equivalent where the foreign currency is that in which the sales are sensitive.

Each of the components in the foreign exchange exposure of the income statement can be expressed in present value terms. Two factors complicate the estimation of the foreign exchange exposure in present terms. The first is the estimation of the revenues associated with each of these activities. The second is the choice of the interest rate used in the present value calculation. The complication is that estimates of some of these components are less certain than estimates of others. (Despite the uncertainty, the firm's confidence in its ability to develop estimates of its future sales is likely to be greater than its confidence in its ability to develop estimates of future exchange rates.)

The firm may have an income-statement exposure in a number of foreign currencies. Eventually, the firm's managers view its foreign exchange exposures in a portfolio context. Managers might group income-statement exposures in various foreign currencies; or instead, they may determine that the firm's aggregate foreign income-statement exposure is the sum of its income-statement exposures in individual foreign currencies. To the extent that the foreign exchange values of different national currencies are highly correlated, the income statement exposures in these currencies can be grouped.

Market Factors and the Currency Denomination of a Firm's Debt

Changes in the currency denomination of the firm's debt and bank loans can reduce or fully neutralize the exposure of its income statement. Alternatively, the currency denomination of the firm's debt and bank loans can be managed to increase the firm's foreign exchange exposure to profit from anticipated changes in exchange rates. Moreover, efforts to arrange the currency denomination of a firm's debt and bank loans to reduce its net interest costs can alter its foreign exchange exposure.

A firm with a foreign exchange exposure increases the sensitivity of its income or its net worth and, perhaps, its market valuation to changes in exchange rates. Because many firms seek to minimize the variance in their income, managers may attempt to reduce their foreign exchange exposures—if other things are equal. But other things are rarely equal— altering the foreign exchange exposure may incur various costs. For the firm, the relevant trade-off is between the cost of reducing (or increasing) its foreign exchange exposure and the benefits of having a smaller foreign exchange exposure—or of not having any foreign exchange exposure.

The firm can alter its foreign exchange exposure through a variety of now traditional techniques, including leading-and-lagging, forward exchange contracts, futures contracts in foreign exchange, options on foreign exchange, and foreign exchange swaps. And some more esoteric techniques are available and may be used when the traditional techniques are not available—these techniques include the pricing of commodity sales transactions, speculation in inventories or real assets and various nonmarket swaps.

Consider a firm that alters its foreign exchange exposure through the purchase of a three-month forward exchange contract. This transaction may reduce or fully neutralize the firm's exposure on its income statement, or increase the firm's exposure. The cost of the purchase of a three-month forward contract is the difference between the amount of domestic currency in settlement of the forward contract and the amount of domestic currency realized when the foreign currency which is taken in delivery in the settlement of the forward contract is immediately sold for domestic currency. This "cost" can be negative or positive. This cost is closely approximated as the difference between the exchange rate in the forward contract and the spot-exchange rate on the date when the forward contract matures.[6] Computation of this cost always involves a comparison between the exchange rate used to effect a change in the firm's foreign exposure with the spot-exchange rate at some future date, usually on the date when the forward exchange contract matures. If the forward exchange rate and the spot-exchange rate at the maturity of the forward exchange rate are not significantly different, there is no cost to altering the firm's foreign exchange exposure by altering the currency denomination of its debt. And the flip side of this statement is that there is no anticipated gain from altering the firm's foreign exchange exposure in anticipation of a profit from an anticipated change in the spot-exchange rate.

That the firm can alter its foreign exchange exposure without cost may seem surprising and comparable to the proverbial free lunch, for even though firms would be willing to pay for the lunch, they are not required to do so. The story is that transactions of U.S. firms to hedge a long foreign exchange exposure in the German mark, and of the German firms to hedge their foreign exchange exposures in the U.S. dollar, tend to be offsetting. Hence, both groups of firms may be able to reduce their foreign exchange exposures in their transactions with each other—and conceivably at no net cost. An insurance analogy is inappropriate because there is no intermediary in the forward exchange market that shares in the risk-reduction activity; instead, the banks act as brokers in the forward exchange market and marry the transactions of the U.S. firms with those of the German firms at a very modest charge—essentially the difference between their buying and selling rates for forward exchange contracts with the two parties.

Similarly, assume managers alter the firm's foreign exchange exposure through leading-and-lagging; the firm borrows in a foreign currency, converts these borrowed foreign funds into domestic currency, and uses the domestic funds to repay its domestic loans. As the firm's interest payments increase in one currency, and its interest payments decline in the second currency, there is likely to be an increase in its interest payments. Moreover, there is a change in the timing of the firm's foreign transactions—the firm enters into a spot-exchange transaction today rather than in three or six months. The cost of leading-and-lagging is the difference between the interest payments during the term of the loan and the amounts of foreign exchange realized on the date when the borrowed funds are converted and on the date when the borrowed funds are repaid. This amount can be approximated as the difference between the interest rate differential and the realized change in the exchange rate over this same interval. If the interest rates on the two loans are not significantly different from the change in the exchange rate in percentage terms, there is no cost to altering the firm's exposure. Again the free lunch question arises, and again the answer involves the impact of the hedging transactions of the U.S. firm and of the German firm on current exchange rates and interest rates. The mirror image of this proposition is that there is a cost to altering the firm's foreign-exchange exposure only to the extent that there is a difference between the two interest rates and the percentage change in the exchange rate. And if the U.S. firm incurs a cost in altering its foreign exchange exposure, the German firm alters its exposure and at the same time realizes a profit—a free lunch.

Because exchange rate movements are volatile, individual forward contracts are poor predictors of the spot-exchange rate on the dates when the forward exchange contracts mature. The central question is whether for a large number of forward exchange contracts in each foreign currency, the forward exchange rate is a biased or an unbiased predictor of the future spot-exchange rate. If the forward exchange rate is an unbiased predictor, then the forecast errors on one side of the spot-exchange rate and the forecast errors on the other side of the spot-exchange rate more or less cancel each other out. The alternative result is that the forecast errors on one side of the spot-exchange rate are substantially larger than the forecast errors on the other side of the spot-exchange rate. If the alternative result is valid, the interpretation might be that investors demand, and receive, a risk premium.

The concept for estimating the costs of altering the firm's exposure is known as Fisher Open; it involves the relationship between interest rates on comparable assets denominated in different currencies and the realized change in the exchange rate over this same holding period. An alternative version is that the Fisher Open involves the relationship between the forward exchange rate and the spot-exchange rate on the date of the maturity of the forward exchange contracts. (These two versions would prove identical in measured costs if domestic and foreign assets were not significantly different in political risk.)

The residual or difference between the two versions can be considered a risk premium, a forecast error, or some combination of both. The forecast error reflects that predicting changes in exchange rates is a risky activity because the movements in spot-exchange rates from one period to the next and from one month to the next may be volatile. Investors do their best to forecast the next period's exchange rate, but frequently they are overwhelmed by unanticipated events and the resulting very large unanticipated movements in the spot-exchange rate. Some investors may be willing to increase their exposure to foreign exchange risk only if they receive an additional payment—a risk premium—for incurring the risks associated with cross-border finance. The economic situation is that the larger the unanticipated movements in the exchange rate, the larger the forecast error and the larger the minimum required risk premium. In a world characterized by a variety of monetary and structural disturbances, there are likely to be large deviations from Fisher Open on a monthly or quarterly basis, with the result that any firm or investor maintaining an exposed position in foreign exchange is likely to realize a significant loss—or gain.

Firms and investors may seek to reduce or minimize their exposure to loss from changes in exchange rates because they believe the cost of the loss dominates the benefits of the gain—even if both are equally probable. Firms and investors would increase their exposure to loss from changes in exchange rates only if they anticipate a large gain in an expected value sense, or at least a savings in interest costs on borrowed funds from maintaining an exposed position in foreign exchange and carrying the associated risk. The implicit proposition is that the cost of reducing or eliminating the exposure is too high relative to the anticipated loss from maintaining an exposed position in foreign exchange and bearing the uncertainty associated with possible changes in the exchange rate. In effect, the firms and the investors carrying foreign exchange exposures self-insure —they believe that the additional income from the savings in interest payments associated with maintaining a foreign exchange exposure is adequate to compensate for the occasional foreign exchange losses and for carrying the uncertainty associated with changes in exchange rates.

Fisher Open has been subjected to many tests, especially in the form of the proposition that the forward exchange rate should be considered an unbiased (or a biased) predictor of the future spot-exchange rate. To a lesser extent, studies have been undertaken to assess the relationship between the difference in interest rates on comparable assets denominated in different currencies, and the observed change in the exchange rate. (If the interest rates are those on Eurodeposits, then the second test is identical with the first.) The general thrust of these studies is that, on average, forward rates are very close to being unbiased predictors of future spot-exchange rates. The economic rationale for this conclusion is that the firms in each of several countries use foreign exchange contracts as a way to reduce their foreign exchange exposures—and the sales of the German mark in the forward market by U.S. firms and the sales of U.S. dollars in the forward market by German firms tend to be offsetting.

The empirical observation that forward exchange rates are unbiased predictors of future spot-exchange rates must be reconciled with the observation that there is a substantial difference among countries in real interest rates. The countries with low real interest rates are the capital-rich countries, while the countries with high real interest rates are the capital-poor countries. The difference in real interest rates can be thought of as the return required for the marginal investor for taking on a foreign exchange exposure.

The combination of competition among the suppliers of these different financial instruments and arbitrage by firms and investors among those for altering exposure ensures that the costs to the firm or investor of using one of these techniques is not likely to differ by a large amount from the costs of some other technique. The cost of altering foreign exchange exposure through the use of forward contracts and through the use of futures contracts is likely to be less than 0.1 percent in a major currency, and perhaps closer to 0.02 or 0.03 percent. Similarly, the cost of forward contracts and the cost of leading-and-lagging are not likely to differ by more than several tenths of 1 percent. Any difference between the cost of these two techniques means that there is a deviation from interest rate parity theorem, and since this concept is based on arbitrage, any observed deviation implies that the financial assets or liabilities used for this comparison are less than perfect substitutes for each other.[7] Arbitrage may be constrained because of exchange controls. Or tax considerations may favor one technique for altering exposure rather than another.

The cost of each of the techniques for altering exposure is an opportunity cost. Hence, the cost of altering the firm's exposure can only be calculated after the end of the investment period, when the spot-exchange rate is known. The cost of altering the firm's exposure is the return for maintaining the exposed position during the period when the exchange rate changes.[8]

The costs of each technique for altering exposure may be compared in a present value analysis. For example, assume a U.S. firm wants to pay £10 million in two years. The U.S. firm can buy British pounds today for delivery in two years; in two years, the firm is obliged to deliver $3.5 million (on the assumption that the forward-exchange rate is $1.75 = £1.00). The present value of $3.5 million in two years can be obtained by using the firm's marginal cost of dollar funds as the interest rate. Alternatively, the firm might lead-and-lag; in this case, the firm uses present value analysis to determine the amount of British pounds that must be acquired today to compound to £2 million in two years; here, present value analysis is applied to the British pound investment.

Firm-Specific Factors and the Currency Denomination of Debt

If the managers of a firm were confident that Fisher Open would remain continuously valid, they would be indifferent about the currency denomination of its debt. The firm might have an income-statement exposure, but the managers would not be able to alter its aggregate foreign exchange exposure by altering the currency denomination of its bank loans and debt. The managers of the firm are concerned about the currency denomination of its debt because they believe there are nontrivial differences from Fisher Open in an ex ante, or anticipated, sense. The inputs to the debt denomination decision include the risk aversion of the firm, the risk the firm associates with particular foreign currencies, the distribution of the firm's income-statement exposure by currency, and the significance of the potential foreign exchange gains and losses to the firm's income, net worth, and market valuation.

Risk Aversion

Individual investors can be ranked by the risk premium that each requires for acquiring or maintaining exposure to loss—and to gain—from unanticipated changes in exchange rates. Similarly, individual firms can be ranked according to their willingness to bear the various cross-border risks.[9] The cliché that is the cornerstone of one view is that "we specialize in producing shoes or machine tools, not in speculating in the foreign exchange." This statement is a cop-out. Almost every firm that takes this view is implicitly speculating in foreign exchange because it has failed not only to devote any resources to measuring its foreign exchange exposure but also to arrange the currency denomination of its debt so that its income statement is not exposed.

For the managers of the firm, the key question is how their risk aversion compares with the risk aversiveness of investors as a group and of firms as a group. In this context, risk aversion is firm-specific and should be distinguished from the risk that each firm encounters because of the set of currencies in which the firm has an income-statement exposure.

For firms and for investors, the relevant risk is that of a portfolio of foreign currencies rather than an individual foreign currency. The less strong the correlation among the changes in the exchange rates of these several foreign currencies, the greater the likelihood that some firms and investors acquire or maintain exposures in each of several different foreign currencies. For these firms and investors, maintaining exposure in a group of foreign currencies leads to a disproportionate increase in the returns relative to the risk; for the firm, the increase in the return is a result of the reduction in interest costs; for the investor, the increase in the return is a result of higher interest income. And by extension, the risk of exposures in various foreign currencies can be grouped with a variety of other financial and nonfinancial risks, on the basis of the same proposition that there is an unusually large increase in the returns relative to the increase in risk as long as the changes in the price of these assets is less than perfectly correlated.

Some firms may manage the currency denomination of their bonds and bank loans to reduce their exposure to foreign exchange risk. In contrast, other firms may manage the currency composition of their debt so that the effect is an increase in their foreign-exchange exposure and increased sensitivity to gain and loss from changes in the exchange rates.

One difference among firms that affects their willingness to maintain a foreign exchange exposure is that their risk aversion may differ. The greater the risk aversion, the less likely is the firm to knowingly maintain a foreign-exchange exposure.

National Domicile

Firms headquartered in different countries may have somewhat similar exposures of their income statements. Consider a U.S. firm with an income-statement exposure in the Canadian dollar and a Canadian firm with an income-statement exposure in the United States. Assume the size of each income statement exposure is similar. Both the U.S. and the Canadian firms are concerned about the debt denomination decision. The Canadian firm could reduce its foreign-exchange exposure by borrowing U.S. dollars, at least to the extent that the increase in the volume of U.S. dollar-denominated loans or borrowings offsets the U.S. dollar exposure of its income statement. The Canadian firm might increase its U.S. dollar borrowings so they exceed the volume of its exposure on its income statement to reduce interest costs; at the same time the firm can reduce both its exposure and net interest costs by borrowing U.S. dollars. In contrast, if the U.S. firm seeks to reduce the exposure of its income statement by borrowing Canadian dollars, it increases its net interest payments. The asymmetry reflects that the difference in interest rates on comparable assets is large relative to the anticipated change in the exchange rate.

Risk of Particular Foreign Currencies and the Portfolio Effect

Individual foreign currencies can be ranked by their riskiness. Risk might be measured by the volatility of the movement of the foreign exchange value of individual foreign currencies, where the volatility might be measured as the range of movement or the standard deviation. Alternatively, the risk might be measured as unanticipated movement in the exchange rate, and either the range or standard deviation of the actual movement about the unanticipated movement.

The firm's attitude toward its exposure might be a function of the riskiness of particular currencies and the cost of altering its exposure. The algorithm is that the firm might maintain exposure in those currencies where the risk is low, and reduce its exposure in those currencies considered very risky. Moreover, this posture toward exposure in particular foreign currencies should be viewed in the context of a portfolio of currencies.

One implication of the portfolio argument is that the larger the firm and the more diverse the array of its foreign exchange exposures, the stronger the case for maintaining these exposures for any given posture toward risk aversion. The rationale is that as the number of currencies in which the firm has income-statement exposures increases, the larger the impact of the inclusion of each additional currency on the firm's income relative to the impact on the riskiness of the firm's portfolio of currencies. The common-sense interpretation is that those firms with income-statement exposures in a diverse group of foreign currencies are best positioned to carry these exposures and "collect" the risk premium in the foreign exchange market.

Materiality

One principle of personal finance is that individuals can increase their incomes by carrying small risks rather than buying insurance against these risks. Thus, individuals may buy automobile and homeowner's insurance with large deductibles; the principle is that they minimize the total cost by self-insuring for small risks. Similarly, individuals may buy major medical insurance and self-insure the cost of smaller medical expenses. The implication is that firms might carry small or modest exposures to their income statements and hedge any exceptionally large exposures. The distinction between large and small is arbitrary and firm-specific; for each firm the question becomes how large a foreign exchange loss it could accept during a quarter or a year, without having any unusual impact on its reported income or its market. The larger the firm, the larger the foreign exchange exposure it might carry.

Conclusions

The key decision in the debt denomination decision is whether the firm should denominate its debt and bank loans in its domestic currency or in a foreign currency. The managers of the firm must decide whether the denomination of debt and bank loans should be managed to increase or reduce the foreign exchange exposure of its income statement. Hence, they must first measure the components of the foreign exchange exposure associated with royalty and licensing income, and the income of the firm's foreign subsidiaries, exports, and domestic sales. Then the managers must address the market factors associated with exchange risk and decide whether they believe that risk premiums are evident in the foreign exchange market. The less convinced they are that risk premiums exist, the stronger the case for hedging the firm's foreign exchange exposure. The flip side of this statement is that the more evident the risk premiums, the larger the possible cost of hedging exposure and the greater the return from carrying the exposure.

Several firm-specific factors affect the firm's posture toward carrying or hedging foreign exchange exposure. A central one is its own attitude toward risk aversion. Moreover, the larger the array of currencies in which the firm has income-statement exposures, the more likely it is to view these exposures in a portfolio context. The firm might hedge only those exposures so large that the foreign exchange losses could have a significant impact on earnings and market value.

Notes

1. The analogy is the foreign exchange exposure or the major international banks on their loans to Mexico, Brazil, and Argentina. These loans were denominated in U.S. dollars, German marks, or Japanese yen; the borrowers acquired the foreign exchange exposure. But when the currencies of Mexico, Brazil, and Argentina depreciated sharply, the debt-servicing burden of the borrowing countries increased significantly and many went bankrupt.

2. The interest rate used in the present value calculation is likely to be the host-country interest rate or to be based on this interest rate.

3. A distinction must be made between the income-statement exposure on anticipated foreign sales and the balance-sheet exposure on sales-financing loans to the importers.

4. The firm's foreign exchange exposure on its export sales is not independent of whether the export sales are invoiced in the firm's currency or in the importer's currency. The rationale is that the volume of exports may decline more rapidly if the importer acquires the foreign exchange exposure than if the exporter does.

5. To some extent, the foreign exchange exposure of the foreign subsidiaries and of the parent may be offsetting.

6. The difference between the cost computed from payments and receipts, and the approximation based on the exchange rate in the futures contract and the spot-exchange rate on the date when the forward contract matures is a set of transactions costs.

7. There may be a difference between the cost of forward contracts and the cost of leading-and-lagging because the financial instruments denominated in different currencies used in leading-and-lagging are less than perfect substitutes for each other in terms of sensitivity to default or the exchange controls.

8. An alternative—and incorrect—approach to measuring the cost or altering the firm's exposure involves the comparison between the today's forward exchange rate and today's spot-exchange rate. This approach confuses the costs of two different techniques for altering foreign exchange exposure.

9. Finance theory stipulates that the managers of the firm should ignore risk in their borrowing and lending decisions. Individual investors can as a group neutralize the risk they associate with particular firms.

References

Aliber, Robert Z. *Exchange Risk and Corporate International Finance*. London: Macmillan, 1978.

Huizinga, John, and F. Miskin. "Inflation and Real Rates on Assets with Different Risk Characteristics." *Journal of Finance*, July 1984, pp. 699–714.

Levi, Maurice D. *International Finance: Financial Management and the International Economy*. New York: McGraw-Hill, 1983.

Levich, Richard N. *The International Money Market*. New York: JAI Press, 1979.

Makin, John H. "Portfolio Theory and the Problem of Foreign Exchange Risk." *Journal of Finance*, May 1978, pp. 517–34.

Oxelheim, Lars. *International Financial Market Fluctuations*. Chichester, England: John Wiley & Sons, 1985.

Papadia, F. "Forward Exchange Rates as Predictors of the Future Spot Rates and the Efficiency of the Foreign Exchange Market." *Journal of Banking and Finance*, June 1981, pp. 217–40.

Wihlborg, Claus. *Currency Risks in International Financial Markets under Different Exchange Rate Regimes*. Stockholm: Institute for International Economics, 1977.

12

Volatile Exchange Rates Can Put Operations at Risk

Donald R. Lessard and John B. Lightstone

Most senior executives understand that volatile exchange rates can affect the dollar value of their companies' assets and liabilities denominated in foreign currencies. Not many, however, understand that exchange rates can have a serious impact on operating profit. Fewer corporations have given managers responsibility for overseeing this operating exposure. Nevertheless, operating exposure is often a large cause of variability in operating profit from year to year, and many decisions depend on a good understanding of it.

In the long run, managers should consider operating exposure when setting strategy and worldwide product planning. In the short run, understanding operating exposure will often improve operating decisions. Also, the evaluation of a business unit and its managers should occur after exchange rate effects have been taken into account since they are outside management's control.

Operating exposure has become more important for several reasons. Exchange rates are more volatile in the world of managed floating rates than they were during the period of U.S. expansion in the international economy. More and more, countries follow divergent monetary policies. At the same time, markets are becoming more global. The United States no longer has a 70% or 80% world market share in key industries but shares markets more equally with Europe and Japan.

Because of these changes, exchange rates affect the operating profits of companies in globally competitive industries, whether or not they export their products. In fact, changes in exchange rates can often affect the operating profit of companies that have no foreign operations or exports but that face important foreign competition in their domestic market.

From *Harvard Business Review*, July/August 1986, pp. 107–114. Reprinted by permission.

By understanding the long- and short-run behavior of exchange rates, we can understand how they affect operating profit. In the long run, changes in the nominal dollar–foreign currency exchange rates tend to be about equal to the difference between the U.S. and foreign inflation rates in the price of traded goods. If the U.S. inflation rate is 4% higher than Germany's during the year, the deutsche mark will tend to strengthen approximately 4% against the dollar. This long-term relationship between exchange rates and price levels—usually called purchasing power parity (PPP)—implies that changes in competitiveness between countries, which would otherwise arise because of unequal inflation rates, tend to be offset by corresponding changes in exchange rates. In the short run of six months to several years, however, exchange rates are volatile and greatly influence the competitiveness of companies selling to the same market but getting materials and labor from different countries.

This short-run change in relative competitiveness results from changes in the nominal exchange rate that are not offset by the difference in inflation rates in the two countries. If the deutsche mark strengthens 4% against the dollar and the German inflation rate is 1%, a U.S. exporter to a German market served primarily by German producers would see its dollar price rise 5%. If, however, the inflation rate in the United States is 4%, or 3% higher than the German inflation rate, the operating margin of the U.S. producer will rise by only one percentage point.

This example shows that the change in relative competitiveness does not depend on changes in the *nominal* exchange rate—the number of deutsche marks obtained for each dollar—but on changes in the *real* exchange rate, which are changes in the nominal exchange rate minus the difference in inflation rates in the two countries. Thus, in the case of the U.S. exporter to Germany, the change in the nominal exchange rate is 4% but the change in the real exchange rate (which then affects operating profit) is only 1%.

Because changes in real exchange rates reflect deviations from PPP, over long periods of time the cumulative change in the real exchange rate tends to be smaller than that of the nominal exchange rate. The volatility of real exchange rates in the time frame of six months to several years, however, causes an exaggerated variability in operating margin.

Operating Exposure

Traditional analysis of currency exposure focuses on contractual items on the balance sheet such as debt, payables, and receivables denominated in a

Table 12.1
Currency exposure

	Accounting exposure	Operating exposure
Financial items considered	Contractual: debt, payables, receivables	Noncontractual: revenue, cost, profit
Inputs to measure exposure	Company's accounting statements	Company's competitive position
Exchange rate that affects profit	Nominal	Real

foreign currency whose dollar value is affected by nominal exchange rate changes (see table 12.1). The company may enter into forward contracts to hedge this contractual exposure.

A traditional analysis recognizes two types of impact on profits. One arises from translation of contractual items outstanding at year end, and the other involves transactions completed during the year. Accounting statements contain the information required to define this contractual or accounting exposure. With the adoption of FASB 52 in 1981, physical assets also enter into the calculation of foreign currency translation gains and losses. In general, however, these gains or losses bear little or no relation to operating exposure.

In economic terms, these contractual items are properly identified as exposed to changes in exchange rates. In many cases, however, this contractual exposure captures only a small part of exchange rates' total impact, which should include the real exchange rates' effect on such noncontractual items as revenues, costs, and operating profit. By hedging its contractual exposure but failing to take operating exposure into account, a company may be raising its total exposure. A company's operating and contractual exposure may have different origins, so that in many cases the two exposures will indeed have opposite signs.

The company must take into account both contractual and operating exposure. Unfortunately, the difference in emphasis in considering each type of exposure tends to make practitioners defensive who are accustomed to dealing with contractual exposure, while operating managers will view it as something outside their responsibility. It is hard to maintain a balanced perspective when the effects of changes in nominal exchange rates are identified separately in the income statement but the effects of changes in real exchange rates on revenues and costs are not.

To overcome these difficulties, companies must ensure that both the operations and the finance divisions understand operating exposure and must define an appropriate sharing of responsibility for its management between the two. We can separate the effects of exchange rates on operating profits into *margin effects* and *volume effects*. We shall illustrate each type of effect with examples based on composites of companies.

Economy Motors, a U.S. small-car manufacturer, sources domestically, sells exclusively in the home market, and has no foreign debt. Traditionalists would say the company has no exposure to changes in exchange rates. The fact is, however, that its operating profit is exposed to changes in the real yen-dollar exchange rate.

The company competes in the United States with Japanese manufacturers who are the market leaders. When setting a dollar price in the United States, the Japanese companies consider their yen costs. Figure 12.1 illustrates the competitive position of Economy Motors. In a year when the yen and the dollar are at parity, Economy Motors' dollar costs equal

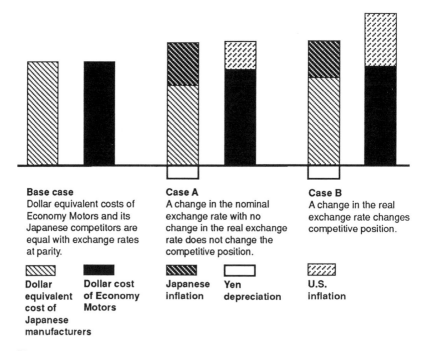

Base case
Dollar equivalent costs of Economy Motors and its Japanese competitors are equal with exchange rates at parity.

Case A
A change in the nominal exchange rate with no change in the real exchange rate does not change the competitive position.

Case B
A change in the real exchange rate changes competitive position.

Dollar equivalent cost of Japanese manufacturers	Dollar cost of Economy Motors	Japanese inflation	Yen depreciation	U.S. inflation

Figure 12.1
The effects of yen depreciation on the competitive position of Economy Motors

the dollar-equivalent costs of its Japanese competitors, and Economy Motors enjoys a normal operating profit margin. The same is true when the dollar costs of Economy Motors in the base year bear their normal relationship—but are not necessarily equal—to the dollar-equivalent costs of its competitors.

If, in a later year, Japan experiences a higher inflation rate than the United States, and if the yen weakens in line with PPP, the competitive position of Economy Motors does not change. The rise in the dollar-equivalent costs of the Japanese companies from Japanese inflation minus the effect of the yen depreciation equals the rise of Economy Motors' costs from domestic inflation. In this case, the nominal exchange rate has changed with no change in the real exchange rate or in Economy Motors' competitive position.

If, however, the yen weakens relative to the dollar by an amount more than required by PPP, the dollar-equivalent costs of the Japanese companies will be less than the costs of Economy Motors and the competitive position of Economy Motors will weaken. This was the case between 1980 and 1984 for many U.S. companies, including Chrysler, RCA, Zenith, and Black & Decker, that compete with Japanese imports.

This example illustrates several characteristics of operating exposure:

• Operating exposure bears no necessary relation to accounting or contractual exposure.

• The structure of the markets in which the company and its competitors source labor and materials and sell products determines operating exposure. Measurement of operating exposure must accordingly take these factors into account. Measurement of accounting exposure has traditionally considered only the company itself.

• The country in which goods are sold or inputs sourced does not necessarily affect operating exposure. As we saw, while it sells only at home, Economy Motors still has a high yen exposure.

• Operating exposure is not necessarily linked to the currency in which prices are quoted.

• Operating profit varies with real exchange rate changes.

Market Structure

The importance of market structure in determining operating exposure is evident in the following two cases:

Specialty Chemicals (Canada), the Canadian subsidiary of a U.S. company, distributes chemicals produced by its parent in the United States. With few fixed assets, it has little debt. It quotes prices in Canadian dollars. A weak Canadian dollar reduces the U.S. dollar value of the company's Canadian dollar receivables, and from an accounting viewpoint Specialty Chemicals is exposed because of these receivables.

Looking beyond the accounting treatment, we see that when the Canadian dollar weakens, Specialty Chemicals' costs will go up in Canadian dollars. This raises a number of questions: Does Specialty Chemicals have a Canadian dollar operating exposure? Should it construct a Canadian manufacturing plant to match revenues and costs? Should the company issue Canadian dollar debt so that if the Canadian dollar weakens, it can reduce the U.S. dollar value of its repayments?

To answer these questions, Specialty Chemicals must examine the structure of the marketplace in which it sells its product. The company and all its competitors import products from the United States. Any rise in Canadian dollar costs is felt equally by everyone, with no change in their relative competitive position, and is reflected quickly in a higher price. This price responsiveness offsets the cost responsiveness so there is no operating exposure except in the very short run. Issuing Canadian dollar debt or building a plant in Canada would introduce a new operating exposure where none existed. This analysis holds in industries in which several U.S. companies collectively dominate the world market, like mainframe computers and, until recently, commercial aircraft.

Operating exposure often differs greatly among companies that appear similar but sell to markets with different structures. As in the previous case, Home Products (Canada), the Canadian subsidiary of a U.S. company, purchases its product from its parent. Its competitors, however, have manufacturing facilities in Canada and have the largest share of the Canadian market. If the Canadian dollar weakens in real terms, the company's Canadian dollar costs will rise without any associated rise in price. Thus cost is responsive without any offsetting price response so that Home Products has a Canadian dollar–U.S. dollar operating exposure.

Home Products can reduce this exposure by building a plant in Canada or by using a financial hedge to offset the effect of the real exchange rate change. Or if Home Products raises its Canadian market share to become the market leader, it may be able to raise prices to offset some or all of the higher Canadian dollar costs caused by a weakening Canadian dollar, thereby reducing its operating exposure. This competitive situation is typical of many companies in the U.S. consumer goods industry, such as Procter & Gamble, Colgate-Palmolive, and Dart & Kraft.

A Canadian exporter to the United States with a small share of the U.S. market will be affected by changes in the real Canadian dollar–U.S. dollar exchange rate in opposite ways to Home Products. When the Canadian dollar weakens in real terms, Home Products' profits will decline but the Canadian exporter's will increase. Table 12.2 summarizes the effect of various combinations of cost responsiveness and price responsiveness on the size of the resulting operating exposure in these examples.

We can apply the same analysis to the more realistic but also more complex case of companies that compete globally rather than in specific national markets. Consider the case of Global Instrumentation (GI), a U.S. company that sells precision measurement instruments worldwide and is its industry's market leader. Since product requirements do not vary from country to country and transshipment costs are a small part of the product's value, its prices are approximately uniform worldwide. Since its products represent a small fraction of its customers' total costs, demand is quite insensitive to price. Nevertheless, GI management does not allow prices

Table 12.2
Operating exposure matrix

		Cost responsiveness		
		Low	Moderate	High
Price responsiveness	Low	Small		Large Home Products
	Moderate		Small	
	High	Large Ecomony Motors		Small Specialty Chemicals

and margins to become so high as to encourage other companies to enter the market. GI sets its prices taking into account its costs and those of actual and potential competitors. If most of its potential competitors are also U.S.-based, its prices in dollars will be quite independent of exchange rates. If GI is attempting to discourage potential competitors in other countries, it will set lower dollar prices in periods of relative dollar strength.

Compare this case with Earthworm Tractors, a U.S.-based manufacturer of heavy construction equipment. Its prices vary somewhat across countries because of high shipping costs and variations in product specifications. It faces two important competitors in Germany and Japan. The cost positions of the three companies are such that exchange rate fluctuations shift cost and price leadership, and so basic world prices, whether measured in dollars, yen, or deutsche marks, respond to exchange rate changes.

These cases illustrate some other characteristics of operating exposure:

• Differences between competitors in sourcing, technology, or country of manufacture introduce operating exposure.

• Market leaders will usually have lower operating exposure.

• Operating exposure is peculiar to particular businesses. A company with subsidiaries in any given country is likely to have several operating exposures, so it must evaluate the exposure of each business unit separately. A standard accounting treatment, by contrast, combines the exposures of the various businesses in an area company.

• Companies facing the same real exchange rate may have opposite operating exposures.

Effects on Volume

In some cases, real exchange rate changes will have their most important impact not on operating margins but on volume. United Kingdom Airways is a fictitious U.K.-based charter airline that sells package tours to the United States. As the pound sterling weakens relative to the dollar in real terms, the company will carry fewer British travelers to the United States. Since the travel cost is less than half the total cost of a vacation, a seller of travel services can do little to offset the rising cost of a trip to the United States.

Laker Airways, a U.K.-based company, seems to have directed its marketing mainly at British travelers. With a marketing strategy more evenly balanced between travel originating in the United States and the United Kingdom, it would have experienced little effect on the demand for total air travel between the two countries due to changes in the real exchange rate. Although fewer British tourists would visit the United States when the dollar was strong, more Americans would travel to Britain. Until 1980, Laker transported a rising number of British tourists. This was mostly because the pound was strengthening beyond its parity with the dollar. In 1980, however, Laker financed new aircraft purchases in dollars, thereby doubling its exposure. When the pound later weakened, Laker was forced into bankruptcy.

Measuring Operating Exposure

A company can readily determine contractual or accounting exposure from accounting statements. Operating exposure, on the other hand, cannot be estimated in this way. The measurement of operating exposure requires an understanding of the structure of the markets in which the company and its competitors obtain labor and materials and sell their products and also of the degree of their flexibility to change markets, product mix, sourcing, and technology.

The estimate of operating exposure will not, however, be as precise as an estimate of contractual exposure. Treasury staff can usually have successful dialogues with operating management to obtain this information. Since most managers have the information to answer these questions but lack the analytical framework to use it themselves, treasury staff will usually have to coordinate the audit process. For many companies this represents a closer involvement of the treasury group with operations and an enlarged treasury responsibility. The treasury function's involvement in operating considerations reflects the fact that the impact of exchange rates on a company's profit is in some sense a financial effect and is to a large extent outside the control of the business, yet it corresponds to an important aspect of the external competitive environment.

The exposure audit with operating management should include the following questions: Who are actual and potential important competitors in various markets? Who are low-cost producers? Who are price leaders? What has happened to profit margins when real exchange rates have shifted markedly? What flexibility does the company have to switch production to countries with undervalued currencies?

Operating management will welcome this dialogue because an understanding of operating exposure can improve operating decisions and, as we will see, can help measure managerial performance. Economy Motors, for example, is likely to gain market share when the dollar is weak and when its Japanese competitors face falling yen-equivalent prices—if management has anticipated these circumstances in its contingency planning.

Managing Exposure

In managing contractual and operating exposure, companies have both business and financial options (see table 12.3). A company may reduce its contractual exposure by changing the invoicing currency, which is a business option. Since contractual exposure is a function of nominal exchange rates, the financial instruments available for offsetting this exposure also involve nominal exchange rates. The company may accordingly manage the exposure by borrowing in a foreign currency or by entering into forward contracts to buy or deliver the foreign currency. Or the company may believe that its knowledge of the future direction of exchange rates is superior to the market's and choose not to cover all or part of its contractual exposure.

In managing operating or noncontractual exposure, the business options are often strategic instead of tactical. And since changes in real, not nominal, exchange rates influence operating exposure, the traditional financial instruments used to manage contractual exposure are not very effective.

Companies have three business options for managing operating exposure:

• A company may choose to configure each of its various businesses to reduce the operating exposure of that business, for example, by carefully selecting manufacturing sites. Or a company may differentiate its product so that it has a smaller operating exposure than a commodity product in an otherwise similar market structure. When a company introduces a new product class, the operating exposure starts out small and then grows as competing products enter the market. These structural hedges generally have an associated cost that reduces the expected rate of return of the business. To limit operating exposure, for example, a company may build plants in many countries and forgo major economies of scale. As a re-

Table 12.3
Exposure management

Exposure	Exchange rate	Financial options	Business options
Accounting	Nominal	Foreward contracts/foreign currency debt	Invoicing currency
Operating	Real	Operating exposure high	Structural hedge

sult, the company reduces both expected cash flows and the degree of exchange-rate-related variability.

• Parent companies may alternatively allow individual businesses to have large operating exposures but may select a portfolio of businesses that have offsetting exposures so that the company as a whole has only a small exposure. With this strategy, management must carefully review the individual business units' operating results after correction for the effects of operating exposure.

• Or the company may choose to exploit exchange rate volatility by configuring its businesses to have the flexibility to be able to increase production and sourcing in countries where currencies become strongly undervalued in real terms. This will tend to add costs of switching locations and building excess capacity, but it will reduce average operating costs across a spectrum of exchange rates. Depending on the trade-off between the additional expense and cost savings, switching locations will represent a good investment for some companies as it will increase average profitability and at the same time reduce exchange-rate-related profit variability. A business may also be able to modify its product and marketing mix to meet changed market conditions.

These business responses differ in important respects. Configuring specific businesses to reduce operating exposure and possibly to exploit exchange rate volatility will alter both average profit levels and exchange-rate-related variability in profits. Hence fairly priced financial options that have zero net present value will not accomplish the same result. The second option, pooling businesses to reduce operating exposure, has no direct impact on expected operating cash flow. Therefore appropriate financial instruments can achieve the same end.

If fairly priced, financial options will have no effect on the company's expected gain or loss. Further, in contrast to business options, which may involve relocating a manufacturing plant, for example, they can be modified to reflect changing circumstances at little or no cost. Thus they clearly are preferable to business options that lower expected profits to reduce exchange-rate-related risk. Given the organizational costs of building a portfolio of businesses with offsetting operating exposures, financial options are also likely to dominate diversification that is undertaken solely to reduce exchange-rate-related variability in profits.

The most common financial option for offsetting operating exposure is to borrow long term in a foreign currency. This borrowing, however, which is equivalent to a dollar borrowing coupled with a long-dated currency swap, is at best an approximate hedge for operating exposure. The dollar cost of foreign currency borrowing fluctuates with the nominal exchange rate, while operating exposure is a function of the real exchange rate. The nominal and real exchange rates often diverge over time. Also, companies are unaccustomed to lending long term in a foreign currency when that is required to offset a cost exposure.

A company can somewhat improve its operating exposure by selling short-term forward contracts on a rolling basis. Although this policy contradicts the conventional wisdom that companies should finance long-term foreign operations with fixed-rate foreign currency borrowing, in most cases it provides a better offset to operating exposures. Existing swap transactions provide no improvement because they essentially replicate either the fixed or the floating rate options, perhaps with lower transaction costs.

In simulations from 1977 to 1985, for example, we found that a U.S. exporter to Germany with a "normal" profit margin of 15% would have experienced swings in profitability ranging from a high of 35% to a low of nearly—30% in line with swings in the real dollar–deutsche mark exchange rate. If the company had attempted to hedge its operating exposure with fixed-rate foreign currency borrowing or its equivalent, a long-dated currency swap, its profit margin would have varied between 8% and 30%. With floating rate borrowing, or rolling sales of short-term forward foreign exchange contracts, these margins would have varied between 17% and 41%. While these higher margins might suggest that this short-term hedge was the best alternative, they actually show that the short-term hedge was a poor counterbalance to the variation in operating profits that might under- or overshoot in the future.

It is possible to design a new kind of financial instrument that meets these objections to the use of existing instruments. Unlike previously available hedges, this one is linked to the real exchange rate and hence is particularly appropriate for offsetting operating exposures. Like existing long-dated currency swaps, it may involve either two industrial counterparties, which in this case have opposite operating exposures, or one party and a financial institution.

It will generally be possible to identify two companies with opposite operating exposures with respect to the same real exchange rate. The operating exposure hedge is a contractual arrangement between two such companies. Operating exposure losses by one party are offset by operating exposure gains of the counterparty. This allows the company to offset closely the variability in operating profits caused by real exchange rate changes. Previously available instruments do not move with changes in the real exchange rate and therefore have limited usefulness in managing operating exposure.

A company entering into this operating exposure hedge has no expected long-run gain or loss because any expected change in the real exchange rate is incorporated in the initial pricing of the contract. On a year-to-year basis, however, any decrease (or increase) in the normal operating profit due to short-run changes in the real exchange rate will be offset by a corresponding gain (or loss) on the hedge contract so as to reduce the variability in operating earnings associated with changes in the real exchange rate. In addition, the termination provisions of this hedge allow the company to retain a strategic flexibility that would not be available with a structural hedge to manage operating exposure.

Measuring Management

When evaluating the quality of a business and its management's effectiveness, executives should consider the effect of exchange rates on a company's operating profit. Changes in real exchange rates cannot usually be predicted over the planning cycle of a business with sufficient accuracy to be useful in developing plans and budgets. It is unreasonable to hold operating managers accountable for the effects of exchange rates on operating profits that are outside their control, so the measurement and incentive compensation of the managers should be based on reported results after correction for operating exposure effects.

A company can accomplish this end in several ways. One is to allow operating managers to enter into hedge contracts with corporate treasury so that they can "contract away" their exposures. This stratagem closely parallels the treatment of transaction exposures in many companies, whereby operating units implicitly sell foreign currency receivables to the treasury function at the forward rate or, in an equivalent transaction, the operating units are charged local currency financing costs on those receivables.

A second method is to adjust the actual performance of the unit for variations in the real exchange rate after the end of the period. A third way is to adjust performance plans in line with variations in the real exchange rate. The third approach is generally preferable to the second since it can measure operations' true profitability as well as the operating manager's contributions to this profit. The choice between the first and third options, however, will depend on the nature of the business and its organization.

Some people argue that a company can overcome this problem by measuring performance on an unadjusted basis in local currency rather than in dollars. The assumption underlying this view is that the unit in question has no operating exposure from a local currency perspective and hence its dollar profits should move one for one with the real exchange rate. This will be true, however, only in special cases where there is little global pricing influence. Every one of these approaches requires before-the-fact estimates of the company's exposure.

To use any of these approaches, the company must understand its operating exposures. Given the complex interactions between currency fluctuations and other factors affecting demand and competitiveness, however, exact models and hence exact performance or budget adjustments will probably be impossible. This uncertainty underscores the need for open and continuing communication between top executives and operating managers to improve understanding of these exposures and also to anticipate responses to possible exchange rate scenarios. This communication not only will provide a better basis for after-the-fact measurement but also will make the company more aware of its potential responses. In the end, a suitable response to the risk of volatile exchange rates will raise profits and reduce risks.

13

International Capital Budgeting

Alan C. Shapiro

Multinational corporations evaluating foreign investments are forced to confront several capital budgeting issues that are rarely, if ever, encountered by wholly domestic firms. Here are just a few: How do foreign tax regulations affect the expected profitability of international investments? Should management evaluate projected cash flows from the standpoint of a foreign subsidiary, and in terms of local currencies, or from the home currency perspective? How can the use of foreign sources of financing be reflected in investment analysis? Should the required rate of return on international investments be raised to reflect risks like expropriation, currency controls, and exchange rate fluctuations? Are there significant benefits to investors from international portfolio diversification? and if so, how does this affect the value of foreign investment by multinationals?

My purpose in this article is to address these issues in the context of modern finance theory, and to present a practical framework that incorporates the special complications of international investment into the standard discounted cash flow (DCF) capital budgeting method. By reducing to a common denominator the effects of these complex factors on the expected profitability of contemplated foreign investments, the framework enables management to evaluate international projects on a uniform basis and, thus, to compare them directly with all other investment opportunities. The principle aim of the framework is to make the greatest possible use of available information about the expected risks and returns of foreign investment. At the same time, it eliminates some of the arbitrary adjustments of cost of capital and cash flow that are now common practice in multinational capital budgeting.

Before turning to the subject of international investment, I want to review the standard DCF method that most companies use to evaluate

From *Midland Corporate Finance Journal*, Spring 1983, pp. 26–45. Reprinted by permission.

their capital investment alternatives. Then I will discuss the modifications of the standard DCF framework necessary to accommodate the special features of foreign project appraisal. This is followed by a discussion of the required rate of return, or cost of capital, for foreign investments. Finally, having proposed a financial framework for quantifying the value of investments, I offer a theoretical rationale for direct foreign investment that attempts to identify the characteristics most likely to distinguish—*prior* to any detailed, systematic financial analysis—profitable from unprofitable foreign projects. Such a rationale should serve as a basic guide for multinational strategic thinking; it can also be used to furnish the criteria for the first screening of foreign investment opportunities.

The Discounted Cash Flow Framework

The standard capital budgeting analysis has two steps. The first, and ordinarily the most time-consuming, is the estimation of expected after-tax cash flows associated with a prospective investment. The second is the discounting of those cash flows back to the present using the company's weighted average cost of capital. If the resulting number, known as the net present value (NPV) of those cash flows, is positive the investment should be undertaken; if negative, it should be rejected.

The weighted average cost of capital (WACC) is conceptually simple and easy to apply. Recall that the calculation of WACC involves weighting the after-tax cost of each component of capital by its proportional representation in the (target) company's capital structure. For a company, with only debt and equity in its capital base, its overall cost of capital and, hence, its required rate of return on normal investments, would be expressed as follows:

WACC = (Cost of Debt × Debt/Total Capital) + (Cost of Equity

× Equity/Total Capital)

The use of the weighted cost of capital is thus predicated on the assumption of a specific financing structure, or debt-equity ratio, *for each individual project*. Consequently, the indiscriminate, corporation-wide use of a single rate is appropriate only when the financial structures and commercial risks are similar for all investments considered. The costs of debt and equity will vary with different project risks. Furthermore, because projects with different risks are likely to have different debt capacities, their required rates of returns should be calculated using not the company's capital structure, but rather the financial structure supported by the project standing apart from the company.

Another objection to the use of a single corporation-wide discount rate —one especially pertinent to foreign investments—is its failure to reflect the availability of project-specific loans at concessionary rates. There also may be cases where the multinational (MNC) may choose to use foreign source funds having a higher cost due to home country exchange controls. The benefits or costs of these unusual sources of financing should be reflected in the analysis.

An Adjusted Present Value Approach

One way to reflect these deviations from the company's typical investment and financing policy is to adjust the company's weighted average cost of capital. But, for some companies, such as those in extractive industries, there is no norm. Project risks and financial structure vary by country, raw material, production stage, and position in the life cycle of the project. Such problems can be dealt with by using an alternative procedure, known as the "adjusted present value" (APV) approach. Developed by Stewart Myers[1] in the early 1970s, the APV approach involves discounting cash flows at a rate that, by removing the effects of financing, reflects only the business risks of the project. This rate, called the *all-equity* rate (also known as the "cost of capital for business risk"), represents the required rate of return on a project financed entirely with equity.

The all-equity rate, c, can be used in capital budgeting by viewing the value of a project as the sum of the following components: (1) the present value of project cash flows after taxes but before financing costs, discounted at c; (2) the present value of the tax savings on debt financing, discounted at the company's normal domestic borrowing rate, b; and (3) the present value of any savings on (or penalties from) interest costs associated with project-specific financing, discounted also at b.[2] This latter differential would generally be due to government regulations and/or subsidies that caused interest rates on restricted funds to diverge from domestic interest payable on unsubsidized, arm's-length borrowings.

In equation form, the APV of a project can be expressed as follows:

$$APV = -I + X/c + [(b \times D) \times t]/b + [(b - b') \times D']/b$$

where:

I is the initial investment, assuming a one-time initial outlay

X is the expected annual operating after-tax cash flow, assuming the
project is financed with all equity (and has an infinite life)

c is the risk-adjusted required rate of return on the specific project, assuming the project is financed solely with equity

b is the company's normal domestic borrowing rate

D is the amount of debt financing supported by the project (assumed to
be constant throughout the project's life)

t is the company's marginal tax rate

b' is the rate of interest (translated into its domestic equivalent) on special foreign source financing

D' is the amount of special foreign source debt financing used (also assumed to be constant throughout)

It should be emphasized that the all-equity cost of capital equals the required rate of return on a *specific* project; this in turn can be broken down
into the riskless rate of interest plus an appropriate risk premium based on
the project's particular risk. Thus c varies according to the risk of the
specific project.

Recall also that, in accordance with the capital asset pricing model
(CAPM), the risk reflected in c is only "systematic risk." As measured by
"beta," systematic risk reflects not the total variability of a company or
project's expected returns, but rather its covariability with market-wide
(e.g., S & P 500) average returns. It is a measure of investors' exposure to
"non-diversifiable" or market risk and, as such, reflects the sensitivity of an
investment's return to general economic conditions which affect all stock
prices.

For project analysis, this means that a project's risk and, thus, its minimum required rate of return should reflect its correlation only with overall
market returns. The interaction of the project's returns with the returns of
the company's other investments is largely irrelevant, and thus should be
ignored, in the valuation and capital budgeting process. The message of
modern finance is that, in well-functioning capital markets, *corporate* diversification does not add value. Why, after all, should investors pay premiums for diversified companies when they can privately and cheaply
accomplish the same end by buying a mutual fund? Casual observation,
combined with what evidence we have on this question, says that the
market doesn't reward companies for diversification it can easily duplicate
at the same or lower cost.

In short, each individual project should be viewed as having its own required return; and this risk-adjusted minimum return, or "cost of capital," is completely unaffected by the composition of the company's portfolio of present and prospective investments.

Issues in Foreign Investment Analysis

With this review of the principles of valuation as background, let's turn to two troublesome issues confronting foreign project analysts:

1. Should expected cash flows be measured from the standpoint of the project (or the foreign subsidiary's managers) or from that of the parent company?

2. Should the uniquely foreign economic and political risks be reflected by raising the required rate of return (or the discount rate) or by adjusting expected cash flows?

Parent Versus Project Cash Flows

Because of tax regulations and exchange controls, a substantial difference can exist between the cash flow of a project and the amount that can be remitted to the parent multinational corporation. Also, many project expenses, such as management fees and royalties, are actually returns to the parent company. And, yet another source of this discrepancy, the *incremental* revenue contributed to the parent MNC by a project can differ from total project revenues if, for example, the project involves substituting local production for parent company exports, or if transfer price adjustments shift profits elsewhere in the system. (It is only incremental revenues, of course, that should be credited to the project.)

Given the appreciable differences between parent and project cash flows likely to exist, what, then, are the relevant cash flows to use in evaluating a foreign project? The managers of a foreign subsidiary can be expected to focus only, of course, on those project cash flows accruing locally. Unless compensated for doing otherwise, they will tend to ignore the consequences of their investment policies on the economic situation of the rest of the MNC.

Partly because of the impracticability of expecting local management to take a global view, and partly out of a desire to decentralize decision-making and offer foreign managers greater autonomy, some have suggested that the effect of restrictions on repatriation be ignored. According to economic theory, however, the value of a project is determined by the net present value of future cash flows *back to the investor*. Thus, the parent MNC should value only those cash flows (net of any transfer costs such as taxes) that are—or, more precisely, *can be*—repatriated. Only remittable funds can be used to pay dividends and interest, to amortize the firm's debt, and to reinvest.[3]

To overcome the problem caused by the difference between project and parent cash flows, I recommend that the financial analysis of foreign investments proceed in three stages. In the first stage, project cash flows are computed solely from the subsidiary's standpoint, as if it were a separate national corporation. In the second stage, the perspective shifts to that of the parent company. This step requires specific forecasts of the amounts, forms, and timing of transfers (assuming all repatriable cash is actually remitted) to headquarters. It also involves gathering information about taxes and other expenses incurred in the transfer process. Third and last, the parent company should take into account the indirect benefits and costs this investment confers or imposes on the rest of the system, such as an increase or decrease in export sales by another affiliate. This, of course, may not be easy to do. In some cases, management may be able to estimate incremental cash flows to the parent only by subtracting worldwide parent company cash flows (without the investment) from post-investment parent company cash flows.

While the principle of adjusting and valuing incremental cash flows is conceptually simple, it can become quite complicated in its actual application. Let's look at how this recommended procedure might be applied, with special attention to the tax question.

Incorporating Tax Factors
Because only after-tax cash flows are relevant, it is necessary to determine when and what taxes must be paid on foreign-source profits. On the basis of existing tax laws, taxes paid are a function of the time of remittance (are profits remitted immediately or are they reinvested?), the form of remittance (whether as dividends, loan repayments, or transfer price adjustments), the foreign income tax rate, the existence of withholding taxes, the treaties between home and host countries, and the existence and usability of foreign tax credits.

Because of these complexities in estimating actual after-tax cash flows back to the parent, I propose a simpler approach for calculating the tax

Box 13.1
Calculation of Marginal Tax Rate

A simple calculation of an MNC's marginal tax rate on remitted foreign-source earnings illustrates the procedure. Suppose after-tax earnings of $120,000 will be remitted by an affiliate to its U.S. parent in the form of a dividend. Assume the foreign tax rate is 40%, the withholding tax on dividends is 4%, and excess foreign tax credits are unavailable. The marginal rate of additional taxation is found by adding the local withholding tax to the U.S. tax owed on the dividend. Withholding tax in this case would equal $4,800 ($120,000 × .04), while U.S. tax owed would be $7,200. (The U.S. tax is calculated as follows. With a before-tax local income of $200,000 ($200,000 × (1 − .4) = $120,000), the U.S. tax owed before foreign tax credits would equal $200,000 × .46, or $92,000. The firm would receive foreign tax credits equal to $84,800, for the $80,000 in local tax paid and the $4,800 dividend withholding tax. This leaves a net of $7,200 owed the IRS.) The incremental taxes on the MNC's remitted foreign-source earnings would thus equal $12,000 ($4,800 + $7,200) and the marginal tax rate would be 10% ($12,000/$120,000).

liabilities on the foreign investment. This approach makes two conservative assumptions: first, the maximum amount of funds available for remittance in each year is actually remitted; second, the tax rate applied to these cash flows is the higher of the home or host country rate. This means that a project is evaluated as if the maximum allowable amount of dividends were repatriated each year.

The fact that there are substantial tax savings from reinvesting locally instead of repatriating can be ignored at this initial stage of the investment analysis. The recognition of excess foreign tax credits and alternative, lower-cost remittance channels should also be deferred. Finally, in order to avoid understating the parent's tax liability (by understating remitted cash flow), all funds expected to be transferred back to the parent in the form of management fees, royalties, and licensing fees are included in this initial stage of the analysis.

The reasoning behind this division of the investment analysis procedure into these stages is straightforward: if the investment is acceptable under conservative assumptions, then it will be acceptable under a more liberal set of circumstances, and it will not be necessary to calculate all the additional tax savings possible. If the initial net present value is negative under these conservative assumptions, then the additional tax savings can be estimated and added back.

Political and Economic Risk Analysis

All else being equal, multinational companies prefer to invest in countries with stable currencies, healthy economies, and minimal political risks. But because all else is usually not equal, management must carefully evaluate the consequences of various political and economic risks for the viability of potential investments.

There are presently, to my knowledge, four practical (though not necessarily correct) methods of incorporating international political and economic risks, such as the risks of currency fluctuations and expropriation, into foreign investment analysis. They are

1. Shortening the minimum payback period.
2. Raising the required rate of return of the investment.
3. Adjusting cash flows for the costs of risk reduction; e.g., charging a premium for overseas political risk insurance.
4. Adjusting cash flows to reflect the specific impact of a given risk.

Adjusting the Discount Rate or Payback Period

The additional risks confronted abroad are usually discussed in general terms rather than in direct relation to specific investments. This rather vague view of risk probably explains the popularity of two questionable approaches to account for the added political and economic risks of overseas operations. One is to use a higher discount rate for foreign operations, the other to require a shorter payback period. For example, if exchange restrictions are anticipated, a normal required return of 15% might be raised to 20%, or, alternatively, a five-year payback standard may be shortened to three years.

Neither of these approaches lends itself to careful evaluation of the actual impact of a particular risk on expected investment returns. Thorough risk analysis requires an assessment of the magnitude and timing of such risks, and their implications for the projection of cash flows. For example, an expropriation expected five years hence is likely to be much less threatening than one anticipated next year, even though there is a higher probability associated with the former. Using a uniformly higher discount rate to reflect these quite different expropriation risks only serves to distort the meaning of the *present value* of a project by penalizing future cash flows relatively more heavily than current ones. It is not a good substitute for careful risk evaluation.

Furthermore, the choice of a risk premium (or risk premiums, if the discount rate is allowed to vary over time), whether 2% or 10%, is an arbitrary one. Adjusting cash flows instead of assigning some more or less arbitrary risk premium makes it possible to make fuller, more specific use of the information available about the effects of a specific risk on the future returns from an investment.

The two principal methods for adjusting cash flow estimates to reflect international risks are (1) uncertainty absorption and (2) adjustment of expected values of future cash flows.

Uncertainty Absorption

Uncertainty absorption is used to quantify the effect of international risk by charging against each year's flows a premium for political and economic risk insurance, whether or not such insurance is actually purchased.[4] Political risks like currency inconvertibility or expropriation can be covered by insurance bought through the Overseas Private Investment Corporation, a U.S. government agency. Economic risks like currency fluctuations can be hedged in the forward exchange market. In the latter case, the uncertainty absorption approach involves adjusting each period's dollar cash flow by the cost of a hedging program (again, regardless of whether the program is put in place).

There is, however, a problem with the uncertainty absorption method: it does not accurately measure the effect of a given political or economic risk on the present value of a project. In the case of expropriation, political risk insurance normally covers only the book value, not the economic value, of expropriated assets. The relationship between the book value of a project's assets and the economic value of a project, as measured by its future cash flows, is at best tenuous. It is worthwhile, of course, to compare the cost of political risk insurance with its expected benefits. But insurance is no substitute for a careful evaluation of the impact of political risk on the expected profitability of a specific project.

As a method for dealing with exchange risk, the uncertainty absorption technique is fine if local currency cash flows are fixed, as in the case of interest on a foreign-currency-denominated bond. But, where income is generated by an ongoing business operation, the operating cash flow in local currency will itself be affected by changes in the exchange rate.[5] This effect is entirely ignored by the uncertainty absorption technique.

Adjusting Expected Values

In 1978, I published a paper recommending that the expected cash flows, not the discount rate, of a project be adjusted to reflect the *specific* impact of each perceived risk. The argument was based largely on my firsthand observation that management typically has more and better information about the effect of a given risk on a project's cash flows, than about its effect on shareholders' required return. Such cash flow adjustments, by assigning probabilities to various economic and political events, will generate an *expected* value for the project; that is, the value resulting from this adjustment will reflect the expected "mean" or average outcome of a number of possible effects on cash flow caused by specific international risks.

In adjusting expected cash flow downward and allowing the discount rate to remain unchanged, this procedure does not assume that shareholders have a neutral attitude toward risk. What it does assume, however, is that either (1) risks such as expropriation, currency controls, inflation, and exchange rate changes are unsystematic or (2) the diversification provided by foreign investment may actually *lower* a firm's systematic risk. If the latter is true (and, as I will argue later, there is some persuasive evidence to support this belief), adjusting only the expected values of future cash flows will yield a *lower bound* on the value of the investment to the firm.

According to modern capital asset pricing theory, adjusting expected cash flows, instead of the discount rate, to reflect incremental risks is justified so long as the systematic risk of a proposed investment remains unchanged. To the extent that these international political and economic risks are unsystematic, there is no theoretical reason to adjust the cost of capital of a project to reflect those risks. The possibility that foreign investments may actually reduce a firm's systematic risk by providing international diversification means that this approach, if anything, underestimates the present value of a project to the parent corporation.[6]

The Impact of Political Risk

In recent years, there has been a significant increase, in developing and developed countries alike, in the kinds and magnitude of political risks that multinational companies have historically faced. Currency controls, expropriation, changes in tax laws, requirements for additional local production or expensive pollution control equipment—these are just some of the more visible forms political risk can take. The common denominator of such risks, however, is not hard to identify: government intervention into the workings of the economy that affects, for good or ill, the value of the firm. While the consequences are usually adverse, changes in the political environment can provide opportunities. The imposition of quotas on autos from Japan, for example, was undoubtedly beneficial to U.S. auto manufacturers.

Measuring Political Risks

A number of commercial and academic political risk forecasting models are available today. These models typically supply country indices that attempt to quantify the level of political risk in each nation. Most of these indices rely on some measure(s) of the stability of the local political regime. Such measures may include the frequency of changes of government, the level of violence in a country (for example, violent deaths per 100,000 population), the number of armed insurrections, conflicts with other states, and so on. The basic function of these stability indicators is to determine how long the current regime will be in power and, equally important, whether that regime will also be willing and able to enforce its foreign investment guarantees.

Other popular indicators of political risk include various economic factors such as inflation, balance of payments deficits or surpluses, and the level and growth rate of per capita GNP. The intention behind these measures is to determine whether the economy is in good shape or requires a "quick fix." Foreign governments with sagging economies often resort to expropriations to increase government revenues, or to measures blocking currency conversions to improve their balance of payments.

Despite the increased sophistication of these models, there is little evidence of their success in forecasting political risk. For one thing, political instability by itself does not necessarily contribute to political risk. Changes of government in Latin America, for example, are quite frequent; yet, most multinationals continue to go about their business undisturbed.

The most important weakness of these indices, however, is their implicit assumption that each firm in a country faces the same degree of political risk. As indicated by the empirical evidence on the post–World War II experiences of U.S. and British MNCs, this assumption is manifestly untrue. The data clearly show that, except in those countries that went Communist, companies differ in their susceptibilities to political risk according to their industry, size, composition of ownership, level of technology, and degree of vertical integration with other affiliates.[7] For example, expropriation—or, its more prevalent form, creeping expropriation—is more likely to occur in the extractive, utility, and financial service sectors of an economy than in the manufacturing sector.[8] Also, the expected effect of currency controls will probably not be the same over the life of an investment. It is only when a project is throwing off excess cash that restrictions on profit repatriation generally become a problem.

Because political risk has a different meaning for, and effect on, each firm, it is doubtful that any index of generalized political risk will be of much value to a company selected at random. The specific operating and financial characteristics of a company will largely determine its susceptibility to political risk and, hence, the effects of that risk on the present value of its foreign investment.

Managing Political Risk

Once a firm has assessed the political environment of a country, it must then decide whether to invest, and if so, how to structure its investment to minimize political risk. The important point to keep in mind, once again, is that political risk is not independent of the firm's activities. The substance and form of the firm's investments will, in large measure, determine their susceptibility to changing government policies. For example, a multinational can reduce the risk of expropriation by keeping the project dependent on affiliated companies for markets, supplies, transportation, and technology. Another defensive ploy is to offer local foreign investors or government agencies a stake in the venture's success.[9] Similarly, a firm can reduce the impact of currency controls by investing in the form of debt rather than equity (because governments are more hesitant to restrict loan repayments than dividends), borrowing locally, and setting high transfer prices on goods sold to the subsidiary while buying goods produced by the subsidiary at lower prices where legally possible.[10] Obviously, it is important to incorporate these methods into a capital budgeting and planning procedure that is completed *before* the initial commitment of funds.

One other point: the automatic inclusion of depreciation in computing cash flows from domestic operations is questionable when evaluating a foreign project. Dividend payments in excess of reported profits will decapitalize the enterprise, thereby inviting closer host government scrutiny. Using depreciation cash flows to service parent company debt, however, is generally more acceptable. Thus, while parent company funds—whether called debt or equity—require the same return, the cash flow from foreign projects could very well be affected by the form of the investment.

Cash Flow Adjustments for Political Risks

To make the greatest possible use of available information, political risks should be incorporated into foreign investment analysis by adjusting the expected cash flows of a project, not its required rate of return. In this section, I want to demonstrate the application of my proposed cash-flow adjustment method using the extreme case of political risk: an expropriation. The aim of this exercise is to illustrate how a multinational investment analyst could quantify the effect of an expropriation (or any other form of political risk) on the present value of a contemplated foreign investment.

Let's assume that, in the absence of expropriation, the expected cash flow of a given project over a specified period is $1 million. Assume also that if expropriation occurs prior to that time, the expected cash flow is zero. If we can assign a probability of expropriation of .25, the expected cash flow during that period would be $750,000 ((.75 × $1,000,000) + (.25 × 0)).[11]

Calculating the probability of expropriation with any level of confidence is of course difficult, if not impossible. In cases of extreme uncertainty about the timing of a possible expropriation, an alternative to assigning probabilities is to use a form of break-even analysis. Suppose, for instance, that management is reasonably certain that expropriation will occur either in the third year of the project, or not at all. If no expropriation occurs, the project's net present value (NPV) is estimated to be $3 million. If an expropriation does occur, however, the expected NPV is $-2 million. In this case, the expected NPV (in millions) equals $-2p + 3(1 - p)$, where p is the unknown probability of expropriation. The value of p at which the project breaks even can be found by solving for p^* where $-2p^* + 3(1 - p^*) = 0$, or $p^* = .6$. Thus, if the probability of expropriation is less than .6, the project will have a positive expected net present value. This probability break-even analysis is often more easily applied because it is normally easier, and certainly requires less information, to ascertain whether p is less or greater than .6, than to decide on the absolute level of p.[12]

Cash Flow Adjustments for Exchange Rate Changes and Inflation

Projected cash flows can be stated in any combination of nominal (current) or real (constant) domestic or foreign currency terms. To ensure comparability among the various cash flows and with today's home currency outlays, however, all cash flows must finally be expressed in real terms; i.e., in units of constant purchasing power. Nominal cash flows can be converted to real cash flows by adjusting either the cash flows or the discount rate. That is, nominal cash flows can be discounted at the nominal discount rate or real cash flows can be discounted at the real discount rate. Both methods yield the same results.[13]

In order to assess the effect of exchange rate changes on expected cash flows, it is first necessary to remove the effect of offsetting changes in inflation and exchange rates. Over the long run, purchasing power parity (or the "law of one price") is a reasonably good approximation of economic reality; and thus, these changes tend to be almost completely offsetting.

But because there is often a lag between a given change in relative rates of inflation and the exchange rate change necessary to maintain international equilibrium, it is worthwhile to analyze each effect separately. This is particularly true when government intervention occurs, such as in a fixed-rate system or a managed float. Furthermore, local price controls may not allow the normal adjustment of internal prices to take place. This will result in relative price changes, leading to deviations from purchasing power parity.

The possibility of relative price changes within a foreign economy can be incorporated easily by altering projected nominal local currency project cash flows. To capture the effect of exchange rate fluctuations, the MNC should list for each period the various possible exchange rates along with the anticipated local currency (LC) cash flow associated with each particular currency scenario. By assigning probabilities to these different exchange rates, management can then calculate for each period an expected home currency cash flow. This can be done by first converting each LC cash flow into its home currency equivalent, and then multiplying by the probability assigned to that scenario.[14]

Thus, the present value of future cash flows from a foreign project can be calculated in a two-stage procedure: (1) convert nominal foreign currency cash flows into nominal home currency terms; and (2) discount those nominal flows at the nominal expected domestic required rate of return. This procedure, to reiterate, will yield the same results as first converting nominal foreign currency cash flows into *real* home currency terms, and then discounting them at the *real* domestic required rate of return.

The Cost of Capital for Foreign Investments

A central question that must be addressed by the multinational corporation is whether the required rate of return on foreign projects should be higher than, lower than, or the same as that for comparable domestic projects. To answer this question, it is necessary to examine one of the most complex issues in international financial management: the cost of capital for multinational firms.

Recall that the opportunity cost of capital for a given investment is the minimum risk-adjusted return required by shareholders of the firm for undertaking that investment. As such, it is the basic standard of corporate performance. Unless the investment generates sufficient funds to provide suppliers of capital with their expected returns, the firm's value will suffer. This return requirement is met only if the net present value of future project cash flows, using the project's cost of capital as the discount rate, is positive. An alternative, and generally equivalent, investment criterion is to use the cost of capital as a cut-off rate for the internal rates of return on proposed investments.

The development of appropriate cost-of-capital measures for multinational firms is tied to how those measures will be used. When used as discount rates to aid in the global resource allocation process, they should reflect the value to firms of engaging in specific activities. Thus, the emphasis here is on the cost of capital for specific foreign projects rather than for the firm as a whole. As pointed out earlier, unless the financial structures and commercial risks are similar for all projects considered, the indiscriminate use of an overall cost of capital for project evaluation is inappropriate. Different discount rates should be used to value prospective investments that are expected to change the risk complexion of the firm.

My approach to determining the project-specific required return on equity is based on modern capital market theory.[15] According to this theory, an equilibrium relationship exists between an asset's required return and its associated risk. This relationship is formulated by the Capital Asset Pricing Model (CAPM). As mentioned earlier, the CAPM is based on the notion that intelligent risk-averse shareholders will seek to diversify their risks and, as a consequence, the only risk that will be rewarded with a risk premium is systematic or "non-diversifiable" risk. Systematic risk, as measured by beta, is the sensitivity of an investment's value to changes in general economic conditions. Statistically, it is the covariance of a security's (or any investment's) returns with broad, market-wide average returns.

Discount Rates for Foreign Investments

The importance of the CAPM for the international company is that the relevant component of risk in pricing a firm's stock is its systematic risk; in other words, that portion of return variability that cannot be eliminated through diversification, whether by investors or corporations. Much of the systematic or general market risk affecting a company, at least as measured using a domestic stock index such as the S & P 500 or the NYSE index, is caused by the cyclical nature of the national economy in which the company is operating. For this reason, it is highly possible that multinationals, by having operations in a number of countries whose economic cycles are not perfectly in phase, may be reducing the variability of their earnings through international diversification.

A number of studies suggest this, in fact, is the case.[16] Such studies suggest that there is little correlation among the earnings of the various national components of MNCs. Thus, to the extent that foreign cash flows are not perfectly correlated with those of domestic investments, the total risk (systematic and unsystematic) associated with variations in cash flows appears to be *reduced*, not increased, by international investment. Furthermore, most of the economic and political risks faced by the multinational corporation appear to be unsystematic and can, therefore, be eliminated through stockholders' diversification.

Rather surprisingly, it is the less-developed countries (LDCs), where political risks are greatest, which are likely to provide the greatest diversification benefits. This is because the economies of LDCs are less closely tied to the U.S., or to any other Western, industrialized, economy. By contrast, the correlation among the economic cycles of developed countries is considerably stronger; and the diversification benefits from investing in industrialized countries, from the standpoint of an American or Western European MNC, are proportionately less.

It should be noted, however, that the systematic risk of projects even in relatively isolated LDCs is unlikely to be far below the average for all projects, because these countries are still tied into the world economy. The important point about LDCs, then, is that their ratio of systematic to total risk is generally quite low; their systematic risk, while perhaps slightly lower, is probably not significantly less than that of industrialized countries.[17]

Even if a nation's economy is not closely linked to the world economy, the systematic risk of a project located in that country might still be rather large. For example, a foreign copper-mining venture will probably face systematic risk very similar to that faced by an identical extractive project in the United States, regardless of whether the foreign project is located in Canada, Chile, or Zaire. The reason is that the major element of systematic risk in any extractive project is related to variations in the price of the mineral being extracted, which is set in a world market. The world market price is in turn a function of world-wide demand, which itself is systematically related to the state of the world economy. By contrast, a market-oriented project in an LDC, whose risk depends largely on the evolution of the domestic market in that country, is likely to have a systematic risk that is small both in relative and absolute terms.

One of the major issues in selecting a discount rate for foreign investments is choosing the relevant market portfolio for evaluating a project's systematic risk, or its beta coefficient. Is the relevant base portfolio against which covariances are measured the domestic portfolio of the investor or the world market portfolio? Selecting the appropriate portfolio is important because a risk that is systematic in the context of the home country market portfolio may well be diversifiable in the context of the world portfolio. If this is the case, then using the domestic market portfolio to calculate beta will result in a higher required return than if risk were measured using the world market portfolio. On the other hand, a risk that is unsystematic in a domestic context may be systematic in a global context, with corresponding implications for the measurement of beta. Thus, the choice of a base portfolio could well affect the present value of a project and, hence, its acceptability.

Which market, then, domestic or global, is the relevant context for measuring the risks of international investment? The appropriate market portfolio to use in measuring beta depends largely on one's view of world capital markets. More precisely, it depends on whether world markets are integrated or not. If they are, then the world portfolio is the correct choice. If they are not, the correct choice is the domestic portfolio. The test of capital markets' integration is whether international assets are priced in a common context; that is, world capital markets are integrated to the extent that security prices offer all investors worldwide the same trade-off between systematic risk and real expected return. In a perfectly integrated market, the risk premium expected by investors for holding a foreign stock would reflect that stock's risk relative only to a globally diversified portfolio.

The truth probably lies somewhere in between.[18] Capital markets are now integrated to a great extent, and can be expected to become ever more so with time. But, due to various government regulations and other market imperfections, that integration is not complete.

Accordingly, my present recommendation to American managers is to measure the betas of international projects against the U.S. market portfolio. My reasons for this are three:

1. It ensures comparability of foreign with domestic projects which are evaluated using betas calculated relative to a U.S. market index.

2. There is as yet no readily accessible global market index.

3. The relatively minor amount of international diversification attempted (as yet) by U.S. investors suggests that the relevant portfolio from their standpoint is the U.S. market portfolio.

International Capital Market Integration and Corporate International Diversification

To the extent that international investments actually reduce the systematic risk of the firm, management is justified in using proportionately lower hurdle rates in evaluating such investments. If, in addition to this condition, capital markets are not fully integrated internationally (so that, say, an American investor seeking to invest in the Brazilian economy could do so only by buying the shares of an American multinational with Brazilian operations), then international diversification by multinationals could be providing investors with benefits they cannot achieve simply by buying foreign securities. This means that, where there are barriers to international portfolio investments, MNCs could accept lower rates of return than firms operating only locally because of their ability to diversify investment risks internationally.

The net effect of such financial market imperfections, then, may be to enable MNCs to undertake overseas projects that would otherwise be unattractive. But if international portfolio diversification can be accomplished as easily and as cheaply by individual investors, then although the required rates of return on MNC securities would be lower to reflect the reduced covariability of MNC earnings caused by international diversification, there would be no further reduction of the discount rate to reflect investors' willingness to pay a premium for the indirect diversification provided by the shares of MNCs.

The fact is, though, very little foreign portfolio investment is actually undertaken by U.S. investors. This lack of investment in foreign securities is normally explained by various legal, informational, and economic barriers that serve to segment national capital markets, deterring investors seeking to invest abroad.[19] These barriers include currency controls, specific tax regulations, relatively less efficient and less developed capital markets abroad, exchange risk, and the lack of readily accessible and comparable information on foreign securities. The lack of adequate information

can significantly increase the perceived riskiness of foreign securities, giving investors an added incentive to keep their money at home.
Furthermore, no other country in the world has the breadth or depth of
industry that the United States has. Hence, to diversify adequately within
foreign economies, it will usually be necessary to acquire shares of multinational firms in industries where indigenous firms do not exist. Diversifying
into the computer industry in Venezuela, for example, means buying the
shares of IBM or some other multinational computer manufacturer with
Venezuelan operations. To the extent that their international investment
opportunities are so restricted, U.S. investors may be able to achieve low-
cost international diversification only by purchasing the shares of U.S.-
based MNCs. Moreover, investors in countries like France and Sweden that
restrict overseas portfolio investment would appear to benefit even more
by being able to purchase shares in domestically based multinationals. All
these conditions would lead investors to pay a premium for the international diversification provided by the shares of multinational corporations.

Because the world's economies are not perfectly synchronized, and also
because of these imperfections in world capital markets, the value of
international diversification to investors appears to be significant. Donald
Lessard[20] and Bruno Solnik,[21] among others, have presented evidence that

Table 13.1
Risk measures for foreign market portfolios

Country	Annualized standard deviation of returns (%)[a]	Correlation with U.S. market[b]	Market risk (beta) from U.S. perspective
France	26.4	.50	.71
West Germany	20.4	.43	.47
Japan	20.1	.40	.43
The Netherlands	21.9	.61	.72
Switzerland	22.7	.63	.77
Great Britain	41.0	.51	1.13
United States	18.5	1.00	1.00

All figures estimated from data for 1973–1977 period.
a. Measured in U.S. dollars.
b. The S & P 500 Stock Index is used to represent the U.S. market.
Source: Donald R. Lessard. "An Update on Gains from International Diversification," 1977.
This table appeared in Donald R. Lessard, "Evaluating Foreign Projects: An Adjusted
Present Value Approach," in Donald R. Lessard, ed., *International Financial Management*
(Boston: Warren, Gorham & Lamont, 1979), p. 590. Reprinted by permission of the author.

national factors have a stronger impact on security returns than any common world factor. In addition, they find that returns from the different national equity markets have relatively low correlations with each other (see table 13.1).

In short, Lessard and Solnik's results suggest that international diversification significantly reduces the risk of portfolio returns. In fact, the variance of an internationally diversified portfolio appears to be as little as 33% of the variance of individual securities (as compared to 50% for a diversified portfolio of U.S. securities alone). In other words, the risk of an internationally diversified portfolio is about one third less than the risk of a domestically diversified portfolio (see figure 13.1).

Thus, the ability of multinationals to provide an indirect means of international diversification should be an important advantage to international investors. As noted earlier, however, such corporate diversification will

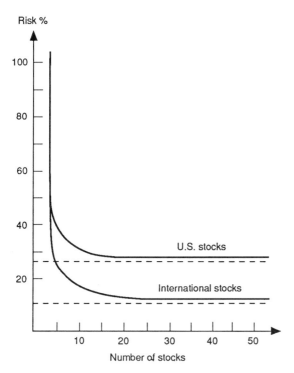

Figure 13.1
The potential gains from international diversification
Source: Bruno Solnik, "Why Not Diversify Internationally Rather Than Domestically?"
Financial Analysts' Journal, July–August 1974, p. 51. Reprinted by permission of publisher.

prove beneficial to MNC share holders only if there are barriers to direct international portfolio diversification by individual investors.

Nevertheless, regardless of whether investors are internationally diversified or not, the apparently lower degree of systematic risk of foreign investments means that the required returns on such projects will still probably be lower, not higher, than required returns on comparable domestic projects. At the very least, therefore, when evaluating prospective foreign investments, executives of multinational firms should seriously question the use of a risk *premium* to account for the added political and economic risks of overseas operations.

International Capital Budgeting and Corporate Strategy

The capital budgeting process typically involves calculation of the net present values of the various investment opportunities, domestic and foreign, facing the firm. Those projects with positive net present values (excess returns) are accepted; those that fail this test are rejected. The emphasis is on estimating future cash flows and required rates of return.

Only rarely, however, is the issue raised as to the origin of investments yielding excess returns. It is taken for granted that they do exist and can be found using fairly straightforward capital budgeting techniques. Yet, it should be recognized that identifying positive net present value projects in this way is very similar to (and as unreliable as) selecting undervalued securities on the basis of fundamental analysis. The latter can only be done with confidence if financial market imperfections exist which prevent asset prices from reflecting their equilibrium values. Similarly, the existence of economic rents—excess returns that lead to positive net present values—results largely from imperfections in real markets. Such imperfections take the form of monopolistic control over product or factor supplies. In less technical terms, companies can have a distinctive superiority in knowledge of specific markets, technological expertise, trademarks, patents—all of which exist in the real as distinguished from the financial sector of the business.

The imperfections that presently characterize world capital markets are not likely to be around for long. But, unlike the financial sector, where prices are continuously and rapidly adjusting to reflect new information, and where all companies can expect to get a fair deal based on their expected risks and returns, imperfections in the real markets may last for some time. Technological edges, production cost efficiencies, superior management capability, vertical integration—all these factors can enable companies to earn consistently abnormal returns. In the long run, though, even such differences can be expected to be neutralized by the inevitable forces of competition.

But, over the short to intermediate term, the availability of positive NPV projects depends largely on a company's ability to exploit imperfections in real markets. The essential focus of the corporate planner should thus be on identifying, strengthening, and then capitalizing on those comparative advantages which distinguish it from its competitors, both actual and potential. A thorough understanding of such imperfections, and the company's ability to exploit them, should provide the qualitative basis for determining—prior to any systematic financial analysis—which foreign investments are likely to have positive net present values.

Various studies of the phenomenon of direct foreign investment[22] have helped to identify those market imperfections that have allowed, or encouraged, firms to become multinational. Among those market imperfections contributing to the rise of the multinational are government regulations and controls, such as tariffs and capital controls, that impose barriers to free trade and private portfolio investment.

Real market imperfections, however, in the areas of firm-specific skills and information are probably the most important single reason for the rise of multinationals. This is the explanation provided by Richard Caves (1971),[23] who sought to understand not only why firms engage in direct foreign investment, but also why they choose that option over licensing or exporting. Caves's work on multinationals, which relies on the theory of industrial organization, points to certain general circumstances under which each approach—exporting, licensing, or local production—will be the preferred alternative for exploiting foreign markets.

According to Caves, multinationals have intangible capital in the form of trademarks, patents, general marketing skills, and other organizational abilities. If this intangible capital can be embodied in the form of products without much adaptation, then exporting will generally be the preferred method of market penetration. Where the firm's knowledge takes the form of specific product or process technologies that can be written down and transmitted objectively, then foreign expansion will usually take the licensing route.

Often, however, this intangible capital takes the form of organizational skills. Among these specialized skills are knowledge about how best to service a market (including new product development and adaptation), quality control, advertising, distribution, after-sales service, and the general ability to read changing market desires and translate them into saleable products. Because it is difficult, if not impossible, to separate these services and sell them apart from the firm, we expect this form of market imperfection to lead to corporate attempts to exert control directly through the establishment of foreign affiliates. There will also, of course, be added costs in establishing and administering an operation overseas. Consequently, as Ian Giddy has pointed out, "The market in an intermediate good (product, factor, service or knowledge) will be internalized if and only if the benefits from circumventing imperfections outweigh the administrative and other costs of central control."[24]

Because local firms have an inherent cost advantage over foreign investors (who must bear the costs of operating in an unfamiliar environment together with the stigma of being foreign), multinationals can succeed abroad only if their monopolistic advantages cannot be purchased or duplicated by local competitors. Eventually, however, all barriers to entry erode, and the multinational firm must find new sources of competitive advantage to defend itself against the inevitable increase in competition both at home and abroad.

My approach to international strategic planning can be reduced to the following four interrelated propositions:

1. Effective corporate planning should be directed toward identifying those investments likely to provide the most profitable returns. (Without suggesting that the firm adopt a myopically short-run view, profitability should be regarded as the prerequisite, not merely a by-product, of multinational survival and expansion.) The strategic response of a firm to a competitive threat, which includes the decision to invest in operations overseas, should be designed to exploit its distinctive advantages. Such advantages will stem, in large part, from imperfections in international product or factor markets. Effective corporate planning, accordingly, should be grounded in a thorough understanding of the company's competitive advantages, and on the associated barriers to entry that would prevent competitors from eroding those advantages.

2. The global approach to investment planning requires a systematic evaluation of individual entry strategies in foreign markets, a comparison of the options, and selection of the best method of entry. Many multinationals seem to disregard the fact that a market's sales potential, and thus its profitability, is at least partly a function of the entry strategy.[25]

3. Investment planning requires a continuous audit of the effectiveness of current entry methods. As knowledge about a foreign market increases, or

sales potential grows, the optimal market penetration strategy will likely change.

4. A systematic investment analysis requires the use of appropriate evaluation criteria. Despite the added complexities of overseas investment evaluation (and perhaps *because* of the difficulties they present), most multinationals continue to use simple rules of thumb in making international investment decisions. Analytical techniques are used only as a rough screening device or as a final checkoff before project approval. While simple rules of thumb are obviously easier and cheaper to use, there is a danger of obsolescence and misuse as the fundamental assumptions underlying their applicability change.

The use of the theoretically sound and recommended present value analysis is anything but straightforward. The strategic rationale underlying many investment proposals can be translated into traditional capital budgeting criteria, but it is often necessary to look beyond the returns associated with the project itself to determine its true impact on the overall, worldwide risk and return of the multinational. For example, an investment made to save a market threatened by competition or trade barriers must be judged on the basis of the sales that would otherwise have been lost. As another example, export creation and direct investment often go hand in hand. ICI, the British chemical company, found that its exports to Europe were enhanced by its strong market position there in other product lines— a position due mainly to ICI's local manufacturing facilities. Such cash flow synergies should be reflected in the capital budgeting analysis.

Summary and Conclusions

Because of the length of this chapter, I want to review a few of the major issues in multinational capital budgeting it examines, and to offer an outline of the solutions it proposes.

The first major complication of international investment addressed is accounting for the significant differences that can arise between project (or foreign subsidiary) and parent cash flows. To deal with this problem, I offered a three-stage procedure for incorporating such differences into the traditional discounted cash flow framework. The first involves the projection of expected after-tax cash flows strictly from the perspective of the local project or subsidiary managers. The second step was to estimate the timing and magnitude of both actual and allowable repatriations (which also gives the multinational's management a means of estimating their marginal tax rate on foreign-source earnings). The final phase attempts to project any effect that the given investment would have on worldwide corporate cash flows.

Next, I offered a rationale for adjusting project cash flows instead of the discount rate to reflect the key political and economic risks that MNCs face abroad. Cash flow adjustments are preferred on theoretical grounds: most distinctively foreign risks are unsystematic or diversifiable, and thus do not raise investors' required rates of return. Adjustments of cash flows are also preferred because management generally has access to more and better information about the specific effect of such risks on cash flow projections. The popular practice of adjusting a foreign project's required rate of return to reflect incremental risk does not usually allow for adequate consideration of the time pattern and magnitude of the risk being evaluated. Using a uniformly higher discount rate to reflect additional risk indiscriminately penalizes future cash flows relative to less distant ones.

Some investments, however, do entail more systematic risk than others, and such risks should be reflected in project discount rates. The key question, therefore, in setting discount rates for foreign projects is whether the incremental risks are systematic. The use of an international risk premium ignores the fact that the risk of an overseas investment (which should be viewed in the context of all other investments of the firm's shareholders, domestic as well as foreign) may be considerably lower than the total risk of the project. For this reason, the automatic inclusion of a premium for risk when evaluating foreign projects is not a necessary element of conservatism. It is instead a management shortcut that may penalize the firm's shareholders by causing management to reject positive net present value foreign investments.

Unlike the diversification sought by wholly domestic conglomerates (especially in the 1960s), there may be significant benefits to multinationals from international diversification. The theoretical justification for such benefits depends on the extent to which international capital markets are imperfectly integrated, thus preventing investors from achieving such diversification on their own. On the assumption that world capital markets are not fully integrated, multinational managers may be justified in actually *lowering* the required rates of return on foreign projects that offer significant additional diversification.

Finally, the article offers a theoretical rationale for the multinational firm, one which should serve as the basis for international strategic planning. Such a rationale should provide the qualitative criteria for the initial screening of foreign investment opportunities. The existence and success of multinationals is attributed largely to their success in defending and exploiting barriers to entry created by product and factor market imperfections. Multinational corporate planning, accordingly, should be based on identifying and preserving those competitive advantages that distinguish it from its competitors. Given the inevitability of competition, and of the eventual lowering of barriers of entry, corporate planners must continually reassess both their competitive vulnerabilities and strengths.

Notes

1. Stewart C. Myers (1974), "Interactions of Corporate Financing and Investment Decisions," *Journal of Finance*, March, pp. 1–26.

2. In a paper published in 1979, Donald Lessard discusses these issues in his extension of the APV approach to foreign project appraisals. See Donald R. Lessard (1979), "Evaluating Foreign Projects: An Adjusted Present Value Approach," in Donald R. Lessard, ed., *International Financial Management*, Boston: Warren, Gorham & Lamont.

3. This principle also holds, of course, for a domestic firm. For example, dividends received by a parent firm from an unconsolidated domestic subsidiary (less than 80% ownership) are taxed at a 15% rate and, hence, should be valued at only 0.85 of the original dividend paid.

4. This is the approach recommended by Arthur Stonehill and Leonard Nathanson (1968) in "Capital Budgeting and the Multinational Corporation," *California Management Review*, Summer, pp. 39–54.

5. As pointed out by Ian Giddy (1976) and a number of others, there is a set of equilibrium conditions in an efficient foreign exchange market that generally cause exchange rate changes and inflation to have only a minimal impact—at least over the long run—on real cash flows. To be more specific, the relative version of purchasing power parity states that changes in the ratio of domestic and foreign prices will equal changes in the equilibrium exchange rate. This means, for example, that the effect on cash flows of a foreign currency depreciation should be largely offset by a higher rate of foreign inflation.

6. Although the suggestion that cash flows from politically risky area be discounted at a rate that ignores those risks is contrary to current corporate practice, the difference may be more apparent than real. In 1979, Donald Lessard observed that most firms evaluating foreign investments discount most likely ("modal") rather than expected ("mean") cash flows at a risk-adjusted rate. If an expropriation or currency blockage is anticipated (though with a probability well under, 50), then the mean value of the probability distribution of future cash flows will be significantly below its mode. Thus, the negative effect of the widespread practice of raising the discount rate may, in the typical case, be offset by the perhaps equally popular practice of using most likely rather than average cash flows. From a theoretical standpoint, of course, cash flows should always be adjusted to reflect

the change in the mean or expected values caused by a particular risk. But such flows, to repeat, should be further discounted only in cases where the attending international risks can be shown to be systematic.

7. See, for example, J. Frederick Truitt (1970), "Expropriation of Private Foreign Investment: Summary of the Post-World II Experience of American and British Investors in the Less Developed Countries," *Journal of International Business Studies*, Fall, pp. 21–34. Also Robert G. Hawkins, Norman Mintz, and Michael Provissiero (1976), "Government Takeovers of U.S. Foreign Affiliates," *Journal of International Business Studies*, Spring, pp. 3–15.

8. See David Bradley (1977), "Managing Against Expropriation," *Harvard Business Review*, July-August, pp. 75–83. Bradley argues that companies whose inputs and services were more easily replaced are more likely to be subject to expropriation.

9. In a paper published in 1981, I provided a framework for the assessment and management of political risk, concentrating on the methods available to reduce the risk of expropriation. See Alan C. Shapiro (1981), "Managing Political Risk: A Policy Approach," *Columbia Journal of World Business*, Fall, pp. 63–70.

10. Numerous other mechanisms available for accessing or otherwise using blocked funds are described in my own paper (1980), "Managing Blocked Currency Funds," University of Southern California Working Paper. They include swap, parallel, and back-to-back loans, leading-and-lagging, purchase of commodities and local services for use abroad, conducting research and development locally, and hosting corporate conventions and business meeting locally.

11. In the event of an expropriation, the expected return is not likely to be zero. Thus, it is also necessary to estimate the expected value of the net compensation provided in such a case. While difficult to foresee with any precision, such post-expropriation compensation can be expected to come from several sources:

• Direct compensation paid to the firm by the local government. (This compensation can be delayed, as in Chile, for example, where many MNGs were expropriated by the Allende government with little or no compensation. When Allende was overthrown, however, his successors began returning property and otherwise compensating these MNGs.)

• Indirect compensation, such as the management contracts received by oil companies whose properties were nationalized by the Venezuelan government.

• Payment received from political risk insurance. (Insurance payments may lag expropriation by several years as well.)

• Tax deductions in the home country associated with such an extraordinary loss.

• A reduction in the amount of capital that must be repaid by the project equal to the unamortized portion of any local borrowing. It is inconceivable that a firm which has had a foreign operation expropriated would pay back any local borrowing except as part of a total compensation package worked out with the government. Suppliers of capital from outside the host country would normally be repaid by the parent company (whether or not loans were guaranteed) in order to preserve the parent's credit reputation.

12. In 1978, I published a paper developing a variety of analytical formulas to deal with the impact of expropriation and currency controls on a project's expected NPV. See Alan C. Shapiro (1978), "Capital Budgeting for the Multinational Corporation," *Financial Management*, Spring, pp. 7–16. In this article, I provide a more complex and less artificial illustration of how such cash flow adjustments for expropriation could be made.

13. See Donald R. Lessard (1979), "Evaluating Foreign Projects: An adjusted Present Value Approach," in Donald R. Lessard, ed., *International Financial Management*. Boston: Warren, Gorham & Lamont; or Alan C. Shapiro (1982), *Multinational Financial Management*. Boston: Allyn and Bacon.

14. It is impossible to do justice to the complex question of exchange risk management in the allotted space. In the third issue of the *Midland Corporate Finance Journal*, Brad Cornell and I will present an extended treatment of this issue alone.

15. For a good review of this theory, see William F. Sharpe (1978), *Investments*, Englewood Cliffs, N.J.: Prentice-Hall.

16. See, for example, Benjamin I. Cohen (1975), *Multinational Firms and Asian Exports*, New Haven, Conn.: Yale University Press; and Alan Rugman (1976), "Risk Reduction by International Diversification," *Journal of International Business Studies*, Fall, pp. 75–80.

17. This point was made by Fischer Black.

18. Michael Adler and Bernard Dumas (1981) discuss this and related issues at great length in "International Portfolio Choice and Corporation Finance: A Survey," a CESA working paper soon to be publisher in *The Journal of Finance*.

19. For a good description of the various barriers to international portfolio diversification, see Gunter Dufey (1976), "Institutional Constraints and Incentives on International Portfolio Investment," *International Portfolio Investment*, U.S. Department of the Treasury, OASIA.

20. Donald R. Lessard (1974), "World, National, and Industry Factors in Equity Returns," *Journal of Finance*, May, pp. 379–391.

21. Bruno H. Solnik (1974), "Why Not Diversify Internationally?" *Financial Analysts Journal*, July-August, pp. 48–54.

22. Direct foreign investment, or DFI, is defined as the acquisition abroad of physical assets such as plant and equipment.

23. Richard E. Caves (1971), "International Corporations: The Industrial Economics of Foreign Investment," *Economica*, February, pp. 1–27.

24. Ian H. Giddy (1978), "The Demise of the Product Cycle Model in International Business Theory," *Columbia Journal of World Business*, Special Issue, p. 93.

25. For example, a study by the Conference Board in 1966 (*U.S. Production Abroad and the Balance of Payments*, New York: The Conference Board) showed that 62 percent of firms surveyed made no attempt to determine the net profits from their existing foreign licensing agreements. Instead, they simply treated these agree-

ments as a free good, ignoring the opportunity costs that would have been revealed by a comparison of alternatives. Similarly, a 1978 survey by David Rutenberg ("Shunning the Risks of Eastern Europe," Queens University Working Paper) of 120 companies disclosed that, on average, these companies accepted only about 11% of the joint venture proposals they received, rejecting 83% out of hand without evaluating them. Also, only one-third had a policy of actively searching for joint venture opportunities.

References

Adler, Michael and Bernard Dumas, "International Portfolio Choice and Corporation Finance: A Survey," CESA Working Paper, *Journal of Finance* (1981, forthcoming).

Caves, Richard E., "International Corporations: The Industrial Economics of Foreign Investment," *Economica* (February 1971), 1–27.

Cohen, Benjamin I., *Multinational Firms and Asian Exports*, New Haven, Conn.: Yale University Press (1975).

Dufey, Gunter, "Institutional Constraints and Incentives on International Portfolio Investment," *International Portfolio Investment*, U.S. Department of the Treasury, OASIA (1975).

Giddy, Ian H., "An Integrated Theory of Exchange Rate Equilibrium," *Journal of Financial and Quantitative Analysis* (December 1976), 883–892.

Giddy, Ian H., "The Demise of the Product Cycle Model in International Business Theory," *Columbia Journal of World Business* (Spring 1978), 90–97.

Hawkins, Robert G., Norman Mintz, and Michael Provissiero, "Government Takeovers of U.S. Foreign Affiliates," *Journal of International Business Studies* (Spring 1976), 3–15.

Lessard, Donald R., "World, National, and Industry Factors in Equity Returns," *Journal of Finance* (May 1974), 379–391.

Lessard, Donald R., "Evaluating Foreign Projects: An Adjusted Present Value Approach," in Donald R Lessard (ed.), *International Financial Management*, Boston: Warren, Gorham & Lamont (1979).

Rugman, Alan, "Risk Reduction by International Diversification," *Journal of International Business Studies* (Fall 1976), 75–80.

Rutenberg, David P., "Shunning the Risks of Eastern Europe," Queens University Working Paper (1978).

Shapiro, Alan C., "Capital Budgeting for the Multinational Corporation," *Financial Management* (Spring 1978), 7—16.

Shapiro, Alan C., "Managing Blocked Currency Funds," University of Southern California Working Paper (1980).

Shapiro, Alan C., "Managing Political Risk: A Policy Approach," *Columbia Journal of World Business* (Fall 1981), 63–70.

Shapiro, Alan C., *Multinational Financial Management*, Boston: Allyn and Bacon (1982).

Solnik, Bruno H. "Why Not Diversify Internationally?" *Financial Analysts Journal* (July-August 1974), 48–54.

Truitt, J. Frederick, "Expropriation of Private Foreign Investment: Summary of the Post-World War II Experience of American and British Investors in the Less Developed Countries," *Journal of International Business Studies* (Fall 1970) 21–34.

IV Multinational Corporate Finance

Key Terms

• debt denomination
• foreign exchange exposure
• foreign exchange risk
• cost of capital
• capital structure
• international diversification
• purchasing power parity
• capital budgeting
• discounted cash flow
• project-versus-parent cash flows

Questions

1. "Canadian borrowers have traditionally denominated a significant proportion of their long-term debt in foreign currencies. As of December 1987, aggregate provincial government and corporate borrowers had over 35 percent of their total outstanding long-term debt denominated in currencies other than the Canadian dollar. However, the extent and mix of foreign denominated debt varies significantly among borrowers." (Don G. Roberts, "The Currency Denomination of Long-Term Debt of Canadian Borrowers," manuscript, University of Chicago, 1989.) Most foreign-currency Canadian debt is denominated in U.S. dollars (see table IV. 1).

a. Why would Canadian corporations want to borrow in foreign currencies, and particularly in U.S. dollars?

Table IV.1
Currency denomination of bonds outstanding in the Canadian private sector (percent,
December 1987)

Industry	C$	U.S.$	Other
Agriculture	100.0	0.0	0.0
Mines and quarries	51.3	33.9	14.8
Energy	57.2	36.1	6.7
Manufacturing	50.1	43.2	6.7
Petroleum products	47.1	50.0	2.9
Forest products	44.1	52.2	3.7
Construction	66.2	33.8	0.0
Transportation, communication, utilities	71.5	23.4	5.1
Wholesale and retail trade	81.5	12.7	5.8
Service (nonfinancial)	80.9	10.0	9.1
Financial	59.7	25.3	16.8

Source: Don G. Roberts, "The Currency Denomination of Long-Term Debt of Canadian
Borrowers," manuscript, University of Chicago, 1989.

b. Table IV.1 lists the currency denomination of bonds outstanding for
different industries in Canada. What might account for the different mix of
foreign-currency-denominated debt across industries?

2. What steps does a multinational corporation go through in evaluating a
foreign investment project? What are the major difficulties that arise in
evaluating a foreign project that do not arise in evaluating a domestic
project?

Suggested Readings

Adler, Michael, and Bernard Dumas, "Exposure to Currency Risk: Definition and
Management," *Financial Management*, Summer 1984, pp. 41–50.

Flood, Eugene, Jr., and Donald R. Lessard, "On the Measurement of Operating
Exposure to Exchange Rates: A Conceptual Approach," *Financial Management*,
Spring 1986, pp. 25–36.

Khoury, Sarkis J., and K. Hung Chan, "Foreign Exchange Risk: Selecting the Optimal Tool," *Midland Corporate Finance Journal*, Winter 1988, pp. 40–52.

Lessard, Donald R., and Alan C. Shapiro, "Guidelines for Global Financing
Choices," *Midland Corporate Finance Journal*, Winter 1983, pp. 68–80.

Levich, Richard M., "Empirical Studies of Exchange Rates: Price Behavior, Rate
Determination, and Market Efficiency," Chapter 19 of *Handbook of International
Economics*, North-Holland, 1985, pp. 979–1040.

Rugman, Alan, "Internalization Theory and Corporate International Finance," *California Management Review*, Winter 1980, pp. 73–79.

Rutterford, Janette, "An International Perspective on the Capital Structure Puzzle," *Midland Corporate Finance Journal*, Fall 1985, pp. 60–72.

Smith, Roy C., "Planning Your Global Financial Strategy," *The Journal of Business Strategy*, September-October 1988, pp. 8–25.

V International Taxation and Accounting

In 1990, corporate tax payments to the U.S. Treasury were of $98 billion—about 2 percent of U.S. national income. The receipts of corporate tax payments range from 1 to 5 percent of national income in most industrial other countries; a sampling is shown in table V.1. The tax rates in most countries are in the range of 30 to 50 percent; the tax rate in Germany is highest, and above these rates. Paradoxically, the ratio of corporate tax payments to Gross Domestic Product is lower in Germany than in every other country except Switzerland.

The myth—the grand myth—is that corporations pay taxes; in reality, only people pay taxes. Corporations obtain funds to pay the taxes either from their customers in the form of higher prices or from their suppliers in the form of lower prices and wages.

Because corporations are obliged to collect funds to pay these taxes from others, the managers of most firms are eager to organize numerous aspects of their activities to minimize their tax payments—or more precisely to maximize their after-tax income. A large number of their decisions—investment decisions, financing decisions, organizational decisions, locational decisions, dividend decisions, and pricing decisions—are affected by the desire to minimize the tax burden.

The investment and financing decisions made by a firm inevitably will reflect the managers' views about the anticipated returns on comparable investments in different countries. These cross-country comparisons are affected by the national differences both in tax systems and in corporate tax rates.

Tax structures and tax rates differ significantly among countries, in part because the role of government is much larger in some countries than in others; the ratio of fiscal revenues to national income is higher in countries with a large government sector. The proportion of direct taxes—personal income taxes, corporate income taxes, and wealth taxes—to total revenues is small relative to indirect taxes—sales taxes, employment taxes, value-added taxes—in those countries that have a large government sector; their governments need (or at least want) all the revenues they can get but are reluctant to raise tax rates on individuals and on firms to levels much higher than in other countries.

Still, tax rates on corporate income tend to be higher in those countries with a relatively large government sector. Yet governments in some countries with high tax rates provide investment tax credits; similarly they allow firms to depreciate the costs of investment in plant and equipment in a short period, much shorter than the economic life of this equipment. The more aggressive a country is in the use of investment tax credits and

Table V.1
Corporate tax rates and payments

	1987 Corporate tax rate	Corporate tax payments/GDP
United States	0.34	0.0203
Canada	0.44	0.0208
Great Britain	0.35	0.0561
Japan	0.42	0.0461
Germany	0.64	0.0124
France	0.42	0.0243
Italy	0.46	0.0266
Sweden	0.52	0.0222
Netherlands	0.42	0.0355
Switzerland	0.35	0.0067

Source: International Monetary Fund, *Government Finance Statistics*.

accelerated depreciation to induce new investments in plant and equipment, the lower its effective corporate tax rate relative to the posted tax rate.

The objective of the corporate manager is to maximize after-tax income. Taxes—more precisely national differences in tax rates—are important in the decisions of which country is most attractive for the location of a new plant; however, the differences among industrial countries in corporate tax rates usually are smaller than the differences among them in production costs. Because the profit rate in most industries is generally low as a percentage of sales or as a return on assets or on the funds invested, small differences among countries in the effective tax rate can make a large difference in the after-tax profit rate. For example, assume the pretax profit rate on an investment in the United States is 12 percent, while the pretax profit rate in Canada is 15 percent. If the U.S. corporate tax rate is 30 percent and the corporate tax rate in Canada is 40 percent, then the after-tax profit rate is 8.4 percent in the United States and 9.0 percent in Canada.

A major complication in the comparison of the managers' views of effective national tax rates on their activities is that most countries tax the foreign income of domestic firms. Virtually every country taxes the domestic income of foreign firms (usually at the same rates as the domestic income of domestic firms); thus the Japanese Government taxes the Japanese income of the local branches and subsidiaries of U.S. and other foreign firms, and the U.S. Government taxes the U.S. income of the local branches and subsidiaries of Japanese and other foreign firms. The United States and

Table V.2
Corporate tax structure

	United States	Canada	Japan	United Kingdom	Germany	Italy	France	Netherlands	Belgium	Switzerland	Sweden
Corporate tax rate (percent)	34	29	37.5	35	58.5	47.8	42	40	41	33.6	30
Loss carryforward (years)	5	7	5	unlimited	5	5	5	8	unlimited	2–6	unlimited
Taxes on foreign incomes (percent)	34	29	37.5	34	50	36	0	0	0	0	30
Withholding tax on dividends (percent)	30	25	20	0	25	32.4	25	25	25	35	30

Sources: Arthur Andersen & Co., *Tax Guide to Western Europe*, 1991, and Organization for Economic Cooperation and Development, *Taxing Profits in a Global Economy*, 1991.

Japan—and most other industrial countries—also tax the foreign income of domestic firms.

The United States has entered into bilateral tax treaties with more than two dozen countries. These treaties provide that the sum of the U.S. and foreign tax rates on a U.S. firm's income cannot exceed the higher of the two rates. The United States taxes the foreign income of U.S. firms when the income is repatriated—when the foreign subsidiary pays a dividend to its U.S. parent—and provides a credit against U.S. tax liability for foreign income taxes paid. The effective U.S. tax rate on the foreign income of U.S. firms depends on when the foreign subsidiaries pay dividends to their U.S. parents; the longer the delay between when the profits are earned by the subsidiaries and when the subsidiaries pay dividends to their parents, the lower the effective U.S. tax rate on foreign income. France does not tax the foreign income of firms headquartered in their jurisdictions. Many countries follow the U.S. approach to the taxation of foreign income; a few follow the French approach.

International tax management involves a set of organizational, locational, pricing, and dividend decisions. The investment decision involves whether the anticipated after-tax return on a new activity exceeds the firm's cost of capital. The financing decision involves both the choice between corporate equities and bonds and other types of debt, and the choice between own finance and leasing; frequently leasing may be less expensive because of tax factors. One of the key organizational decisions is whether the foreign business activity should be organized as a branch or as a subsidiary; the losses of foreign branches can be grouped with the profits of the parent and hence taxable domestic income is reduced. Another organizational decision is whether the firm should establish subsidiaries in low tax foreign jurisdictions, which might be used to "park" income. The locational decisions involve where to produce; some countries such as Ireland provide tax holidays (a period during which the effective tax rate will be low) to attract investment in plant and equipment by foreign firms. The pricing decisions involve intra-firm transactions, and the scope for shifting income to low tax jurisdictions from the high tax jurisdiction; some of these low tax jurisdictions may be tax havens. The dividend decision involves selecting which of the several foreign subsidiaries should pay a dividend to the parent; the sooner a dividend is paid, the sooner the parent will be obliged to pay a tax on foreign income to its domestic tax authority.

The first article in part 5, "Taxing International Income: An Analysis of the U.S. System and Its Economic Premises" by Hugh J. Ault and David F.

Bradford, provides an overview and evaluation of international tax principles. Although the article focuses on the U.S. tax system and recent changes in tax law, the implications are more widely applicable. Ault and Bradford begin by explaining the foreign tax credit, allocation of income and deductions, tax implications of establishing branches and subsidiaries, and transfer pricing. They go on to analyze the implications of the tax system with respect to capital allocation.

No discussion of international taxation would be complete without thorough consideration of transfer prices on goods and services traded internally within a corporation. Suk Hi Kim, in "International Transfer Pricing," provides a concise analysis of the objectives of, and legal limits in, transfer pricing for U.S. firms—both in the presence and absence of import duties and governmental restrictions. He evaluates three approaches to transfer pricing accepted by the U.S. Internal Revenue Service: the "comparable uncontrolled price" method, the "resale price" method, and the "cost-plus" method.

Clyde P. Stickney's article on "Accounting Considerations in International Finance" provides a tool kit on accounting methodologies and tax reporting for U.S. firms—and hence the basis for the accounting approach to the measure of foreign exchange exposure. The translation of financial statements reported in foreign currencies into U.S. dollars is governed by Statement No. 52 of the Financial Accounting Standards Board (FASB-52); the objective of FASB rules is to ensure that accounting statements convey the economic circumstances of the firm. FASB-52 focuses on the functional currency concept to determine which currency is the most reasonable benchmark, which then determines the method of translation. Stickney notes that the approach of translating foreign income into domestic income to arrive at U.S. tax liability differs modestly from the approach recommended by FASB-52. Stickney also provides a brief introduction to international accounting harmonization.

14

Taxing International
Income: An Analysis of
the U.S. System and Its
Economic Premises

Hugh J. Ault and
David F. Bradford

International tax policy has been something of a stepchild in the tax legislative process. The international aspects of domestic tax changes are often considered only late in the day and without full examination. As a result, the tax system has developed without much overall attention to international issues. This paper is an attempt to step back and look at the system that has evolved from this somewhat haphazard process.

We will describe in general terms the basic U.S. legal rules that govern the taxation of international transactions and explore the economic policies or principles they reflect. Particular attention will be paid to the changes made by the Tax Reform Act of 1986, but it is impossible to understand these changes without placing them in the context of the general taxing system applicable to international transactions.[1] The first part (secs. 1–4) contains a description of the legal rules, and the second part (secs. 5–9) undertakes an economic analysis of the system. We have tried to make both parts intelligible to readers with either legal or economic training.

1 Basic Jurisdictional Principles

1.1 Domiciliary and Source Jurisdiction

U.S. persons are subject to tax on a worldwide basis, that is, regardless of the geographic "source" of their income. Traditionally, this principle has been referred to as "domiciliary"- or "residence"-based jurisdiction since it is based on the personal connection of the taxpayer to the taxing jurisdiction. In contrast, foreign persons are subject to tax only on income from

From *Taxation in the Global Economy*, Assaf Razin and Joel Slemrod, editors, University of Chicago Press, 1990, pp. 11–46. Reprinted by permission.

"U.S. sources" and then only on certain categories of income. Individuals are considered U.S. persons if they are citizens of the United States (wherever resident) or if they reside there.[2] Corporations are considered U.S. persons if they are incorporated in the United States. The test is purely formal, and residence of the shareholders, place of management of the corporation, place of business, and so forth are all irrelevant. "Foreign persons" are all those not classified as U.S. persons.

As a result of the rules outlined above, a foreign-incorporated corporation is treated as a foreign person even if its shareholders are all U.S. persons. The foreign corporation is taxed by the United States only on its U.S.-source income, and the U.S. shareholder is taxed only when profits are distributed as a dividend. Thus, the U.S. tax on foreign income of a foreign subsidiary is "deferred" until distribution to the U.S. shareholder. A special set of provisions introduced in 1962 and modified in 1986, the so-called Subpart F rules, limits the ability to defer U.S. tax on the foreign income of a U.S.-controlled foreign corporation in certain circumstances.[3]

This pattern of tax rules depends crucially on identifying the source of income. A complex series of somewhat arbitrary rules is used to establish sources. For example, income from the scale of goods is sometimes sourced in the country in which the legal title to the goods formally passes from the seller to the buyer.

1.2 Overlapping Tax Jurisdiction and Double Taxation

Where several countries impose both domiciliary- and source-based taxation systems, the same item of income may be taxed more than once. For example, if a U.S. corporation has a branch in Germany, both the United States (as the domiciliary country) and Germany (as the country of source) will in principle assert the right to tax the branch income. It has been the long-standing policy of the United States to deal with double taxation by allowing U.S. taxpayers to credit foreign income taxes imposed on foreign-source income against the otherwise applicable U.S. tax liability. The United States as domiciliary jurisdiction cedes the primary taxing right to the country of source. Nevertheless, the United States retains the secondary right to tax the foreign income to the extent that the foreign rate is lower than the U.S. rate. Thus, if a U.S. taxpayer realizes $100 of foreign-source income subject to a 50 percent U.S. rate and a 30 percent foreign rate, the entire foreign tax of $30 could be credited and a residual U.S. tax of $20 would be collected on the income. If the foreign rate were 60 percent, $50 of the $60 of foreign taxes would be creditable. Thus, subject to a number of qualifications discussed below,[4] the amount of foreign taxes currently creditable is limited to the U.S. tax on the foreign income. The credit cannot offset U.S. taxes on U.S.-source income. If the U.S. taxpayer pays "excess" foreign taxes—that is, foreign taxes in excess of the current U.S. tax on the foreign-source income—the excess taxes can be carried back two years and forward five years, but they can be used in those years only to the extent that there is "excess limitation" available, that is, to the extent that foreign taxes on foreign income in those years were less than the U.S. tax. In effect, the carryforward and carryback rules allow the U.S. taxpayer to average foreign taxes over time, subject to the overall limitation that the total of foreign taxes paid in the eight-year period does not exceed the U.S. tax on the foreign-source income.

The foreign tax credit is also available for foreign income taxes paid by foreign corporate subsidiaries when dividends are paid to U.S. corporate shareholders, the so-called deemed-paid credit.[5] Thus, if a foreign subsidiary earns $100 of foreign income, pay $30 of foreign taxes, and later distributes a dividend of $70 to its U.S. parent, the parent would include the $70 distribution in income, "gross up" its income by the $30 of foreign tax, and then be entitled to credit the foreign tax, subject to the general limitations discussed above, in the same way as if it paid the foreign tax directly itself.

It should be emphasized that the credit is limited to foreign income taxes and is not available for other types of taxes. The determination of what constitutes an income tax is made under U.S. standards, and detailed regulations have been issued to provide the necessary definitions (Treasury Regulations, sec. 1.901-2). In general, the foreign tax must be imposed on net realized income and cannot be directly connected with any subsidy that the foreign government is providing the taxpayer. Special rules allow a credit for gross-basis withholding taxes.

1.3   Source of Income Rules

The source rules are central to the taxing jurisdiction asserted over both U.S. and foreign persons. For foreign persons (including U.S.-owned foreign subsidiaries), the source rules define the U.S. tax base. For U.S. persons, the source rules control the operation of the foreign tax credit since they define the situations in which the United States is willing to give double-tax relief.[6] In general, the same source rules apply in both situations, though there are some exceptions. The following are some of the most important of the source rules.

Sale of Property
As a general rule, the source of a gain from the purchase and sale of personal property is considered to be the residence of the seller. Gain on the sale of inventory, however, is sourced where the legal title to the good passes. If the taxpayer manufactures and sells property, the income is allocated by a formula that in effect allocates half the income to the jurisdiction where the sale takes place and half to the place of manufacture.[7] Sales of financial assets are generally sourced at the residence of the seller, with an exception for the sale of stock in a foreign affiliate of a U.S. resident.

Interest
Interest received on an obligation issued by a U.S. resident (including the federal government) is U.S.-source income unless the payor has derived more than 80 percent of its income over the last three years from an active foreign trade or business. Interest paid by a foreign obligor in general has a foreign source, except that interest paid by a U.S. branch of a foreign corporation is U.S. source. In addition, in the case of a foreign corporation that has 50 percent or more U.S. shareholders,[8] a portion of the interest will be treated as U.S. source for foreign tax credit purposes if the foreign corporation itself has more than 10 percent of its income from U.S. source.

Dividends
All dividends from U.S.-incorporated corporations are U.S.-source income regardless of the income composition of the corporation. Dividends paid by foreign corporations are in general foreign source unless the corporation has substantial U.S.-source business income, in which case the dividends are treated as partially from U.S. source.[9] As in the case of interest, a special rule preserves the U.S. source (for foreign tax credit purposes) of dividends paid by a U.S.-owned foreign corporation that itself has U.S.-source income.

Rents and Royalties and Services
Rents and royalties from the leasing or licensing of tangible or intangible property have their source where the property is used.[10] If a transaction involving intangible property is treated as a sale for tax purposes, the royalty source rule applies to the extent that any payments are contingent on productivity. Services income has its source where the services are performed.

The source rules put a great deal of stress on the appropriate categorization of a particular item of income. For example, is the granting of a letter of credit the performance of a service, the extension of credit, or something else?[11]

1.4 Allocation of Deductions

The source rules apply only to establish the source of gross income. Gross income must be reduced by the appropriate deductions to arrive to net foreign-source income and net U.S.-source income. In 1977, the Treasury Department issued a set of specific and quite detailed rules dealing with the allocation of deductions (Treasury Regulations, sec. 861-8). In general, the regulations look at the factual relation between particular costs and the appropriate income categories.

Special rules apply for interest and for research and development expenses. Interest is allocated on the theory that money is fungible and thus that interest expense should be allocated to all categories of gross income and apportioned on the basis of foreign and domestic assets.[12] Technical changes in the allocation rules made by the 1986 Act have required more interest expense of U.S. corporate groups to be allocated to foreign-source income, thus reducing the amount of net foreign-source income and hence the ability to use foreign tax credits.[13]

Research and development costs are allocated to broad categories and then apportioned in part on the basis of where the research took place and in part on the basis of the relative amount of sales (i.e., U.S. or foreign) involved.[14]

1.5 Foreign-Exchange Rules

Before 1986, there were no specific statutory rules dealing with the calculation of foreign-exchange gain or loss or the appropriate method for translating into dollars the gain or loss realized in transactions denominated in foreign currency. As a result, taxpayers had considerable flexibility in the treatment of the foreign-currency aspects of international transactions. The 1986 Act established a fairly extensive set of rules governing these matters.

All U.S. taxpayers initially must establish a "functional currency" in which their income or loss must be calculated. The dollar is presumptively the functional currency, but the taxpayer can alternatively establish as its functional currency for its "qualified business units" the currency in which the unit's activities are conducted and in which its financial books and records are kept. Thus, for example, if a U.S. corporation has a branch in Switzerland and another branch in the United Kingdom, the dollar will be the functional currency of the U.S. head office, the Swiss franc the functional currency for the Swiss office, and the pound the functional currency for the British office. The Swiss and British offices will calculate their income initially in the appropriate functional currency, and this amount will then be translated into dollars at an appropriate exchange rate to determine the U.S. tax liability.[15] For foreign-tax-credit purposes, foreign taxes are translated at the rate in effect at the time the taxes are paid or accrued.[16]

The 1986 Act also provided rules for the treatment of gain or loss arising from certain transactions undertaken by the taxpayer in a "nonfunctional currency." Generally, direct dealings in nonfunctional currency, such as borrowing or lending, can result in foreign-currency gain or loss that is treated as ordinary income and has its source in the taxpayer's country of residence. This means, for example, that, if a U.S. taxpayer with the dollar as its functional currency realizes a foreign-currency gain on the repayment of a foreign-currency loan, the gain will be taxable as ordinary income with a U.S. source. Regulations may be issued that will treat the gain as interest income in certain circumstances.[17] A special and complex set of rules applies to "hedging" transactions involving foreign currency whereby the taxpayer is seeking to reduce the risk of currency fluctuations.

2 Some Aspects of the Taxation of U.S. Business Operations Abroad

The following material discusses some more specific applications of the general principles outlined above. The focus is on the effect of the tax rules on patterns of U.S. foreign investment. Particular reference is made to the 1986 Act's changes and perceived responses to those changes.

2.1 Branch versus Foreign Subsidiary Operation

In General

If foreign operations are undertaken by a branch (i.e., without the interposition of a foreign subsidiary), any income generated will be subject to U.S. taxation currently (with a credit for any foreign income taxes paid), and any foreign losses will likewise be currently deductible.[18] If operations are carried out through a foreign subsidiary, the income will be subject to U.S. tax only when distributed[19] (with a deemed-paid credit for foreign taxes), and operating losses will not be currently deductible. Before the 1986 Act reduction in U.S. rates, these rules favored the organization of subsidiaries in those jurisdictions where the foreign effective rate was lower than the

U.S. rate. The potential tax attributable to the difference between the U.S. rate and the foreign rate could be deferred until the income was distributed as a dividend. When U.S. rates were reduced, the advantages of deferral were obviously reduced. Since most of the tax preferences (e.g., investment tax credit, accelerated depreciation) that were eliminated by the 1986 reform had not in any case been available for foreign income, the effect of the associated reductions in statutory tax rates was also to reduce the effective rate of U.S. tax on foreign income. As a result, foreign effective rates in general are today in excess of U.S. rates, and many U.S. taxpayers are in "excess credit" positions.

Despite the reduction or elimination of the advantage of deferral of income recognition, there is still a tax incentive to use foreign subsidiaries. If operations are in the form of a branch, the "excess" foreign tax credits go into the carryforward and carryback mechanism immediately, and, if they cannot be used within the carryover period, they are lost completely. On the other hand, foreign taxes paid by a foreign subsidiary and creditable under the deemed-paid rules begin to toll the carryover period only when the corresponding dividends are distributed. Thus, in the post-1986 world, use of a foreign subsidiary may allow the deferral of excess credits instead of the deferral of U.S. taxes.

Subpart F

The ability to defer current recognition of income of a U.S.-controlled foreign corporation (CFC) is limited by the Subpart F provisions.[20] Income subject to Subpart F is in effect treated as if it had been distributed as a dividend to the U.S. shareholder and then reinvested. A foreign tax credit is available for the income that is currently includible; it parallels the deemed-paid credit for dividend distributions. Later distributions of the previously taxed income can be made tax free and are "stacked" first.

The Subpart F rules apply to certain classes of income received by a CFC. In general terms, the rules affect dividends, interest, and other forms of passive or investment-type income, income from financial services, and income from certain dealings with related parties. The latter category covers situations where the foreign corporation is in effect used as a conduit to sell goods outside its country of incorporation. For example, if a U.S. parent corporation manufactures widgets with a cost of $100 and sells them to its Swiss sales subsidiary for $120 (an arm's-length price) and the Swiss subsidiary sells the widgets to German customers for $150, the $30 of profit in the Swiss subsidiary will be taxed directly to the U.S. parent. On the other hand, income from sales in Switzerland would not be taxed currently. Neither would income derived by the Swiss corporation from the manufacture and sale of widgets using component parts purchased from the parent company.[21] Similar rules apply to the provision of services on behalf of related parties. The 1986 Act expanded the scope of Subpart F somewhat by extending the rules to financial services income and shipping income.

Subpart F also contains rules that in effect treat as a dividend distribution any transaction by a CFC that indirectly makes its earnings available to the U.S. shareholder. This is clearest in the case in which the CFC makes a loan to the U.S. shareholder or guarantees a loan by a third party, but the rule also applies to other investments in U.S. property by the CFC.

Note that, to the extent that the objective of Subpart F is to oblige companies to repatriate earnings not currently used in the active conduct of a business, it is not strictly sufficient to tax the passive income generated by earnings retained abroad. Thus, for example, where a foreign subsidiary defers U.S. tax by retaining active income earned abroad and investing instead in assets generating passive income (e.g., interest), subjecting the passive income to current U.S. tax is not enough to produce the equivalence of repatriation of the original active income because the passive income is itself partially earned on the initially deferred taxes.

The role of Subpart F after the 1986 Act rate reductions is somewhat unclear. The provisions were originally enacted to limit the ability to defer U.S. tax through the use of a foreign subsidiary where foreign rates were typically lower than U.S. rates. At present, however, deferral is an advantage in only a limited number of cases. In fact, in some cases CFCs are intentionally creating Subpart F income to use foreign tax credits without paying the additional foreign withholding tax that would be due on an actual dividend distribution of non–Subpart F income. Deferral is still significant in tax haven operations that slip through the Subpart F definitions and in situations where the foreign jurisdiction has a low rate of tax on certain operations (e.g., a tax holiday in a developing country).

2.2   Foreign Tax Credit Planning after the 1986 Act

Background
As discussed in general terms in section 1.1.2, the foreign tax credit is limited to the U.S. tax applicable to foreign-source income. But the credit does not attempt to "trace" foreign taxes to particular items of foreign income to determine if the foreign tax exceeds or is less than the corre-

sponding U.S. tax. Rather, the credit is limited by the following fraction: [(foreign-source taxable income)/(worldwide taxable income)] × (U.S. tax liability). This approach in principle allows an averaging of foreign taxes where foreign effective rates are above and below U.S. rates. This means that a U.S. corporation with high-taxed foreign-source income (e.g., dividends from an operating subsidiary in Germany) would have an incentive to create low-taxed foreign-source income to use the excess credits it has with respect to the high-tax source income. On the other hand, a U.S. corporation with low-taxed foreign income is not deterred from investing in a high-tax country since it can absorb the high tax against the excess limitation created by the low-tax income and "average out" to the U.S. rate.

Limits on Averaging
The 1986 Act placed a number of restrictions on the ability to average high- and low-taxed foreign income. It was anticipated that the rate reductions would place many companies in an excess credit position and would encourage them to attempt to create additional low-tax foreign-source income. Accordingly, the Act adopted a sort of schedular system that requires that foreign income be classified into a number of separate "baskets" or categories and prohibits the averaging of foreign taxes across baskets. Averaging is still permitted for active business income but is otherwise substantially restricted. Thus, if a U.S. corporation has high-taxed foreign-source manufacturing income, it can average the taxes on that income with the taxes on low-taxed foreign sales income.[22] On the other hand, it could not average high-tax manufacturing income with low-tax foreign-source portfolio interest or dividend income.

In applying the basket system, dividends, interest, and royalties from CFCs (and amounts subject to the deemed distributed requirements of Subpart F) are subject to a "look through" rule, which categorizes the payments according to the character of the underlying income out of which they are made. Thus, for example, interest normally falls in the passive basket and cannot be grouped with business income.[23] But interest from a CFC that has only active business income would go into the business income basket. A special rule places interest from export financing in the business basket. Income from banking is in a separate basket and cannot be combined with other business income. In addition, dividends from foreign corporations in which the U.S. corporate shareholder owns less than 50 percent go in a separate basket "per corporation" and cannot be used to average at all.

Reducing Foreign Effective Rates

A U.S. parent corporation can affect the form in which it gets its returns from its foreign subsidiaries. These income flows can take the form of dividends on equity investment, interest on loans, royalties on licenses, or payments for management services. Payments in the form of interest, royalties, or service fees can in principle reduce the foreign tax base and hence the overall effective rate of foreign tax. This is true, of course, only if the foreign fiscal authorities accept the characterization of the payments and do not treat them as disguised dividend distributions. Within certain broad limits, however, a range of deductible payments is possible. The 1986 Act rate reductions and the corresponding excess credit position of many companies have encouraged greater use of nondividend forms of returns that have the effect of reducing taxable income (and therefore tax) from the point of view of the foreign jurisdiction, but not of reducing foreign-source income for purposes of calculating the creditable portion of the foreign tax. Under the "look through" rule discussed above, the nondividend payments from a CFC still fall in the business income basket (assuming that the foreign subsidiary has active business income) and allow the U.S. company to reduce the overall effective foreign rate to the U.S. rate so that the foreign taxes are more likely to be fully creditable.

Pooling of Foreign Earnings

Before the 1986 Act, the deemed-paid foreign tax credit was calculated on the basis of an annual calculation of the earnings and taxes of the foreign subsidiaries, with the most recently accumulated earnings (and associated taxes) deemed to be distributed first. This procedure gave an incentive to make dividend distributions in years in which foreign rates were high and to skip distributions in low-tax years (assuming that the higher credit could be used currently). This was especially the case in foreign system in which the effective tax rate could be substantially influenced by the taxpayer, for example, by taking or not taking optional depreciation deductions. The foreign subsidiary could have an artificially high tax rate in one year by taking no depreciation deductions and paying a dividend in that year and then reducing its foreign taxes in the next year through higher depreciation and paying no dividend. Through a judicious use of this so-called rhythm method of distributions, foreign tax credits could be accelerated when compared to those that would have resulted in a level distribution of the same total amount.

The 1986 Act responded to this problem by requiring a pooling of earnings for foreign-tax-credit purposes for years after 1986. In effect, foreign earnings and taxes are calculated on a cumulative rather than an annual basis for purposes of determining how much foreign tax credit a dividend distribution brings with it.

Allocation of Costs
The numerator of the foreign-tax-credit fraction is taxable foreign-source income. The more costs allocated to foreign to foreign-source income, the smaller the fraction, with a corresponding reduction in the available credit. The 1986 Act in general requires a greater allocation of expenses to foreign-source income. In the first place, expenses (in particular, interest expense) must be calculated on a consolidated basis, taking into account all the members of the U.S.-affiliated group. Previously, interest calculations were made company by company. Thus, borrowing for the group could be isolated in an affiliate corporation that had no foreign-source income, and as a result the consolidated taxable foreign-source income of the group would not be reduced by the interest expense. Similarly, other expenses could be "loaded" in affiliates that had no foreign-source income. Requiring consolidated calculations has eliminated these manipulations.

Summary and Evaluation
The present structure of the credit is extremely complex. In order to apply the credit, the following operations are necessary:

1. segregate items of gross income into U.S. and foreign sources;
2. segregate foreign-source income into the appropriate categories;
3. allocate and apportion expenses to each category;
4. determine the creditable foreign taxes attributable to each category;
5. "pass through" these attributes through the various tiers of foreign subsidiaries involved; and
6. compute a separate carryover mechanisms for each category.

Even considering that the addressees of these rules are for the most part large multinational corporations with substantial resources and computer capacity, one can question whether the welter of technical complexity does not try to fine tune the system to too great an extent.

2.3   Some Specific Subsidy Provisions

In addition to the general structural rules outlined above, the U.S. tax system has some explicit subsidy provisions in the international area. The most important are the rules for Foreign Sales Corporations (FSCs) and so-called possessions corporations operating in Puerto Rico.

Foreign Sales Corporations
Since 1971, the U.S. tax system has contained several tax regimes intended to promote U.S. exports. The original provisions involved the tax treatment of Domestic International Sales Corporations (DISCs). In essence, a DISC was a paper U.S. company through which export sales could be channeled. If the appropriate formalities were followed, a portion of the U.S. tax normally due on the export income could be deferred. In 1976, a GATT panel found that the DISC provisions violated the prohibition on export subsidies, and as a result the provisions were effectively repealed in 1984 and replaced by the FSC rules.[24]

The FSC provisions attempt to subsidize exports while at the same time technically complying with the GATT rules. As Congress interpreted the GATT rules, an exemption from tax on export income is not a prohibited subsidy if the economic processes that generate the income take place outside the country of export. The FSC rules try to meet that test by requiring that an FSC (unlike a DISC, a foreign company) have "foreign management" and engage in certain foreign activities.[25] Special provisions in effect waive the normally applicable arm's-length pricing rules in determining the amount of income attributable to the FSC and hence qualifying for the exemption. Under various complex pricing formulae, the overall tax saving from the exemption is generally not more than 5 percentage points of tax on the export income. Whether the current FSC rules are compatible with GATT principles has not yet been determined.[26]

Possessions Corporations
In order to encourage economic development in Puerto Rico, a variety of tax subsidies have been offered over the years to U.S. corporations investing in Puerto Rico and other U.S. possessions. In its present form, the subsidy consists of a tax credit that in effect eliminates the U.S. tax on income arising in Puerto Rico. In order to qualify for the credit, the corporation must derive the bulk of its income from sources within Puerto Rico and be engaged in an active trade or business there.

Special rules apply to the income from intangibles (patents, knowhow, etc.) involved in the Puerto Rican activities. In the past, some of the most important intercompany pricing issues have involved possessions of corporations and the amount of intangible income appropriately allocated to them.[27] In 1982, Congress enacted provisions limiting the amount of intangible income that can qualify for the possessions tax credit.[28]

During the preliminary considerations of the 1986 Act, a proposal was made to repeal the possessions tax credit and replace it with a temporary credit (inexplicably, in view of the underlying policy justification for a subsidy) tied to the amount of wages paid in Puerto Rico, but the proposal was ultimately rejected.[29]

3   Taxation of Foreign Persons on U.S.-Source Income

The U.S. system of source-based taxation is substantially less developed technically than the system of domiciliary-based taxation, reflecting presumably the history of the United States as a capital exporting country. The system is essentially schedular; it distinguishes among three basic categories of U.S.-source income: investment returns ("fixed or determinable annual or periodic income"), business income (income "effectively connected with a U.S. trade or business"), and capital gains. The 1986 Act expanded source-based taxation is several ways. It retained the prior tax rate on investment income received by foreign persons (while reducing domestic rates), limited the role of tax treaties in reducing U.S.-source-based taxation, and imposed a new layer of tax on foreign branch operations in the United States.

3.1   Investment Income

Investment income is taxed at a statutory 30 percent gross rate and is collected through withholding by the U.S. payor. The rate is often reduced, sometimes to zero, through bilateral income tax treaties in which both contracting states agree to a reciprocal reduction in source-based taxation. Representative types of income subject to the 30 percent rate are dividends, interest from related parties, royalties, and rents.[30] The theory of this form of taxation is that it is impossible administratively to calculate the deductions of the recipient that net-based taxation would require. Accordingly, a lower gross rate of tax is applied as a surrogate for net-based taxation. The basic statutory rate of 30 percent, however, was not changed when rate on domestic taxpayers were reduced in 1986, and the arguable result is overtaxation of investment in situations in which the 30 percent rate is applicable.[31]

Several categories of investment income are exempt by statute. The most important is portfolio interest, essentially interest paid by U.S. borrowers (including the U.S. government) to unrelated foreign lenders other than banks lending in the normal course of business.[32] Interest on deposits by foreign persons with U.S. banks is also exempt.

3.2 Capital Gains

In general, capital gains are not subject to tax unless the foreign taxpayer is engaged in a U.S. trade or business and the gains are "effectively connected" with that trade or business. Statutory provisions make it comparatively easy for foreign investors to avoid trade or business status for their stock-trading activities in the United States unless they are dealers in securities with their principal office is the United States.

Special rules apply to gains from the sale of real estate or the shares of U.S. corporations that have substantial investments in real estate. Such gains are taxed regardless of whether or not the foreign investor is otherwise engaged in a U.S. trade or business. The tax is enforced through a withholding mechanism that requires the buyer of a U.S. real property interest to withhold tax on the sale proceeds if the seller is a foreign person.

3.3 Business Income

"Normal" business income of a U.S. trade or business operated by a foreign person is taxed at the usually applicable individual or corporate rates on a net basis in the same way as corresponding income earned by a U.S. taxpayer. In the case of corporations, the income is also subject to a second layer of tax, the so-called branch profit tax.[33] Income that would usually be classified as investment income or capital gain is treated as business income if it is deemed to be "effectively connected" with the foreign taxpayer's U.S. trade or business. For example, interest income on trade accounts receivable would be taxed as business income rather than as interest income subject to 30 percent gross withholding. Similarly, the capital gain on the sale of a business asset would be taxable, but an unrelated capital gain would be exempt from tax. Complex rules define the line between effectively connected and noneffectively connected income.

3.4 Forms of Business Investment

Different patterns of taxation apply, depending on whether a foreign person invests in the United States through a U.S. corporation or directly through a U.S. branch. If the investment is through a U.S. corporation, all the income realized by the corporation will be subject to the normal tax rules applicable to U.S. persons because, technically, the foreign-owned

U.S. corporation is simply a U.S. taxpayer subject to tax on its worldwide income. Dividends paid by the U.S. corporation to the foreign shareholder are subject to the 30 percent gross withholding tax (reduced by treaty). Interest paid by the corporation on shareholder loans is subject to withholding tax as well. Shares of the corporation could be sold without U.S. tax as long as the corporate investment was not primarily in real estate. A sale of the assets followed by a liquidation of the corporation would result in tax at the corporate level but no tax at the shareholder level.[34]

If the foreign corporate investor formed a U.S. branch, the net business income of the branch (and any investment-type income that was effectively connected) would be taxed at normal U.S. rates. Deductions would be allocated to the U.S. operations under roughly the same rules used to make similar allocations for purposes of the foreign-tax-credit fraction. In addition, to the extent that the branch did not reinvest its net profit in the U.S. branch operation, a second level of tax would be imposed on the corporate profits. This "branch profits tax," enacted by the 1986 Act, is intended to replicate the shareholder-level dividend tax that would have been applicable if the investment had been made through a U.S. corporation that then distributed its net profit as a dividend. The branch analog to a dividend distribution is the failure to reinvest the branch profits in the U.S. business. Thus, if a foreign-owned U.S. subsidiary has $100 of pretax profit and pays $34 of corporate level tax, a distribution of the $66 after-tax profit is subject to the dividend withholding tax. Similarly, if the U.S. branch of a foreign corporation has $100 of pretax profit and does not reinvest the $66 of after-tax profit in the U.S. business, the branch profits tax is applicable. If the branch profits tax has been avoided in past years through reinvestment and in a subsequent year the U.S. business investment is reduced, the tax becomes due at the time of disinvestment.

The branch profits tax replaced a largely ineffective withholding tax on dividend distributions by foreign corporations with substantial U.S. business income. It represents a more serious attempt to establish the U.S. claim to two levels of source-based taxation on U.S.-generated corporate profits. The treaty aspects of the branch profits tax are discussed below.

4 Other International Aspects of the 1986 Act

4.1 Transfer Pricing for Intangibles

Under section 482, the income arising out of transactions between related parties must be determined on an "arm's length" basis, that is, as if the various parties were not related. Thus, if a U.S. parent sells manufactured products to a foreign subsidiary, the price charged (which will determine the amount of income that the United States will tax currently to the parent) must be that which would have been charged to an unrelated third party. The same principles apply to sales by a foreign parent to its U.S. subsidiary. In the absence of any comparable third-party sales, regulations provide for a number of different methods for constructing an appropriate intercompany price. These rules have been very hard to administer and have resulted in extensive administrative and judicial disputes. Problems have arisen, in particular, with the transfer and licensing of intangibles.

In response to these difficulties, Congress in 1986 amended section 482 as it applied to intangibles by specifically providing that, in the case of a transfer or license of an intangible, "the income with respect to such transfer or license shall be commensurate with the income attributable to the intangible." This language was intended to mandate an approach that looks to the actual profit generated by the intangible and the relative economic contribution that each of the related parties involved has made to the income that has been generated. The "commensurate with income" standard applies to all intangible transactions, but it was particularly aimed at the transfer of intangibles with a high profit potential, so-called crown jewel intangibles.

A congressionally mandated Treasury Department study (1988)—the "White Paper"—has been issued in connection with the 1986 Act change in the treatment of intangibles. It contains an extensive analysis of the issues involved in developing the commensurate-with-income standard. The White Paper starts from the premise that, if an "exact comparable" in fact exists, an arm's-length price should be based on that comparable. That comparison gives the best evidence of what unrelated parties would have done in the situation under examination. If, as generally will be the case, there is no exact comparable, several alternative approaches are suggested. One is to attempt to find an "inexact comparable," one that differs in significant respects from the intangible transaction in question, and then to make appropriate adjustments. The White Paper, although it in general accepts the principle of looking to inexact comparables, finds that in the past their use has led to "unpredictable outcomes" and downplays such comparisons. It stresses instead a method that looks to arm's-length rates of return rather than arm's-length prices.

The arm's-length rate of return method begins by identifying the assets and other factors of production the related parties will be using in the line of business in which the intangible will be used. This determination involves a functional analysis of the business. Then a market rate of return is assigned to each of the identified functions, based on the rates of return in unrelated transactions. This analysis will give the appropriate amount of the income generated in the line of business that is attributable to all the quantifiable factors of production. All the remaining income is allocated to the intangible. For example, assume that P has developed a patent for the manufacture of a product that will be manufactured under a license by an affiliate. The transaction will generate $500 of income, and, at a market rate of return on the tangible assets involved, $300 of the income would be allocated to the tangible assets. The remaining $200 would be allocated to P's intangible as the commensurate amount of intangible income.

The example above assumes that the manufacturing intangible was the only intangible involved in the line of business and that the returns on the tangible assets could be determined. In more complex cases where both of the related parties have intangibles, for instance, where the foreign affiliate has marketing intangibles, the White Paper approach is to apply the arm's-length rate of return analysis to the extent possible and then split the residual income based on the relative values of the intangibles involved. Thus, in the example above, the residual $200 of income would be split in some fashion between the manufacturing intangible and the marketing intangible. The White Paper recognizes that "splitting of intangible income ... will largely be a matter of judgment" (U.S. Treasury Department 1988, 101). Nevertheless, some guidance may be got from unrelated parties that use similar intangibles.

The legislative history of the 1986 changes in the treatment of intangibles indicates that the income from the intangible subject to allocation under section 482 should reflect the "actual profit experience realized as a consequence of the [license or transfer]."[35] The White Paper takes the position that this language justifies periodic adjustments to intangible returns to reflect changes in levels of profits that occur after the original transaction. Such periodic adjustments will be required only in situations in which third parties dealing at arm's length would have normally included provision for them. In practice, this may mean that licenses for "normal" intangibles will not be subject to periodic adjustment but that such adjustment would be required in situations involving intangibles with unusually high profit potential.

4.2 Tax Treaties

As indicated above, bilateral income tax treaties can affect the basic pattern of domestic tax rules. In general, the treaties typically do not have any effect on the U.S. taxation of U.S. persons but may reduce the taxes imposed by the source country treaty partner. This will be especially significant in the future, when many U.S. taxpayers will be in excess credit positions. The treaty may also provide that a foreign tax that might not otherwise be creditable as an income tax will qualify for the credit.

For foreign persons, the treaties can reduce the U.S. source-based tax that would normally be applicable. For example, many treaties eliminate the 30 percent tax on nonportfolio interest entirely and reduce the dividend tax to 15 or 5 percent in the case of parent-subsidiary dividends. Treaties may also prevent the imposition of the 1986 branch profits tax. Most treaties contain a so-called nondiscrimination clause, under which the United States agrees not to subject foreign persons to taxation "more burdensome" than the taxation imposed on similarly situated U.S. persons. As described above, the branch profits tax is imposed on foreign corporations doing business in the United States but not on U.S. corporations. This difference in treatment is viewed as violating nondiscrimination clauses and prevents the application of the branch tax in many treaty situations.[36]

A number of recent treaties contain provisions to prevent so-called treaty shopping, that is, the use of a treaty country corporation by third-country investors to obtain a reduction in U.S. source-based taxation that they could not have received directly because there was no treaty (or a less favorable treaty) between their country and the United States. In addition, the 1986 Act specifically denied treaty benefits in some circumstances to foreign corporations that are treaty shopping.[37] In particular, treaty-shopping foreign corporations are prohibited from claiming relief from the branch profits tax under a treaty nondiscrimination clause.

5 Recapitulation of Present Policy

The tax treatment of international income flows reflects a variety of policy objectives, so it is difficult to discern the policy principles in the actual rules—to state the optimizing problem to which the rules are the solution.[38] Broadly speaking, though, the regime for taxing international transactions can be understood as springing from a fundamental principle that U.S. citizens and residents should be taxed on all their income. Coupled with this basic premise, in a multijurisdictional system, is the principle that people should not be taxed twice on the same income. Both principles reflect notions of equity. The first reflects the conception of income as a measure of ability to pay—since the source of income has no bearing on its validity as a measure of ability to pay, the tax burden should be based on "worldwide income" But the tax burden is not simply imposed by the home government; if two people with the same income are to pay the same tax, the amount extracted by a foreign jurisdiction must be counted equally with that taken by the home government.

These simple and superficially plausible normative conclusions are buttressed by a similarly plausible efficiency criterion, that of capital export neutrality. A nation's tax rules satisfy capital export neutrality if the choice of a domestic taxpayer between foreign and domestic investment is unaffected by tax considerations and depends only on the relative level of before-tax rates of return. Of course, an efficiency criterion is itself at heart an expression of an equity objective, that of maximizing the size of the economic pie. If all the tax authorities in the international system adhere to export tax neutrality, a perfectly competitive international capital market will leave no gain from reallocation of (any *given* stock of) world capital unexploited.

In the context of real-world politics and practical tax administration, the two foundation stones of U.S. international income tax policy, taxation on the basis of worldwide income and capital export neutrality, give rise to a continually evolving set of rules. The most recent version has been described in sections 1–4. Much as we can think of the domestic personal income tax as an accretion income tax with certain exceptions and the basic corporate tax as a "classical" second-level tax on corporations, we can broadly describe the current treatment of international business as follows:

1. U.S. corporations are taxed on their income wherever earned. The "income" of a U.S. corporation attributable to its holdings of shares in a foreign company (even a controlled subsidiary) is basically interpreted as the dividends received, when received. Hence, there is "deferral" of U.S. tax until repatriation.

2. Sovereign governments have the first claim to tax income created within their borders. This principle applies to the taxation of U.S. corporations operating abroad and to foreign corporations operating in the United States.

3. To alleviate the "double taxation" of income arising from activities abroad, the United States allows U.S. taxpayers to credit foreign *income* taxes paid against their U.S. tax liabilities. The foreign tax credit should not be seen to reduce the tax on income created by a company in the United States; hence, the credit is limited to the amount of U.S. tax that would have been collected on the foreign income. U.S. companies should not be inhibited by tax considerations from using foreign subsidiary corporations

to do business abroad. Therefore, a credit against U.S. income tax is allowed to U.S. corporate shareholders for foreign taxes actually paid by foreign corporations.

4. Certain payments to foreigners (mainly dividends and interest) are subjected to a withholding tax that mimics the tax that would be paid by a U.S. individual recipient. The withholding tax is eliminated or reduced mutually by bilateral treaty agreement with other governments.

5. Certain tax rules are intended to encourage investment in the United States (now, mainly, accelerated depreciation). Generally, these rules do not apply to investment abroad.

As the discussion of the legal rules in sections 1–4 makes clear, implementing these general principles is far from straightforward. The present system is the result of a long process of successive "loophole closing" efforts, as the tax policy makers have discovered one way after another in which taxpayers (or foreign governments) can organize their affairs to take advantage of the U.S. rules. The 1986 changes are the latest in the series, with particular attention to the implications of the substantial lowering of U.S. tax rates incorporated in the reform.

The thrust of the 1986 changes with respect to U.S. firms operating abroad was to scale back deferral through expansion of the Subpart F provisions that require immediate taxation of "tainted" forms of income, to limit further the creditability of foreign taxes through wider use of "baskets" of income by type, and to reduce the relative attractiveness of domestic investment through elimination of the investment tax credit and slowdown of depreciation allowances.

With respect to foreign firms operating in the United States, the 1986 Act introduced a branch profits tax, whose objective was to put branches of foreign corporations and U.S. subsidiary corporations of foreign corporations on a more similar footing. The branch profits tax corresponds to the withholding tax on the dividends paid by U.S. corporations to foreign shareholders. For foreign firms, the second main thrust of the 1986 changes was the consequence of *not* changing the rate of withholding tax at the same time domestic rates were being cut; the effect was to the disadvantage of foreign relative to domestic ownership.[39]

6   Do the Bricks Lack Straw?

Before we turn to some of the more specific policy issues raised by these rules, it may be useful to devote a bit of critical attention to the two basic building blocks of worldwide taxation and the foreign tax credit.

6.1   Worldwide Taxation

The argument underlying the principle of worldwide taxation—taxation of income from whatever source—appears to be motivated by a conception of income as a given attribute of an individual or a firm. If A and B have the same income, they should pay the same tax. But income for tax purposes is not an abstract flow. Rather, it is an accounting construct built up by adding and subtracting amounts paid and received (or accrued, to make matters worse). The banal fact that an income tax is based on *transactions* (admittedly, the transactions are sometimes subjected to very complicated transformations) has destructive implications for the equity case often made for tax rules. It also has profound implications for tax design, implications that have as yet been only partially digested in academic economic thinking and that are only beginning to be felt in the making of tax policy.

The equity proposition that it is unfair for two people with equal incomes to pay different amounts in tax would perhaps be persuasive if income were an attribute with which in individual is endowed. But it is generally fallacious when income is an aggregation of transactions entered into by the taxpayer. To take an obvious example, if two people have the same amount of money to invest, it is of no equity consequence that one chooses tax-exempt bonds and pays no tax and the other chooses taxable bonds and pays tax. Since either could make the same choice as the other, no inequity can be said to result from the fact that they send different amounts of money to the tax collector.[40]

Equity arguments based on the view of income as an exogenous attribute are particularly misleading in the context of capital markets. In part, this is because the opportunities of participants are to a considerable degree unrelated to a meaningful measure of their ability to pay: people differ in their wages but not in the rate of interest that they can earn on savings. More important, as the tax-exempt interest example illustrates, is the fact that determining the actual tax burdens (in economists' jargon, the *incidence* of taxes) requires a difficult analysis of the effect of the rules in the context of strong forces tending to equate the rate of return on investment for a given taxpayer at all margins of choice. In capital markets, those margins are extraordinarily varied and simultaneously available to many participants.

The more profound consequence of the view of income as an aggregation of transactions is to place income tax policy in the framework of taxes on transactions more generally. The more complex uses of transaction data in the income tax context concern purchases and sales of claims on goods at different times or under different contingencies. In mundane terms, the hard part of income taxation is to use transactions to measure "income from capital." But, when these transactions are viewed like other purchases and sales of goods, the case for employing the peculiarly complex procedures of income accounting (rather than much more simple rules) in order to achieve various equity objectives becomes much less clear than it appears when income is viewed as an abstract attribute. A striking instance of how little it is recognized that an income tax consists of a collection of taxes on transactions is the almost total lack of connection between the making of international income tax policy and the making of international trade policy.[41]

6.2   Credit for Foreign Income Taxes

Recognizing that an income tax is levied on the basis of voluntary transactions, not exogenously determined attributes of individuals and firms, upsets the equity argument for crediting foreign income taxes as well. As first glance, if A and B have the same income but B is subjected to a foreign income tax, it seems fair to allow B's foreign tax to count against an overall burden. But, if B's wealth can alternatively be allocated between a foreign asset and a domestic one, it is clear that allowing or not allowing a credit for the foreign tax will affect the location of B's wealth, not B's tax burden.

7   International and Foreign Transactions in a System of Accretion Income Accounting

The traditional literature on income taxation begins with a discussion of the accretion income concept, generally known in the jargon of the trade as Haig-Simons or Schanz-Haig-Simons (SHS) income.[42] SHS income is defined to be the sum of consumption and the change in net worth (at market value) of a person over some specified period. A natural question is how the rules relating to international income relate to this fundamental income notion.

7.1   Source of Income and Allocation of Deductions

Accounting for Personal Income
The idea that income has a locatable source seems to be taken for granted, but the source of income is not a well-defined economic idea. The SHS definition describes a quantity that is, in principle, measurable, whatever the practical problems may be (and they are substantial). The emphasis

placed by tax reform advocates on the objective of taxing income "from whatever source" has obscured the fact that the SHS income concept is not susceptible to characterization as to source at all. Income in this definition attaches to someone or something that consumes and that owns assets. Income does not come from some place, even through we may construct accounts to approximate it by keeping track of payments that have identifiable and perhaps locatable sources and destinations. To the extent that income describes an activity, it is not that of production but that of consumption and wealth accumulation, and its location is presumably the place of residence of the person doing the consuming and accumulating.

Naturally, calling a tax an income tax does not imply that it will or should embody the SHS norm. The fact is, however, that something like the SHS income norm does appear to motivate much of the U.S. system. More important, the objective of increasing wealth is rather persuasively the motivator of investment decisions. Large changes in wealth occur continually by virtue of changes that have no natural locational aspect. Examples are the discovery of a new drug formula or new consumer good. Even more significant are simple changes in expectations and beliefs about the future, which can result in large changes in asset values. Attaching locations to these phenomena inevitably involves arbitrary line drawing, with its attendant controversy. (See the discussion in secs. 1–4 of transfer pricing of intangibles.)

The view of income as a payment for factor services (rather than as the sum of saving and consumption) may appear to offer a firmer basis for attribution of source. The reasoning that leads to an SHS concept, however, emphasizes that the payment actually received by a person has to be interpreted in terms of some notion of accruing benefit. In crude terms, the normative notion of income must be net of the "costs of earning" any payments. That is why is seems correct to deduct employee business expenses from wages; the same line of argument may justify a deduction for medical expenses as well (they do not buy consumption in a normative sense).

As we have emphasized, an income tax in practice is built up from transactions. It would be very difficult to construct a system of accounts that would give a close approximation to SHS income. Actual income accounts do not even attempt it. When one then adds the necessity of attaching a locational label to the transactions, an operation that is not itself based on a well-defined economic question, complexity and arbitrariness are hard to avoid.

In many cases, amounts paid and received can be rather readily given a location by association with a process of production or similar activity. A practical consequence is that the transaction becomes susceptible to monitoring by a particular local jurisdiction and thereby becomes a potential basis for taxation. The association is so obvious that it is apparently taken for granted that a government has the "right" to levy a tax based on a measure of the profits earned by a production activity physical carried on within its jurisdiction. One may speculate that force majeure has been as important as any ethical conception of sovereignty in producing a general acceptance of the priority of the "source" jurisdiction to tax particular transactions.

Income of a Corporation
For a corporation, the analog of personal consumption is distributions to shareholders. The corporation tax treatment of particular transactions, such as receipt of a dividend or of the proceeds of the sale of an asset, has to be understood as a piece of a system of accounts designed to capture the sum of distributions to shareholders and increase in net worth. A dividend, itself, is not SHS income; it may be used to measure income, but, if the change in value of the stockholder's remaining claim on the corporation is ignored, the accounts will produce a bad approximation to SHS income (Bradford 1986, chap. 3). The defective accounts will either over- or understate the taxpayer's SHS income; typically, such mismeasurement sets up opportunities for tax-motivated arbitrage with balancing transactions that involve different mismeasurement.

The economist is struck by the frequency with which one encounters in the law legal and institutional distinctions without an economic difference. As a result, the rules frequently prescribe different tax consequences for economically equivalent (or nearly equivalent) transactions. Where this is the case, there is an opportunity for arbitrage profit. The efforts of the policymakers to limit arbitrage profit (without actually instituting consistency) have much to do with the evolution of the rules.

As a simple example, consider the distinction between distributed and undistributed earnings of a wholly owned foreign subsidiary. In one case, the sub sends the parent a dividend. In the second case, the sub simply retains the earnings but lends the parent money. The bundle of real claims owned by the parent is the same after the transactions are completed in both cases. Yet before 1962 the tax results were very different. It then might have made sense for the sub never to pay the parent a dividend since the exactly equivalent cash flow could have been effected with a lower tax penalty by the lending route. The policy response: a rule treating loans to the parent as dividends and a series of subrules dealing with transactions similar to loans, for example, the sub's guarantee of a loan to the parent. This is an example of the problems created by inconsistency of the tax treatment of transactions with similar economic effects. Such inconsistency is ubiquitous in the implementation of the income tax. Although the point is a simple one and even well known, it is still insufficiently appreciated by policymakers. The difficulty of designing rules to implement equal tax treatment for economically equivalent results is severe in the case of an income tax, basically because of the difficulty of measuring accruing changes in value. These difficulties are compounded when the ill-defined criterion of location of income is added.[43]

7.2 Deduction or Credit for Foreign Taxes?

Discussions of the foreign tax credit are often cast in a framework in which the tax at issue is on the capital income of domestic residents. Viewed as an element of a set of accounting rules to approximate the sum of a person's consumption and increase in net worth during the period, the foreign tax credit makes little sense. True, the payment of taxes might be regarded as a use of buying power that is not consumption (although the point is arguable; see Bradford et al. 1984), and it certainly is not evidence of an increase in net worth. But SHS income tax principles would seem to imply, at most, deductibility of taxes paid to other jurisdictions by persons otherwise regarded as within the income tax net.

8   Economic Analytical Problems Posed by Actual Policies

In the discussion of the economics of the international tax rules so far, we have attempted to relate them to philosophical objectives. We turn now to economic issues more directly related to the actual system as it has evolved.

8.1   International Tax Rules as Taxes on Capital Flows

Most economic modeling related to international tax policy assumes that the implementation problems have been solved. Specifically, analysts take for granted the existence of a measurable quantity called capital (K) that can be located in a particular country and whose ownership can be observed. Also assumed observable is the measurable return (rK) accruing to capital in each country. As we have emphasized, actual tax rules depend on a variety of observable transactions, none of which corresponds neatly to the accruing return on capital.[44] Before we turn to a closer look at problems associated with particular aspects of the rules, however, we may note a troublesome problem of consistency that is likely to present itself quite apart from matters of definition and measurement. This problem, which has been emphasized by Slemrod (1988), can be described as one of tax harmonization. It arises when the tax rules applied by different countries to investors in different countries are not appropriately coordinated.

We can best express this problem in a setting in which risk is assumed away and investors are indifferent between returns arising in different countries (no bias toward returns in one's own country). Then investors will move their capital around to achieve the highest return after all taxes. A condition of equilibrium is that the rate of return after all taxes be simultaneously equal in all countries for residents of each country. In a two-country case, let r_d be the domestic rate of return before taxes and r_f the return in the foreign country. Let t_{ijk} be the tax levied by country i on investors resident in country j on returns to capital they own in country k, where i, j, and k can be either d (domestic) or f (foreign). Then there are eight possible tax rates. If we rule out the taxation by one country of the income of residents of the other country earned on capital in that country (t_{dff} and t_{fdd} are zero), there are six tax rates. If domestic investors are to be indifferent between investing at home and abroad, it must be true that

$$r_d(1 - t_{ddd}) = r_f(1 - t_{ddf} - t_{fdf}).$$

Similarly, in order for foreigners to be indifferent between investing in their own country and abroad, it must be true that

$$r_d(1 - t_{dfd} - t_{ffd}) = r_f(1 - t_{fff}).$$

Taking the ratio of the two conditions, we see that together they imply

$$\frac{(1 - t_{ddd})}{(1 - t_{dfd} - t_{ffd})} = \frac{(1 - t_{ddf} - t_{fdf})}{(1 - t_{fff})}.$$

This is one condition on six tax rates. The difficulty is that there is very little assurance that it will be satisfied by the rules chosen by any given pair of countries (much less that the corresponding generalization will be satisfied for various pairwise linkings of several countries). If the condition is not satisfied, one or the other after-tax equalization condition must fail. The difficulty that this failure creates for economic modeling is clear (we would say that the markets have no equilibrium), but the world was not created to satisfy the modelers. Actually, some process will balance the demands and supplies—probably some combination of transactions cost, nonlinearity of tax rates (e.g., the nonlinearity that results from the fact that taxes are nonrefundable), and special "patches" in the tax rules designed to limit the arbitrage between more and less favorable jurisdictions.[45]

8.2 Incentives for Business Location: Form and Substance

Place of residence and even citizenship are choices. Since the U.S. tax laws make distinctions on the basis of place of residence and citizenship, we may expect the laws to influence the choices. Clearly, in exceptional cases (movie stars, for instance), taxes influence people's domicile and citizenship. But for most people in the range of tax regimes that is typically encountered, we expect little elasticity of domicile or citizenship to changes in tax policy, and therefore distinctions based on residence of people will be of a lump-sum character.

One might expect the choice of place of incorporation to be much more responsive to variations to tax rules. The U.S. policy of distinguishing between U.S. and foreign corporations must have effects, either on the choices or on the rules enacted (having in mind their effect on place of incorporation). If the people choosing the location of incorporation are U.S. taxpayers and they want to be able to control the management of the operation located abroad, they have two basic options: to incorporate (or even not to incorporate but to operate in noncorporate form) in the United States and run the foreign activity as a branch or to incorporate abroad while maintaining significant ownership interest. These two forms of organization are economically virtually equivalent. In addition, there are such less perfectly substitutable alternatives as a noncontrolling interest in a foreign corporation ("portfolio investment") and royalty and similar contingent claims. Note that a capital market "imperfection" is implicit in the observation that one cannot create a perfect substitute for a controlling interest through an appropriate combination of available securities. A controlling interest in a corporation could presumably in principle be reproduced by a sufficiently complicated contract that could be marketed as a portfolio security. The cost of writing and monitoring such contracts is required for a distinction between controlling and portfolio investment.

The basic policy toward residence of corporations is an extension of the legal doctrine that the corporation is a separate person. A corollary of the distinction between U.S. and foreign persons is the deferral of tax on the earnings of foreign subsidiaries of U.S. corporations. For U.S. corporations that own other U.S. corporations, the tax accounts are consolidated. Dividends passing from the sub to the parent have no tax consequences. By the same logic, dividends paid from one company to another ought not to be taxed when both corporations are separately U.S. taxpayers but not in a relation of parent and sub. (In fact, a fraction of dividends received by a U.S. corporation from another U.S. corporation, other than a controlled sub, is included in the recipient's tax base. The fraction was increased by the 1986 Act.)

In the case of a subsidiary that is not a U.S. taxpayer, the policy that springs from the treatment of a corporation as a person is to tax the parent only on "income" as measured by dividends, that is, in the cash-flow sense of income often encountered in the U.S. income tax. No one suggests "integrating" corporate and shareholder income accounts in the case of portfolio investment, so deferral, which is a much debated policy, might seem a sensible way of avoiding a sharp break in tax treatment at the point at which the shareholder's interest is regarded as crossing the boundary to "control." The main effect, however, of this extension of the metaphor of corporation as person and of the use of dividends as a measure of income arises precisely with control because the policy puts a great deal of tax weight on a decision that is under the U.S. taxpayer's control. In this connection, the critical choice is probably not between retention of funds and their distribution as dividends. More important is the choice between dividends and distribution in other forms, such as share repurchase, royalties, favorable loan terms, or manipulation of other intercompany prices ("transfer prices").

8.3 The Foreign Tax Credit as an Implicit International Agreement

As has been mentioned, the creditability of foreign income taxes is usually justified on the equity grounds of avoiding double taxation and on the efficiency grounds of capital-export neutrality, which requires that taxes should not influence the country of location of capital. The credit is supposed to make U.S. tax burdens independent of the location of investment, thereby assuring that a U.S. firm will not be influenced in its investment decisions by differences between U.S. and foreign taxes.

It is difficult to construct an optimizing model from a national perspective that implies capital-export neutrality, even if it could be achieved without sacrificing revenue to foreign governments. Optimal tariff considerations (whereby a large country seeks to exploit its monopoly advantage by, in effect, raising the prices of its exports and forcing down the prices of its imports through the use of tariffs) would generally imply that foreign investment should be discouraged relative to the level implied by unobstructed competitive capital markets.[46] It is even more difficult to justify crediting taxes paid to foreign governments as a method of achieving capital-export neutrality, as long as the policies of foreign governments are taken as given. The reason is simple. The foreign government collects the taxes on the investment. The yield to the domestic economy is net of foreign tax, whereas the yield of domestic investment is gross of domestic tax. National self-interest would seem to imply something like deduction of foreign taxes.

It is a serious error, though, to view the choice of policy as made in an international vacuum.[47] Since the tax policy of foreign governments cannot be taken as a given, an analysis of the national interest that neglects their reactions is fundamentally flawed. Like free trade, capital-export neutrality has to be understood as an international discipline or standard that may leave all participants better off than they would be under likely noncooperative alternatives.[48] That is, a policy of capital-export neutrality by all countries may lead to an outcome that is better for all than would obtain if policy were made separately on the assumption of no foreign interactions.

Unfortunately, this hypothetical possibility is merely that. The suggested policy that makes the economic pie as big as possible (and note that, since the taxes affect the level as well as the allocation of capital, there is no assurance that universal capital-export neutrality would be better than, for example, no taxation of capital) also affects who gets what part of the pie. Characteristically of efficiency rules in general, capital-export neutrality as a desideratum of policy makes no reference to who gets what share of the world economic pie (or even of the world's tax revenues).

We have described above the equity principle that it is unfair to tax income that has already been subjected to tax. This may be called the "intranational" equity principle in that it concerns fair treatment of two apparently similarly situated U.S. taxpayers. As has been emphasized, if we put to one side issues of transitional incidence (thereby probably putting aside the bulk of tax politics), the argument for the foreign tax credit based on the individual equity principle is surely fallacious. It is a condition of equilibrium that investors obtain the same rate of return after all taxes at all margins of investment. It therefore cannot be inequitable to subject certain forms of investment to higher or lower rates of tax, although it may be wasteful.

One encounters in this context, though, another notion of equity that is focused less on the U.S. taxpayer per se and more on the obligations of a tax jurisdiction toward the other members of the community of jurisdictions. This "international" equity principle is that each jurisdiction has an obligation to provide relief from double taxation up to the level of tax that would be levied on a taxpayer with purely domestic-source income. If we think of equity in terms of outcomes for individuals, the international equity principle seems a rather odd precept. But it is different from the intranational equity principle. For example, the international equity principle would be satisfied by exempting foreign-source income from domestic tax, provided the basic premise holds—that income is an exogenous attribute of taxpayers. Even more than the intranational equity principle, the international equity principle suffers in implementation from its definition in terms that are purely institutional rather than more fundamentally in terms of outcomes or even alternatives for individuals. For the latter purposes, it is not important whether something is taxed more than once or whether the burden is imposed by an income or by a sales tax. All the same, it is significant that the international principle carries with it a notion of obligations of good jurisdictional citizenship that is missing altogether from the intranational equity principle.

There is a further justification for the foreign tax credit suggested by the view of the corporate tax as a substitute for accrual accounting for income at the individual shareholder level. If the basic function of the "double taxation" of corporate income is to impose single taxation on the income of shareholders, something like the foreign tax credit is clearly necessary to dilute the strong incentive that would otherwise arise for individuals to hold shares directly rather than indirectly via U.S. corporations. If the nationality of the controlling corporation is a matter of indifference, such a policy as substituting a deduction for the credit would presumably result in significant shifts in portfolio form, little extra revenue, and the economic value loss that would result from inhibiting direct control.

Rather little attention has been paid to the implications of confining creditable foreign taxes to "income" taxes. The basis for the limitation is legal and institutional rather than economic. That is, the allowable credit is not determined by asking whether the incidence or other economic effect of the foreign tax or other policy is like that of the U.S. income tax. Instead, implementation depends on the foreign tax having various institutional features that make it look like the U.S. income tax (a VAT of the income type, for example, would not be creditable). As a result, it would be quite possible for a foreign government that desired to do so to implement simultaneously a capital subsidy and a formal income tax in such a way that the tax is "paid" by the U.S. government (through the credit) while the effective tax burden on investment is zero. U.S. law disallows the credit in cases where there is a direct connection between a subsidy received by a company and its tax obligations. it would not be difficult, however, to circumvent this rule (Gersovitz 1987).

So far we have not commented in detail on another important feature of U.S. law with respect to the crediting of foreign taxes, namely, the limitation of the credit, in effect, the the amount that would have been collected on the same income under U.S. law. The logic of the foreign tax credit as an intranational equity-based adjustment in a corporation's U.S. liability would imply no such limitation. Nor would the efficiency-oriented principle of capital-export neutrality. A more obvious justification has to do not with the behavior or burdens of taxpayers but with the behavior of governments. A country that is host to a large amount of activity owned by a U.S. corporation could obviously impose a tax at a virtually unlimited rate if the difference between its tax and the U.S. tax on the same income would be paid by the U.S. Treasury. Naturally, this reasoning is not confined to the issue of crediting foreign taxes in excess of U.S. rates. It applies as well to crediting taxes up to U.S. rates. Canadian tax policy analysts, for example, regard the Canadian corporate tax primarily as an instrument for absorbing the U.S. tax credit.

It is difficult to exaggerate the complexity that has been introduced to the U.S. rules by the need to limit the foreign tax credit. The present international tax rate constellation, in which a large number of U.S. taxpayer corporations find themselves with excess credits, sets up strong pressures on governments. Those with tax rates in excess of that in the United States, still an extremely important source of direct investment, will find themselves under pressure to reduce rates to the U.S. level. The stock of excess credits, though, will imply additional pressure for some countries to reduce rates below the U.S. level. Ironically, the foreign tax credit will become increasingly a source of capital-export nonneutrality, as firms find opportunities in low-tax jurisdictions artificially enhanced by the option that they provide to use up excess credits on the U.S. tax books.

8.4   International Taxation as Conditioned on Control

In the literature on international income taxation, most attention has been paid to the way in which the taxes influence the decision of an investing individual or firm to locate capital. Here, too, though, there has perhaps been too little focus on the actual transactions taxed, which are not flows of income in the abstract but dividend, royality, interest, and other "payments" (perhaps just on the books), and on the distinctions that influence the amount of tax (e.g., the distinction between a portfolio and a controlling investor).

One of the more elusive aspects of the rules for taxing international business is their reliance on discrimination among degrees of *control* of activities carried on abroad. Thus, the deemed-paid credit for foreign corporate income taxes is entirely denied to corporate portfolio investors, that is, corporate shareholders owning an insignificant fraction of the stock of the foreign company. To qualify, the U.S. corporation must own at least 10 percent of the voting stock. Even at this level of control, the foreign tax credit is limited according to the various "baskets" of income types, foreign company by foreign company. When the level of control rises to the level of a CFC, the foreign tax limits are determined by aggregates of foreign income by type. (Reminder: a CFC is a foreign corporation in which U.S. shareholders each owning at least 10 percent of the voting stock together own at least 50 percent of the voting stock.)

The most obvious manifestation of the importance placed by the tax law on control of a foreign business activity is the distinction between active and passive income (in its various forms). The distinction (which is found in the purely domestic tax sphere as well) has no place in the SHS income conception, nor is it readily modeled in the usual capital-flow model (of the sort outlined earlier in connection with the problem of international tax harmonization). Yet control and taxes are the two most obvious bases for the existence of multinational corporations.

We have discussed as length the traditional concept of capital-export neutrality, which (among other things) can an least be understood in the context of conventional capital flow models. Introducing the notion of control as an economic phenomenon provides a context for mentioning another traditional neutrality concept. "Capital-import neutrality" refers to the nationality of ownership of firms.[49] It obtains when there is no tax-based difference in circumstances of firms operating within a given country associated with the nationality of the firm's owners. The U.S. policy of deferring income tax on the earnings of foreign subsidiaries (thereby subjecting those earnings to the local tax system alone, until repatriation) can be thought of as applying the standard of capital-import neutrality to retained foreign earnings. (Arguably, the U.S. tax that will be due on repatriation is an unavoidable toll charge that has no influence on the foreign investment decision; see Hartman 1984.) The usual models of international capital-flows do not allow one to address the justification for capital-import neutrality effectively. The nationality of the owners of capital is not generally associated with economically significant consequences (apart, perhaps, from portfolio diversification).

The study of control promises to be an interesting one. In particular, it appears to be the obvious place to bring the notion of international competitiveness into the analysis in a meaningful way, one different from a mere identification with capital importation. (See, e.g., Summers 1986.) Control is, however, not easily given a rigorous economic interpretation—note, for example, that the extent of control of the corporate sector of an economy can range from 0 to 100 percent according to the degree of portfolio diversification by shareholders.

9 Concluding Comments

The conventional analysis of the broad economic principles traditionally said to underlie the basic structure of the U.S. system for taxing foreign income is fairly straightforward. A system of worldwide taxation combined with a foreign tax credit for taxes paid to other governments is asserted to achieve capital-export neutrality and the most efficient international allocation of investment. From the perspective of the domestic investor, the choice at the margin between foreign and domestic investment should be unaffected by tax considerations and should respond to the international levels of before-tax rates of return. This system will create an efficient worldwide allocation of resources and maximize world welfare. At the same time, some assert that national welfare will also be maximized when the overall effects of foreign investment are taken into account.

Although this theoretical analysis is relatively straightforward, as the preceding sections have shown, the implementation of these general principles in the real world of tax rules is enormously complex, and the results often inconsistent. Some of the sources of this complexity can be identified relatively easily. In the first place, capital-export neutrality under the current system is present only when the U.S. tax rate exceeds the foreign rate. When the foreign rate of tax exceeds the U.S. rate, the theory of capital-export neutrality in principle would require the United States to credit the taxes against the U.S. taxes paid on U.S.-source income and, if necessary, refund the excess. If this step is not taken, then investment is discouraged in countries with rates of tax higher than that of the United States. In view of the revenue cost of such a policy, however, particularly when the possible reactions of foreign governments are taken into account, the credit has historically been limited to the U.S. taxes attributable to foreign-source income, though the form of the limitation has varied over the years. The failure to refund excess foreign taxes was less significant before 1986 since most companies then could fully use their foreign tax credits. Now, however, the majority of firms are in an excess credit position, and the limitations on the availability of the credit have led to much of the complexity of the legal rules.

More important, perhaps, the present form of the limitation has led to significant "second-best" issues. For example, under the current rules, averaging of foreign taxes is allowed for active business income. This means that a U.S. company that is currently paying high foreign taxes with respect to one active business investment is encouraged at the margin to undertake a new business investment in a low-tax foreign country rather than in the United States. The excess credits on the high-tax investment can in effect shelter all (or at least some) of the U.S. tax burden on the low-tax investment. In the extreme case where the foreign country does not tax the investment at all—for example, under a tax holiday—the U.S. firm is comparing the before-tax rate of return in the foreign country with the after-tax rate of return on a domestic investment. Thus, an imperfectly pursued policy of capital-export neutrality can lead to results exactly the opposite of those the policy was intended to achieve.

Similar issues arise with respect to the taxation of income earned though U.S.-controlled foreign subsidiaries. A fully implemented policy of capital-export neutrality would tax the subsidiary income to the U.S. shareholder as it accrues. On the other hand, a fully implemented policy of capital-import or competitive neutrality would lead to the complete exemption of foreign income. Historically, Congress has accepted business arguments that current U.S. taxation adversely affects the competitive position of U.S. companies in foreign markets. It has allowed the deferral of U.S. tax on subsidiary income until repatriation, but only as long as that income fell into certain categories. On repatriation, capital-export considerations reassert themselves, and the income is then taxed, with the allowance of the "deemed" foreign tax credit for the foreign taxes paid by the subsidiary. This "hybrid" mixture of capital-import and capital-export considerations again has led to the complex dividing lines required by Subpart F to sort out income into deferral and accrual categories as well as the convoluted "pass through" of baskets for foreign-tax-credit purposes.

Another perspective from which to view the international rules is taxpayer equity. How should traditional notions of horizontal equity be applied in connection with foreign income? The exemption of foreign-source income would clearly seem inconsistent with any equity criterion based on ability to pay or well-being, assuming that income is taken to be an exogenous characteristic of taxpayers. An SHS approach to income definition would seem to imply inclusion of foreign income and a deduction for foreign taxes as a cost of producing income.

On the other hand, many have argued that a credit for foreign taxes is required by what we have called international equity considerations. The U.S. taxpayer who is subject to tax both here, because of a domiciliary connection, and in the foreign jurisdiction where the income arises is, some assert, not similarly situated when compared with a U.S. taxpayer who has income only from U.S. sources. The United States as the country of domicile has an internationally recognized responsibility to relieve the burden of international double taxation arising because of the overlapping assertions of taxing jurisdiction by the United States and the source country. Having chosen initially to tax foreign-source income, the United States has an accompanying responsibility based on equity considerations to relieve double taxation through the credit.

On the other hand, if the responsibility of the domiciliary country to relieve international double taxation is recognized, a foreign tax credit is not the only means available. An alternative would be a "territorial" system that left out of account both foreign income and foreign taxes. Such an approach, in turn, would lead back to the question of the relative merits of capital-export and capital-import neutrality and reintroduce the appropriateness from an equity perspective of eliminating from the tax base a receipt that clearly would be included under traditional income notions.

In short, as in so many other tax policy issues, the possible theoretical starting points for analysis in the international area lead to quite different results, and the real-world phenomena are often "noisy" and inconsistent with any single overarching approach. The most important task for policy analysis at this point is to try to determine with more accuracy exactly what effect the complex system of rules has on the form and extent of international activity.

Notes

The authors would like to thank Daniel Frisch, James Hines, Thomas Horst, Richard Koffey, Joel Slemrod, Emil Sunley, and participants in the NBER Conference on International Aspects of Taxation for helpful discussions of various aspects of this research, and the National Bureau of Economic Research for financial support. This paper was completed while Bradford was a fellow at the Center for Advanced Study in the Behavioral Sciences. He is grateful for the Center's hospitality and for financial support arranged by the Center from the Alfred P. Sloan Foundation and the National Science Foundation (grant # BNS87-00864). Bradford would also like to acknowledge financial support provided by Princeton University and by the John M. Olin Program at Princeton University for the Study of Economic Organization and Public Policy.

1. For a fuller exposition of the applicable U.S. tax law, see McDaniel and Ault (1981). For the details of the Tax Reform Act of 1986, see U.S. Congress (1987) and U.S. Congress, Joint Committee on Taxation (1987).

2. The Internal Revenue Code provides a series of mechanical rules for determining residence of aliens; see sec. 7701(b). Special rules exempt certain amounts of earned income received by citizens residing abroad; see sec. 911.

3. The Subpart F rules are described in more detail in sec. 2.1 below.

4. The foreign tax credit mechanism is discussed in more detail in sec. 2.2 below.

5. The U.S. shareholder must be a corporation and must own at least 10 percent of the voting stock of the foreign corporation. The deemed-paid credit is also available for taxes paid by lower-tier foreign subsidiaries under certain conditions as income is distributed up a chain of foreign corporations to the U.S. shareholder.

6. That is, the credit is limited to foreign taxes on income that is determined by the United States to be from a foreign source. If a foreign country imposed a tax on an item of income that under the U.S. source rules is determined to be U.S. source, the credit is in effect not available (unless there are other items of income from foreign sources that create excess limitation; see the discussion in sec. 2.2).

7. More technically, if there is no independently determined factory price, half the income is allocated to the location of the assets used in the production and sale and half to the place of sale. In practice, this means that, if property is manufactured in the United States and sold abroad with no sales assets located abroad, half the income is foreign source even though it is unlikely that any foreign jurisdiction will tax it (Treasury Regulations, sec 1.836-3(b)).

8. Treasury Regulations, sec. 904(g).

9. Such dividends are not subject to tax when received by nonresident aliens or foreign corporations if the dividend-paying corporation is subject to the branch profits tax discussed in sec. 3.4 below.

10. The determination of where an intangible is used is obviously not always easy.

11. See Bank of America v. U.S., 680 F.2d 142 (Ct. Cls. 1982).

12. Treasury Regulations, secs. 864(e), 1.861-9T. Special rules apply for the allocation of the interest expense of a foreign corporation with a U.S. branch that in effect try to take into account the relation between interest rates and exchange rate gain or loss (Treasury Regulations, sec. 1.882-5).

13. See the discussion in sec. 2.2.

14. The regulations originally provided that 30 percent of research and development costs would be allocated to the place in which more than 50 percent of the

research costs were incurred. Congress enacted a moratorium on the application of the regulation and allocated all research and development expenses incurred in the United States to U.S.-source income. For 1987, 50 percent (rather than 30 percent) allocation was established by the 1986 Act and subsequently modified. Additional legislative action is anticipated.

15. For the branch operations described above, the translation rate is the average exchange rate for the year. Calculation of income under this so-called profit and loss method means that unrealized foreign-exchange gains or losses in the tax-payer's invested capital are not taken into account currently. Special rules apply to taxpayers who do business in "hyperinflationary economies," which in effect allow changes in the dollar value of invested capital to be accounted for currently.

In the case of a distribution of income from a foreign subsidiary that has a foreign currency as its functional currency, the translation rate is the spot rate in effect at the time of the distribution.

16. Appropriate adjustments are made if there is a difference between the amount accrued and the amount actually paid.

17. The legislative history of the 1986 Act recognizes the economic connection between exchange gain and interest income.

18. If the losses reduce U.S. income, i.e., if there is an overall foreign loss, adjustments are later required in the foreign-tax-credit faction to limit the creditability of foreign taxes on an operation that, from the U.S. perspective, has not generated any net income.

19. Subject to the limitations of Subpart F discussed in sec. 3.2.

20. The rules apply to any foreign corporation in which "U.S." persons" own more than 50 percent of the voting power or value of the outstanding stock of the corporation. A "U.S. person" is defined as a U.S. individual or corporation that owns 10 percent or more of the voting stock of the foreign corporation.

21. The regulations have extensive rules defining the types of activities that constitute manufacturing as contrasted with mere assembly and packaging. In addition, the income would not be taxed currently if it bore a rate of foreign tax that approximated the U.S. rate.

22. This makes the source rule discussed in sec. 1.3 extremely important. This rule sources income from sales of inventory in the jurisdiction in which title is passed. That rule makes it possible to create income that is technically foreign source but is unlikely to attract any foreign taxes. As a result, the foreign taxes on high-tax foreign-source income can become currently creditable.

23. A special rule applies to interest that is subject to a high withholding tax. Such interest is segregated in its own basket to prevent averaging with other normally low-taxed passive income.

24. Technically, the DISC provisions were retained in a limited form, and an interest charge was imposed on the deferred tax liability. Thus, the taxpayer may still benefit from an indirect loan from the government at a potentially favorable rate of interest.

25. Treasury Regulations, sec. 924(d)–(e). In fact, since the FSC can "contract out" the foreign activities to related parties, its actual foreign presence can be minimal.

26. See U.S. Congress, Joint Committee on Taxation (1984, 1042). The European Community has "raised questions" about the FSC provisions under GATT.

27. See, e.g., Eli Lilly v. Commissioner, 84 T.C. 996 (1984).

28. See Treasury Regulations, sec. 946(h).

29. See U.S. Treasury Department (1984, 2:327–30). The Treasury analysis of the possessions tax credit estimated that the average tax benefit for corporations taking advantage of the possessions tax credit was $22,000 per employee, while the average employee wage was only $14,210.

30. Rental income from real property is in principle taxed at the 30 percent gross rate, but the foreign taxpayer can elect to have the income treated as business income so that deductions such as depreciation, taxes, and interest are available. The resulting net income is taxed at normal U.S. rates.

31. As indicated below, very often the 30 percent rate is eliminated or reduced by treaty, and several important categories of income are exempt. Nonetheless, the existence of the high withholding rate can be significant in some circumstances.

32. The exemption for portfolio interest was added in 1984. Certain formalities must be complied with to ensure that the portfolio debt will not be acquired by U.S. taxpayers. Before the exemption in 1984, U.S. corporations could in effect issue tax-exempt bonds to foreign lenders through a convoluted technique involving the use of wholly owned finance subsidiaries organized in the Netherlands Antilles. The transactions took advantage of a tax treaty between the United States and the Antilles. These structures originated in the 1970s with the blessing of the Treasury Department to encourage U.S. corporations to borrow abroad during a period of balance-of-payments difficulties. The direct exemption for portfolio interest has made them obsolete, and the treaty on which they were originally based has been terminated.

33. See the discussion in sec. 3.4 below.

34. Although a sale of the shares would result in no current U.S. tax, presumably a purchaser would discount the purchase price for the shares to reflect the fact that it could get a stepped-up basis in the underlying assets of the corporation only by paying the corporate-level tax. Thus, the two methods of disposition would have roughly the same after-tax consequences to the seller.

35. H. Rep. 99-426, 99th Cong., 1st sess. (1985), 425.

36. The branch profits tax is only a surrogate for the tax on a dividend distribution to the foreign shareholder, but it technically falls on the foreign corporation, and thus the nondiscrimination clause is applicable.

37. A foreign corporation is deemed to be treaty shopping if more than 50 percent of its stock is owned by nontreaty country residents, with an exception for publicly traded corporations.

38. For an overview of the economics of international income taxation, see Adams and Whalley (1977), Sato and Bird (1975).

39. Grubert and Mutti (1987) present an analysis of the economic effects of the 1986 changes.

40. For a clear development of this point, see Bittker (1980).

41. In his elegantly clear exposition of tax policy in open economies, Dixit (1985) makes no mention at all of income taxes. For promising beginnings at integration of the two subjects, see the papers by Frenkel, Razin, and Symansky and by Gordon and Levinsohn in *Taxation in the global economy*, ed. Assaf Razin and Joel Slemrod, Chicago: University of Chicago Press, 1990.

42. For an extended discussion of income concepts and references to the literature, see Bradford (1986) or Institute for Fiscal Studies (1978).

43. Within the United States, income is typically allocated to different jurisdictions by formula. Formula apportionment solves some problems but introduces others. See Gordon and Wilson (1986).

44. Newlon's (1987) analysis of the taxation of multinationals provides a nice illustration of the importance of looking closely at the rules relating to specific transactions (such as payment of interest).

45. For a model that takes into account the imperfect substitutability of assets in different countries in investor portfolios, see Mutti and Grubert (1985).

46. This conclusion has long been recognized. See, e.g., Richman (1963) and Musgrave (1969). Feldstein and Hartman (1979) present a formal analysis.

47. For a forceful statement of this viewpoint, see Ross (1983).

48. For an analysis of tax policy determination as an international noncooperative game, see Gordon and Varian (1986).

49. Hufbauer and Foster summed up the law in 1976 as follows: "Both in legislation and in bilateral tax treaties, the United States has attempted to ensure the type of neutrality appropriate to different situations, while at the same time protecting U.S. tax revenue. Thus, United States taxation of the foreign income of U.S. owned firms embodies a mixture of capital-export neutrality, capital-import neutrality, and revenue protection clauses" (1976, 15).

References

Adams, J. D. R., and John Whalley. 1977. *The international taxation of multinational enterprises in developed countries.* Westport, Conn.: Greenwood.

Bittker, Boris I. 1980. Equity, efficiency, and income tax theory: Do misallocations drive out inequities? In *The economics of taxation*, ed. Henry J. Aaron and Michael J. Boskin, 19–31. Washington, D.C.: Brookings.

Bradford, David F. 1986. *Untangling the income tax.* Cambridge: Harvard University Press.

Bradford, David F., and the U.S. Treasury Tax Policy Staff. 1984. *Blueprints for basic tax reform.* 2d ed., rev. Arlington, Va.: Tax Analysts.

Dixit, Avinash. 1985. Tax policy in open economies. In *Handbook of public economics*, ed. Alan J. Auerbach and Martin S. Feldstein, 1:313–74. New York: Elsevier.

Feldstein, Martin, and David Hartman. 1979. The optimal taxation of foreign source investment income. *Quarterly Journal of Economics* 93 (November): 613–29.

Gersovitz, Mark. 1987. The effects of domestic taxes on foreign private investment. In *The theory of taxation for developing countries*, ed. David Newbery and Nicholas Stern, 615–35. New York: Oxford University Press.

Gordon, Roger H., and Hal R. Varian. 1986. Taxation of asset income in the presence of a world securities market. NBER Working Paper no. 1994. Cambridge, Mass.: National Bureau of Economic Research, August.

Gordon, Roger H., and John D. Wilson. 1986. An examination of multijurisdictional corporate income taxation under formula apportionment. *Econometrica* 54 (November): 1357–73.

Grubert, Harry, and John Mutti. 1987. Taxes, international capital flows and trade: The international implications of the Tax Reform Act of 1986. *National Tax Journal* 40 (3): 315–29.

Hartman, David. 1984. Tax policy and foreign direct investment in the United States. *National Tax Journal* 37: 475–87.

Hufbauer, Gary, and David Foster. 1976. U.S. taxation of the undistributed income of controlled foreign corporations. In *Essays in international taxation: 1976.* Washington D.C.: U.S. Treasury Department, U.S. Government Printing Office. Institute for Fiscal Studies. 1978. *The structure and reform of direct taxation: The report of a committee chaired by Professor J. E. Meade.* London: Allen & Unwin.

McDaniel, Paul R., and Hugh J. Ault. 1981. *Introduction to United States international taxation.* 2d rev. ed. Boston: Kluwer.

Musgrave, Peggy B. 1969. *United States taxation of foreign investment income: Issues and arguments.* Cambridge: Harvard Law School.

Mutti, John, and Harry Grubert. 1985. The taxation of capital income in an open economy: The importance of resident-nonresident tax treatment. *Journal of Public Economics* 27 (3): 291–309.

Newlon, T. Scott. 1987. Tax policy and the multinational firm's financial policy and investment decisions. Ph.D. diss., Princeton University.

Richman, Peggy Brewer. 1963. *Taxation of foreign investment income: An economic analysis.* Baltimore: Johns Hopkins University Press.

Ross, Stanford G. 1985. A perspective on international tax policy. *Tax Notes* 26 (18 February): 701–13.

Sato, Mitsuo, and Richard Bird. 1975. International aspects of the taxation of corporations and shareholders. IMF Staff Papers no. XII-2. Washington, D.C.: International Monetary Fund.

Slemrod, Joel. 1988. International capital mobility and the theory of capital income taxation. In *Uneasy compromise: Problems of a hybrid income-consumption tax,* ed. Henry J. Aaron, Harvey Galper, and Joseph A. Pechman. Washington, D.C.: Brookings.

Summers, Lawrence H. 1986. Tax policy and international competitiveness. NBER Working Paper no. 2007. Cambridge, Mass.: National Bureau of Economic Research, August.

U.S. Congress. 1987. *Tax Reform Act of 1986.* Washington, D.C.

U.S. Congress. Joint Committee on Taxation. 1984. *General explanation of the revenue provisions of the Deficit Reduction Act of 1984.* Washington, D.C.

U.S. Congress. 1987. *General explanation of the Tax Reform Act of 1986.* Washington, D.C., 4 May.

U.S. Treasury Department. 1984. *Tax reform for fairness, simplicity, and economic growth.* Vol. 1, *Overview.* Vol. 2, *General explanation of the Treasury Department proposals.* Vol. 3, *Value-added tax.* Washington, D.C.: U.S. Government Printing Office, November.

U.S. Treasury. 1988. *A study of intercompany pricing.* Washington, D.C., 18 October.

15   International Transfer Pricing

Suk Hi Kim

Transfer prices are prices of goods and services bought and sold between parent companies and subsidiaries. Internal transfers include raw materials, semifinished goods, finished goods, allocation of fixed costs, loans, fees, royalties for use of trademarks, and copyrights. International transfer pricing policies become increasingly complex as companies increase their involvement in international transactions through foreign subsidiaries, joint ventures, and parent-owned distribution systems. Discrepancies between transfer pricing methods used by companies and those allowed by taxing agencies take place because taxing agencies and companies have different objectives. For example, multinational companies try to maximize profits and improve performance evaluation by manipulating internal transfer prices. Taxing authorities, on the other hand, try to allocate through fair market prices the profit of a sale between their country and other countries. Thus, multinational financial managers must understand transfer pricing objectives and their impact on transfer prices.

This chapter has three sections. The first section discusses the major objectives of transfer pricing. The second section describes Section 482 of the Internal Revenue Code and its implications for international transfer pricing. The third section covers foreign sales corporations because Section 482 affects them and because they have significant tax advantages.

Transfer Pricing Objectives

Transfer pricing strategies are sensitive internal corporate issues, because successful pricing is a key element in achieving profits. Transfer pricing also helps multinational companies determine how company profits are allo-

From *Global Corporate Finance*, Copley Publishing Group, 1991, pp. 371–384. Reprinted by permission.

cated across divisions. Governments show interest in transfer pricing, because these prices will decide tax revenues and other benefits. So, many
host governments have policing mechanisms to review the transfer pricing
policies of multinational companies.

Transfer pricing has the following objectives:

1. Income tax minimization.

2. Import duty minimization.

3. Avoiding financial problems.

4. Adjusting for currency fluctuations.

Income Tax Minimization

A number of researchers such as Jeffrey Arpan and Lee Radebaugh have
singled out tax minimization as the most important variable influencing
international transfer pricing decisions. Their finding is not surprising because transfers between related business entities account for approximately
40 percent of total world trade. Economic benefits are immediate if transfer
prices can shift profits from a country with a higher tax rate to a country
with a lower tax rate. Yet, a company using transfer pricing for maximized
profits must balance this approach by having prices consistent with the
regulations of taxing authorities.

Example
To illustrate the tax effects of a change in transfer prices on corporate
earnings, assume the following: (1) Affiliate A is in a low-tax country (20%
tax rate) and affiliate B is in a high-tax country (50% tax rate). (2) Affiliate
A produces 100 radios for $5 per unit and sells them to affiliate B. (3)
Affiliate B sells these radios for $20 per unit to an unrelated customer.
Table 15.1 shows the tax effects of low versus high transfer price on
company earnings.

Under the low transfer price, A pays taxes of $60 and B pays taxes of
$300 for a total tax bill of $360 and a consolidated net income of $450.
Under the high transfer price, A pays taxes of $160 and B pays taxes of $50
for a total tax bill of $210 and a consolidated net income of $690. Earnings
before taxes are the same of $900 despite the different prices at which the
radios transfer from A to B. Still, the higher transfer price reduces total
taxes by $150 ($360–$210) and increases consolidated net income by the
same amount ($690–$540).

Table 15.1
Tax effect of low versus high transfer price

	Low tax A	High tax B	Combined A + B
Low transfer price			
Sales price	$1,000	$2,000	$3,000
Cost of goods sold	500	1,000	1,500
Gross profit	$ 500	$1,000	$1,500
Operating expenses	200	400	600
Earnings before taxes	$ 300	$ 600	$ 900
Taxes (20%/50%)	60	300	360
Net income	$ 240	$ 300	$ 540
High transfer price			
Sales price	$1,500	$2,000	$3,500
Cost of goods sold	500	1,500	2,000
Gross profit	$1,000	$ 500	$1,500
Operating expense	200	400	600
Earnings before taxes	$ 800	$ 100	$ 900
Taxes (20%/50%)	160	50	210
Net income	$ 640	$ 50	$ 690

Import Duty Minimization

Affiliate A sells goods to affiliate B. The rule of thumb for income tax minimization is: (1) set the transfer price as high as possible if A's tax rate is lower than B's rate and (2) set the transfer price as low as possible if A's tax rate is higher than B's tax rate. The introduction of import duties complicates this rule because multiple objectives could conflict. For example, a lower transfer price reduces import duties, but it increases income taxes. A higher transfer price reduces income taxes, but it increases import duties. Suppose that B must pay import duties at the rate of 10 percent. Import duties are normally levied on the invoice (transfer) price. The higher transfer price raises tariffs by $50 ($1,500 × 0.10 − $1,000 × 0.10), thus offsetting tax effects of $50 in terms of increased tariffs.

Import duty minimization is easy, but tax reductions, which have offsetting effects, may complicate it. Moreover, a country with low import duties may have high income taxes, while a country with high import duties may have low income taxes. If multinational companies use low or high transfer prices in certain countries, they have to balance import duties and income taxes to maximize a combined benefit from tariff and income tax reductions.

Avoiding Financial Problems

Transfer prices can avoid financial problems or improve financial conditions. Transfer pricing often avoids economic restrictions and exchange controls that host countries place on multinational companies. For example, some developing countries restrict the amount of profits that can leave the country. An obvious way around this restriction is to charge high prices for imports. Thus, countries with such restrictions watch import and export prices closely.

Some countries do not allow multinational companies to charge certain expenses against taxable income. For instance, they do not permit expenses for research and development done elsewhere. Royalty fees a parent company charges against its subsidiary income are often not allowed. Because the host country does not allow them, they can be recaptured by increasing the transfer price of goods shipped into the country.

Transfer prices also channel profits into an affiliate to bolster its financial condition, thus presenting a favorable profit picture to satisfy earnings criteria set by foreign lenders. So, the parent company does not need to commit much capital to its foreign subsidiary even though the subsidiary may be required to secure the loan. Besides, low transfer prices give the subsidiary a competitive edge it might need starting a new venture or reacting to an economic downturn.

Adjusting for Currency Fluctuations

A wide range of currency fluctuations may influence the performance reports of foreign subsidiaries. Many U.S. multinational companies evaluate the performance of foreign subsidiaries with reports stated in U.S. dollars. If currency exchange rates fluctuate, it may be difficult to evaluate the performance of the subsidiary. Management of the subsidiary often prefers to evaluate its performance with reports stated in local currency rather than U.S. dollars. Adjusting transfer prices for currency fluctuations can solve this performance evaluation problem. But, performance evaluation is difficult when the objective is tax minimization or when currency fluctuates. One subsidiary's profit in one country may be greater than another subsidiary's profit in another country, not because of better management but because of the transfer price. One way to solve this problem is to maintain two sets of books: one for foreign authorities and another set for performance evaluation purposes.

Summary of Transfer Pricing Objectives

This section discussed several transfer pricing objectives such as minimizing income taxes and import duties, avoiding financial problems, and adjusting for currency fluctuations. Minimizing income taxes and import duties is important. Taxing agencies in many countries usually pay close attention to companies transferring profits to countries with lower taxes. As some unfortunate companies discovered, overzealousness may have short-run gains but long-run losses. Many multinational companies have also manipulated transfer prices to avoid financial problems of a foreign affiliate. They adjust for currency fluctuations to evaluate affiliate performance. Based on our discussion, changes in transfer prices seem to attain transfer pricing objectives easily. Yet, rules in many countries regulate how transfer prices must be set. A company should balance its transfer pricing objectives by making its transfer pricing policies consistent with the regulations of host countries.

As this discussion shows, international transfer pricing must meet the objectives of management control and other objectives. These other objectives are sometimes so important that goal congruence (profit maximization) and performance evaluation are secondary or unachievable. Thus, multinational companies must establish an efficient transfer pricing system. Wagdy Abdallah suggests five criteria for an efficient international transfer pricing system:

1. The transfer pricing system should measure profits of subsidiaries and their managers, including controllable divisional contributions.

2. The transfer pricing system should supply top management information for guidelines in managerial decision making.

3. The transfer pricing system should improve company performance.

4. The transfer pricing system should motivate subsidiary managers to increase efficiency and maximize divisional profits in harmony with the objectives of top management.

5. The transfer pricing system should minimize international transaction costs by reducing border and income tax liabilities, foreign exchange losses, and currency manipulation losses.

Empirical studies reveal some interesting findings about the practices of U.S. companies in international transfer pricing. Researchers single out income tax minimization as the most important objective of transfer pricing. Still, other studies find that the influence of a given variable differs according to environments. For example, Jane Burns surveyed 62 U.S. companies with subsidiaries in industrialized countries to identify the importance of 14 variables influencing transfer pricing decisions. Seung Kim and Stephen Miller surveyed 342 U.S. companies with subsidiaries in eight developing countries to obtain the perceived importance of nine variables in transfer pricing decisions. According to Burns, the five most important influences on transfer pricing decisions were: (1) market conditions in the foreign country, (2) competition in the foreign country, (3) reasonable profit for foreign affiliates, (4) U.S. federal income taxes, and (5) economic conditions in the foreign country. Kim and Miller found that the five most important objectives were: (a) profit repatriation restrictions within the host country, (b) exchange controls, (c) joint-venture constraints within the host country, (d) tariffs/customs duties within the host country, and (e) income tax liability within the host country.

Minimizing income tax ranked fourth highest in Burns' survey and fifth highest in Kim-Miller's survey. One problem with making a transfer pricing decision is that multiple objectives could conflict with each other. Other objectives often are so important that profit maximization and performance evaluation seem secondary or unachievable. Therefore, multinational financial managers must understand transfer pricing objectives and their effect on transfer prices.

Section 482 and Transfer Pricing

International transfer pricing decisions have a major impact on global sales, tax liabilities, and profits of multinational companies. Tax authorities of most countries require multinational companies to use fair market prices as the transfer pricing policy. Their objectives are (1) to prevent multinational companies from reducing tax liabilities by shifting profits from one country to another; (2) to allow tax authorities to adjust income and deductions to reflect the correct taxable income within territories; and (3) to counter abusive transfer pricing policies.

Few governments are similar. Nor are they all equally concerned about the effects of transfer prices. The United States, Canada, and developing countries show the most concern. In the United States, for example, Section 482 of the Internal Revenue Code (IRC) permits the Internal Revenue Service (IRS) to "distribute, apportion, or allocate gross income, deductions, credits, or allowances" between related companies to prevent tax evasion. The IRS prefers that all transfers among related parties take place at an "arm's length" price, which is the price that would take place between unrelated parties. Section 482 of the 1986 Internal Revenue Code compares intragroup transfer prices with arm's-length prices. The IRS monitors transfers in the following five areas:

1. Loans and advances.

2. Performance of services.

3. Use of tangible property.

4. Use of intangible property.

5. Sale of intangible property.

This chapter deals with only (3), which covers transfer pricing of tangible property.

Section 482 assumes that subsidiaries are legally and economically separate from their parent corporation. On the other hand, it fails to consider that multinational companies may base their intercompany prices on the assumption that the organization is one economic unit. The fundamental difference—the source of recent controversy—has caused severe discrepancies between the transfer pricing methods the IRS will accept and those U.S. multinational companies use.

An important feature of minimizing taxes is the assurance that transfer prices reflect arm's-length transactions as much as possible. Section 482 and other regulations allow U.S. companies to use four pricing methods in determining the arm's-length price for the sale of tangible property. These methods are the comparable uncontrollable price method, the resale price method, the cost-pull method, and other acceptable methods.

Comparable Uncontrolled Price Method

Under this method, uncontrolled sales are compared to controlled sales if their physical property and circumstances are nearly identical with the physical property and circumstances of controlled sales. This method most accurately approximates an arm's-length standard because it reflects (1) the price of sales made to unrelated customers, (2) the price of sales from unrelated sellers to the company, and (3) the price of sales between other unrelated parties. The comparable uncontrolled price is similar to the prevailing market price when markets are perfectly competitive. Section

482 allows an adjusted market price if markets are less than perfectly competitive.

Though simple in theory, the comparable uncontrolled price method is often impractical. Perfectly competitive markets rarely exist for products transferred between related entities. There are many cases where no useful evidence of uncontrolled transactions is available. The goods transferred between related parties are so special to the group that there is no open market for them. This may be the case for semifinished products or for transfers of technology. Without perfectly competitive markets, adjustments can be made easily for such items as freight and insurance. But they cannot be made accurately for other items such as trademarks and brand names.

Resale Price Method

Under this method, an arm's-length price is obtained by subtracting an appropriate markup from the applicable sale price. The applicable sale price is the price at which a buyer resells goods obtained in a controlled sale. A company must use the resale price method only when the following three conditions exist: First, there are no comparable uncontrolled sales. Second, an applicable resale price is available. Third, the buyer adds only an insubstantial amount to the value of the property.

Markup percentages should be derived from the uncontrolled purchases and resales of a reseller who acts in the controlled sale. But markup percentages may be obtained from the resale of other resellers if the same reseller makes the sale. Although the resale price method is applicable to most market operations, the IRS may reject it on the basis that it is difficult to find which markups are appropriate. In other words, the IRS may reject this method when a reseller adds to the value of the product.

Cost-Plus Method

Under this method, an arm's-length price is determined by adding an appropriate markup to the seller's cost. Markup percentages are determined by referring to similar transactions with or between unrelated entities. The IRS, besides, stipulates that costs must be according to accounting practices that neither favor nor burden controlled sales. The IRS selects the cost-plus method instead of the resale price method if the cost and profit of a seller are easier to evaluate than the cost and profit of a reseller. Thus, the cost-plus method is useful when a reseller adds a substantial value to property before resale. Such situations occur when related parties sell semi-finished products or when one entity acts as a subcontractor for a related entity.

As some court cases show, the cost-plus method is arbitrary. It is difficult to assess the cost of the product and to figure out the appropriate markup percentage. The Internal Revenue Code does not define full cost given. It also does not give a uniform formula for prorating shared costs over joint products. Thus, multinational companies manipulate the markup percentage over cost.

Other Methods

The IRS had allowed companies to use only these three transfer pricing methods until 1968, when it permitted a fourth choice but only in cases where the three other methods did not apply. The fourth alternative may be entirely distinct from the three already described in the regulations. How far the IRS wishes to allow other methods is unknown. But it is likely that the taxpayer's method will be analyzed to see whether it results in an arm's-length price. Some of these methods are the rate-of-return on investment, the proportionate profit method, and the appraisal method. The rate-of-return method is a variation of the resale price and the cost-plus methods. Under the rate-of-return method, the markup percentage depends on a certain rate of return on total assets. The proportionate profit method allows companies to allocate total profits among segments, using full cost as the allocation basis. Under the appraisal method, the arm's-length price is the price at which an unrelated party would agree to buy the products in an uncontrolled sale.

Summary of Transfer Pricing Methods

The Tax Reform Act of 1986 reduced U.S. corporate tax rates from 40 percent to 34 percent on domestic corporations and branches of foreign corporations. These U.S. tax rates fall below those of other industrial countries. Thus, most accounting practitioners and international business executives believe that these lower rates will encourage U.S.-based multinational companies to bring more taxable income to the United States. Section 482 still insists on the use of arm's-length prices for intercompany transactions.

The IRS may decide that the price for merchandise sent to an affiliate is below an arm's-length price—the amount that unrelated parties would charge in an independent transaction. As a result, the agency would adjust upward the taxable income of the parent company to reflect this higher arm's-length price. The affiliate, in effect, incurs double taxation since it would have used the lower price when computing the cost of goods sold in estimating its foreign tax. Foreign tax credit provisions of the United States partially offset this problem. Foreign income is taxed at the same rate as domestic income, and credit is given for any taxes paid to a foreign government according to domestic tax neutrality. Not many cases of double taxation are completely resolved, however, because there are many departures from this theoretical norm of tax neutrality.

The threat of double taxation is no longer as great as it was before the U.S. government agreed to many bilateral tax treaties. In a fashion similar to Section 482 of the Internal Revenue Code, many foreign governments have recognized the principle of allocating income and deductions among related parties. The IRS allocates income and deductions among related parties when it thinks that intracompany dealings are not at arm's-length. The provisions also recognize the right of another country to make allocations that will reflect arm's-length dealings based on its domestic laws.

The IRS requires that companies must follow a specific order for finding arm's-length prices. No pricing method can be used unless a preceding one is unsuitable. According to the Internal Revenue Code, the first method is the comparable uncontrolled price method, followed by the resale price method. The third method is the cost-plus method if the first two are unsuitable. If none of these three options apply in a particular case, another method, including a variation of the first three, may be used.

Comparison of Transfer Pricing Methods in Use

Suk Kim surveyed business executives from 168 U.S. firms to find out how the IRS applied the methods outlined in Section 482. His findings reveal that many firms did not practice the pricing methods they should have used. As table 15.2 shows, approximately 69 percent of exports to subsidiaries were products sold to unrelated customers while 31 percent were sold to related customers. Two-thirds of the products were either components or semifinished, and one-third were finished goods.

Though 69 percent of export sales qualified for a comparable uncontrolled price, only 17 percent of the respondents used it for intercompany exports. Furthermore, while only ten percent of exports to subsidiaries seemed to qualify for a resale price, 27 percent of the respondents used it for intercompany sales. The variation is more dramatic for the cost-plus

Table 15.2
IRS transfer pricing methods and their uses

	Comparable uncontrolled price	Resale price	Cost-plus price	Other price
Pricing methods that seem most appropriate, according to types of intercompany sales	69%	10%	21%	
Pricing methods used by 168 sample companies	17%	27%	47%	9%

method: 47 percent of the respondents used it even though only 21 percent of exports to subsidiaries seemed to qualify for the cost-plus method. Jane Burns has found that about 10 percent of the IRS audits on intercompany prices was based on the resale price method, 25 percent depended on the comparable uncontrolled price method, and the remaining 65 percent relied on the cost-plus method or other method. These studies suggest that the IRS does not follow regulations when assessing additional taxes or settling disputes. Several arguments support the popular cost-plus method. Being liberal, this approach can be easily justified to tax authorities. In perfectly competitive markets, a company can justify its departure from prevailing prices because of product differentiation. When there is no identical market price, a company can argue for its transfer prices on available data. Next, the cost-plus method avoids internal friction of arbitrary systems. Most multinational companies are highly decentralized. So, each unit's manager is in the best position to estimate the cost of products and their appropriate profit markup. This method also safeguards against manipulation in transfer pricing.

Section 482 White Paper

On October 18, 1988, the IRS issued its findings and recommendations from its study of intercompany pricing—the so-called Section 482 White Paper. The study outlines four key concepts:

1. At the time a tax return is filed, the taxpayer should document contemporaneous pricing or significant mispricing.

2. The IRS should aggressively pursue pricing information through administrative summons and Section 982 formal document requests. IRS economists and counsel should become involved early in the case.

3. The procedures for determining the appropriate transfer price of intangibles should be revised, and appropriate pricing readjustments should be made over time.

4. The rules for acceptable cost-sharing agreements should be made more specific. They should require an arm's-length "buying" charge for pre-existing unshared research.

The full impact of the paper will not be known for years. Still, renewed IRS interest in intercompany pricing may be the most significant tax issue that U.S. and foreign multinational companies will confront for the rest of this century. Foreign countries have already expressed concern over proposals in the White Paper. First, these proposals fail to recognize that an arm's-length price is not a single specific number. The IRS is trying to require one specific price. Second, taxpayers must involve tax economists/ Section 482 specialists early on when making their pricing decisions. Third, the IRS will create a confrontational climate with taxpayers and foreign fiscal authorities. Fourth, the proposals may ultimately result in final outcomes of intercompany pricing disputes which are not any different from solutions before the White Paper.

The Foreign Sales Corporation (FSC)

Although this chapter does not discuss foreign sales corporations in detail, we mention them because they are affected by Section 482 and have significant tax advantages. ... the purpose of a FSC is to encourage U.S. manufacturers to increase exports by providing them with substantial tax benefits. The basic tax advantage is the exemption of federal income tax on a significant portion of the FSC's earnings.

The difficult part of the 1985 FSC Act is determining the FSC's income. Because the parent company usually owns the FSC which sells its merchandise, the price of the merchandise is a transfer price. Transfer prices are subject to artificial manipulation. According to this legislation, the price should be an actual arm's-length transfer price or a formula price designed to fit the definition of a transfer price set forth by the General Agreement on Tariffs and Trade.

Thirty-four percent of the income from transactions is exempt from federal taxes if the transfer price of the merchandise is an arm's-length price. Seventy-four percent of the income from the transaction is exempt if the transfer price is based on the special administered pricing rules.

Administrative pricing guidelines allow two pricing methods: the combined taxable income method and the gross receipts method. Under the combined taxable income method, the transfer price to the FSC is the sales price less the FSC expense and 23 percent of the combined taxable income. Under the gross receipts method, the transfer price to the FSC is the sales price less the FSC expense and the lesser of 1.83 percent of foreign trading gross receipts or twice the allowable FSC profit under the combined taxable income method.

Assume that an FSC buys export property from a related supplier and sells it for $1,000. The FSC incurs expenses of $200, and the supplier's cost of goods solid is $600. In selling the export property to the FSC, the supplier incurs a cost of $100. Table 15.3 shows transfer prices under the two administrative pricing guidelines.

Foreign trading gross receipts include the sales of export property, the lease or rental of export property, services related to the sale or lease of export property, engineering and architectural services, and export management services. These transactions must take place outside the United

Table 15.3
Administrative pricing guidelines

(a) Combined taxable income:	
FSC foreign trading gross receipts	$1,000.00
Cost of goods sold of related supplier	− 600.00
Combined gross income	$ 400.00
Direct expenses of related supplier	− 100.00
Direct expenses of FSC	− 200.00
Combined taxable income	$ 100.00
(b) Transfer price under combined taxable income method:	
Sales price	$1,000.00
Direct expenses of FSC	− 200.00
FSC profit (23% of combined taxable income)	− 23.00
Transfer price to FSC	$ 777.00
(c) Transfer price under gross receipts method:	
The allowable FSC profit is 1.83% of foreign trading gross receipts ($18.30) or twice the amount in (b) above ($46).	
Sales price	$1,000.00
Direct expenses of FSC	− 200.00
FSC profit	− 18.30
Transfer price to FSC	$ 781.70

States in order to qualify. If 50 percent of the direct costs for a transaction takes place in a foreign location, the transaction qualifies as a foreign trading gross receipt.

Summary

Many international transactions take place between members of the group —sales of goods, the provision of services, the licensing of patents and know-how, and the granting of loans. The prices for such transfers do not necessarily result from the free play of market forces. They may diverge considerably from the prices that unrelated parties would agree on. Although minimizing income tax is the most persuasive objective influencing transfer prices, other objectives often dominate. Among these objectives are import duty minimization, avoidance of financial problems, and adjustment of currency fluctuations for performance evaluation.

Minimizing income tax takes place by an allocation of profits among the countries involved in the production and sale of the product. In the United States, Section 482 of the Internal Revenue Code regulates the allocation of profits. Section 482 specifies three methods of determining transfer prices: the comparable uncontrolled price method, the resale price method, and the cost-plus method. In addition, taxpayers may be allowed to use any other method if they can convince the IRS that the other method is more appropriate than any of these three methods.

The Foreign Sales Corporation Act became effective as of January 1, 1985. The Act encourage U.S. companies to increase exports by giving them substantial tax benefits. Foreign sales corporations have major tax advantages if they meet certain conditions in Section 482 of the Internal Revenue Code and other regulations.

References

Wagdy M. Abdallah, *International Transfer Pricing Policies: Decision-Making Guidelines for Multinational Companies* (New York: Quorum Books, 1989).

Jeffery S. Arpan and Lee H. Radebaugh, *International Accounting and Multinational Enterprises* (New York: John Wiley & Sons, 1985), pp. 261–263.

Ralph L. Benke and James D. Edwards, *Transfer Pricing: Techniques and Uses* (New York: National Association of Accountants, 1980), Chapter 6.

Jane O. Burns, "How the IRS Applies the Intercompany Pricing Rules of Section 482: A Corporate Survey," *Journal of Taxation* (May 1980), pp. 308–314.

Jane O. Burns and Ronald S. Ross, "Establishing International Transfer Pricing Standards for Tax Audits of Multinational Enterprises," *Journal of International Business Studies* (Fall 1980), pp. 23–39.

Robert G. Eccles, *The Transfer Pricing Problem: A Theory for Practice* (Lexington, Mass.: Lexington Books, 1985).

Seung H. Kim and Stephen W. Miller, "Constituents of the International Transfer Pricing Decision," *Columbia Journal of World Business* (Spring 1979), pp. 69–77.

Suk H. Kim, "International Transfer Pricing for Tangible Property and Section 482 of the Internal Revenue Code," *The Journal of Business Issues* (Fall 1988), pp. 23–26.

Lynette L. Knowles and Ike Mathur, "Designing International Transfer Pricing Systems," *Managerial Finance* (Summer 1985), pp. 21–24.

Thomas Pugel and Judith L. Ugelow, "Transfer Pricing and Profit Maximization for the Multinational Firm," *Journal of International Business Studies* (Spring/Summer 1982), pp. 115–119.

Guenter Schindler, "Intercompany Transfer Pricing After the Tax Reform Act of 1986," *Tax Planning International Review* (November 1987), pp. 9–10.

Roger Y. Tang, "Environmental Variables of Multinational Transfer Pricing: A U.K. Perspective," *Journal of Business, Finance, and Accounting* (Summer 1982), pp. 179–189.

16

Accounting Considerations in International Finance

Clyde P. Stickney

In an international setting, as in a domestic setting, economic considerations should play the dominant role in business decisions. Yet, because
accounting affects the manner in which the results of business decisions
are reported to investors, creditors, and others, business managers must
be cognizant of the impact of the required accounting and weigh its importance in structuring business activities. This chapter explores three accounting issues relevant to international managers: (1) foreign currency
translation, (2) hedging foreign exchange risk, and (3) alternative accounting principles across countries.

Foreign Currency Translation

The foreign currency transactions of a U.S. parent company, as well as the
operations of foreign branches and subsidiaries, must be translated into
U.S. dollars both for preparing financial statements for shareholders and
creditors and for measuring taxable income and tax liabilities. This section
describes and illustrates the translation methodology and discusses the
implications of the methodology for managing international operations.

Functional Currency Concept

Central to the translation of foreign currency items is the functional currency concept. This concept is embedded both in Financial Accounting
Standards Board (FASB) Statement No. 52 which governs financial reporting and in Section 985 of the Internal Revenue Code which governs tax
reporting.[1]

From *The Handbook of International Financial Management*, Dow Jones-Irwin, 1989, pp. 342–
372. Reprinted by permission.

Foreign entities (whether branches or subsidiaries) are of two general types:

1. The operations of a foreign entity are a direct and integral component or extension of the parent company's operations. In this case, the U.S. dollar is the functional currency.

2. The operations of a foreign entity are relatively self-contained and integrated within a particular foreign country. In this case, the functional currency is the currency of that foreign country.

FASB Statement No. 52 sets out characteristics for determining whether the U.S. dollar or the currency of the foreign unit is the functional currency.[2] Table 16.1 summarizes these characteristics. The signals indicating which currency is the functional currency are mixed in some cases, and management judgment is required to determine which functional currency best captures the economic effects of a foreign entity's operations and financial position. As discussed later in this section, management may wish to structure certain financings or other transactions to swing the balance in favor of either the U.S. dollar or the foreign currency as the functional

Table 16.1
Factors determining functional currency of foreign unit

	U.S. dollar is functional currency	Foreign currency is functional currency
Cash flows of foreign entity	Receivables and payables denominated in U.S. dollars and readily available for remittance to parent	Receivables and payables denominated in foreign currency and not usually remitted to parent currency
Sales prices	Influenced by worldwide competitive conditions and responsive on a short-term basis to exchange rate changes	Influenced primarily by local competitive conditions and not responsive on a short-term basis to exchange rate changes
Cost factors	Labor, materials, and other inputs are obtained primarily from the United States	Labor, materials, and other inputs are obtained primarily from the country of the foreign unit
Financing	Financing denominated in U.S. dollars or ongoing fund transfers by the parent	Financing denominated in currency of foreign unit or foreign unit is able to generate needed funds internally
Relations between parent and foreign unit	High volume of intercompany transactions and extensive operational interrelations between parent and foreign unit	Low volume of intercompany transactions and little operational interrelations between parent and foreign unit

currency. Once the functional currency of a foreign entity has been determined, it must be used consistently over time unless changes in economic facts and circumstances clearly indicate that the functional currency has changed.

FASB Statement No. 52 provides one exception to the guidelines in table 16.1 for determining the functional currency. If the foreign entity operates in a highly inflationary country, its currency is considered too unstable to serve as the functional currency, and the U.S. dollar must be used instead.[3] A highly inflationary country is one that has had cumulative inflation of at least 100 percent over a three-year period. Most South American countries and many developing nations fall within this exception and pose particular problems for the U.S. parent company, as discussed later.

The Tax Reform Act of 1986 specifies the methodology for translating foreign currency amounts when measuring taxable income. It borrowed the functional currency concept from Statement No. 52. Sections 985(b)(1), (2), and (3) of the Code state that the U.S. dollar is the functional currency when the activities of a foreign entity (referred to as a "qualified business unit") are conducted "primarily" in U.S. dollars. If such activities are not conducted primarily in U.S. dollars but "significantly" in a foreign currency, then the foreign currency is the functional currency. Important factors for determining the functional currency are (1) the principal currency in which revenues are earned and expenses are incurred, (2) the principal currency in which the foreign unit borrows and repays its debt, (3) the currency in which the books are kept, and (4) the functional currency of other foreign units of the firm.[4] It has been suggested that the first two factors probably dominate the functional currency determination.[5] The third factor is not discriminating, as the books of foreign units are often kept in both U.S. dollars and the foreign currency. The fourth factor envisions consistency in the application of the criteria across economically similar foreign units.

The criteria for determining the functional currency for financial and tax reporting are sufficiently similar that the functional currency for any particular foreign unit is likely to be the same for both reporting purposes.

Translation Methodology—Foreign Currency Is Functional Currency

When the functional currency is the currency of the foreign unit, the all-current translation method is followed. Table 16.2 summarizes the translation procedure for both financial and tax reporting.

Table 16.2
Summary of translation methodology when the foreign currency is the functional currency

	Financial reporting	Income tax reporting
Income statement	Revenues and expenses as measured in foreign currency are translated into U.S. dollars using the average exchange rate during the period. Income includes (1) realized and unrealized transaction gains and losses, and (2) realized translation gains and losses when foreign unit is sold	Branch. Revenues and expenses as measured in foreign currency are translated into U.S. dollars using the average exchange rate during the period. Income includes (1) realized, but not unrealized, transaction gains and losses and (2) realized transaction gains and losses when the foreign unit remits dividends or is sold

Subsidiary. Only dividends are included in taxable income, translated using the exchange rate on the date distributed |
| Balance sheet | Assets and liabilities as measured in foreign currency are translated into U.S. dollars using the end-of-the-period exchange rate. Use of the end-of-the-period exchange rate gives rise to unrealized transaction gains and losses on receivables and payables requiring currency conversions in the future. An unrealized translation adjustment on the net asset position of the foreign unit is included in a separate shareholders' equity account and not recognized in net income until the foreign unit is sold | No translation of balance sheet accounts is permitted or required |

Financial Reporting

Revenues and expenses are translated at the average exchange rate during the period, and balance sheet items are translated at the end-of-the-period exchange rate. Net income includes only *transaction* exchange gains and losses of the foreign unit. That is, a foreign unit that has receivables and payables denominated in a currency other than its own is presumed to make a currency conversion at the time the account is settled. The gain or loss from changes in the exchange rate between the time the account originated and the time when it is settled is a transaction gain or loss. This gain or loss is recognized during the periods while the account is outstanding.

When a foreign unit is operated more or less independently of the U.S. parent and the foreign currency is therefore the functional currency, only the parent's equity investment in the foreign unit is presumed to be subject the exchange rate risk. A measurement of the effect of exchange rate changes on this investment is made each period, but the resulting "translation adjustment" is included in a separate account in the shareholder's equity section of the balance sheet rather than being included in net income. The rationale for this treatment is that the investment is presumed to be made for the long term; short-term changes in exchange rates should not, therefore, affect periodic net income. The cumulative amount in the translation adjustment account is taken into consideration in measuring any gain or loss when the foreign unit is sold or liquidated.

Tax Reporting
The amount included in the U.S. tax return of a parent company for earnings of a foreign unit depends on whether the foreign unit is operated as a branch or a subsidiary of the parent.

If the foreign unit is operated as a branch, then the all-current method of translation is followed.[6] However, there are three important differences from the procedures followed for financial reporting:

1. Only realized, or settled, transaction gains and losses from receivables and payables are included in taxable income. Thus, their recognition is delayed for tax reporting relative to financial reporting.

2. An exchange gain or loss is recognized if the exchange rate changes between the time earnings are generated by the foreign branch and a dividend is remitted. This gain or loss is a component of the translation adjustment account for financial reporting but is not recognized for financial reporting prior to complete liquidation of a foreign unit. Thus, exchange gains and losses incurred prior to the remission of earnings as a dividend are recognized earlier for tax than for financial reporting.

3. There is no translation of the balance sheet for tax reporting.

If the foreign unit is operated as a subsidiary, none of the income of the foreign unit is included in the taxable income of the U.S. parent. Only dividends received from this subsidiary are included. The dividend is translated into U.S. dollars using the exchange rate on the date of distribution.[7] Unlike the case for a foreign branch, no exchange gain or loss arises for exchange rate changes between the time earnings are generated by the foreign subsidiary and the dividend is paid.

Illustration

Table 16.3 illustrates the all-current method for a foreign unit during its first year of operations. The exchange rate was $1 : FC1 on January 1, $2 : FC1 on December 31, and $1.5 : FC1 on average during the year.

For financial reporting, all assets and liabilities on the balance sheet are translated at the exchange rate on December 31. Common stock is translated at the exchange rate when it was issued; the effects of changes in exchange rates on this investment by the parent are included in the translation adjustment amount. The translated amount of retained earnings is computed by translating the income statement and dividends. Note that all revenues and expenses of the foreign unit are translated at the average exchange rate. The foreign unit realized a transaction gain during the year and recorded it on its books. In addition, an unrealized transaction gain is reflected in the translated amounts for the foreign unit arising from exposed accounts that are not yet settled. Note a to table 16.3 shows the computation of translated retained earnings. The dividend was paid on December 31. Note b shows the calculation of the translation adjustment. By investing $30 in the foreign unit on January 1 and allowing the $24.5 of earnings to remain in the foreign unit throughout the year while the foreign currency was increasing in value relative to the U.S. dollar, the parent has a potential exchange "gain" of $35.5. This amount is reported in the separate shareholders' equity account on the balance sheet. For tax reporting, the U.S. parent includes $47.5 in taxable income if the foreign unit is operated as a branch and $10 if it is operated as a subsidiary. The taxable income of the branch excludes the unrealized transaction gain but includes a $2.5 gain on the dividend remittance. Note a to table 16.3 shows that the foreign unit generated earnings while the exchange rate was $1.5 : FC1 but paid a dividend when the exchange rate was $2 : FC1. By delaying the payment of the dividend and holding the funds in a currency that increased in value relative to the dollar, an exchange gain of $2.5 is recognized. That is, if the FC5 of earnings had been remitted when earned, the dividend would have been $7.5 $(= $1.5 \times FC5)$. The actual distribution was $10, composed of $7.5 of earnings distribution (dividend) and $2.5 of exchange gain. When the foreign unit is operated as a branch, the dividend is not included in taxable income. When the unit is operated as a subsidiary, the full amount received of $10 is included in taxable income of the U.S. parent.

Table 16.3
Translation methodology when the foreign currency is the functional currency

	Foreign currency	Financial reporting		Tax reporting	
Balance sheet					
Assets					
Cash	FC 10	$2:FC1	$ 20.0	Not applicable	
Receivables	20	$2:FC1	40.0		
Inventories	30	$2:FC1	60.0		
Fixed assets (net)	40	$2:FC1	80.0		
Total	FC100		$200.0		
Liabilities and shareholders' equity					
Accounts payable	FC 40	$2:FC1	$ 80.0		
Bonds payable	20	$2:FC1	40.0		
Total	FC 60		$120.0		
Common stock	FC 30	$1:FC1	$ 30.0		
Retained earnings	FC 10		14.5[a]		
Unrealized translation Adjustment	—		35.5[b]		
Total	FC 40		$ 80.0		
Total	FC100		$200.0		
Income statement					
Sales revenue	FC200	$1.5:FC1	$300.0	$1.5:FC1	$300.0
Realized transaction gain	2[c]	$1.5:FC1	3.0[c]	$1.5:FC1	3.0[c]
Unrealized transaction gain	—[d]	—	2.0[d]	—	—[d]
Remittance transaction gain	—[e]	—	—[e]	—	2.5[e]
Cost of goods sold	(120)	$1.5:FC1	(180.0)	$1.5:FC1	(180.0)
Selling and administrative expense	(40)	$1.5:FC1	(60.0)	$1.5:FC1	(60.0)
Depreciation expense	(10)	$1.5:FC1	(15.0)	$1.5:FC1	(15.0)
Interest expense	(2)	$1.5:FC1	(3.0)	$1.5:FC1	(3.0)
Income tax expense	(15)	$1.5:FC1	(22.5)	Tax. inc. (if branch)	$ 47.5
Net income	FC 15		$ 24.5		

Table 16.3 (continued)

	Foreign currency		U.S. dollars
a. Retained earnings, January 1	FC 0.0		$ 0.0
Plus net income	15.0		24.5
Less dividends	(5.0)	$2:FC1	$(10.0)
Retained earnings, December 31	FC10.0		$ 14.5
b. Net asset position, January 1	FC30.0	$1:FC1	$ 30.0
Plus net income	15.0		24.5
Less dividends	(5.0)	$2:FC1	$(10.0)
Net asset position, December 31	FC40.0		$ 44.5
Net asset position December 31	FC40.0 ⟶	$2:FC1	80.0
Unrealized transaction "gain"			$ 35.5

c. The foreign unit had receivables and payables that were denominated in a currency other than its own. When these accounts were settled during the period, a currency conversion was required and resulted in a realized transaction gain of FC1. This realized exchange gain is recognized for both financial and tax reporting.

d. The foreign unit has receivables and payables outstanding that will require a currency conversion in a future period when the accounts are settled. Because the exchange rate changed while the receivables/payables were outstanding, an unrealized transaction gain is recognized for financial reporting. It will not be recognized for tax reporting until the accounts are settled in the future.

e. The foreign unit earned $24.5 during the period. If the $2 unrealized transaction gain is excluded because it is a timing difference, its retained earnings for tax purposes (called earnings and profits) is $22.5. The foreign unit waited until the end of the year to pay out one-third of these earnings as a dividend. Because the foreign currency increased in value during the year, an exchange gain of $2.5 [= (.33 × $22.5) − $10] must be included in taxable income if the unit is operated as a branch.

Table 16.4
Summary of translation methodology when the U.S. dollar is the functional currency

	Financial reporting	Income tax reporting
Income statement	Revenues and expenses are translated using the exchange rate in effect when the original measurements underlying the valuation were made. Revenues and most operating expenses are translated using the average exchange rate during the period. However, cost of goods sold and depreciation are translated using the historical exchange rate appropriate to the related asset (inventory, fixed assets). Net income includes (1) realized and unrealized transaction gains and losses, and (2) unrealized translation gains and losses on the net monetary position of the foreign unit.	Branch. The translation procedure is the same as is done for financial reporting. However, only realized transaction gains and losses are included in taxable income. Unrealized transaction and translation gains and losses are not included, nor is any gain or loss on dividend remittances. Subsidiary. Only dividends are included in taxable income, translated at the exchange rate on the date distributed.
Balance sheet	Monetary assets and liabilities are translated using the end-of-the-period exchange rate. Nonmonetary assets and equities are translated using the historical exchange rate.	No translation of balance sheet amounts is permitted or required.

Translation Methodology—U.S. Dollar Is Functional Currency

When the functional currency is the U.S. dollar, the monetary/nonmonetary translation method is followed. Table 16.4 summarizes the translation procedure for both financial and tax reporting.

Financial Reporting
The underlying premise of the monetary/nonmonetary method is that the translated amounts reflect amounts that would have been reported if all measurements had originally been made in U.S. dollars. To implement this underlying premise, a distinction is made between monetary items and nonmonetary items.

A monetary item is an account whose amount is fixed in terms of a given number of foreign currency units regardless of changes in the exchange rate. From a U.S. dollar perspective, these accounts give rise to exchange gains and losses as exchange rates change because the number of U.S. dollars required to settle the fixed foreign currency amounts fluctuates over time. Monetary items include cash, receivables, accounts payable, and other accrued liabilities and long-term debt. These items are translated using the end-of-the-period exchange rate and give rise to translation gains and losses. These translation gains and losses are recognized each period in determining net income, regardless of whether an actual currency conversion is required to settle the monetary item.

A nonmonetary item is any account that is not monetary and includes inventories, fixed assets, common stock, revenues, and expenses. These accounts are translated using the historical exchange rate in effect when the measurements underlying these accounts were initially made. Inventories and cost of goods sold are translated using the exchange rate when the inventory items were acquired. Fixed assets and depreciation expense are translated using the exchange rate on the date the fixed assets were acquired. Most revenues and operating expenses other than cost of goods sold and depreciation are translated at the average exchange rate during the period. The objective is to state these accounts at their U.S. dollar-equivalent historical-cost amounts. In this way the translated amounts reflect the U.S. dollar perspective that is appropriate when the U.S. dollar is the functional currency.

Income Tax Reporting

When a foreign unit is operated as a branch, the translation procedure for the income statement follows the procedure followed for financial reporting with two important exceptions: unrealized transaction and translation gains and losses are not included in taxable income. In addition, unlike the case where the foreign currency is the functional currency, no exchange gains or losses are recognized on dividend remittances.[8] When the foreign unit is operated as a subsidiary, taxable income includes only dividends received.

Illustration

Table 16.5 shows the application of the monetary/nonmonetary method to the data considered earlier in table 16.3.

For financial reporting, net income again includes both realized and unrealized transaction gains and losses. However, net income in this case also includes a $24.5 translation loss. As table 16.6 shows, the firm was in a net monetary liability position during a period when the U.S. dollar

Table 16.5
Translation methodology when the U.S. dollar is the functional currency

	Foreign currency	Financial reporting		Tax reporting	
Balance sheet					
Assets					
Cash	FC 10	$2.0:FC1	$ 20.0	Not applicable	
Receivables	20	$2.0:FC1	40.0		
Inventories	30	$1.5:FC1	45.0		
Fixed assets (net)	40	$1.0:FC1	40.0		
Total	FC100	$2.0:FC1	$145.0		
Liabilities and shareholders' equity					
Accounts payable	FC 40	$2.0:FC1	$ 80.0		
Bonds payable	20	$2.0:FC1	40.0		
Total	FC 60		$120.0		
Common stock	FC 30	$1.0:FC1	$ 30.0		
Retained earnings	FC 10		(5.0)[d]		
Total	FC 40		$ 25.0		
Total	FC 60		$145.0		
Income statement					
Sales revenue	FC200	$1.5:FC1	$300.0	$1.5:FC1	$300.0
Realized transaction gain	2[a]	$1.5:FC1	3.0[a]	$1.5:FC1	3.0[a]
Unrealized transaction gain	—[b]	—	2.0[b]		—[b]
Unrealized transaction loss	—	Table 16.6	24.5[c]		—
Cost of goods sold	(120)	$1.5:FC1	(180.0)	$1.5:FC1	(180.0)
Selling and administrative expense	(40)	$1.5:FC1	(60.0)	$1.5:FC1	(60.0)
Depreciation expense	(10)	$1.0:FC1	(10.0)	$1.0:FC1	(10.0)
Interest expense	(2)	$1.5:FC1	(3.0)	$1.5:FC1	(3.0)
Income tax expense	(15)	$1.5:FC1	(22.5)	Tax. inc. branch	$ 50.0
	FC 14		$ 5.0		

a. Realized transaction gains and losses are included in income for both tax and financial reporting.

b. Unrealized transaction gains and losses are included only in income for financial reporting.

c. Income for financial reporting includes any unrealized translation gain or loss for the period. The translation gain or loss is based on the net monetary position of a foreign unit during the period. The foreign unit was in a net monetary liability position during a period when the U.S. dollar decreased in value relative to the foreign currency. More U.S. dollars, $24.5, are required to settle the net monetary liability position at the end of the year than if settlement had been made throughout the year before the exchange rate changed. The calculation is shown in Table 16.6.

Table 16.5 (continued)

	Foreign currency		U.S. dollars
d. Retained earnings, January 1	FC 0	—	$ 0.0
Plus net income	15		5.0
Less dividends	(5)	$2:FC1	(10.0)
Retained earnings, December 31	FC10		$ (5.0)

Table 16.6
Calculation of unrealized translation loss when the U.S. dollar is the functional currency

	Foreign currency		U.S. dollars
Net monetary position, January 1	FC 0.0	—	$ 0.0
Plus:			
Issue of common stock	30.0	$1:FC1	$ 30.0
Sales for cash and on account	200.0	$1.5:FC1	300.0
Settlement of exposed receivable payable at a gain	2.0	$1.5:FC1	$ 3.0
Unrealized gain on exposed receivable/payable	—		3.0
Less:			
Acquisition of fixed assets	(50.0)	$1:FC1	(50.0)
Acquisition of inventory	(150.0)	$1.5:FC1	(225.0)
Selling and administration costs incurred	(40.0)	$1.5:FC1	(60.0)
Interest cost incurred	(2.0)	$1.5:FC1	(3.0)
Income taxes paid	(15.0)	$1.5:FC1	(22.5)
Dividend paid	(5.0)	$2:FC1	(10.0)
Net monetary liability position, December 31	(30.0)		$ (35.5)
	⌊⟶ $2:FC1		60.0
Unrealized translation loss			$ 24.5

Table 16.7
Summary of translation results

	Functional currency	
	Foreign currency	U.S. dollar
Net Income	24.5	$ 5.0
Total assets	200.0	145.0
Shareholders' equity	80.0	25.0
Return on assets	12.3%	3.4%
Return on equity	30.6%	20.0%

decreased in value relative to the foreign currency. Because more U.S. dollars are required to settle these foreign-denominated net liabilities at the end of the year than would have been required if the net liability position had been discharged before the exchange rate changed, an exchange loss is recognized.

For tax purposes only, the realized transaction gain of $3 is included in taxable income under a branch arrangement and $10 is included under a subsidiary arrangement.

Implications of Functional Currency Determination

As these illustrations demonstrate, translated financial statement amounts for a foreign unit can be significantly different depending on the functional currency and related translation method used. Some summary comparisons are shown in table 16.7.

These differences arise for two principal reasons:

1. Current exchange rates are used in translation when the foreign currency is the functional currency, while a mixture of current and historical rates is used when the U.S. dollar is the functional currency. Not only are net income and total asset amounts different, but also the relative proportions of total assets made up of receivables, inventories, and fixed assets are different, debt/equity ratios are different, and gross and net profit margins are different. When the all-current translation method is used, the translated amount reflect the same financial statement relationships (e.g., debt/equity ratios) as when measured in the foreign currency. When the U.S. dollar is the functional currency, financial statement relationships get remeasured (in U.S. dollar-equivalent amounts) and financial ratios differ from their foreign currency amounts.

2. The other major reason for differences between the two translation methodologies is the inclusion of unrealized translation gains and losses in net income under the monetary/nonmonetary method. Much of the debate with respect to the predecessor to FASB Statement No. 52, which was Statement No. 8, involved the inclusion of this unrealized translation gain or loss in net income. Many argued that the gain or loss was a bookkeeping adjustment only and lacked economic significance. This criticism was particularly justified when no currency conversion was required to settle a monetary item. Also, its inclusion in net income often caused wide, unexpected swings in earnings, particularly in quarterly reports.

As discussed earlier, the manner in which a particular foreign unit is organized and operated affects the determination of its functional currency. In many cases, the signals are mixed, and management judgment is required. For reasons discussed previously, most firms prefer to use the foreign currency as the functional currency because the all-current method generally results in fewer earnings surprises. Some of the actions that management might consider to swing the balance of factors in favor of the foreign currency as the functional currency include:

1. Decentralize decision making into a foreign unit. The greater the degree of autonomy of the foreign unit, the more likely its currency is to be the functional currency. The U.S. parent company can design effective control systems to ensure that corporate objectives are achieved while at the same time permitting the foreign unit to operate with considerable freedom.

2. Minimize remittances/dividends. The greater the degree of earnings retention by the foreign unit, the more likely is its currency to be the functional currency. It may be possible to get cash out of a foreign unit and into the parent's hands indirectly rather than directly (through remittances or dividends). For example, a foreign unit whose signals about its functional currency are mixed might, through loans or transfer prices for goods or services, send cash to another foreign unit whose functional currency is clearly its own currency. This second foreign unit can then remit it to the parent. Other possibilities for interunit transactions are possible to ensure that *some* foreign currency rather than the U.S. dollar is the functional currency.

3. Denominate borrowing in some currency other than the U.S. dollar. The borrowing need not be in the currency of the foreign unit. Although such a strategy may result in having the second foreign currency be the functional currency, at least the all-current translation would still be used.

4. Transform any U.S. dollar borrowing into some other currency through currency swaps.

In some cases, a firm has no choice but to use the U.S. dollar as the functional currency. This may be because the balance of characteristics of the foreign unit clearly requires it or because the foreign unit operates in a highly inflationary country. Because of the possibly significant and often unexpected earnings effects of including the unrealized translation gain or loss in earnings, it is advantageous to neutralize its impact. Because the translation gain or loss usually lacks economic substance, it is not desirable to enter into hedging actions that have economic cost. Rather, a firm should endeavor to manage with a net monetary position as close to zero as possible. Any change in exchange rates when applied to the small net monetary position results in insignificant translation gains or losses.

For most foreign unit, cash and receivables are offset by current payables; thus, the net current monetary position is close to zero. However, long-term debt financing is often denominated in the currency of the foreign unit, resulting in a net overall monetary liability position. Some avenues for minimizing the amount of long-term liabilities for the foreign unit that enter into the calculation of the translation gain or loss are as follows:

1. Denominate borrowing in U.S. dollars. Recall that monetary items represent amounts that are receivable or payable in a fixed number of foreign currency units, regardless of changes in exchange rates. U.S. dollar-denominated debt does not satisfy the definition of a monetary item and is, therefore, excluded from the computation of the translation gain or loss.

2. Structure leases for the use of property so they do not qualify as capital leases. Using regular debt denominated in the foreign currency to finance fixed assets increases monetary liabilities. By leasing the asset and accounting for it as an operating lease, the lease obligation is kept off the balance sheet. To treat leases as operating leases, the lessor must assume most of the risk. This means that the lessee is likely paying a larger amount than if the lessee assumed the risks. As stated earlier one must be careful not to incur real economic cost to neutralize a bookkeeping translation gain or loss.

3. Structure a borrowing transaction so that the debt gets reported on the books of some other entity. The myriad off-balance-sheet financing techniques that can be used in a domestic setting may be equally applicable in an international setting and may have the added value of minimizing translation gains and losses.[9]

Accounting for Hedging Transactions

Firms often engage in transactions to neutralize their exposure to exchange (transaction) gains and losses. This might take the form of forward contracts, currency swaps, tax straddles, or other mechanisms. The treatment of gains and losses on these contracts for both financial and tax reporting is discussed in this section. The key issue is whether gains and losses from the neutralizing device should be accounted for and recognized independent of the transaction that gave rise to the need for the neutralizing device or whether the two activities are integrated.

Financial Reporting

FASB Statement No. 52 sets out the requiring accounting for forward contracts in foreign currency. These requirements apply to currency swaps and other hedging instruments. Table 16.8 summarizes the required accounting.

A forward contract that does not hedge an exposed position but is entered into as an investment is considered a speculative contract.[10] Such contracts are revalued each period; the change in value since the previous valuation date is recognized as a gain or loss. The revaluation is computed based on the foreign currency amount of the contract and the forward rate available on the market for the remainder of the contract. The contract is essentially market to market each period.

All other forward contracts are presumed to be entered into to hedge either a specific or general exposed position. Two computations are needed: the initial discount or premium on the contract and the periodic gain or loss. The calculation of these amounts is summarized in table 16.9.

The discount or premium is viewed the same as the discount or premium on any monetary asset or liability: it is amortized over the life of the contract as interest revenue or expense. The effective interest method of amortization is used unless the results from using the straight line method are not materially different.[11]

With the three exceptions discussed next, the gain or loss is recognized each period in measuring net income. Recall from the earlier discussion that unrealized transaction gains or losses are recognized each period as they arise, regardless of whether the all-current or monetary/nonmonetary method of translation is followed. Any offsetting gains or losses on forward contracts are effectively matched against these transaction gains or losses. The net income measure, therefore, indicates the extent to which the exposed position has been neutralized, although few companies provide

Table 16.8
Accounting for forward contracts for financial reporting

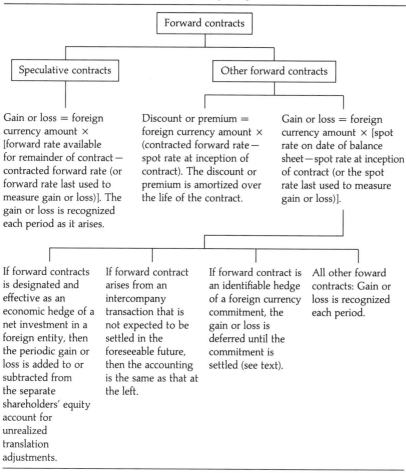

```
                          ┌──────────────────┐
                          │ Forward contracts │
                          └──────────────────┘
          ┌─────────────────────────┴─────────────────────────┐
┌──────────────────────┐                      ┌──────────────────────────┐
│ Speculative contracts │                     │ Other forward contracts   │
└──────────────────────┘                      └──────────────────────────┘
```

| Gain or loss = foreign currency amount × [forward rate available for remainder of contract − contracted forward rate (or forward rate last used to measure gain or loss)]. The gain or loss is recognized each period as it arises. | Discount or premium = foreign currency amount × (contracted forward rate − spot rate at inception of contract). The discount or premium is amortized over the life of the contract. | Gain or loss = foreign currency amount × [spot rate on date of balance sheet − spot rate at inception of contract (or the spot rate last used to measure gain or loss)]. |

| If forward contracts is designated and effective as an economic hedge of a net investment in a foreign entity, then the periodic gain or loss is added to or subtracted from the separate shareholders' equity account for unrealized translation adjustments. | If forward contract arises from an intercompany transaction that is not expected to be settled in the foreseeable future, then the accounting is the same as that at the left. | If forward contract is an identifiable hedge of a foreign currency commitment, the gain or loss is deferred until the commitment is settled (see text). | All other foward contracts: Gain or loss is recognized each period. |

sufficient detail in their published financial statements for the user to make this assessment.

1. If the forward contract is designated as, and is effective as, an economic hedge on the net investment in a foreign entity, then the gain or loss each period is not recognized in determining net income but instead is added to or subtracted from the separate shareholders' equity account for unrealized translation adjustments.[12] Recall that hen a foreign unit operates more or less independently of the U.S. parent, the functional currency is usually the currency of the foreign unit and the all-current translation method is used.

Table 16.9
Calculation of discount or premium and gain or loss

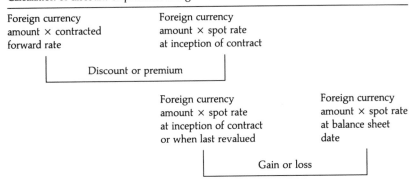

From the parent's perspective, the foreign unit is viewed more as an invest-ment than as an integral part of the parent's operations. Any effect of exchange rate changes on the parent's investment is not recognized cur-rently because the investment is viewed as a long-term commitment. Thus, the "gain" or "loss" from exchange rate changes is not recognized until the investment is liquidated. Instead it is accumulated in a separate share-holders' equity account. If a parent enters into a formal contract to hedge its exposed position, any offsetting gain or loss on the contract is not recognized in net income each period but is likewise accumulated in the separate shareholders' equity account, based on the matching principle of accounting. To the extent that the gain or loss on the contract exceeds the adjustment from translation, however, that portion of the gain or loss is recognized in computing net income each period.

2. If the forward contract is intended to hedge a long-term intercompany transaction, such as a long-term advance to or from the parent, then the gain or loss is assigned to the separate shareholder's equity account.[13] The rationale for this treatment is that the advance is part of the parent's invest-ment in the foreign unit; the accounting for such advances is, therefore, the same as the accounting for the parent's equity investment.

3. If the forward contract is intended to hedge a foreign currency commit-ment, then the gain or loss is deferred and included in the measurement of the commitment when it is satisfied.[14] For example, suppose a firm commits to purchase an item of equipment and denominates the price in a currency other than its own. To neutralize its exposed position, the firm takes out a forward contract. Under generally accepted accounting princi-ples, commitments such as these are not usually recognized as liabilities.

Poor matching would result if the gain or loss were recognized on the forward contract but the effect of the purchase commitment were not recorded in the accounts until the commitment was satisfied (i.e., the equipment was acquired). To the extent that the forward contract amount exceeds the commitment amount, any gain or loss on such excess is not deferred but recognized currently in determining net income.

It is evident that the required accounting for gains and losses on forward contracts closely parallels the accounting for exchange rate gains and losses (both transaction and translation) that gave rise to the need for a forward contract. The underlying principle is the matching of revenues and gains with associated expenses and losses.

Income Tax Reporting

The tax treatment of forward contracts, currency swaps, tax straddles, and similar instruments has been clarified by the Tax Reform Act of 1986. Table 16.10 summarizes the relevant provisions of the Code.

The major addition to the Code is Section 988. A Section 988 hedging transaction is one that effectively converts nonfunctional currency borrowing or lending into functional currency borrowing or lending. The general principle underlying Section 988 is that the transaction giving rise to the need for the hedge and the hedge transaction are considered one integrated unit. Any gain or loss on the hedge instrument is recognized in the same period as the gain or loss on the exposed asset or liability. Because transaction gains or losses are usually not recognized for tax purposes (in contrast to financial reporting) until they are closed or settled, the gain or loss on the hedge contract is generally recognized at that time.

Two categories of Section 988 hedging transactions are envisoned: fully hedged and partially hedged. Fully hedged transactions perfectly neutralize an exposed position on an asset or liability. This requires that the amount of the forward contract or other hedging instrument equals the amount of the exposed asset or liability and that the time period underlying each financial contract be the same. In partially hedged transactions, one or both of these criteria are not met. Fully hedged Section 988 transactions follow the rules previously stated. The Internal Revenue Services has not yet issued regulations pertaining to partially hedged Section 988 transactions, but the rules are expected to follow the principles just described.

A forward or other contract that does not meet the criteria for a Section 988 transaction is next judged as to whether it is a Section 1256 contract.

Table 16.10
Accounting for forward contracts for income tax reporting

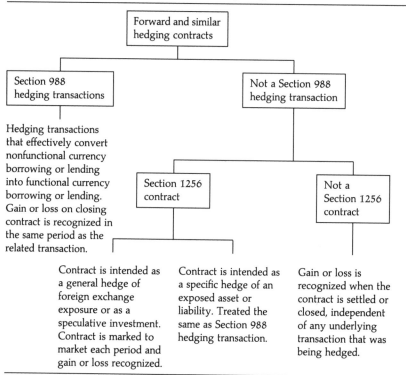

Section 1256 applies to contracts in currencies traded through regulated futures contracts. Market values for these contracts are readily available at all times. With one exception discussed next, these contracts are marked to market each period, and gains and losses recognized as market values change. This tax treatment is applicable to contracts acquired as an investment for speculative purposes as well as contracts acquired to hedge general exposure in a currency. If the contract is acquired to hedge a specifically identified exposed asset or liability and the firm identifies and accounts for it as such, then the contract is not marked to market each period. Instead, any gain or loss on settling the contract is recognized in the same period as the gain or loss on the exposed asset or liability, usually when the latter is closed. This treatment is similar to that for Section 988 hedging transactions.

A gain or loss on a forward or other contract that is not part of either a Section 988 transaction or a Section 1256 contract is recognized when it is closed or settled independent of the gain or loss on any underlying transaction that gave rise to the need for the contract.

As is the case for financial reporting, the recognition of gains and losses on hedging contracts for tax purposes follows a matching principle. Because transaction gains and losses are generally recognized when settled or closed, offsetting gains and losses on hedging contracts are treated similarly. When the hedging contract can be clearly linked with a specific exposed asset or liability, the matching takes place when the exposed asset or liability is settled. When the linking is not clear-cut, the gain or loss is recognized when the hedging contract is closed. The only exception occurs for publicly traded contracts acquired either for speculative reasons or to hedge general business exposures. These contracts are marked to market each period and any changes in market value recognized as gains or losses as they arise.

Alternative Accounting Principles

When analyzing and interpreting the financial statements of a foreign entity, whether it be a subsidiary of a U.S. parent or an unaffiliated foreign firm, recognition must be given to the accounting principles or methods that underlie those statements. Differences in acceptable accounting methods across countries can make intercompany comparisons meaningless. This section discusses the nature and extent of such differences and describes recent efforts toward harmonization.

Differences across Countries

There have been numerous efforts in recent years both to catalog differences in accounting principles across countries[15] and to classify countries into various groups based on the nature of the accounting principles or the process through which they are set.[16] Two major drawbacks of these lines of research are as follows:

1. A substantial amount of effort is required to identify the accounting principles followed by various countries around the world. During the last five years, there has been a rapidly increasing degree of harmonization of accounting principles. By the time that studies describing differences in accounting principles are published, the data are usually highly inaccurate.

2. Because of the rapid degree of harmonization, efforts to classify countries according to the nature of the standard-setting process or the resulting

Table 16.11
Evolutionary process of the setting of accounting principles

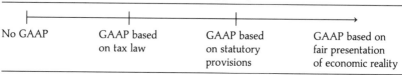

| No GAAP | GAAP based on tax law | GAAP based on statutory provisions | GAAP based on fair presentation of economic reality |

specific accounting principles have had mixed results. As discussed later, the standard-setting process in most countries follows a fairly predictable evolutionary process. A specific country's stage in this evolutionary process is a moving target, particularly so in recent years.

Table 16.11 depicts the stages in the evolutionary process of accounting standard setting. In the early stages of economic development of a country, no established mechanism exists for setting accounting principles. Soon after the economic development process begins, however, local governments institute various sales, income, and property taxes. The methods of accounting required for computing tax liabilities often become the methods used for financial reporting to creditors, owners, and others. During this phase, most businesses are closely held and use bank financing. Analysis of financial statements tends to focus on the availability of liquid assets relative to the amount of obligations. That is, there is more of a balance sheet than an income statement orientation.

As economic development evolves further, businesses tend to access the public debt and equity markets to a greater extent. Financial statement analysis during this phase shifts more to the income statement and the ability of operations to generate profits and needed cash. During this stage the deficiencies of an income measure defined to raise tax revenues and accomplish certain governmental policy objectives arise. Recognition is given to the need for an income measure that reflects the economic effects of transactions. Generally accepted accounting principles (GAAP) during this phase are typically set by a governmental legislative process. This occurs both because governmental units have previously been involved in the process of defining the tax base and because the accounting profession within the country is just beginning its own evolutionary development.

As economic development within a country matures, one typically finds sophisticated capital markets and active professional accounting organizations. Deficiencies in using the governmental legislative process to establish acceptable accounting principles become recognized, and standard setting is turned over to the accounting profession. There is much greater emphasis on accounting principles that capture the economic effects of transactions. Lacking the enforceability of governmentally imposed principles, more effort is devoted to gaining acceptance of accounting principles enunciated by private-sector standard-setting bodies.

Most major countries involved in international business fall into the third and fourth stages of table 16.11. The United States, United Kingdom, and Canada are probably in the fourth stage. West Germany, France, and Japan are closer to the third stage, but rapidly evolving toward the fourth. Most developing nations are in the second or third stages. The wide array of accounting principles that have been cataloged in the studies cited earlier reflect the differing stages of economic development and the related evolutionary stages of standard setting, as well as differences in culture, language, and similar factors. Table 16.12 lists some of the important differences in accounting principles for major trading nations.

Efforts toward Harmonization

Extensive efforts have been made in recent years to harmonize divergent accounting principles. Harmonization is not the same as standardization. Wilson provides the following definition:

The term harmonization as opposed to standardization implies a reconciliation of different points of view. This is a more practical and conciliatory approach than standardization, particularly when standardization means that the procedures of one country should be adopted by all others. Harmonization becomes a matter of better communication of information in a form that can be interpreted and understood internationally.[17]

Much of the work of harmonization has been undertaken by the International Accounting Standards Committee (IASC). Established in 1973, the IASC is now composed of members from 91 organizations from 66 countries. These members are pledged to exert their best efforts to get pronouncements on accounting standards from the IASC established as the acceptable methods of accounting in their countries. Thus, the pronouncements of the IASC have no enforceability on their own.

The IASC has issued accounting standards on a wide range of topics, including consolidated financial statements, segment reporting, leases, inventory valuation, and cost flow assumption.

Many of these pronouncements do not take a definitive position on a reporting issue. Rather, they describe alternative ways of accounting for a particular item (e.g., income taxes) to enhance understanding of the finan-

Table 16.12
Summary of alternative accounting principles in major international trading nations

Item	United States	Canada	United Kingdom	West Germany	France	Japan
Inventory cost flow assumption	FIFO LIFO Wt. avg.	FIFO LIFO Wt. avg.	FIFO — Wt. avg.	FIFO LIFO Wt. avg.	FIFO — Wt. avg.	FIFO LIFO Wt. avg.
Segment reporting	Sales, income, and assets by product and geographical location	Sales, income, and assets by product and geomgraphical location	Sales, income, and assets by proudct and geographical location	Not required	Not required	Sales by product and geographical location
Research and development costs	Expensed in period incurred	Expensed in period incurred	Expensed in period incurred	Expensed in period incurred	Deferred and amortized in certain circumstances	Deferred and amortized in certain circumstances
Goodwill arising from business combinations	Amortized over maximum of 40 years	Amortized over maximum of 40 years	Amortized over maximum of 20 years (exposure draft)	No specific maximum period for amortization	No amortization required	Amortization over 5 years
Capitalization of finance leases	Yes	Yes	No	No	No	No
Foreign currency translation	Combination of all-current and monetary/nonmonetary methods	Similar to U.S. but translation gains and losses on long-term debt amortized over life of issue	Similar to U.S.	No specific requirements	No specific requirements	Monetary/nonmonetary method

cial statement effects of the alternatives, and the manner in which financial statements prepared on one basis can be reconciled to those prepared on another basis. Harmonization does not eliminate differences in accounting principles but may be a necessary step in the process of establishing more uniform accounting principles in an international setting. Kirkpatrick states: "Harmonization must be identified as a gradual, though positive, process that with goodwill, common sense and acceptance of user needs, and preparer recognition of these, will pass through the phases of compatibility, comparability, and eventually conformity."[18]

Reporting Requirements for Foreign Registrants in the United States

Foreign corporations desiring to raise capital in U.S. markets are required to conform to two important Securities and Exchange Commission (SEC) requirements:

1. The foreign entity must either (a) present a reconciliation, using Form 20F, of net income and balance sheet amounts computed using GAAP of the foreign entity with net income and balance sheet amounts based on U.S. GAAP, or (b), if such a reconciliation cannot be meaningfully compiled, then a full set of financial statements and related disclosures conforming to U.S. GAAP must be provided.[19]

2. The financial statements for the most recent three years must be audited in conformance with U.S. generally accepted auditing standards.

The position of the SEC is that differences in accounting principles can be reconciled, but differences in auditing standards cannot.[20]

Summary

Accounting issues facing international managers are in different stages of development. Since the issuance of FASB Statement No. 52, the methods of translating the financial statements of foreign branches and subsidiaries for the purpose of consolidation with a U.S. parent are well settled. Except for operations in highly inflationary countries, most foreign operations are translated using the all-current method. Transaction exchange gains and losses enter into the computation of net income each period, while unrealized translation exchange adjustments are shown in a separate shareholders' equity account and do not affect net income each period. The accounting for forward contracts and other hedging devices for financial reporting has also been settled since Statement No. 52 was issued.

The method of foreign currency translation and the accounting for hedging contracts for income tax purposes was set out in provisions of the Tax Reform Act of 1986. The treatment of these items for tax purposes closely parallels their treatment for financial reporting, except that transaction exchange gains and losses are not recognized for tax purposes in most cases until closed or settled. Given the recent change in the tax law, the Internal Revenue Service has not yet issued full regulations to implement the new tax law.

The topic of international differences in accounting principles is in a stage of rapid change. As capital markets around the world become increasingly more integrated, efforts to harmonize and even conform accounting principles across countries have accelerated. The International Accounting Standards Committee continues to issue new pronouncements that attempt to narrow differences in accounting principles. The IASC has no enforcement power, however, and must rely on the accounting profession within each country to get its pronouncements adopted. The internationalization of securities markets will be a major force in accelerating the pace at which standardization of accounting principles is realized.

Notes

1. Financial Accounting Standards Board, "Foreign Currency Translation," *Statement of Financial Accounting Standards No. 52* (1981).

2. Ibid., para. 42.

3. Ibid., para. 11.

4. House Report No. 426, 99th Congress, 1st Session 472 (1985); Senate Report No. 313, 99th Congress, 2d Session 457 (1986).

5. Hals K. Dickenson, "New Foreign Currency Translation and Transaction Rules," *Taxes—The Tax Magazine* (July 1987), pp. 463–77.

6. *Internal Revenue Code*, Sec. 987.

7. *Internal Revenue Code*, Sec. 986.

8. *Internal Revenue Code*, Sec. 986.

9. See D. L. Landsittel and J. E. Stewart, "Off-Balance-Sheet Financing: Commitments and Contingencies," in *Handbook of Modern Accounting*, 3d ed., ed. S. Davidson and R. Weil (New York: McGraw-Hill, 1983).

10. FASB, *Statement No. 52*, para. 19.

11. FASB, *Statement No. 52*, para. 18.

12. FASB, *Statement No. 52*, para. 129.

13. FASB, *Statement No. 52*, para. 131.

14. FASB, *Statement No. 52*, para. 21.

15. Ernst & Whinney, *International Accounting Standards: Synopes, Multinational Comparisons and Disclosure Checklist* (Cleveland, 1986); F. D. S. Choi and V. B. Bavishi, "International Accounting Standards: Issues Needing Attention," *Journal of Accountancy* (March 1983), pp. 62–68.

16. For a summary and review of these efforts, see A. Belkaoui, *International Accounting: Issues and Solutions* (Westport, Conn.: Quorum Books, 1985), pp. 28–49.

17. J. A. Wilson, "No Need for Standardization of International Accounting," *Touche Ross Tempo* (Winter 1969), p. 40.

18. J. L. Kirkpatrick, "The Gaps in International GAAP," *Corporate Accounting* (Fall 1985), p. 4.

19. Securities and Exchange Commission, Rule 4-01 (a)(2) [17 CFR 201.4-01].

20. Securities and Exchange Commission. *Internationalization of Securities Markets* (1987), pp. iv–29.

References

Belkaoui, A. *International Accounting: Issues and Solutions*. Westport, Conn.: Quorum Books, 1985.

Choi, F. D. s., and V. B. Bavishi. "International Accounting Standards: Issues Needing Attention." *Journal of Accountancy* (March 1983), pp. 62–68.

Dickenson, H. K. "New Foreign Currency Translation and Transaction Rules." *Taxes—The Tax Magazine* (July 1987), pp. 463–77.

Ernst & Whinney. *International Accounting Standards: Synopes, Multinational Comparisons and Disclosure Checklist*. Cleveland, 1986.

Financial Accounting Standards Board, "Foreign Currency Translation." *Statement of Financial Accounting Standards No. 52* (1981).

Kirkpatrick, J. L. "The Gaps in International GAAP." *Corporate Accounting* (Fall 1985).

Securities and Exchange Commission. *Internationalization of Securities Markets*. Washington, D.C.: Securities and Exchange Commission, 1987.

V   International Taxation and Accounting

Key Terms

• transfer pricing
• dividend repatriation

- withholding taxes
- worldwide system
- territorial system
- comparable uncontrolled price method
- resale price method
- cost-plus method
- tax havens
- branch vs. subsidiary
- tax holiday
- tax deferral
- functional currency
- FASB-52
- translation exposure

Questions

1. Gizmo International is a U.S.-based multinational corporation that ships gizmos to its subsidiaries in Canada, Mexico, and Australia. The marginal profits tax rate is 34 percent in the United States, 30 percent in Canada, 50 percent in Mexico, and 40 percent in Australia. The subsidiaries in all three foreign countries are profitable and able to remit dividends. The U.S. taxes foreign income only when repatriated, and allows a credit for foreign taxes paid.

   a. Gizmo can justify setting a transfer price anywhere between $20 and $25 per gizmo and can determine this price separately for gizmos shipped to Canada, Mexico, and Australia. What should the transfer price for gizmos shipped to each location be, and why?

   b. Gizmo decides to repatriate $1 million in profit from one of its subsidiaries. Which subsidiary should pay the dividend, and why?

2. Harpoon, Inc., is a U.S. multinational corporation that ships small appliances to its subsidiary in Austria. The marginal profits tax rate in the United States is 34 percent, and in Austria 55 percent. The United States taxes foreign subsidiary income only when repatriated, and allows a credit for foreign taxes paid. Austria has a 20 percent withholding tax on dividend payments, for which the United States gives a complete tax credit. Harpoon's accountant has just informed you that he can justify setting a

transfer price anywhere between $100 and $150 on microwave ovens shipped to Austria.

a. What should the transfer price be?

b. If Austria introduces an import tariff of 25 percent on microwave ovens, and permits this to be a deductible expense in figuring the subsidiary's income tax, what should the transfer price be?

c. If $100 in pretax profits is repatriated from Austria, how much cash does the parent receive? (Ignore the import tariff introduced in question 2b.)

d. If $100 in pretax profits is repatriated from Austria, what is Harpoon's additional U.S. tax burden or excess tax credit? (Again, ignore the import tariff introduced in question 2b.)

Suggested Readings

Choi, Frederick D. S., and Vinod B. Bavishi, "Financial Accounting Standards: A Multinational Synthesis and Policy Framework," *The International Journal of Accounting: Education and Research*, Fall 1984, pp. 159−184.

Fowler, D. J., "Transfer Prices and Profit Maximization in Multinational Operations," *Journal of International Business Studies*, Winter 1978, pp. 9−26.

Hall, Thomas W., and H. Jim Snavely, "Translated Financial Statements Can Be Meaningful," *The International Journal of Accounting: Education and Research*, Fall 1984, pp. 153−170.

VI

Political Risk

One of the major questions that concerns firms involved in foreign investments is whether the returns will be sufficient to compensate for the exceptional risks, and especially for the losses incurred when the host-country
governments change the terms initially adopted to attract foreign firms. In
the late 1970s many U.S., European, and Japanese firms incurred large
losses on their investments in Iran following the departure of the Shah and
the coming to power of the Islamic Revolutionary Government. In the
1960s and 1970s many international oil companies were obliged to sell
their production units in Venezuela, Saudi Arabia, Indonesia, and other
oil-producing developing countries to host-country governments. In the
1960s U.S. firms with assets in Cuba lost control of these assets soon
after Castro assumed power. Firms headquartered in Great Britain, France,
Belgium, and the Netherlands incurred significant losses soon after their
countries' colonies became independent, when the governments in many of
these countries nationalized properties of the firms headquartered in their
former metropoles. And firms with operations in Kuwait and Iraq incurred
losses following the Iraqi invasion of Kuwait and the subsequent bombing
of Baghdad and other Iraqi cities.

In many cases firms incur losses because host-country governments—or
individuals acting in the name of the governments—adopt measures that
reduce anticipated profits. These firms may feel obliged to increase employment of host-country nationals, or to increase purchases from local firms—
some of which are importers. In some cases host-country governments may
set price ceilings for the products made or imported by foreign firms.

Foreign firms incur exceptional risks when governments in the host
countries change, because incoming governments may adopt more restrictive policies toward foreign investors.

The most dramatic examples of political risk involve expropriation of
the assets of foreign firms without compensation. At times compensation
may be paid, but usually the amount of compensation is much smaller than
what the firms believe appropriate. Most of the large losses from expropriation have been incurred on investments in the developing countries, and
especially by firms involved in petroleum and other resource-extraction
industries; losses incurred by firms in manufacturing have been much
smaller.

The business risks attached to foreign investment are more or less identical with those attached to domestic investment. Political risks for foreign
investments are distinctly greater than for domestic, because foreign investors are at a substantial disadvantage relative to domestic investors in
attempting to use both the political and the judicial processes in host

countries to protect their interests—and these measures are likely to be much more expensive for foreign firms than for domestic firms.

Political risk management involves estimating the risk attached to foreign investments, and developing a low-cost approach toward reducing both the risk and the losses associated with it. Some firms are so concerned about the likelihood and scale of losses that they have forgone opportunities in many developing countries that were otherwise attractive. Some firms enter into joint ventures with partners headquartered in other industrial countries, in the belief that the host-country governments will be less likely to harass or interfere with a firm that has parents headquartered in two foreign countries. Some firms enter into joint ventures with firms headquartered in the host country, in the belief that the local partner will be much more effective in coping with the demands of the host country government. Some firms develop a diversified portfolio approach to political risk—they believe that the losses they may incur in a few countries because of the arbitrary actions of host-country governments will be smaller than the amounts saved by not undertaking any special measures to reduce the likelihood of these losses. Some firms devise one set of policies for countries with large domestic markets, and another set for the much larger number of countries with small domestic markets.

Back-of-the-envelope calculations suggest that the costs firms incur as a result of host-country government actions are much smaller than the income they forgo when they reduce their investments or undertake other measures to avoid such losses. If these calculations are anywhere near correct, the implication is that political risk analysis may help management enhance their net returns on foreign investment.

"Political Risk Analysis and Direct Foreign Investment: Some Problems of Definition and Measurement" by S. Prakash Sethi and K. A. N. Luther discusses several methods of evaluating political risk. Sethi and Luther develop an analytical approach to political risk, and highlight ways to gather and interpret data dealing with political risk. They emphasize firm-specific and industry-specific measures of political risk rather than generic country index measures.

Thomas A. Poynter's "Managing Government Intervention: A Strategy for Defending the Subsidiary" examines changes in the bargaining power of multinationals and of host-country governments; political incidents are more likely to happen when the bargaining power of the host-country government exceeds that of the multinational firm. Managers are encouraged to enhance the firm's bargaining power so as to reduce its sensitivity to political risk, perhaps by enhancing dependence on the firm for new technologies. However, the cross-country implications are weak because governments with the most bargaining power are often not the most politically risky. Poynter specifically implies that, because of its immense bargaining power, Brazil would be riskier than Bolivia; in reality, most observers would give Brazil higher marks for its investment climate and shun Bolivia.

"Foreign Ownership: When Hosts Change the Rules" by Dennis J. Encarnation and Sushil Vachani applies bargaining power analysis to the case of forced equity dilution in India. Encarnation and Vachani outline three alternative approaches toward the political risk encountered by foreign investors: (1) sell a share of the equity to Indian investors; (2) withdraw from India; or (3) expand the operation by issuing new equity to Indian investors. They suggest that forced equity dilution may be surprisingly favorable if firms follow the third approach, because they will profit from new product lines and markets.

17

Political Risk Analysis and Direct Foreign Investment: Some Problems of Definition and Measurement

S. Prakash Sethi and K. A. N. Luther

One of the major uncertainties and risks associated with foreign investments—portfolio, direct, or loan—involves the political developments occurring in the international arena and in both the host and home countries of multinational business operations. The impact of these political developments on the safety and profitability of foreign investments is quite often far greater than the normal uncertainties and risks associated with overseas developments, for example:

• In the international organizations, less-developed countries (LDCs) have become more strident in their demands for shifts in economic resources from the developed countries under the rubric of the "New International Economic Order," or the North-South conflict.

• Private lenders have substantially increased their loans to both the LDCs and socialist countries in the Eastern Bloc. The interest payments of these loans are absorbing a large portion of these countries' foreign exchange resources and more loans are being advanced just to meet the interest payments.

• The oil-rich countries of the Middle East are displaying increasing instability while at the same time creating greater trade and investment links and dependencies with the developing countries.

• Protectionist sentiments in the economies of the West have made them more reluctant to open their doors to exports from LDCs.

• The combined population pressures, the lack of economic growth, and the totalitarian and often inefficient political orders and governmental bureaucracies create a need for dependence and foreign aid. However, international lending institutions (e.g., the World Bank) are tightening their

From *California Management Review*, Winter 1986, pp. 57–68. Reprinted by permission.

lending criteria, and developed countries led by the U.S.A. are pulling back on their government-to-government direct aid.

All these factors, along with the happenings in Iran, El Salvador, and Nicaragua, highlight the importance of political events to business decision making. It is, therefore, no wonder that corporations and lending institutions have been paying more attention to the analysis of the impact of political risk on their current and potential foreign investment decisions.

Political Risk Analysis—The State of the Art

A survey of current scholarly and professional literature would also indicate a significant increase in the research and analysis of political risk. The current state of research, however, is faced with a number of problems that are likely to limit severely the relevance of the concept both as an analytical tool and as a practical guide to business decision making. These problems are broadly those of definition and measurement.

Without quite specifying it, most writers tend to use "political risk" as a catchall term for the risk dimensions of political events which have an impact on business decisions. As such, it is replete with definitional incongruities. Political risk is generally equated with political instability and is analyzed along those lines. However, political risk, as it affects business investment decisions, cannot be equated simply with political instability such as a change in government. Furthermore, political instability has different connotations in different sociocultural frameworks. Thus, any measure of political risk based on some index of political instability would most likely lead to erroneous findings of dubious practical value.

Consider, for example, the case of Italy and the United Kingdom. If one were to measure changes in government as proxy for political instability, ten changes in Italy would not mean the same thing as ten changes in the government of the United Kingdom during the same period; yet the index would not be able to differentiate between the two conditions. Similarly, there may be frequent changes in the military strong men running a government; but so long as the government is controlled by the army, the changes in government would have little practical impact on economic activity. Also, it is not certain that the process of economic development, which leads to environmental changes, is the cause of political instability—as argued in some studies.[1] Political stability can be found in some of the fast-growing nations (such as South Korea, Malaysia, and Taiwan) and in some of the low achievers (like Cuba, Zaire, Kenya, and Tanzania).

It seems that in much of the research effort on political risk, not enough attention has been paid to the development of concepts and definitions that capture the breadth of the problem. Unless the definitions are clear, other methodological issues are not likely to be resolved. The penchant is for quantification. This process has led to unrealistic expectations about the usefulness of the results. Given the poor definitions of the concept to begin with, the results provide the wrong answers. The problems are compounded by inconsistent interpretations, limitations in technical skills, and, given the lack of a "real feel" for the country being analyzed, misperceptions of possible uses of the data.

Questions of definition and measurement are fundamental to the use of effective political risk analysis by business entities. There is a tendency to proceed with the analysis as if a commonly agreed upon definition of the phenomenon existed. The result is that while there may be a great deal of dialogue or "noise," there is little understanding of the problem. A fuzziness in the definition invariably leads to the wrong selection of data, the inappropriate choice of analytical tools, and the interpretation of findings and solutions that have little, if anything, to do with the original problem.

Professor Kobrin has stated this impasse in his review essay on the subject: "We need better definitions of the phenomena, a conceptual structure relating politics to the firm, and a great deal of information about the impact of the political environment. The three are, of course, related."[2]

The first objective of this article is to develop a structure of political risk such that it would lend itself to systematic analysis of its various dimensions in terms of degree and type of risk and the modes of containment measures that can be undertaken by the investors. The second objective is to identify certain approaches for the measurement and interpretation of data pertaining to different categories of risk.

Problems of Definition

The term "political risk" has had various interpretations in the literature. Most studies define it as unanticipated government actions that have an impact on business operations.[3] National governments by their actions might prevent business transactions, change terms of agreements, or even expropriate business units. Other studies have defined political risk on the basis of environmental changes due to political developments (like acts of violence, instability, riots, and so on) that have repercussions on business activity.[4] These two distinct definitions of political risk—one deliberative and the other environmental—are interdependent. Environmental changes can prompt government actions as much as government activity can provoke environmental developments.

An operational definition of political risk such as that offered by Robock (who refers to it as being "discontinuities in the business environment" and "difficult to anticipate"[5]) is, of course, correct but not very useful. A business entity needs to have an understanding of the,sources of risk to take a proactive stand against such risks or initiate measures to contain them. Adequate responses from corporations require an understanding of the total environment of political risk.

It is clear that political risks emanate from different sources and have an impact on a business entity in a manner different from pure market developments. They threaten both profitability and satisfactory repatriation of profits of a direct foreign investment. The risk potential faced by a business is influenced by: entry conditions in terms of magnitude and types of investment; ownership patterns, in as much as expatriate versus local participation is a factor; type of product lines and operations, where the relative technological and human skills sophistication of production processes and final products play a part; and government instruments and directives both of host and parent countries that would ensure or hinder freedom and safety of operations. This means that country, industry, and firm characteristics all influence the potential vulnerability and intensity of political risk for a business firm.[6]

The difficulty of political risk assessment is further compounded by distinctions between macro dimensions (which affect all business enterprises in general) and micro political risks (which selectively affect specific business activities).[7] Political instabilities, government actions, or other factors might translate into either one of these two types of risks and it is not possible a priori to identify outcomes.

These considerations, therefore, warrant a more extensive classification of political risks than prevalent in the literature. But if the term political risk is not going to be "overly constrained from both an analytical and operational viewpoint," we need to be concerned with not political events "but their potential manifestations as constraints upon foreign investors."[8] This again requires an understanding of the sources of political risk. It is this concern that leads us to argue for a more encompassing identification of the types of risks that are generated by events that have political dimensions.

In table 17.1, various dimensions of political risk are identified along with different avenues of containment. Such a matrix helps in the task of political risk assessment by making explicit the multidimensional nature of the political risk problem. Possible strategies can then be identified for a

Table 17.1

Matrix of risk and containment

Sources of political risk	Methods of containment		
	International	Home country	Host country
Host country conditions:			
Political	• Insurance against political risk	• Foreign aid • Military aid	• Joint ownership • Shorter payback period
Economic	• International/ multilateral agreements	• Foreign aid restrictions on technology transfer • Bilateral agreements	• Higher ROI restrictions on technology transfer
Sociocultural	• Changes in public opinion	• Maintain a low profile • Posture of non-involvement	• Change in product design
Home country conditions:			
Political	• Use of international organizations • Pressure from other countries	• Lobbying for change in laws and government policy • Threat of international reparations	• Insulate local subsidiaries from home country laws • Be a good corporate citizen
Economic	• International/ multilateral agreements	• Coalition of businesses with common interests	• Increase economic benefits and host country dependence on foreign enterprise
Sociocultural	• International public opinion	• Create positive public opinion towards needs and aspirations of people in the host country	• Be a good corporate citizen • Maintain a low profile

business unit, particularly if it is going to be proactive rather than reactive in making decisions pertaining to foreign direct investment.

In the matrix, risk to foreign enterprises is viewed as a combination of three interrelated factors: political, economic, and sociocultural.

• The *political* dimension refers to events that arise from power or authority relationships, which can stem from many different sources. Political instability can refer to cataclysmic events, such as violent changes in government, assassinations, and riots. It can also refer to gradual events that have implications for business decisions, such as the effect of growing national pride on the ownership of business entities or the gradual undermining of the power base of the current leadership by ideological and institutional developments.

• *Economic* factors also play a role in bringing about political risks. As has been noticed in the literature, the distinction between purely political and economic risks breaks down at the operational level because of the interdependence of economic and political phenomena.[9] However, the distinction is useful insofar as it identifies the root cause of the problem being tied to economic conditions (such as poor economic management, low employment, high inflation rates, balance of payments problems, and inequities in income and wealth distributions). Furthermore, to the extent to which national governments modify economic arrangements to accommodate political pressure (as in the case of protectionism and foreign exchange controls), political risk dimensions are accentuated in business decision making. Because they engage in the import and export of finished products, foreign direct investment units are vulnerable to trade-related disruptions caused by the political influence of pressure groups.

• Finally, political risk dimensions may also result from *sociocultural* developments. The Iranian experience is a case in point: the rapid pace of Westernization created social tensions and cultural conflicts which resulted in the fundamentalist revolution.

In general, the risks posed by host-country developments are adequately covered in the political risk literature, but risks emanating from parent- or home-country policies are ignored. For example, export controls have become increasingly important as instruments of foreign policy. Other examples of economic alternatives that are used by parent countries to bolster political influence include trade embargoes, sanctions, and controls on the transfer of technology and goods to unfriendly nations. Foreign entities of domestic enterprises are affected by these restrictions since they infringe on the free flow of goods and services from the headquarters to the foreign subsidiary.

Two examples illustrate the interdependence of international, home-country, and host-country government policies on the one hand, and political, economic, and sociocultural factors on the other hand. The cases in point are investments in South Africa and the sale and marketing of infant formula in less-developed countries. There are conflicting crosscurrents between the policies of various U.S. administrations in terms of the degree of compliance with various U.N. resolutions on these issues. There are also different types of pressures by vested interest groups, especially religious groups, on U.S. corporations both to refrain from investing in South Africa and to comply with the WHO code on marketing practices for the sale of infant formula in less-developed countries. The response of U.S. multinationals in both these cases is invariably complicated by their vulnerability to U.S. domestic pressures; pressures from other countries, where they have operations; their global market shares and international production strategy; and their relative investment exposure in South Africa and third-world countries. It should, therefore, be clear that any analysis of risk that ignores these interdependencies is likely to have little practical value for MNCs in assessing relative investment or operational risks in their overseas operations.

The analysis can be further extended by considering possible avenues of containment for political risk problems. Each of the risks mentioned can involve a composite of responses for containment. International treaties, concessions, and pacts can safeguard against some aspects of risk. Parent countries can choose less interventionist measures to influence foreign policy objectives or respond by withholding foreign aid or arms if the risk emanates from the host country. Considerable responsibility for reducing political risk for business might be in the hands of the host country, which has to guarantee a favorable business climate despite political and sociocultural pressures that potentially may be destabilizing.

Corporate response to these pressures is also important. By anticipating possible sources of conflict, corporations can make adjustments in their business practices and ownership patterns (such as permitting greater local participation) and, hence, can take a proactive stance. The common reactive stance seems to occur because assessment resources are limited and therefore are used sparingly. A proactive stance would entail anticipating the political risk problem well in advance and taking measures to lessen social conflict. Quite apart from "self-insurance" through a shorter payback period or higher rate of return, an activist strategy can diffuse potential sources of conflict for corporate management.

Although not all of the cells of the matrix are of relevance for every strategy of containment, the schema enables decision makers to have a sense of the alternatives involved. Careful identification of the sources of risks will go a long way in suggesting possible strategies of containment against political risks. Definitions that do not take into account the broad spectrum of the political risk problem are not likely to be useful for formulating responses. To focus upon just political instability defined in a narrow manner leads either to empirical studies that show political factors as not being a major determinant for foreign direct investment or to assessments which claim that "political instability is neither a necessary nor a sufficient condition for changes in policy relevant to foreign investment."[10]

Problems of Measurement

Political risk assessment, besides requiring comprehensive definitions, demands reconciliation of numerous problems of measurement. These range from problems with data (in terms of collection and quality) to problems of analysis and interpretation of findings.

General Problems of Data Collection

It is well known that problems of data severely limit the predictability of models of political risk. Data deficiencies exist for even the simplest of tests, leave alone sophisticated assessment techniques like Delphi, time series analysis, and regression models. Data collection of a political nature is not only difficult and time-consuming but is likely to be biased as the local people respond guardedly to sensitive questioning. Problems are further compounded by censorship of published sources and records. Whatever data are available are likely to be haphazard and not in a format readily usable by a multinational corporation. The risk-averse proclivities of the bureaucrats who gather information lead to "bad" information being hidden. Official data-gathering agencies like the United Nations and the State Department might be susceptible to a great deal of "doctoring" of data that have been supplied voluntarily by country bureaucrats to create positive, as opposed to truthful, country images.

More fundamentally, however, it could be argued that the data that are available for political risk assessment suffer because they are not collected with respect to a specific strategic position of a business entity. The decision-related dimension of political risk assessment does not feature in the collection stage. Pursuance of a particular strategy generates its own unique risk exposure, and correct evaluation of this risk requires not just general or broad data, but rather strategy-specific information. Furthermore, data have to be somewhat firm- and industry-specific. The issue of data collection, therefore, is ultimately tied to strategic containment avenues that are contemplated by a business. An emphasis on collecting data that are strategy-specific and micro-oriented should yield more focused information gathering and eliminate some of the problems outlined above.

Problems of Analysis and Interpretation

Quite apart from data problems, there are problems of analysis and interpretation once the data have been collected. Until recently, impressionistic and qualitative assessments of political risk were made. But now, more and more sophisticated and quantitatively oriented techniques are being used. In the literature, models range from subjective assessments (such as the Delphi method with its reliance on expert opinions) to those that use quantitative indicators of political and environmental instability. Models have been employed both to gauge the extent of political risks and to forecast the likelihood of these risks.

Haner has constructed indices of instability on the basis of expert opiniond and assigning of probabilistic weights to a number of variables to arrive at the prospect for political risk.[11] The technique provides a collective impressionistic assessment by a panel of experts. But the multidimensionality of the risk function is glossed over in the aggregation process, which attempts at generating a single scale of potential risk.

A more sophisticated version is provided by Rummel and Heenan, who break up the risk dimension into components (domestic instability, foreign conflict, political and economic climate) and assign probability values based on insight and intuition for each of them.[12] Although this is an improvement in terms of having a broader focus on risks and a finer distillation of information, it still suffers from too much aggregation.

Researchers have also attempted to compute political instability indices for different national environments. Variables (such as number of years of independence, number of changes in government, and number of deaths by political violence) are used to arrive at an index of instability. Weights are also ascribed to variables to convey intensity. Cluster analyses are used to enable grouping of countries so as to generate experience from one country to another in light of poor data availability.[13] This approach is most helpful in enabling a generalization of characteristics in a particular country across a cluster of countries that are similar and where data and operational and other difficulties do not permit a country-by-country analysis. The technique offers an effective method of getting around data limitations with respect to political risk assessment. However, problems of definition of variables, limited applicability of an extrapolation of the past into the future in dynamic environments, and a lack of consensus on what variables constitute political instability restrict the usefulness of these approaches.

More sophisticated techniques are suggested by Stobaugh, who deals with a range of estimates and methods for risk exposure.[14] Political risks are accounted for by adjusting "the present value of expected cash flows, or the internal rate of return from the investment project under consideration" so as to "reflect the timing and magnitude of risk probabilities." Further extensions of this approach involve adjusting incremental cash flows to allow for the political uncertainty faced on a per period basis. But as suggested by Kobrin, these judgements on adjustments of cash flows or discount rates are "determined by one's judgements to (1) the applicability of the Capital Asset Pricing Model and (2) whether the risk is systematic or not."[15] There are also immense problems of data availability and estimation of various probabilities. The real danger is that a sophisticated approach for political risk assessment would be used by corporate managements as a "black box," giving interpretations that are questionable and based on data that are very dubious to begin with.

Inasmuch as formal models of the political risk process enable corporate planners to state some of the subjective probabilities that are associated with corporate decisions, these models are useful. They demand a formal accounting of dimensions which otherwise might have been ignored with qualitative assessments. However, there is also the danger that an elaborate and complex model would be treated as a substitute for reality. The political risk assessment process could be seriously misleading if "mechanistic" reliance is placed on mathematical models.

Empirical research has shown that few companies use these sophisticated techniques regularly.[16] The organization of the political assessment function appears to be quite varied, ranging from informal assessment by top management to a formal "unit with five or more professionals, who are charged with developing and implementing an assessment methodology."[17] When scanning the external environment, managers tend to rely heavily on interpersonal contact for their information sources.[18] The integration of the assessment of political risk into the decision-making process, therefore, tends to be informal and unsystematic.[19]

In general, narrow definitions of the political risk concept have led to techniques that can help operationalize the political risk issue. But the very process of simplification demanded by formal models makes the exercise less beneficial; since the complexity of the problem is assumed away. These models, based on limited definitions, assume deterministic relationships between, for example, political instability and political risk. In reality, the causation is a result of numerous sources of risk—and not at all determinable in the fashion demanded by the formal techniques.

Conclusions

Notwithstanding the problems of definition, measurement, analysis, and interpretation, multinational corporations must cope with the evaluation of political risks involved in their overseas investments. Some of these issues could be solved with further research. For multinationals, a five-step approach is suggested here to deal with political risk assessment:

• Broad measures of political risk, based on secondary data, should be used, but only as a first step in political risk assessment. Since the quality of these data is likely to be highly inconsistent, any conclusions derived from these measures should be taken with a large dose of skepticism.

• To the extent that global or regional scales of political risk are developed, emphasis should be placed on ensuring that the data are consistent across countries, not only in terms of inputs (i.e., number of changes in governments, number of assassinations, etc.), but also, more importantly, in terms of measures of output (i.e., degree of political instability, internal turmoil, etc.).

• These global-regional measures must be supplemented with current analysis or country-specific information for both the host countries and home country of the MNC parent.

• Global-regional and country-specific information must be evaluated in terms of a company's strengths and weaknesses in dealing with a particular type of political risk emanating from one or more of the three sources. Each company's potential for political risk absorption would be different based on its global investment strategy, technological lead, and market position.

• Individual investment strategies would depend on a careful analysis of the sources of political risk, avenues of containment available to the MNC, and the MNC's bargaining and negotiating skills.

There is no substitute for solid experience, deep familiarity with the economic, social, and political environment (as well as the political leadership) of the countries involved, a willingness to look at the long-term prospects of direct foreign investments, and an appreciation of the legitimate needs and aspirations of the host-country governments and people.

Businesses need to devote greater effort to trying to work out their differences with host governments and anticipate home-country and international developments. The proactive approach entails a strategy formulation in advance of political risk problems. Thus, collection of information for an assessment of risk exposure is done with respect to a particular strategy of containment.

Research activity in the area of political risk needs to move towards an evaluation of both the substantive and symbolic relationships between governments and multinational companies. Such a move would be desirable because the complexity of the phenomena tends to undermine existing approaches to the problem and because of the firm-specific nature of the political risk question. Creative conflict-management activity seems to be the desired area of extension for political risk analysts.

Notes

1. Robert T. Green, *Political Instability as a Determinant of U.S. Foreign Investments*, Studies in Marketing, No. 17, Bureau of Business Research, Graduate School of Business, University of Texas at Austin, 1972; Lee C. Nehrt, "The Political Climate for Private Investment, Analysis Will Reduce Uncertainty," *Business Horizons* (June 1972), pp. 51–58; Franklin R. Root, "Analyzing Political Risks in International Business," in Ashok Kapoor and Phillip D. Grub, eds., *The Multinational Enterprise in Transition* (Princeton, NJ: Darwin Press, 1972); A. Van Agtmael, "How Business Has Dealt with Political Risk," *Financial Executive* (January 1976), pp. 26–30.

2. Stephen Kobrin, "Political Risk: A Review and Reconsideration," *Journal of International Business Studies*, Vol. X, No. 1 (Spring/Summer 1979): 77.

3. John Fayweather, "Nationalism and the Multinational Firm," in Ashok Kapoor and Phillip D. Grub, eds., op. cit.; Robert T. Green, "Political Structure as a Predictor of Radical Political Change," *Columbia Journal of World Business*, Vol. IX, No. 1 (Spring 1974):28–36; Stephen Kobrin, "Political Assessment by International Firms: Models or Methodologies," *Journal of Policy Modeling* 3/2 (1981):251–270; I. C. MacMillan, "Business Strategies for Political Action," *Journal of General Management* (Autumn 1974).

4. Robert T. Green. op. cit. (1972); Robert T. Green, op. cit. (1974); Robert T. Green and Christopher M. Korth, "Political Instability and the Foreign Investor," *California Management Review* (Fall 1974), pp. 23–31; A. Van Agtmael, op. cit.

5. S. Robock, "Political Risk: Identification and Assessment," *Columbia Journal of World Business* (July/August 1971), p.7.

6. Ibid.; Franklin R. Root, op. cit. (1972); F. Root, "U.S. Business Abroad and Political Risks," *MSU Business Topics* (Winter 1968), pp. 73–80.

7. Robock, op. cit.

8. Kobrin, op. cit. (1979), p. 71.

9. Root, op. cit. (1972).

10. Kobrin, op. cit. (1979), p. 74.

11. F. T. Haner, "Business Environmental Risk Index," *Best's Review* (Property Liability ed.) (July 1975).

12. R. J. Rummel and D. A. Heenan, "How Multinationals Analyze Political Risk," *Harvard Business Review* (January/February 1978), pp. 67–76.

13. S. Prakash Sethi, "Comparative Cluster Analysis of World Markets," *Journal of Marketing Research* (August 1971); S. Prakash Sethi and David L. Curry, "Variable and Object Clustering of Cross-Cultural Data: Some Implications for Comparative Research and Policy Formulation," *Journal of Comparative Political Studies* (October 1972); S. Prakash Sethi and Richard H. Holton, "Country Typologies for the Multinational Corporation: A New Basic Approach," *California Management Review* (Spring 1973).

14. R. Stobaugh "How to Analyze Foreign Investment Climates," *Harvard Business Review* (September/October 1969), pp. 100–107.

15. Kobrin, op. cit. (1979). p. 72.

16. J. LaPalombara and S. Blank, *Multinational Corporations in Comparative Perspective* (New York: The Conference Board, 1977); F. Root, op. cit., (1968).

17. Stephen J. Kobrin, "The Environmental Determinants of Foreign Direct Manufacturing Investment: An ExPost Empirical Analysis," *Journal of International Business Studies*, Vol. 7, No. 2 (Fall/Winter 1976):35.

18. F. J. Aguilar, *Scanning the Business Environment* (New York: Macmillan, 1967); W. Keegan, "Multinational Scanning A Study of Information Sources Used by Headquarters Executives in Multinational Companies," *Administrative Science Quarterly* (September 1974). pp. 411–421.

19. S. Kobrin, J. Basek, S. Blank, and J. LaPalombara, "The Assessment and Evaluation of Non-Economic Environments by American Firms: A Preliminary Report," *Journal of International Business Studies* (Spring/Summer 1980).

18

Managing Government Intervention: A Strategy for Defending the Subsidiary

Thomas A. Poynter

Managers in multinational enterprises are concerned and frustrated by governments which force unwanted changes in their preferred method of operations. Host governments intervene in subsidiaries of multinational enterprises (MNEs) by restricting foreign ownership and control; regulating financial flows, foreign management and technical fees; and instituting requirements for local content and minimum export levels. Historically, MNEs have responded by trying to negotiate changes in either the intervention laws or their implementation; by attempting to bypass the laws; or by reducing their exposure in nations with a record of frequent interventions.

Academics and consultants have been examining the intervention experiences of MNEs. This effort has produced several ideas and approaches for improving the MNE's management of intervention. The purpose of this paper is to summarize these findings and examine how they can be incorporated into a strategy for defending the MNE from unwanted intervention.

While parent companies are usually the focus of attention in such discussions, the focus here is on the subsidiary. This is not only for the obvious reason that subsidiaries are more exposed to the policies of host governments. It is because intervention policies are, in fact, determined less by ideology, politics, and economics, and more by the character of the subsidiary itself. While ideology, political stability, and the supply of hard currency reserves set the stage, the foreign subsidiary is the actor.

Given the crucial role of the subsidiary, managers should refocus their attention on subsidiary strategies. This paper proposes a general strategy for defending the subsidiary, concentrating on a strategy that can be implemented by most manufacturing multinationals without dramatic changes in

From *Columbia Journal of World Business*, Winter 1986, pp. 55–65. Reprinted by permission.

their existing organization and operation. Empirical support for this strategy is based on the study of several hundred subsidiaries, while implementation issues come from a study of fifteen U.S., U.K., French, Swiss and
German MNEs and their subsidiaries conducted between 1980 and 1983.

Intervention Management: a Shift

Traditional political risk analysis no longer meets the needs of MNEs.
Historically, political risk analysis focused on assessing political instability.
While international banks find this analysis still appropriate to their needs,
multinational manufacturing firms know this kind of information is not
particularly useful in managing their political risks. Political instability
forms only a small portion of all the risks faced by multinational enterprises.[1] Instead, MNEs find that actions like forced joint ventures, unilateral
contract renegotiations, and regulations calling for increased local value-
added top their list of concerns. Even when revolutions and similar shocks
occur, they do not necessarily affect all firms equally.

While some nations intervene more than others, avoiding intervention
by predicting a nation's intervention behavior is ineffective. "Safe" countries like Brazil and Mexico often turn into hotbeds of intervention, while
host countries led by unrepentant Marxists provide profitable opportunities. It appears that almost all countries, even fellow members of the Western bloc, intervene in the operations of foreign-owned firms.

How then does the foreign-owned firm defend itself? One dominant
characteristic of host government intervention behavior leads the way
toward a solution: governments discriminate. They force some subsidiaries
into unwanted joint ventures, and impose taxes and limit prices, while
allowing others 100% foreign ownership and financially supporting them.
Even when legislation calls for the equal treatment of all foreign firms, as in
Nigeria, discriminatory enforcement is often the norm.

The basis of this discrimination lies in the differing characteristics of
subsidiaries. Case studies, casual observation, and large-scale empirical in-
vestigations conducted by several observers lead to substantial agreement
on this issue.[2] A key element is the bargaining power associated with each
subsidiary. In this context, bargaining power refers to the control the MNE
parent has over those resources necessary to operate the *subsidiary* successfully. Intervention occurs when domestic firms, entrepreneurs, or government officials feel they have sufficient resources (e.g., technology, export
markets, raw material or components, etc.) to operate part or all of the
activities of the subsidiary without assistance from the MNE. In other

words, local groups will press the government to intervene on their behalf when continued MNE support no longer is required to keep the subsidiary profitable. At that point, the MNE's bargaining power is low. Negotiations usually occur no matter what the bargaining power of the subsidiary, but the level of bargaining power is a good predictor of the outcome of the negotiations.

The bargaining power of the host nation comes from two sources. One source directly counters the power of the MNE, namely the host nation's ability to replace the business resources normally supplied by the MNE. The nation's stock of managerial, technical, and similar resources is either internally generated, or is obtained through consultants, license agreements, and the like. Given, for example, the recent ability of South Koreans to operate complex petrochemical plants, the Brazilians to manufacture digital integrated circuits, and the Canadians to fund and technologically support frontier oil exploration, the capabilities of host nations are growing at rates not predicted a decade ago.[3]

The second source of host nation bargaining power comes from their control over the subsidiary's access to the host nation's market, raw materials, labor, and capital.[4] As these factors grow in importance, more MNEs compete to locate there, thus maximizing the bargaining power of the host nation. Hence, the larger and more attractive the local market becomes, the more intervention the firm will experience, all things being equal. For example, identical firms operating in the Ivory Coast and Nigeria, two countries with roughly equivalent domestic business capabilities, will find a greater amount of intervention in Nigeria due to the power that country derives from its large domestic market.

Summarizing the bargaining power (BP) model algebraically, intervention will *not* occur under the following circumstances:

Subsidiary $BP_{Business\ Resources} >$ Nation's $BP_{Business\ Resources}$

$+$ Nation's $BP_{Market\ Attractiveness}$

In this model bargaining power is derived from two sources, the availability of business resources needed to operate the subsidiary and, for the host nation only, the attractiveness of its market.

It is important here to reiterate the source and applicability of this model. It is based on the intervention experiences of many individual subsidiaries. The model shows what circumstances are typically found when intervention occurs. In practice, low subsidiary bargaining power sets into motion actions by domestic entrepreneurs, government officials, and the like, who actually bring about intervention. This process is described else-where.[5] One must also agree that this model does not examine why one nation would intervene on average more than another.[6] For example, one of the reasons Nigeria intervenes more than the Ivory Coast may have to do with the latter's more open market, which is less distorted by government intervention. But this article is about reducing the level of intervention relative to all other firms in a nation. Given that one must choose to operate in a particular nation, defending the subsidiary against high levels of intervention is a key managerial activity.

The subsidiary's defense strategy is based on the bargaining model presented above, coupled with other subsidiary characteristics which also affect the level of intervention. Because the firm's bargaining power can usually be changed, firms can now manage intervention.[7]

Applicability of the Strategy

Not all kinds of intervention, nor all kinds of MNEs, are covered here. The proposed strategy is only applicable to unwanted interventions and not interventions represented by inducements such as tax holidays, subsidies, etc. Interventions that take place before the investment is made, such as Singapore's list of businesses restricted to local ownership, are not included either. On the corporate side, the strategy is restricted to manufacturing MNEs and not to those in the service sector or those involved in activities of a project nature.

The strategy applies to a wide selection of nations, developed and less-developed alike. Only in those select nations where discriminatory legislation against foreign firms is nonexistent, either because of judicial restraints or because the presence of overwhelming bilateral exchanges mitigates against intervention, does this strategy not apply. While this list of nations varies, three of the more stable members would be the U.K., West Germany, and the U.S.

This paper is also not concerned directly with organizational and integration issues within the MNE. While this exclusion is due mostly to space considerations, it is also affected by a feeling that a well-defined and productive system for managing intervention often paves the way for integration into a firm's organizational structure. For example, the historical failure of political risk analysis to be institutionalized within the MNE has more to do with its perceived disabilities than with any organizational weakness within MNEs.[8]

Defense Strategies

Successful strategies are based on two separate activities: profitably increasing the subsidiary's bargaining power; and adapting its political behavior to its political profile. In addition, several ineffective yet popular strategies are also discussed. Finally, modifications to the basic defense strategy are described.

Maximizing Subsidiary Bargaining Power

The most frequently used method of increasing the bargaining power of the subsidiary is to stay ahead of the technical and managerial capabilities of the host nation. Over time this is operationalized by *significant technological upgrades* within the existing product line. Alternatively, if the speed of technological change is not rapid enough to outrun the domestic learning rate, or if the level of technology is not sufficiently complex, then staying ahead will require the *introduction of new products*.

The purpose of these upgrades is to keep bargaining power high by maintaining the gap between the capabilities of local entrepreneurs and businessmen, and the capabilities needed to operate the subsidiary. While this gap is maintained, the subsidiary is still dependent on the MNE, creating a bargaining disadvantage for local interventionists.

Another means of increasing bargaining power is through *significant exports*. To be effective these must either be to a market where the MNE has a strong competitive advantage, or they must be so price-sensitive that continued MNE manufacturing support is a prerequisite. While providing rapid and visible bargaining power, the successful implementation of this strategy is also the most demanding of the defense strategies.

The final major source of bargaining power stems from MNE *sourcing or vertical integration*. Obviously, there are strong disincentives for local business or government to intervene in a firm that, say, imports a proprietary one-third-completed product for further assembly, with sales locally and to other parts of the MNE. While obvious examples occur in the auto industry, manufacturers of industrial tools, of some specialized chemicals, and of electronics, can implement this strategy as well. Japanese MNEs are frequent users of this strategy, using world-scale plants and trading houses. To guarantee effectiveness, multiple sourcing of the same components or products within the MNE system is necessary to ensure that the subsidiary will not be held hostage by a government taking advantage of its role as a sole supplier within the multinational system.

Threats to the Strategy
The effectiveness of these strategies for increasing the subsidiary's bargaining power can be reduced in two ways. The first comes from the existence of significant foreign competition either within the host nation, or outside, and wishing to enter the host nation. Such competition reduces the nation's dependence on one MNE to supply the resources needed to operate the subsidiary. In effect, such competition forces individual MNEs to build a stronger bargaining position than would otherwise be necessary. Examples of products where this competition occurs are 16-bit computers, automobile tires, textiles, and toiletries.

An even greater and more recent threat to these strategies comes from the growth of alternative suppliers of complete technology. These firms supply host nation companies, eroding the role of the MNE as the exclusive supplier of such resources, and reducing the bargaining position of the foreign direct investor. These suppliers are usually small firms, from developed nations, and tend to specialize in a complex product which they sell worldwide.

In the computer industry, for example, stepper motors for disc drives are manufactured by a small, 100-employee firm in Ohio. This rather complex motor is extremely difficult to engineer and manufacture, and was formerly only supplied by, or available to, computer MNEs. Now this firm makes its motor available worldwide to local firms, increasing their ability to displace MNE producers. This firm in Ohio, and others like it supplying digital chips, computer manufacturing and marketing expertise, and the like, contribute to the very high level of intervention in the foreign-owned computer and electronics industries in nations like Brazil.

Implementing the Strategy
Successful implementation revolves around two management issues: knowing *when* to upgrade or increase the subsidiary's bargaining power, and successfully *installing* the upgrade (new process, a profitable export market, etc.) in both the subsidiary and the MNE's worldwide organization.

Basic to the successful management of costly intervention is the determination of the subsidiary's bargaining position vis-á-vis any potential interventionist. In other words, to what extent can the MNE contribution be replaced, in whole or in part, by domestic firms? Knowing one's bargaining position helps one assess the probability of intervention and the need for a bargaining power upgrade.

Figure 18.1 illustrates in a conceptual sense the subsidiary's intervention management problem. Upon entry into the host nation, the subsidiary's

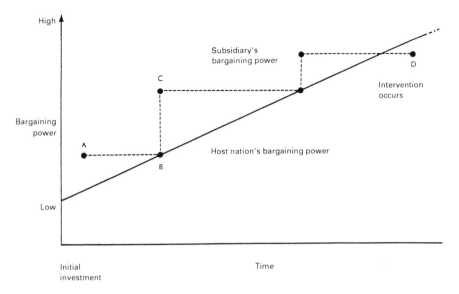

Figure 18.1
Relative bargaining power over time

bargaining position is usually high (A). The subsidiary's level of technology and management skill is generally higher than the capabilities resident in the host country. Over time, this gap decreases, as host nationals learn directly from the subsidiary or from other foreign firms, training, overseas education, etc. This learning reduces the dependence on the MNE as the supplier of these resources which ensure the continued success of the subsidiary. In other words, the relative bargaining power of the MNE dissipates over time as the skills are learned by host nationals.[9]

Conceptually, the ideal time to upgrade, or increase one's bargaining power, is just before the host nation's bargaining power is "equal" to the firm's (point B in figure 18.1). At this point, the host nation government or interest groups begin to believe that they can replace the MNE contribution with domestic technology, management, sourcing, etc., without too great a loss. By this time, MNE threats to withdraw services or skills in the hope of preventing intervention are less of a deterrent to domestic entrepreneurs and others who have been pushing for government intervention.

A bargaining power upgrade at point B would include any of the items noted earlier in this paper. To illustrate this point, for a subsidiary importing electronic components for assembly into a mature electromechanical device, an upgrade could involve the domestic manufacture of the more sophisticated electronic components not easily available in the host country. This tactic could raise the subsidiary's position to point C. Failure to upgrade one's bargaining position will eventually result in some form of costly intervention (point D), such as a forced joint venture, forced local-sourcing of components, etc.[10]

Operationally, to determine each subsidiary's bargaining power requires a measurement of the local firm's ability to provide the following resources:

- technology (process/product)
- management skill
- ability to replace MNE sourcing (inputs-outputs)

Collecting these data requires specific management resources. Executives capable of monitoring the activities, growth, and capability of existing or potential interventionists are required. Not only does this monitoring require considerable senior management time, but these executives must be familiar with, and be able to obtain intelligence on, local competitors. Most U.S. MNEs are particularly hard hit by the latter requirement, given their personnel strategy of frequently relocating executives.

MNEs have developed various mechanisms to collect these data. Some use staff specialized in competitor analysis, while others have the subsidiary general manager develop appropriate procedures. Generally, it appears to require a couple of years before the mechanism works well, but there are some tangible short-term benefits. The approach immediately focuses management attention—albeit without precision—on the single most important aspect of their intervention environment: existing or potential domestic competitors.

The second management issue associated with implementing the defense strategy involves the successful installation of the bargaining power upgrade. On one level, upgrading the technological and managerial complexity of the subsidiary by introducing new processes or products is strategically straightforward. Managerially, in order to extract a profitable return from the upgrade, the challenge is to find and train staff to handle the new activities. MNEs already accustomed to rapid technical change have a special advantage here. The container manufacturer who can progress from cork-lined to plastic-lined bottle caps, to three-seam cans, seamless cans, pressurized cans, all the way up to the sale and maintenance of complex bottling equipment, is a classic example of a firm in which one product line allows for a natural progression up the scale of technological complexity. Preparing managers and technical staff to handle those upgrades is much easier than preparing staff to handle brand new products or highly complex technologies.

Exporting as a defense mechanism is often noted by executives and observers, but very difficult to implement successfully. To be successful, production must be at world prices, with the attendant world-scale plant. While these stringent demands can be partially allayed by generous host government capital, operating subsidies, and export assistance, often the success of this strategy is mitigated by the unavailability of competitively priced inputs, uncompetitive wage and productivity rates, and managers more accustomed to operating behind tariff walls than over them.

Such an export strategy can be successful if one constructs a portfolio of different businesses with high *average* bargaining power. Multiproduct firms can establish a single export plant in a host country, providing both high bargaining power and foreign exchange. Other operations, such as the local manufacture—or even importation—of a mature product, can be grouped with the export plant and hence be protected. Viewed in this manner, the lower intervention risk—but often lower profits—offered by the export operation when matched with the high profits obtained from imported or protected products provides an acceptable overall strategy.

The implementation problems associated with intra-MNE component and product sourcing are not unlike those associated with exporting. While the need to match the world price is slightly relaxed when sales are to associate firms, additional resources are spent ensuring that product specifications, supply, and so forth are accepted worldwide. As with exports, the ability to append products with less bargaining power, but more profit, makes this strategy more attractive.

Reducing Barriers to Successful Implementation
Several multinationals have had problems successfully implementing some of the strategies recommended in this article. The difficulties appear to be of two different kinds: first, a scarcity of personnel appropriate to the new strategy; and second, the fact that this strategy runs completely counter to the MNE's traditional response to intervention.

The defense strategies call for more managerial and technical capabilities to be located in subsidiaries. Not only do export strategies, technology upgrades, and intra-MNE sourcing call for more technical skills, but—as all observers of the international scene suggest—increased numbers of politically attuned executives can be profitably used in subsidiaries too. The high cost of the former, and the scarcity of the latter, deter some MNEs.

These implementation difficulties are not found in all MNEs, however. Some MNEs appear to have far fewer problems in obtaining executives willing to spend most of their careers in subsidiaries. While the source of their success is not yet clear, differences in control systems, executive recruitment policies, promotion patterns, and perceived subsidiary autonomy are often mentioned. In addition, there is a strong suggestion that most MNEs have great difficulties managing both technologically adept executives and politically adept executives in the same organization. It appears that organizational structures, as well as promotion and reporting relationships, cannot easily adjust to dealing with such diametrically opposed executives. In a technology-driven MNE, executives with considerable political or country-based skills often find themselves in ineffectual staff positions. Such executives seem to be more active and to hold line positions in MNEs where knowledge of domestic markets, distribution channels, and so forth is the driving force behind the company, as in the consumer packaged foods industry, for example.

While these so-called consumer-driven firms seem to be the main benefactors of the politically adept executive, the technology-driven MNEs do not automatically suffer from increased intervention as a result of their absence. The reason, of course, lies in the latter's use of changing technology as a source of bargaining power, a defense infrequently available to consumer-driven firms.

Successful MNEs are able either to accommodate both kinds of executives in the same organization (examples would include Nestlé, Crown Cork and Seal, Sandoz and Rhone-Poulenc), or to recognize clearly their intolerance for such accommodation and to behave accordingly. These latter firms decide which kind of executive their firm needs and then organize to keep a steady supply available. Consumer-driven MNEs hire, train, and promote politically skilled executives with local market knowledge who defend the subsidiary primarily through the addition of new products and adroit intervention forecasting. These executives tend to remain in particular subsidiaries for long periods. Technology-driven firms concentrate on executives who are good "transporters of technology," as one MNE called them, and who tend to treat the world as one market. These MNEs tend to develop subsidiaries with export markets, complex technologies, and proprietary sourcing.

The second problem which makes MNEs hesitate to implement the defensive strategy is the complete reversal it represents from the traditional MNE response to intervention. For much of their history most MNEs responded to threats by *reducing* their asset exposure and speeding up profit repatriation. They justified this response by referring to the highly unpredictable nature of government intervention. This response also paralleled the behavior—and won the approval—of international bankers. In contrast, new subsidiary defense strategies call for *increased* investment when intervention threatens.

Many MNEs also find the decision to increase the managerial and technical capabilities of subsidiary personnel to have a double edge. Because these capabilities can be partially acquired by potential interventionists by hiring away personnel, MNEs sometimes see the training of subsidiary personnel as a threat to their bargaining power. Some MNEs think it is best to withhold training. In reality, though, such "leakage" of capabilities and technology from the subsidiary to potential interventionists will always occur without regard to the level of capabilities. Unfortunately, the MNE does not have an option, because withholding training and new equipment only serves to reduce the MNE's bargaining power even further.

Optimum Political Strategy

The choice of political strategy is determined by the political profile the subsidiary exhibits. This political profile seems to be determined by the size of the firm and the firm's strategic importance to the host country.[11] Action against a large employer provides greater publicity impact, allows greater opportunities for implementing political directives, and, in some nations, satisfies trade unions. For similar reasons, firms in strategically important industries such as natural resources, banking, insurance, and public utilities, also have a high political profile.

The political strategy for very high-profile firms tries to affect the political as well as the economic costs of intervention. Political involvement is necessary because raising the *economic* costs of intervention alone is frequently not sufficient to offset the high *political* benefits that accrue to interventionists. Under this strategy some MNEs establish joint ventures involving firms from several nations, and use similarly syndicated project finance. This transnational web of MNEs and financial institutions, which raises the political as well as the economic cost of intervention, is growing in usage.[12] The object of such equity and financial participation is to involve nations which are the export markets, suppliers, bankers, political supporters, and aid donors of the host government. This type of deterrent is subject to much criticism from host governments, but appears to be the only defense available to firms with a high political profile.

Most subsidiaries, however, do not have a high political profile and hence do not automatically provide large political benefits to interventionists. Unlike the high-profile ones, these subsidiaries have a whole range of political strategies available to them. They may remain uninvolved, initiating no contacts with the host government, and when interaction is necessary, use the local Board of Trade instead of direct interaction. The more active alternative involves the maintenance of working relationships with several ministers and senior civil servants.

The optimum political behavior strategy is, again, determined by company characteristics. Research in several nations suggests that only small, nondescript subsidiaries should be politically noninvolved. Here the ability of the firm to remain anonymous is *enhanced* by its lack of political involvement. But all others, it is suggested, will benefit from political involvement.[13] Politicians and civil servants can be briefed on the MNE's contribution to the subsidiary's success—its bargaining power. More importantly, such relationships can help the subsidiary identify proponents of intervention, providing the opportunity to offer arrangements satisfactory to the interventionist but less costly to the subsidiary.[14]

Ineffective Strategies

The rhetorical preoccupations of politicians, civil servants, and most critics of MNEs are not useful guides to the formulation of successful strategies. Cries for appropriate technology, for the creation of foreign exchange, for an often-cited but undefined good corporate citizenship, for licensing, and for joint partnerships do not lead to a parallel reduction in the intervention experiences of MNEs which so accommodate their hosts.[15]

While some of these recommended strategies are harmless, others have the opposite effect and cause governments to intervene at an accelerated rate. Some MNEs respond to requests for "appropriate technology" only to find that their labor-intensive, low-to-moderate technology facility has been taken over, or duplicated, by a domestic firm. Voluntary joint ventures, while providing several advantages to both partners, also provide an ideal opportunity for an active domestic partner to learn the latest technology and management skills, hence reducing the MNE's bargaining power.[16] Some domestic partners go on to compete with their MNE partners. Italian scooter manufacturers are facing competition from their Indian ex-partners, as are U.S. petrochemical firms from South Korean ex-partners.

To offset this leakage of technology in joint ventures, the defensive strategies are usually restricted to intra-MNE sourcing, and, to a lesser extent, exporting to protected markets. However, Japan's Nippondenko reportedly maintained complete control over its Philippine joint venture by continually changing the production process—reducing the ability of local personnel to gain experience—while Tata-Elxsi, a U.S.-Indian joint venture in Singapore, reportedly attempted to achieve the same by restricting participation in local research activities to expatriates.[17]

Modifications to the Basic Strategy

While the basic defense strategy is similar for most manufacturing MNEs, modifications are required depending on the host country. The main source of the variation is the difference in bargaining power of each host nation. While empirical proof is lacking, one could suggest that for many reasons individual nations are at different positions on the bargaining power ladder.[18] One could also postulate that nations move up the bargaining power ladder at different rates. For example, the high speed at which Brazil is acquiring technological and managerial skills, coupled with its large market, gives it a stronger bargaining position than, say, Turkey or Bolivia. Therefore, subsidiaries in nations like Brazil will have to upgrade their bargaining position frequently. In Brazil, certain segments of the chemical industry have had to increase their product selection, level of exports, etc., every three to four years to keep intervention at a lower level. Bolivia's circumstances, on the other hand, have not required such high frequencies.

Figure 18.2 illustrates the point. The level of sophistication, complexity, and technology (all determinants of a firm's bargaining power) necessary for a plant in Bolivia (point A1) is generally lower in Brazil (point A2) for the same bargaining advantage over domestic interventionists. Moreover, because of the higher "learning" rate in Brazil, its bargaining power (its ability to replace the MNE) rises faster than Bolivia's, requiring more frequent bargaining upgrades (points B).

Other modifications to the basic strategy are possible if MNEs have unique skills or business strategies. MNEs without access to more complex technology, export markets, or proprietary intra-firm sourcing, resort to innovative techniques for increasing their bargaining power. For example, a small Canadian MNE, Canada Wire and Cable (CWC), manufactures a number of non-proprietary products of low to moderate complexity, such as wire cables and cable harnesses. Despite the apparent lack of bargaining power provided by such product and industry characteristics, this company has a large international operation with a relatively small incidence of intervention. Almost all of CWC's foreign direct investments are minority

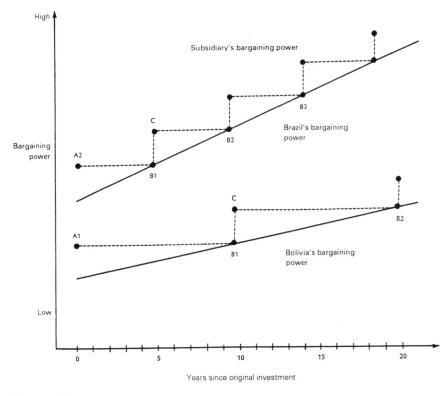

Figure 18.2
Bargaining power: Rate of change in different nations

joint ventures, a mode of operation CWC prefers. The strength of the strategy lies not with the joint venture per se—many would suggest the opposite outcome with joint ventures—but with the choice of partner. In all cases, CWC insists on an aggressive domestic entrepreneur, who is neither particularly wealthy nor politically well connected, and who is usually without experience in CWC's industry. This partner becomes the general manager of the venture.

The subsidiary defense model would predict that after the local partner has mastered the stable and uncomplicated technology for manufacturing the product, CWC would likely be squeezed out by the partner and its government. However, by judiciously selecting an aggressive, hungry partner, CWC finds that the partner continually comes back to CWC for help in attaining marginal improvements in production costs, the product offering, computer systems, export markets, etc. In other words, the local partner is not satisfied with the present level of profits and sees his interest best served by increasing the overall level of profits with CWC's help, rather than by trying to acquire unilaterally CWC's share of the profits.

CWC vigorously supports its partner's perspective with an active and multinational headquarters staff whose sole responsibility is the joint venture. Joint venture partners are provided with whatever resources they need from CWC's domestic divisions and, when CWC does not have the required product or skill, CWC obtains it from some other source, even if it is some other MNE. The result is a rather diverse set of joint ventures but with a very low rate of joint venture failure.

Implications for MNE Parents

The proposed strategy for defending the subsidiary affects the MNE's allocation of human, technical, and capital resources, and introduces new managerial activities to the parent's organization.[19] The new strategy must also be institutionalized, or integrated into the MNE's organization.

The greatest implication of this strategy is that each subsidiary will require a greater amount of capital (machinery, working capital, etc.) and a larger number of better-trained technicians and managers. For the majority of MNEs such increased subsidiary needs can be so high as to be unaffordable. They face a choice of retaining either the existing number of intervention-prone subsidiaries around the world, or of supporting fewer subsidiaries but with an effective defense strategy. The trade-off is difficult for many MNEs, and, again, runs counter to the intuitively appealing strategy of a larger diversified portfolio of subsidiaries. The subsidiary defense strategy, on the other hand, calls for a smaller portfolio containing less risky subsidiaries.

New activities, such as intervention management, have to fit into existing organizational and decision-making structures of the MNE in order to be effective. While the existing organizational structures may not be optimal, organizations do not easily change structures to accommodate new activities. Those MNEs implementing this strategy find that requests for bargaining power upgrades are presented in much the same way as capital budget requests. However, the similarities end there. The staff in most MNEs have little experience in evaluating such bargaining upgrade requests; moreover, most upgrades will affect other subsidiaries as well. Export and sourcing strategies, for example, can affect the product offering of the whole MNE system.

Table 18.1
Kind of MNE

	Global	Multidomestic
Defense strategy	State-of-the-art technology Exports Intra-MNE sourcing	Introducing new products Better intervention forecasting
Political strategy	Lower priority	High local political knowledge and interaction
Staffing	Short-term technologically oriented	Long-term, politically oriented

Intra-MNE trade in machinery, products, processes, and managers will experience a significant increase under the defense strategy. Consequently, another managerial activity is the coordination of subsidiaries which now trade with each other. Agreements must be made on product characteristics, price, and quantity, and when problems arise they must be perceived as being equitably resolved.

Several MNEs have centered many of the management activities in newly revived area headquarters. This is the point in the organization where there appears to be the best supply of pertinent product and country information, all of which is necessary to perform the allocation and integration activities required of the defense strategy.

While MNEs vary in how they defend their subsidiaries from intervention, some patterns are emerging. The patterns can be observed in table 18.1, which divides MNEs into those which follow a global strategy and those which follow a multidomestic strategy.

Summary and Conclusion

A better understanding of the changing world of government-MNE relations has prompted a shift in political risk analysis. Multinational manufacturing firms now find that assessing the vulnerability of each subsidiary to intervention is far more important than assessing broad political shocks. While very few nations offer a safe haven from intervention, certain kinds of subsidiaries do. This paper suggests that MNEs should decrease their emphasis on choosing the right country and instead develop strategies to defend individual subsidiaries from intervention.

There are several strategies which constitute a successful defense. Strategies calling for manufacturing activities requiring continued MNE technological or managerial input, intra-MNE sourcing of proprietary components and end products, and exporting are the more successful ones. The success of these strategies is facilitated as new processes and products are introduced, technological upgrades take place, and scale efficiencies allow for intra-MNE sourcing and exporting. These strategies increase the cost to interventionists of unilaterally increasing their share of a foreign-owned operation.

These strategies have their roots in a defense system, and they do not always produce short-term financial or technical benefits. One may have to say "no" to the engineers and the finance department, and instead structure the subsidiary's activities in a way that always leaves the MNE with something to offer either when the technology matures or after a coup, when vulnerability is inevitable.

Another requirement of a successful defense is to adapt the subsidiary's political behavior to its political profile. Only small or extremely strong subsidiaries without any strategic importance can afford the luxury of avoiding political interaction.

Like most strategies, implementation is a difficult phase. Capital, machinery, technicians and managers who are well trained and politically adept, export markets, and area coordinators are the scarce resources necessary to make the defense strategy work. While the scarcity of resources poses surmountable obstacles for most MNEs, the bigger obstacle is the psychological turnaround this defense mechanism represents. While traditional strategies call for assets reduction and country diversification, this new strategy usually demands an increase in the assets at stake in each country, often necessitating a commensurate decrease in the number of countries served. MNEs, for good business reasons, have difficulty accommodating dramatically different strategic responses. Change will be slow.

MNEs which compete globally will find this defense strategy relatively easy to accommodate and implement. Three popular means of defense—intra-MNE sourcing, exports, and state-of-the-art technology—are characteristic of such MNEs. MNEs which compete on a country-by-country basis tend to rely on introducing new products, building alliances with domestic firms, and better forecasting of when upgrades are necessary.

The importance of proper management of intervention is emphasized when one considers that the same qualities which make nations such as Indonesia, Nigeria, Brazil, and Mexico attractive to MNEs also increase those nations' bargaining power, and hence their tendency to intervene. If MNEs react to intervention by withdrawing or reducing their exposure, or by trying to confront and obstruct host government policies, they may foreclose potentially attractive investment opportunities.

The result of such a strategy for the host nation is a higher average level of technology transfer, and more foreign direct investment. For the MNE, the results include a lower level of intervention, stable profits, and less frustrated executives. Upon closer examination, for MNEs accustomed to serious competition in their home market, this is a more familiar strategy than the traditional one of forecasting political stability and ideology.

Notes

1. Much of this general argument has been stated by Theodore H. Moran, "International Political Risk Assessment: Corporate Planning and Strategies to Offset Political Risk" in *Managing International Political Risk: Strategies and Techniques*, ed. Fariborz Ghadar, Stephen J. Kobrin, and Theodore H. Moran (Washington, D.C.: The Landegger Program in International Business Diplomacy, Georgetown University, 1983). pp. 158–66.

2. The concept of "bargaining power" finds its roots in the work of Raymond Vernon, *Sovereignty at Bay: The Multinational Spread of U.S. Enterprises* (New York: Basic Books, 1971), and was further developed using natural resource firms by Theodore H. Moran, *Multinational Corporations and the Politics of Dependence: Copper in Chile* (Princeton: Princeton University Press, 1974). The comments in this article are based on the substantially similar findings of four independent projects examining the causes of intervention. For further details of these projects see David G. Bradley, "Managing Against Expropriation," *Harvard Business Review*, July-August 1977; Thomas A. Poynter, "Government Intervention in Less Developed Countries: The Experience of Multinational Companies" *Journal of International Business Studies*, Spring-Summer 1982; Nathan Fagre and Louis T. Wells, Jr., "The Bargaining Power of Multinationals and Host Government," *Journal of International Business Studies*, Fall 1982; Donald J. Lecraw, "Bargaining Power, Ownership and Profitability of Subsidiaries of Transnational Corporations in Developing Countries," *Journal of International Business Studies*, Spring-Summer 1984. These four projects used different indicators of the amount of intervention experienced. Fagre and Wells, and Lecraw used the foreign equity percentage, Bradley used the expropriated/not expropriated dichotomy, while Poynter used a series of indicators which represented the amount of forced change a firm had to undergo due to intervention.

3. The least known of these examples concerns the alleged action taken in late 1983 by the Brazilian government in concert with two local firms to squeeze several MNEs, including a Ford Philco–RCA joint venture, out of the digital chip manufacturing business. The $30 million Philco-RCA plant was forced to close barely two years after it started producing chips. Siemens' Brazilian subsidiary may be forced into a similar decision when the manufacture of digital controls is reserved for Brazilians. These actions were reported to be a result of Brazilian nationalism and not a result of the narrowing of the gap between Brazilian and foreign manufacturing capabilities in digital products. See "Tough Choices in Brazil: As the

Junta Squeezes High-Tech Multinationals," *Business Week*, 19 December 1983, p. 44.

4. For a detailed discussion of sources of a nation's bargaining power see Thomas A. Poynter, *Multinational Enterprises and Government Intervention* (New York: St. Martins Press; London: Croom Helm, 1985) pp. 57–68.

5. See Poynter, op. cit., pp. 25–38.

6. See Poynter, op. cit., pp. 61–66; pp. 101–106.

7. These comments, parts of the strategy, and the implementation issues described here are based on discussions and research cases with over 140 subsidiaries and many of their 70 U.S., U.K., Canadian, French, German, Swiss, Dutch and Japanese parents. These discussions took place between 1976 and 1984. See Poynter, op. cit., and Poynter, "Multinational Enterprises and Political Risk in Less-Developed Countries: An Analysis of the Corporate Determinants of Host Country Intervention," Ph.D. Diss., London Business School, 1978, and Poynter, "The Strategic Response to Government Intervention in Developing Countries: Lessons from Research" in Thomas L. Brewer, ed. *Political Risks in International Business* (New York: Praeger, 1985).

8. For a discussion of some of the implementation and integration difficulties encountered by this kind of activity see Stephen J. Kobrin, *Managing Political Risk Assessment* (University of California Press, 1982). For an excellent case history of the problem associated with political risk forecasting in large, complex MNEs see John S. Schwendiman "Managing Environmental Risk: Cases and Lessons for Corporate Strategy," in Fariborz Ghadar and Theodore H. Moran, eds., *International Political Risk Management: New Dimensions* (Washington, D.C.: Ghadar Associates, 1984).

9. The histories of the British and Dutch East Indies Companies are replete with descriptions of this activity. Recent writers first noted the trend by looking at the growth of local independent contractors which used ex-employees of the MNE subsidiary. See Raymond Vernon, op. cit., p. 59.

10. An excellent illustration of this intervention process is provided by the case "Panelec Argentina, S.A." (Harvard Business School, Revised 6/74; ICCH 4-370-077).

11. For further details on the roles of size and strategic importance, see Poynter 1982, pp. 18, 19.

12. For further discussion of this role of project finance see Theodore H. Moran with Debbie Havens Maddox, *Transnational Corporations in the Copper Industry* (New York: U.N., Centre on Transactional Corporations, 1981) and Moran's outline of possible complications facing U.S. MNEs in Ghadar, Kobrin, and Moran, op. cit., p. 164. A superb example is provided by Kennecott, which organized a project in Chile so as to have a large number of supporters should expropriation be threatened. Using such a strategy, Kennecott fared much better than Anaconda. For a complete description see Theodore H. Moran, "Transnational Strategies of

Protection and Defense by Multinational Corporations: Spreading the Risk and Raising the Cost for Nationalization in National Resources," *International Organization*, Vol. 27, No. 2, 1973; pp. 273 et seq.

13. For a description of the relationships between intervention, political profile, and political behavior, see Poynter 1982, pp. 19–20, and Poynter 1985, pp. 25–35. A discussion of alternative strategies available concerning the use of lobbyists, and the effect on intervention, is contained in Poynter 1985, p. 75–78.

14. For a more general discussion of the organizational issues involved when MNEs deal with host governments, see Amir Mahini, "The Management of Government Relations in U.S., Multinationals," D.B.A. Dissertation, Harvard Business School, 1982.

15. In an examination of over 100 subsidiaries, no relationship was noted between intervention and the subsidiaries' effects on the host nation's trade balance; taxes paid; personnel training; profit repatriation; external funding; and proportion of host nationals and management. See Poynter 1982.

16. For a detailed treatment of the subject of managing joint ventures see J. Peter Killing, *Strategies for Joint Venture Success*, (New York: Praeger, 1983). For a description of the ability of domestic joint venture partners to learn from their MNE partners see p. 21.

17. See *The Economist*, 28 April 1984, p. 75.

18. John M. Stopford and Louis T. Wells Jr., *Managing the Multinational Enterprise*, (New York: Basic Books 1972), have some data which support this suggestion, pp. 155–156.

19. For a description of how MNE parents vary in their management of intervention see Y. L. Doz and C. K. Prahalad, "How MNEs Cope with Host Government Intervention," *Harvard Business Review*, March-April 1980.

20. For definitions of global and multidomestic MNEs see Thomas Hout, Michael E. Porter, and Eileen Rudden, "How Global Companies Win Out," *Harvard Business Review*, September-October, 1982, p. 103.

19

Foreign Ownership: When Hosts Change the Rules

Dennis J. Encarnation and Sushil Vachani

Political pressure for national control of multinational corporations is on the rise, and few MNCs are unaffected. Whether the company under duress is Unilever in Canada, Coca-Cola in India, IBM in France, or Ford in Mexico, the story remains the same. Governments of every political stripe are vying for greater domestic ownership of foreign operations within their borders.

Constraints on foreign ownership have taken many forms: Canada's former Foreign Investment Review Act, France's nationalization schemes, Korea's foreign remittance regulations, and "Mexicanization" programs with correlates throughout the world. But even though these policies differ, common features are discernible, particularly when it comes to exemptions. In general, the greater the level of exports, R & D expenditures, foreign exchange savings, and high technology associated with a project, the greater the probability that prohibitions on majority foreign holdings can be relaxed. Yet even then, governments increasingly insist on the diminution of foreign holdings over a specified period or proscribe majority foreign participation in new projects.

In responding to demands for equity dilution, MNCs have a range of strategic options from which to choose, in part because administrative discretion in implementing regulations provides leeway for negotiation. But this flexibility is not always apparent to managers at the parent's headquarters or at the subsidiary. As a result, many companies fail to turn a potentially adverse situation to their competitive advantage.

Nowhere is the regulation of foreign equity participation more encompassing—and, some would say, more onerous—than in India, the focus of our study (see insert). Yet the constraints MNCs face there are representative of those they encounter else-where Focusing on corporate responses

From *Harvard Business Review*, September/October 1985, pp. 152–160. Reprinted by permission.

to India's equity regulations thus teaches lessons that managers throughout the world can apply.

A Portfolio of Responses

India's Foreign Exchange Regulation Act, or FERA, of 1973 restricts foreign equity participation in local operations to 40%. As in other countries, however, several exemptions can apply. If the company operates in high-priority industries that require "sophisticated technology," for example, or exports a "significant proportion" of output, officials may grant an exemption of up to 74%. And if the company exports its entire output, 100% foreign equity may be allowed. But intense negotiations between country managers and government regulators invariably precede extension of these exemptions.

India's rationale for regulating foreign investment this way is similar to that found elsewhere. The perceived economic benefits that flow from retaining more corporate earnings and the managerial control that presumably would follow a change in ownership are among the chief arguments for forced equity dilutions. In addition, such regulation responds to pressure from local competitors who invoke nationalistic sentiment to support their claims on the government.

Managers compelled to reduce foreign equity holdings have at least four options: strict compliance, exit, negotiation, and preemptive action.

Option 1: Follow the Law to the Letter

Companies that sought to maintain existing operations typically sold a majority of their foreign shares to local investors and kept total equity constant. This strategy allowed Colgate-Palmolive (India) to continue producing and marketing a low-technology product line, toothpaste, for which local substitutes existed. Without reclassification as an Indian-owned company, Colgate could not continue to operate in India. By diluting its foreign equity to 40%, it officially became an Indian company and could thereby maintain its dominant position in a profitable and growing market, well protected by entry barriers. (By law, an "Indian" company is one in which the foreign equity share is 40% or less.)

Option 2: Leave the Country

As the widely publicized divestitures of IBM and Coca-Cola illustrate, Indian local ownership requirements forced some companies to leave the country during the late 1970s. Still, exit was not the managers' first choice at any of these companies. Rather, the decision followed a long process of negotiation with government agencies. Consider what happened in the computer industry.

Before 1977, IBM, two other multinationals, and an Indian government-owned company battled for an expanded role in the Indian market. To maintain its competitive advantage, IBM tried to apply FERA selectively. It offered to establish two separate companies: one, a wholly foreign-owned branch for marketing, maintaining, and manufacturing export items; the other, a 40% foreign-owned affiliate to handle data center operations in India. Shares in the affiliate would be widely distributed locally.

Burroughs, a relative newcomer to the Indian market, offered an alternative, proposing to set up a joint venture with an Indian company controlled by the country's second largest business conglomerate, Tata. British-owned International Computer also proposed to set up a minority foreign-owned joint venture with a large-scale private Indian manufacturer, Bharat Electronics. In opposition, the government-owned Electronics Corporation urged that all three foreign companies be shut out of the market, which it alone should dominate.

The government rejected both the Electronics Corporation and IBM proposals. It allowed multinationals to operate in the country but it insisted on equity dilution for manufacturing operations. Burroughs and International Computer decided to go ahead with their plans, while IBM chose to leave the country. Presumably IBM's management thought it would lose more by setting a precedent for shared control with local partners than it could gain from continued operations under the new rules. IBM therefore had few options.

Option 3: Negotiate under the Law

For some MNCs, the equity dilution requirement became an opportunity to grow and diversify because their managers used it as a negotiating tool to raise funds, obtain government licenses, and win approval for new product lines.

Issuing fresh equity exclusively to local investors and leaving the absolute number of shares held by the parent constant was the most common dilution scheme. In this way, Purolator, Ciba-Geigy, and other MNCs used dilution to raise funds for expansion. Ciba-Geigy's dilution scheme, for example, increased the total equity base of its subsidiary, Hindustan Ciba-Geigy, by 27% to $17.7 million. The funds from the new equity, which sold at 40% over book value, contributed nearly one-third of the total capital necessary to undertake expansion in 1983 and 19S4.

Ciba-Geigy's management also used equity dilution as a lever to expand its product lines. By law the company only had to reduce its equity in Hindustan Ciba-Geigy from 65% to 51% since it operated in a high-technology industry. Ciba-Geigy volunteered to dilute its equity to 40%, however, so that its subsidiary could benefit from classification as an Indian company. In return, the company was free to produce pharmaceutical formulations valued at ten times the sale of its bulk drugs, or twice the manufacturing capacity permitted non-Indian producers. Thus Hindustan Ciba-Geigy's dilution strategy cleared the way for it to double its pharmaceutical sales.

Like Ciba-Geigy, Chesebrough-Pond's reduced its holdings in its wholly owned branch to 40% by issuing new equity exclusively to Indian investors. Three production and marketing changes followed this infusion of new capital in its subsidiary, Pond's (India). First, its manufacturing operation expanded from one plant to four in the next five years. Because these factories were located in backward regions, where the government encouraged investment through tax holidays, subsidized loans, and other incentives, the subsidiary's effective tax rates and cost of capital plummeted. Second, in those same five years, the company stopped relying exclusively on the Indian domestic market and began exporting 30% of its sales. Third, by 1983, the company was poised to diversify its product line by introducing clinical thermometers destined for the U.S. market.

As Ciba-Geigy's experience indicates, negotiations over equity dilution are invariably linked to negotiations over other regulatory policies—of which India has many. Indeed, India's regulatory regime has been euphemistically called the "licensecum-permit Raj" to highlight the myriad directorates, departments, secretariats, and ministries whose approval must be secured for operations to proceed. Yet even these obstacles may beget opportunities for MNCs.

For example, India's industrial licensing system prohibits a company from expanding capacity beyond approved limits or entering new product lines or markets without permission. Yet if a company can secure a license previously denied, the system turns around: the new license serves as an entry barrier to domestic competitors, just as India's import restrictions serve as barriers to foreign competition. So if management can secure an industrial license as a negotiating concession, the benefits derived from expansion and diversification may offset the costs of dilution to the parent corporation.

Moving from expansion to diversification was a common strategy. Both steps often occurred simultaneously. Consider the most ambitious equity dilution scheme undertaken in India, a strategy devised by Gabriel India Limited, a subsidiary of Gabriel International (Panama) and, by merger, the Maremont Corporation (USA).

Gabriel India was one of the country's largest manufacturers of shock absorbers even before equity dilution. When it agreed in 1978 to reduce its foreign stake from 50% to 39%, the government granted the company licenses to double production of shock absorbers. In addition, the company received permission to diversify into engine bearings with the technological collaboration of a new American partner, Federal Mogul.

Federal Mogul made several demands, including an equity position in a recapitalized Gabriel India, that countered regulations. It also insisted that Gabriel India remit dividends during the new partnership's first year, even though none of its earnings would come from manufacturing bearings. Finally, Federal Mogul demanded that royalties and technical fees be paid sooner and at higher rates than normally permitted. After heated negotiations, the government consented to all of Federal Mogul's demands—in exchange for equity dilution of Gabriel India and larger output of two products in chronically short supply.

To finance this investment and dilute foreign holdings, Gabriel India nearly doubled its equity to $2.6 million, through a complex series of transactions. By selling fresh equity to Federal Mogul and local investors, the company generated nearly one-fifth of the capital needed for expansion. Simultaneously, Gabriel International and its original Indian partner sold existing shares to government-run financial institutions. These institutions, in turn, financed the remaining new investment through a mix of commercial and concessional loans, supplemented by government subsidies. When the dust settled, Indian investors held 61% of Gabriel India, Gabriel International held 25%, and Federal Mogul held 14%.

Option 4: Take Preemptive Action

Unlike the companies described so far, some MNCs initiated defensive strategies, such as preemptive diversification, phased "Indianization," and joint partnerships, well before FERA's final passage. Still others, like Cummins Engine, deflected political pressure by continuously updating their technology and bringing in valuable foreign exchange through exports.

Preemptive Diversification
Hindustan Lever developed a four-pronged strategy to avoid equity dilution. That strategy allowed it to retain majority ownership of a subsidiary
whose business portfolio differed from its own. At the core of this strategy
were sustained efforts to increase high-technology production and export
sales. First, during the 1970s, management added basic chemicals to the
detergents, soaps, and other consumer goods that made up its product
lines. This addition both reflected the high priority given such manufacture
by the government and fit Hindustan Lever's plan for backward integration. Then, in 1983, the company further increased the proportion of high
technology in its business portfolio by selling its food business to a second
Unilever subsidiary, Lipton India.

Local R & D efforts made up the third feature of Hindustan Lever's high-
technology strategy. As a result of these R & D investments, products like
detergent could be classified as "high technology." Further, the company's
research facility, one of the largest in India's private sector, found ways to
substitute locally abundant oils for imported tallow in the manufacture
of high-quality soaps. This substitution saved scarce foreign exchange,
another government priority.

The fourth prong of Hindustan Lever's strategy also focused on foreign exchange. To boost earnings, the government offered incentives to
large companies that would establish export houses as channels for smaller
manufacturers unable to export on their own. Hindustan Lever, already a
licensed export house selling a variety of other companies' products overseas, took steps to increase the proportion of exports in its sales. Export
sales then grew rapidly, more than tripling in five years to reach $62
million in 1982. In that year, the government decided to allow Unilever to
retain its majority ownership of Hindustan Lever since 60% of the subsidiary's activities generated foreign exchange, involved high technology, or
operated in high-priority sectors.

Phased Indianization
At ITC, a subsidiary of the British-American Tobacco Company, the quest
for new capital and businesses entailed a strategy of phased Indianization.
During the late 1960s, ITC's management realized that the government
was unlikely to grant majority foreign ownership rights for a product—
cigarettes—that was closely tied to agriculture, required little new technology or large capital investments, and had minuscule prospects for export.
Because internal and foreign funds for diversification were limited and gov-

ernment licenses were increasingly reserved for Indian companies, management chose to look for new opportunities through voluntary divestment. Through sale of fresh equity and existing stock, the company reduced its foreign ownership from 94% in 1968 to 75% in 1969, 60% in 1974 (following FERA), and 40% in 1976. Moves to diversify ITC's business accompanied each of these divestments. In 1971, the company began to export products, ranging from frozen shrimp to hand tools to handwoven carpets, that it did not manufacture. By 1973, it had obtained government approval to enter the hotel business (ten years later owning 3 luxury hotels and managing a chain of 18 others). And in 1976, it decided to promote a capital-intensive paperboard venture. By 1982, ITC had diversified in two important ways: from manufacturing to service industries and from local marketing of a single product to exporting various products.

Joint Partnerships
For another group of companies, neither diversification nor dilution was necessary even after FERA's passage. These multinationals already satisfied its requirements because they either continuously updated technology in a politically salient industry or earned sufficient foreign exchange. After 1973, the principal strategy of such joint ventures as Kirloskar-Cummins, Tata-Burroughs, and TAFE (a subsidiary of Massey-Ferguson) was to maintain existing operations. The 50% share of equity held by Cummins Engine, the 50% share held by Burroughs, and the 49% share held by Massey-Ferguson were secure, provided that the technological content of the products remained high and export sales did not decline.

Kirloskar-Cummins, for example, kept on adding larger horsepower products to its line of sophisticated diesel engines. Because it was the only producer of one particular engine, the Cummins subsidiary also had a secure, albeit small, export market. Burroughs likewise staved off equity dilution pressure through its high-technology products and growing computer-software export sales. (Burroughs's wholly owned subsidiary in the Santa Cruz Export Processing Zone contributed significantly to India's burgeoning sales of labor-intensive software design and data-entry operations to overseas clients.)

Reaping the Benefits

Companies that negotiated dilution packages after FERA was enacted or took preemptive action before its passage were able to retain majority

ownership or at least maintain managerial control, diversify risk, and ultimately raise the profits of the parent or the subsidiary.

Retaining Majority Ownership

A few MNCs succeeded in keeping majority ownership of their subsidiaries
even after FERA's passage. Although all met at least one of the act's criteria
for exemption, what usually tipped the scale was the parent's supply of
high technology in a favored industry. Some of these MNCs had earlier
formed joint partnerships with Indian companies. Occasionally, however,
the high technology was homegrown by country managers, such as those
at Hindustan Lever, who invested heavily in local R & D.

Maintaining Managerial Control

Majority ownership is only one means of exercising control, as executives
in India long ago recognized. In each divestiture cited, foreign equity holdings were reduced without compromising MNC control over the subsidiary. When fresh equity was issued to local investors (the most common
financial response) or existing foreign shares were sold, the equity was
dispersed widely among many individual shareholders, each with a small
holding. In 1980, for example, 89,000 Indians held Hindustan Lever's stock.
Smaller MNCs were similarly able to maintain control: more than 11,000
Indian nationals owned 57% of Pond's (India) after the parent reduced its
share to 40%.

    In all these cases, large blocks of shares were seldom, if ever, sold to a
single private Indian enterprise. The only big institutional buyers were
public sector financial agencies—often the largest single Indian shareholders after dilution. And even they were reluctant to intervene in day-to-day
operations, generally deferring to managers installed by the MNC. In this
way, managerial control remained unchanged after dilution.

Diversifying Risk

Subsidiaries and parents that maintained control also benefited by diversifying the risks of operation. For example, MNCs that reduced their foreign holdings to 40% were assured "national treatment" under the law.
Pond's (India) was thereby allowed to build new plants to expand production; Gabriel India could diversify into an industry protected by high technological entry barriers; and ITC could enter a business in which its parent

had no experience. Through these moves, the MNCs diversified the risks associated with narrow product lines, limited production facilities, and restricted markets. Even more important, the government licenses they secured let them hurdle entry barriers that kept out potential competitors, foreign and domestic.

Increasing Profits

The benefits of retained ownership and control show up on the income statement of the parent, the subsidiary, or both. Even the simplest response to FERA, complying with the letter of the law to maintain operations, yielded benefits for Colgate-Palmolive (India), which thereby retained its 50% to 60% share of a fast-growing, highly protected market. By 1982, the subsidiary's revenues had reached $77.6 million, having grown along with net worth at an annual rate of 18% since 1973. During the same period, after-tax profits increased 11% per annum and dividends rose 9%. Dilution of foreign equity in 1978 did, however, depress the level of dividends allotted to the parent in the next few years. But pretax dividends in the four years after dilution, plus pretax value of the sale of equity, exceeded the parent's pretax receipts in the four years preceding dilution by roughly 25%. Moreover, the parent's share in the subsidiary's net worth grew at an annual rate of nearly 8% between 1973 and 1982.

The benefits of negotiation were even more impressive for companies that linked equity dilution to expansion. At the recapitalized and diversified Pond's (India), for instance, after-tax profits grew 57% annually, sales grew 27%, and dividends to the parent grew 49% in the first four years after the company's legal status changed from branch to subsidiary. The increase in profits over sales reflected local management's effective use of tax holidays, subsidized credit, and other incentives available through negotiation with government agencies seeking investment in underdeveloped regions. It is unlikely that this subsidiary would have been allowed to diversify and grow at rates anywhere near as high without diluting its equity.

Preemptive strategies designed to increase the parent's bargaining power yielded similar financial results. By 1982, two years after equity dilution, Hindustan Lever could report that after-tax profits had reached $22.2 million, having grown at an annual rate of 24% over the previous nine years, more than double the rate of inflation. During the same period, sales and dividends rose 16% and 12% respectively. By diversifying into new products and markets, Hindustan Lever not only warded off further equity dilution but also reaped greater financial rewards.

Earnings at companies that avoided equity dilution altogether also grew unimpeded after FERA's passage. Kirloskar-Cummins secured several new licenses for capacity expansion and technological collaboration between 1973 and 1982. During that period, after-tax profits rose at a compound annual rate of 39% to $8.2 million, while revenues rose 24% to $89.5 million. Dividends to the parent grew significantly too, rising 25% annually to reach $820,000 by 1982. The parent's earnings were also boosted by technical fees, which grew at a compound annual rate of 23% to $1 million in 1982.

Limits to Choice

While creative responses to forced equity dilution can yield profitable results, practical considerations and constraints often deny managers the luxury of choosing freely from this portfolio. Factors that limit the range of available options include: the implications of setting a precedent, the MNC's decision-making structure, the level of bargaining power, the political environment, and management's attitudes.[1]

Precedent Setting

Because a single government's actions can affect other parts of a company, few multinational managements can safely ignore the implications of business-government negotiations in any one country. First, in some cases, what matters to one government has a direct impact on the operation of subsidiaries elsewhere. Local-content legislation or minimum export requirements, for example, may force a multinational to reconfigure its international sourcing arrangements. IBM in India rejected both demands on the ground that they would disrupt its global operations.

Second, and probably more important from IBM's perspective, a decision in one country can set a precedent for demands from other governments. Even though Indian operations made up an insignificant part of IBM's global activities, it devoted a great deal of management time to the issue of equity dilution. As a compromise, IBM finally offered to reduce its ownership of the local sales operations to 40%. But it would not budge from its corporate policy of 100% ownership of manufacturing subsidiaries. And when this proved unacceptable, IBM withdrew rather than yield to pressure that could undermine its policies elsewhere. Soon thereafter, the company left Nigeria over the same issue.

IBM was not alone in trying to keep important corporate policies intact. Coca-Cola left India (and other countries) to avoid disclosing its famed formula to a local partner. And petroleum and mining companies must likewise consider the wider implications of their negotiations, lest they grant one country concessions that all may demand.

Centralized Decision Making

MNCs deeply concerned about precedents usually keep decision making centralized. IBM, for example, gave authority for all equity dilution decisions to its Corporate Management Committee, consisting of the company's top five executives. Coca-Cola adopted a similar approach. These decisions were not made lightly because centralization almost completely disenfranchises subsidiary or other front-line managers responsible for the unit's profits, knowledge of local conditions, and day-to-day management tasks. For certain MNCs, however, larger corporate strategic issues, such as protecting intangible assets, make centralized control essential.

Other companies try to coordinate business-government negotiations with less centralized decision-making structures. Like IBM, pharmaceutical companies know that governments are almost certain to have a close interest in their industry and its activities. So these companies often try to apply one subsidiary's experience to another to maintain important corporate policies, including majority ownership. (Given the proprietary nature of technology, patents, and trademarks, drug companies generally try to maintain majority equity holdings in their foreign subsidiaries.)

For these reasons, Ciba-Geigy's corporate management was surprised by the recommendation of its Indian subsidiary that it voluntarily reduce its foreign equity, not to the 51% approved by the Indian government, but to 40%. To prevail, local management had to demonstrate that the new avenues for higher profits resulting from classification as an Indian company justified dilution of foreign equity in a subsidiary already generating impressive earnings from existing operations.

The degree of autonomy accorded local managers, of course, differs greatly, even among MNCs engaged in similar businesses. The U.S. headquarters of Colgate-Palmolive controls decision making tightly, and it would be unlikely to allow its subsidiaries to diversify into unfamiliar product lines. Decision making at Unilever is decentralized, and Hindustan Lever's managers (encouraged by the Indian government) are able to choose from a wider range of strategic options and thereby introduce new product lines.

Bargaining Power

IBM's ability to hold the Indian government at bay for more than a decade reflects the strength of its bargaining position. Yet the IBM story also reminds us that a corporate nonnegotiation policy cannot remain intact forever. Agreements reached at the preinvestment stage, when a company's bargaining position is usually strongest, will become obsolete over time.

The greater an MNC's bargaining power, the less its need to respond to government demands. In general, a foreign company's bargaining power is likely to increase if it:

• Exports a large part of its output and can control the market downstream from the production site.

• Uses factors of production, such as unskilled labor, that can be easily substituted across countries.

• Occupies a monopolistic or dominant oligopolistic position in the industry.

• Uses high technology that has few substitute sources.

• Produces highly differentiated products that require large marketing or R & D expenditures.

• Requires no capital-intensive facilities expenditures that once in place are difficult to liquidate or move.[2]

These factors are not immutable. As we have seen, Unilever's local management hiked the company's bargaining power by transforming a low-technology, domestic producer of limited consumer goods into an exporting, F & D-intensive, high-technology diversified company. But to do this, management had to avoid relying on old bargains that time and events were eroding.

Political Environment

All such strategies could be for naught, of course, given the vicissitudes of politics. IBM, for example, suffered from several political liabilities. It had a high profile; it was identified as a U.S. company at a time when relations were strained; and in the view of the new government that came to power suddenly in 1977 it was closely associated with the earlier Gandhi regime. Moreover, party stalwarts used the case as a litmus test of policy changes

and pressed the new government to penalize IBM for its violations of
FERA. Still, the new government acted only after it was sure that substitute
products were readily available. Much the same could be said for Coca-
Cola. In both cases, the political environment probably exacerbated other
constraints noted previously.

As IBM's experience suggests, the political environment limits managements' options in important ways. Yet politics alone is not enough to
explain corporate choices. Burroughs was one of several U.S. companies
that stayed in India after IBM left; indeed, it took advantage of that departure. Other companies, like Unilever, Colgate-Palmolive, and Chesebrough-
Pond's, also had strong domestic competitors that applied political pressure
to oust them from markets where foreign ownership was harder to justify.

Management's Attitudes

Finally, executives' own spectacles can limit the options they perceive. In
many cases, overseas managers receive their assignments because of their
skills in marketing, production, or other functional areas. Experience in
government relations is rarely part of their background, especially if they
have been transferred from domestic operations in the United States. Further, without special effort from higher up, the managers often have little
chance to learn from their peers' experience in other countries.

Lacking experience or shared information, managers commonly assume
that government, virtually by definition, impedes private business. And the
"license-cum-permit Raj" that is India only reinforces this view. Yet to
undertake the creative responses we have outlined, managers had to overcome these biases. Otherwise they could not have converted government
constraints into business assets.

Ironically, even success can constrain a company's responses, unless its
management guards against the inertia bred by good performance. At
Ciba-Geigy, for instance, the reasons for Indianization would not have
been obvious to headquarters, since its government-approved operation
was already very profitable. But local management saw opportunities in the
FERA regulations and persuaded the parent to pursue them with even more
profitable results for all.

Lessons for Managers

The experiences of MNCs in India teach important lessons for managers
worldwide who must respond to host country regulatory policies:

1. Look at the range of strategic possibilities. The 12 MNCs that we studied unequivocally show that no single strategy works best in a single country or even a single industry. And we can assume that the same conclusion holds true across countries as well. To beat the competition, both parent and subsidiary managements must assess the full portfolio of responses. If you don't, your competitor may. In India, it has proved difficult for Colgate-Palmolive to move into detergent, a product it markets worldwide, partly as a result of Unilever's aggressive marketing and R & D strategy.

2. Use the law to further your own ends. Unilever, Chesebrough-Pond's, and Gabriel India were among the companies that turned adversity into opportunity. By satisfying government demands, such companies availed themselves of government concessions—new licenses to expand or diversify, subsidized loans, and tariff protection. As a result, they transcended some barriers erected by the government controls and also reduced their cost of capital. Other competitors, unable to obtain similar concessions, faced higher entry barriers than these multinationals. Moreover, the additional earnings and risk diversification offset the costs to the parent of complying with the regulations. In short, these MNCs exploited the opportunities that flow from administrative discretion in implementing regulatory and incentive policies.

3. Create future bargaining chips. By linking regulations to concessions, many of these companies reversed the process of obsolescence that inevitably afflicts negotiated settlements. Unilever, for example, could no longer be treated like any other foreign producer of mass consumer goods once it had reconfigured its operations in response to FERA. Rather, its technology and exports were now critical to "self-reliant development"—the byword of India and many other countries. Before the government can again demand that Unilever reduce its majority foreign holdings, substitutes for its products and alternatives to its operations must materialize. But in the meantime, Unilever is seen as a good corporate citizen, and it will be in an even better negotiating position the next time around.

4. Anticipate government policy changes. Building bargaining chips takes time. Of the 12 MNCs we examined, ITC and others that took the initiative had greater freedom to shape their operations than those who waited to act until after FERA had passed. Moreover, some strategies like phased Indianization and preemptive diversification work better when management still has greater control over the timetables for equity dilution, capital infusion, new investment, and so on. Often, government agencies grant special consideration to companies that act early, viewing them as good corporate citizens. And finally, time is critical to bring about changes in the local subsidiary and between the subsidiary and its parent. Internal negotiations are often as crucial as negotiations between the company and the government, and the time they require can best be bought by anticipating government action.

5. Listen to your country managers. Local managers deserve top management's ear for several reasons. They are likely to know when issues are arising, they understand the political environment better, and they are more familiar with the intricacies of the law. Managers who have spent several years in a country may even know government leaders and other important officials.

Further, as the people likely to be most affected by the outcome of negotiations, country managers have a strong incentive to make recommendations that are beneficial to the subsidiary's interests. What is good for the subsidiary may not be good for the MNC as a whole, of course.

The dictum to obtain the country manager's advice does not mean that it must always be heeded. Yet the experience of these 12 companies suggests that it is the country manager who can best turn adversity into opportunity through creative responses in a hostile environment.

Notes

A note on the research: To explore the range of responses available to managements under pressure to dilute their equity ownership in local subsidiaries, we studied 12 companies operating in India during the late 1970s. Each of these MNCs—Unilever, Purolator, Massey-Ferguson, Maremont, IBM, Cummins Engine, Colgate-Palmolive, Coca-Cola, Ciba-Geigy, Chesebrough-Pond's, Burroughs. and British-American Tobacco—faced similar demands in other countries. And each has had to develop a strategy for meeting this threat worldwide. Our analysis draws on the companies' public financial documents as well as interviews with corporate executives and Indian government officials. These interviews took place in three stages, beginning in 1977 and ending in 1983.

1. For a discussion of precedents and centralized decision making, see Amir Mahini and Louis T. Wells, Jr., "Managing Government Relations in Multinational Enterprises," paper presented at the Colloquium on Competition in Global Industries, Harvard Business School, April 1984.

2. For a summary of the literature from which these findings are drawn, see Dennis J. Encarnation and Louis T. Wells, Jr., "Competitive Strategies in Global Industries: A View from the Host Country," paper presented at the Colloquium on Competition in Global Industries, Harvard Business School, April 1984.

VI Political Risk

Key Terms

- political exposure
- political risk
- nationalization
- expropriation
- risk containment
- bargaining power
- equity dilution

Questions

1. Which industries are susceptible to the largest political risk, and why?

2. Consider a firm which contemplates the same investment in a large number of different countries. How would you rank these countries? How would you rank these countries in terms of political risk? Please explain the basis for the rankings.

3. Why are pharmaceutical firms likely to be less sensitive to political risk than firms that produce basic organic chemicals?

4. Why might joint-venture investments be less sensitive to political risk?

Suggested Readings

Austin, James E., and John C. Ickis, "Managing after the Revolutionaries Have Won," *Harvard Business Review*, May-June 1986, pp. 103–109.

Chaudhuri, Adhip, "Multinational Corporations in Less-Developed Countries: What Is in Store?" *Columbia Journal of World Business*, Spring 1988, pp. 57–63.

Kim, W. Chan, "Competition and the Management of Host Government Intervention," *Sloan Management Review*, Spring 1987, pp. 33–39.

Simon, Jeffrey D., "Political Risk Assessment: Past Trends and Future Prospects," *Columbia Journal of World Business*, Fall 1982, pp. 62–71.

Index